"Hatred ever kills, love never dies, such is the vast difference between the two. What is obtained by love is retained for all time. What is obtained by hatred proves a burden in reality, for it increases hatred."

Mohandas Karamchand Gandhi

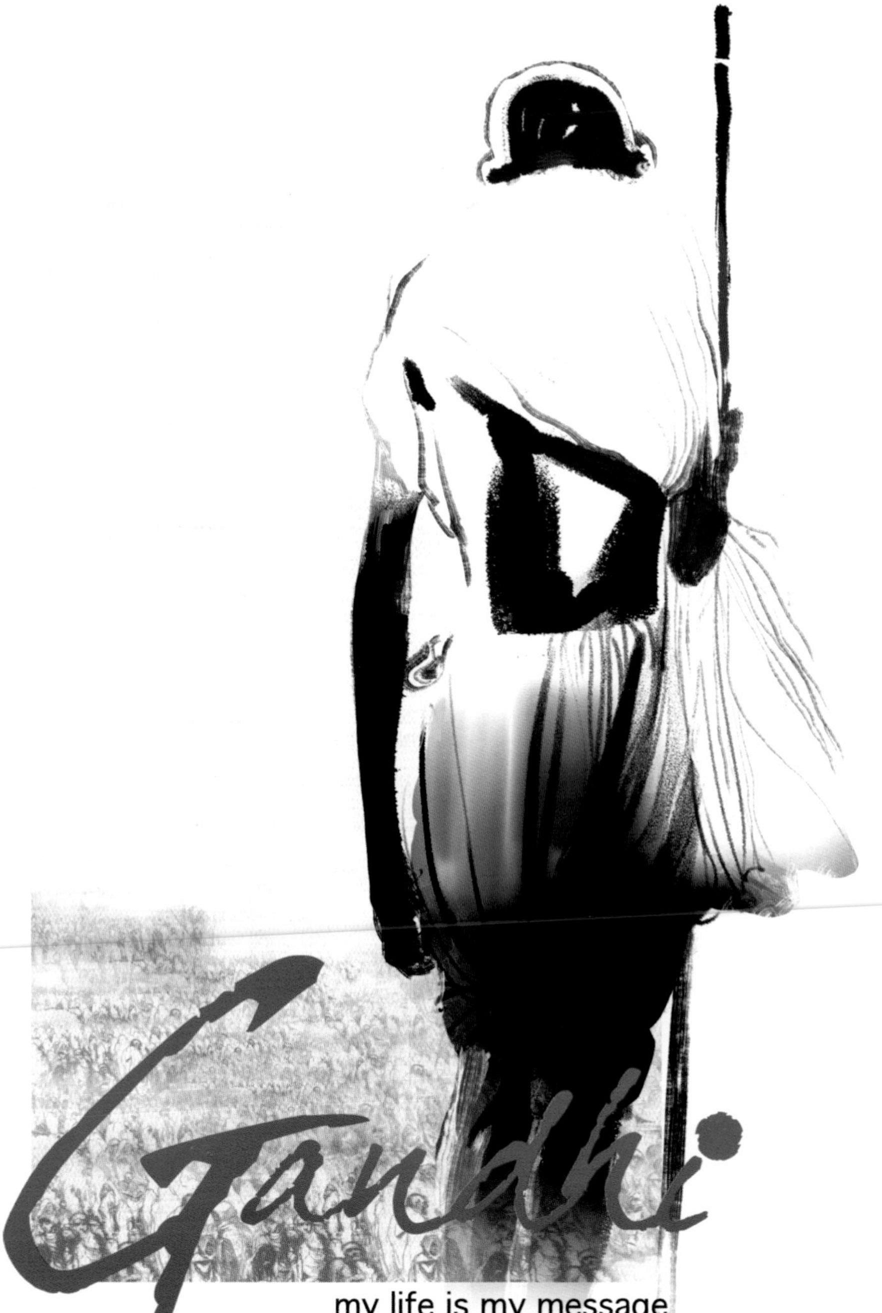

Gandhi

my life is my message

CAMPFIRE®

KALYANI NAVYUG MEDIA PVT LTD

Gandhi

my life is my message

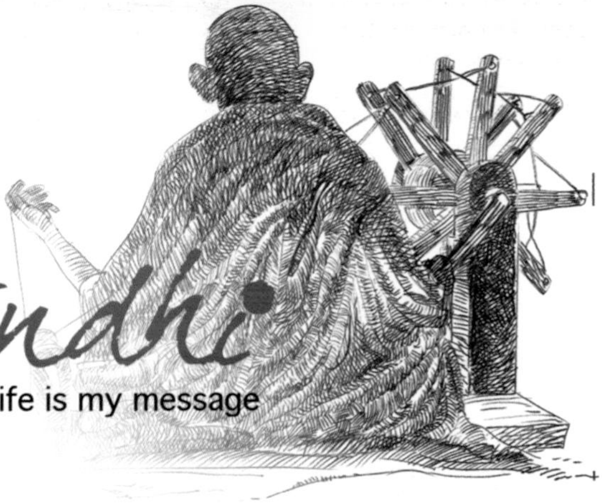

Written by:	Jason Quinn
Illustrated by:	Sachin Nagar
Colorists:	Sachin Nagar, Vijay Sharma, Pradeep Sherawat
Editors:	Jason Quinn, Sourav Dutta
Lettering:	Bhavnath Chaudhary
Cover Art:	Sachin Nagar

Acknowledgement

The author would like to thank Professor Rajmohan Gandhi whose book *Mohandas: A True Story of a Man, his People and an Empire*, proved a great source of inspiration and gave an invaluable insight into Gandhi as a human being.

Published by Kalyani Navyug Media Pvt Ltd
101 C, Shiv House, Hari Nagar Ashram,
New Delhi 110014, India

ISBN: 978-93-80741-22-2

Printed in India

Mission Statement

To entertain and educate young minds by creating unique illustrated books that recount stories of human values, arouse curiosity in the world around us, and inspire with tales of great deeds of unforgettable people.

CAMPFIRE®

www.campfire.co.in

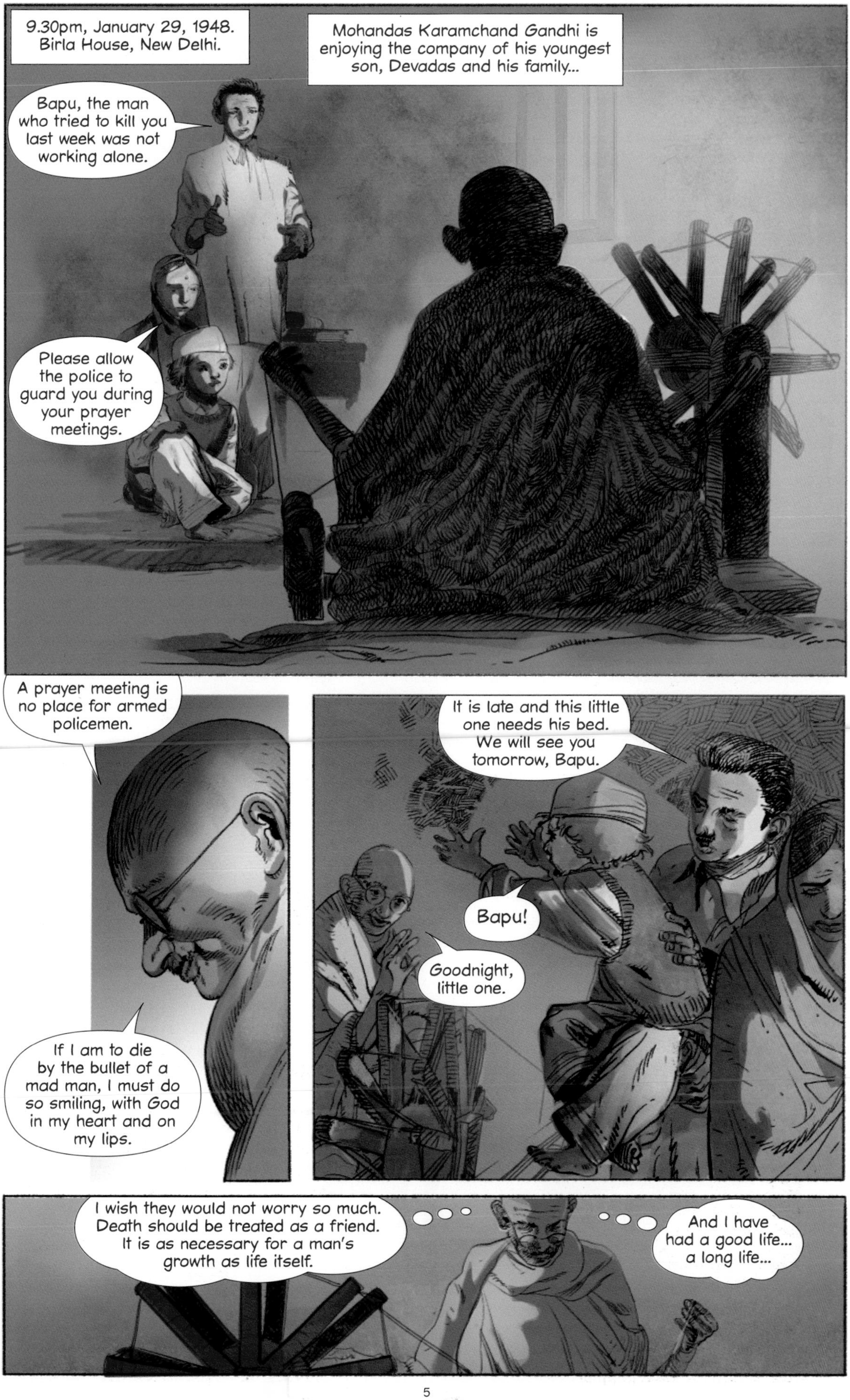
9.30pm, January 29, 1948. Birla House, New Delhi.
Mohandas Karamchand Gandhi is enjoying the company of his youngest son, Devadas and his family...
Bapu, the man who tried to kill you last week was not working alone.
Please allow the police to guard you during your prayer meetings.
A prayer meeting is no place for armed policemen.
If I am to die by the bullet of a mad man, I must do so smiling, with God in my heart and on my lips.
It is late and this little one needs his bed. We will see you tomorrow, Bapu.
Bapu!
Goodnight, little one.
I wish they would not worry so much. Death should be treated as a friend. It is as necessary for a man's growth as life itself.
And I have had a good life... a long life...

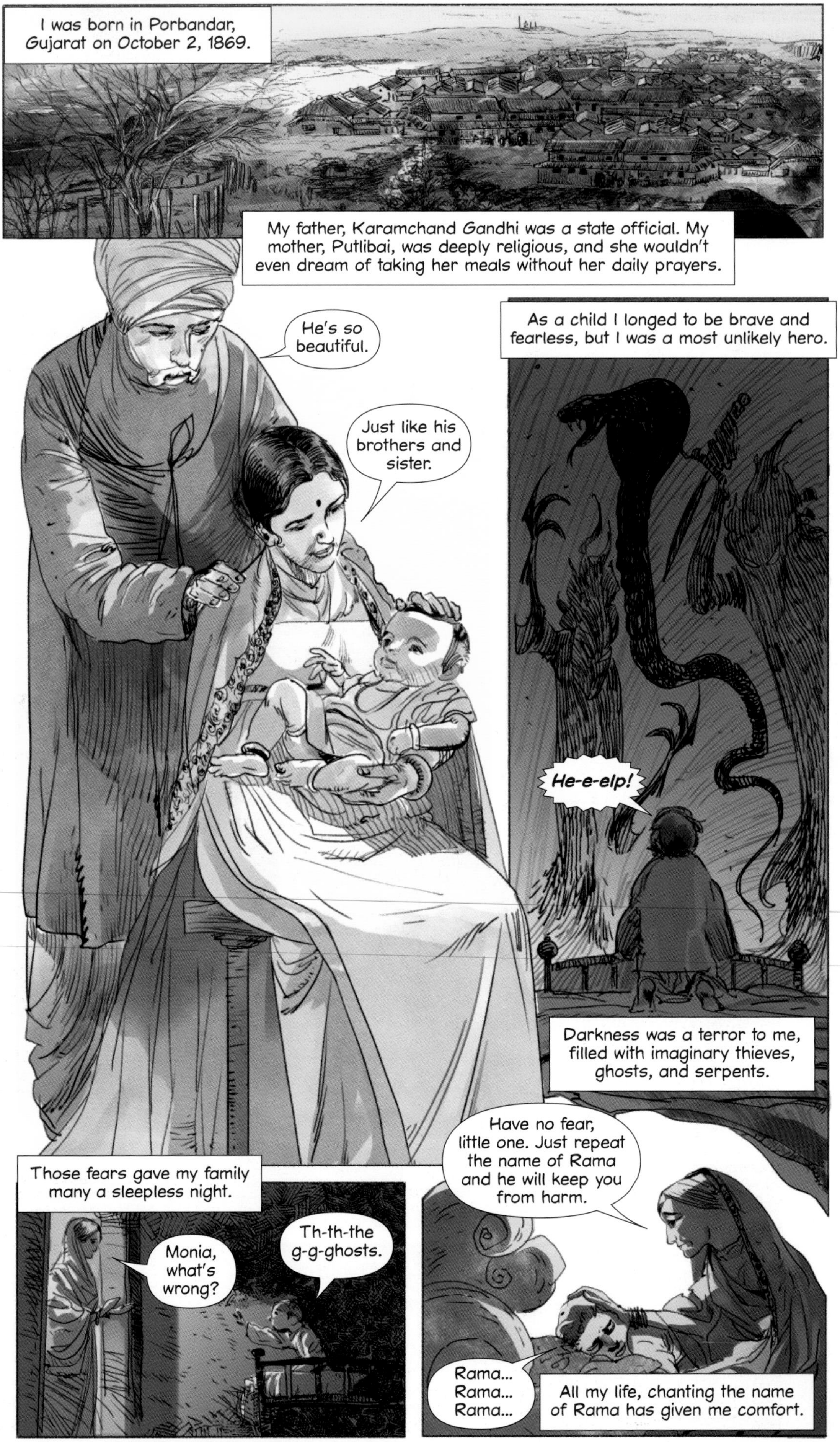
I was born in Porbandar, Gujarat on October 2, 1869.
My father, Karamchand Gandhi was a state official. My mother, Putlibai, was deeply religious, and she wouldn't even dream of taking her meals without her daily prayers.
He's so beautiful.
Just like his brothers and sister.
As a child I longed to be brave and fearless, but I was a most unlikely hero.
He-e-elp!
Darkness was a terror to me, filled with imaginary thieves, ghosts, and serpents.
Those fears gave my family many a sleepless night.
Monia, what's wrong?
Th-th-the g-g-ghosts.
Have no fear, little one. Just repeat the name of Rama and he will keep you from harm.
Rama... Rama... Rama...
All my life, chanting the name of Rama has given me comfort.

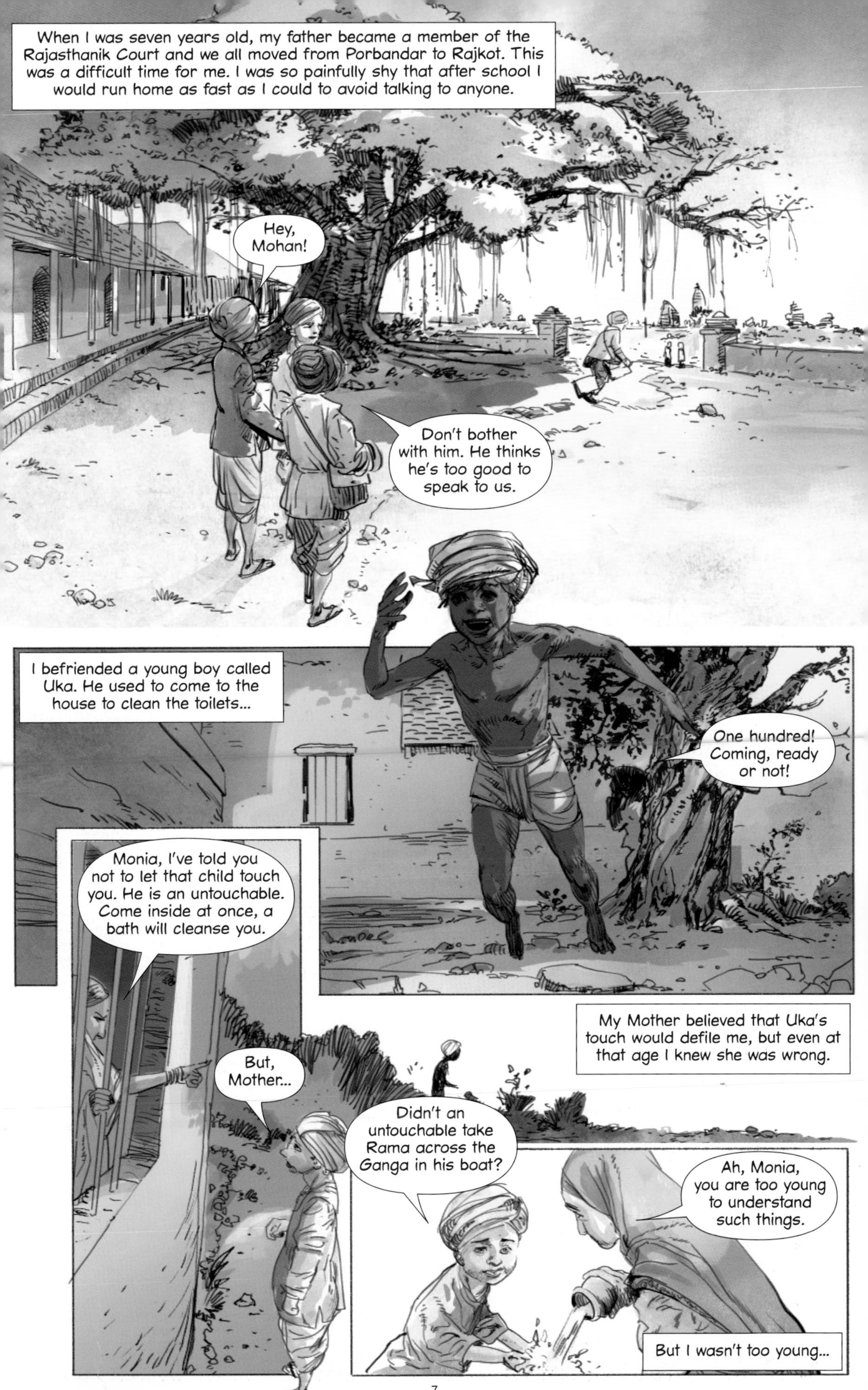

When I was seven years old, my father became a member of the Rajasthanik Court and we all moved from Porbandar to Rajkot. This was a difficult time for me. I was so painfully shy that after school I would run home as fast as I could to avoid talking to anyone.
Hey, Mohan!
Don't bother with him. He thinks he's too good to speak to us.
I befriended a young boy called Uka. He used to come to the house to clean the toilets...
One hundred! Coming, ready or not!
Monia, I've told you not to let that child touch you. He is an untouchable. Come inside at once, a bath will cleanse you.
My Mother believed that Uka's touch would defile me, but even at that age I knew she was wrong.
But, Mother...
Didn't an untouchable take Rama across the Ganga in his boat?
Ah, Monia, you are too young to understand such things.
But I wasn't too young...

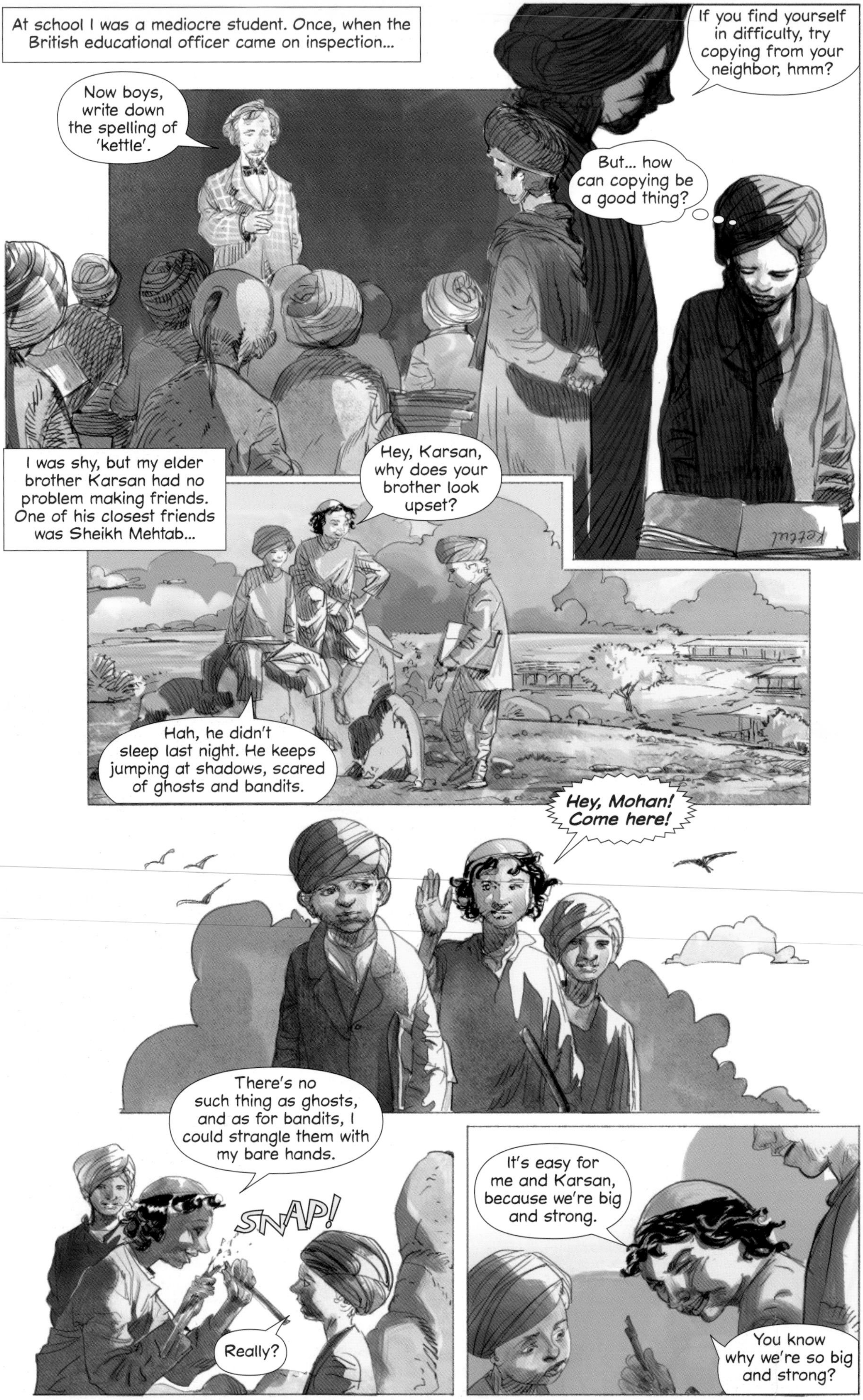
At school I was a mediocre student. Once, when the British educational officer came on inspection...
Now boys, write down the spelling of 'kettle'.
If you find yourself in difficulty, try copying from your neighbor, hmm?
But... how can copying be a good thing?
I was shy, but my elder brother Karsan had no problem making friends. One of his closest friends was Sheikh Mehtab...
Hey, Karsan, why does your brother look upset?
Hah, he didn't sleep last night. He keeps jumping at shadows, scared of ghosts and bandits.
Hey, Mohan! Come here!
There's no such thing as ghosts, and as for bandits, I could strangle them with my bare hands.
SNAP!
Really?
It's easy for me and Karsan, because we're big and strong.
You know why we're so big and strong?

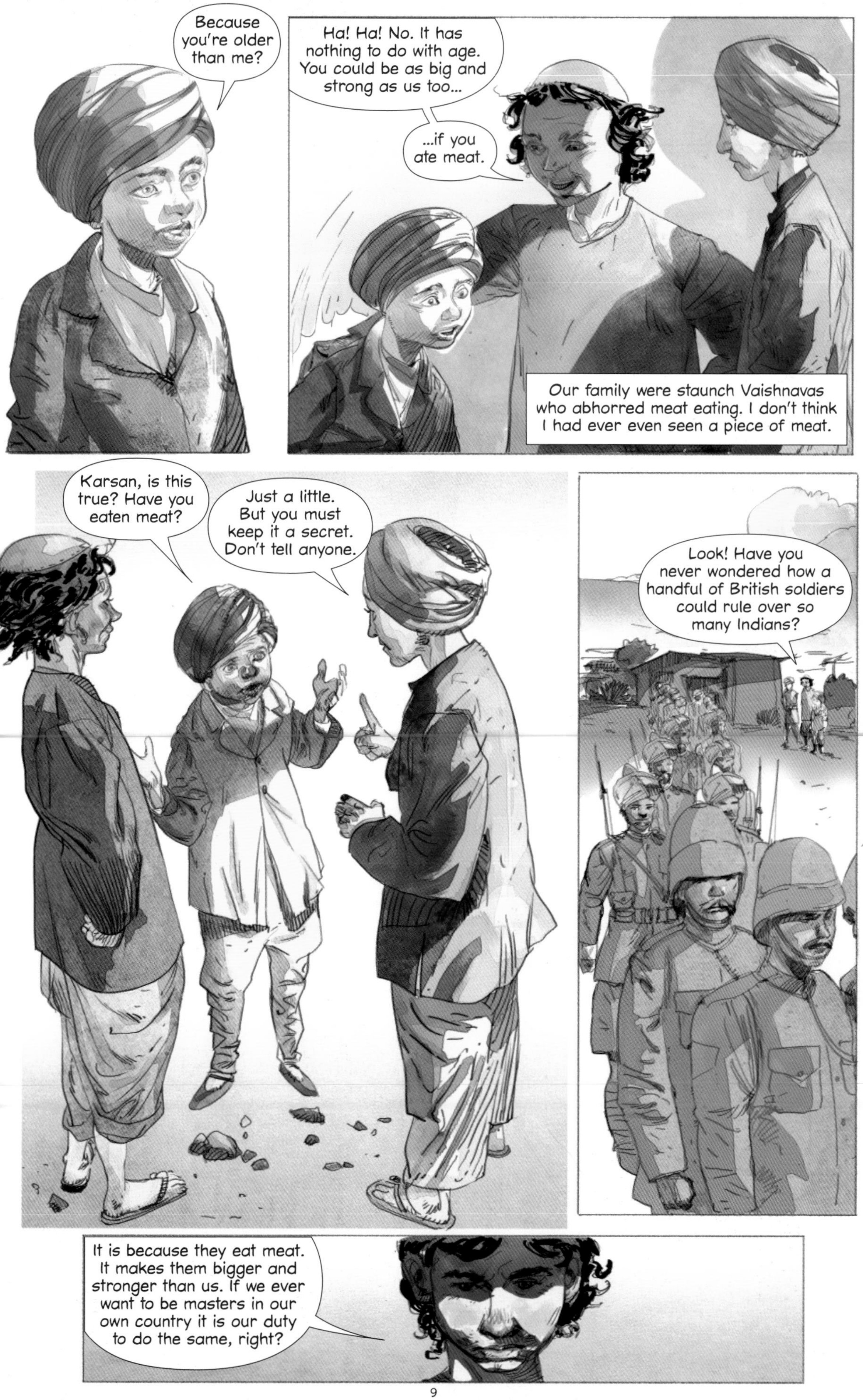

Because you're older than me?
Ha! Ha! No. It has nothing to do with age. You could be as big and strong as us too...
...if you ate meat.
Our family were staunch Vaishnavas who abhorred meat eating. I don't think I had ever even seen a piece of meat.
Karsan, is this true? Have you eaten meat?
Just a little. But you must keep it a secret. Don't tell anyone.
Look! Have you never wondered how a handful of British soldiers could rule over so many Indians?
It is because they eat meat. It makes them bigger and stronger than us. If we ever want to be masters in our own country it is our duty to do the same, right?

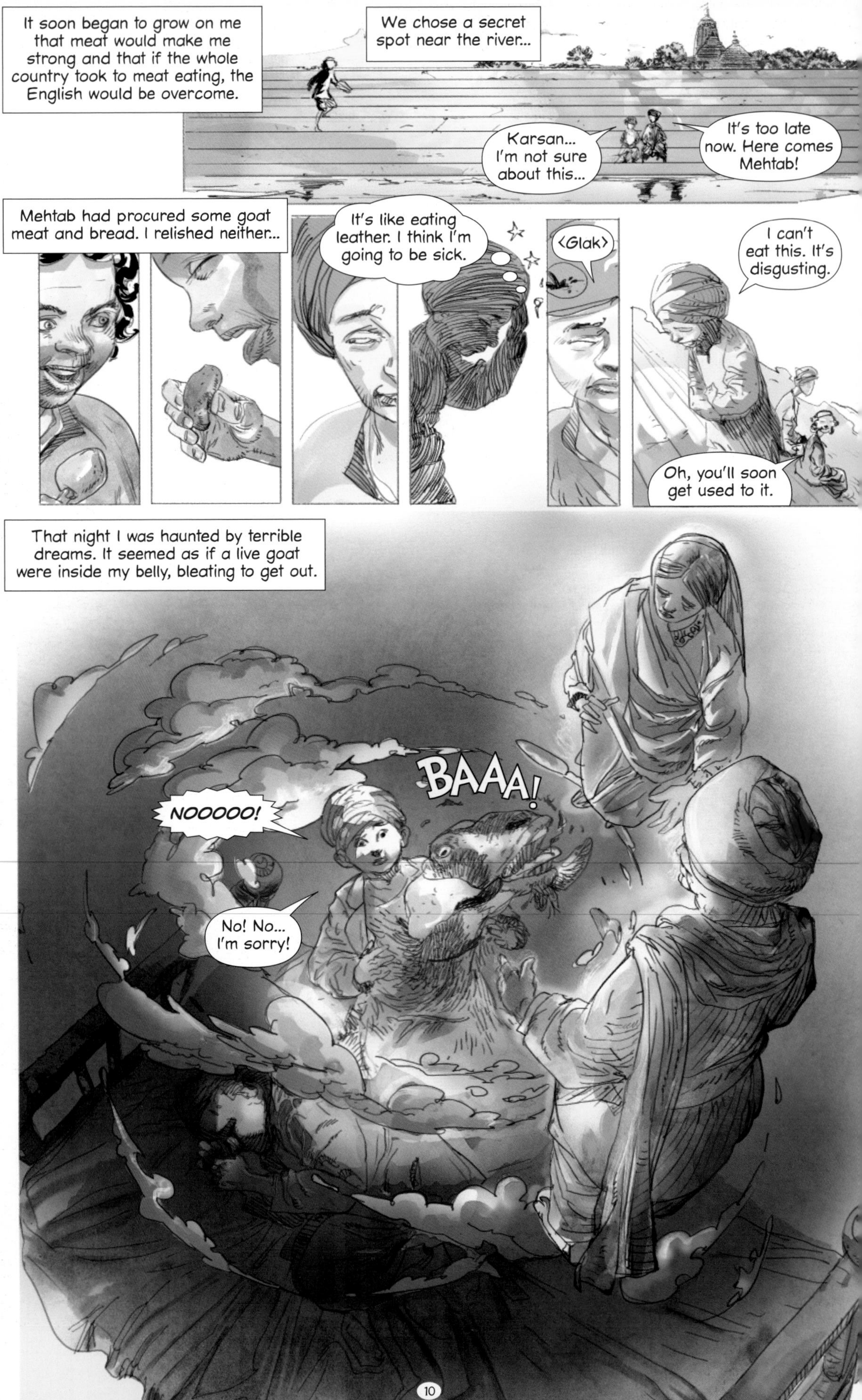

It soon began to grow on me that meat would make me strong and that if the whole country took to meat eating, the English would be overcome.
We chose a secret spot near the river...
Karsan... I'm not sure about this...
It's too late now. Here comes Mehtab!
Mehtab had procured some goat meat and bread. I relished neither...
It's like eating leather. I think I'm going to be sick.
<Glak>
I can't eat this. It's disgusting.
Oh, you'll soon get used to it.
That night I was haunted by terrible dreams. It seemed as if a live goat were inside my belly, bleating to get out.
BAAA!
NOOOOO!
No! No... I'm sorry!

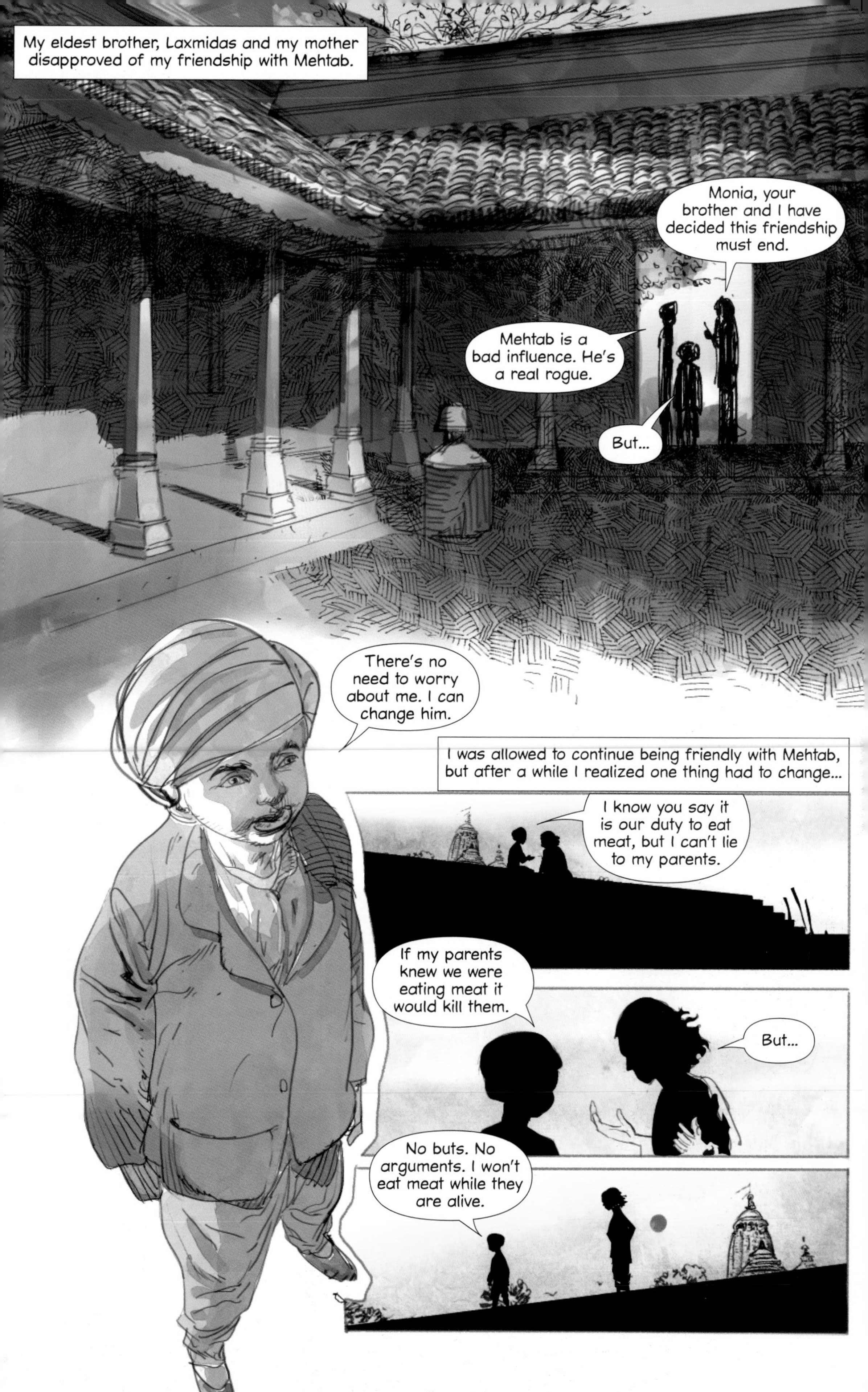

My eldest brother, Laxmidas and my mother disapproved of my friendship with Mehtab.
Monia, your brother and I have decided this friendship must end.
Mehtab is a bad influence. He's a real rogue.
But...
There's no need to worry about me. I can change him.
I was allowed to continue being friendly with Mehtab, but after a while I realized one thing had to change...
I know you say it is our duty to eat meat, but I can't lie to my parents.
If my parents knew we were eating meat it would kill them.
But...
No buts. No arguments. I won't eat meat while they are alive.

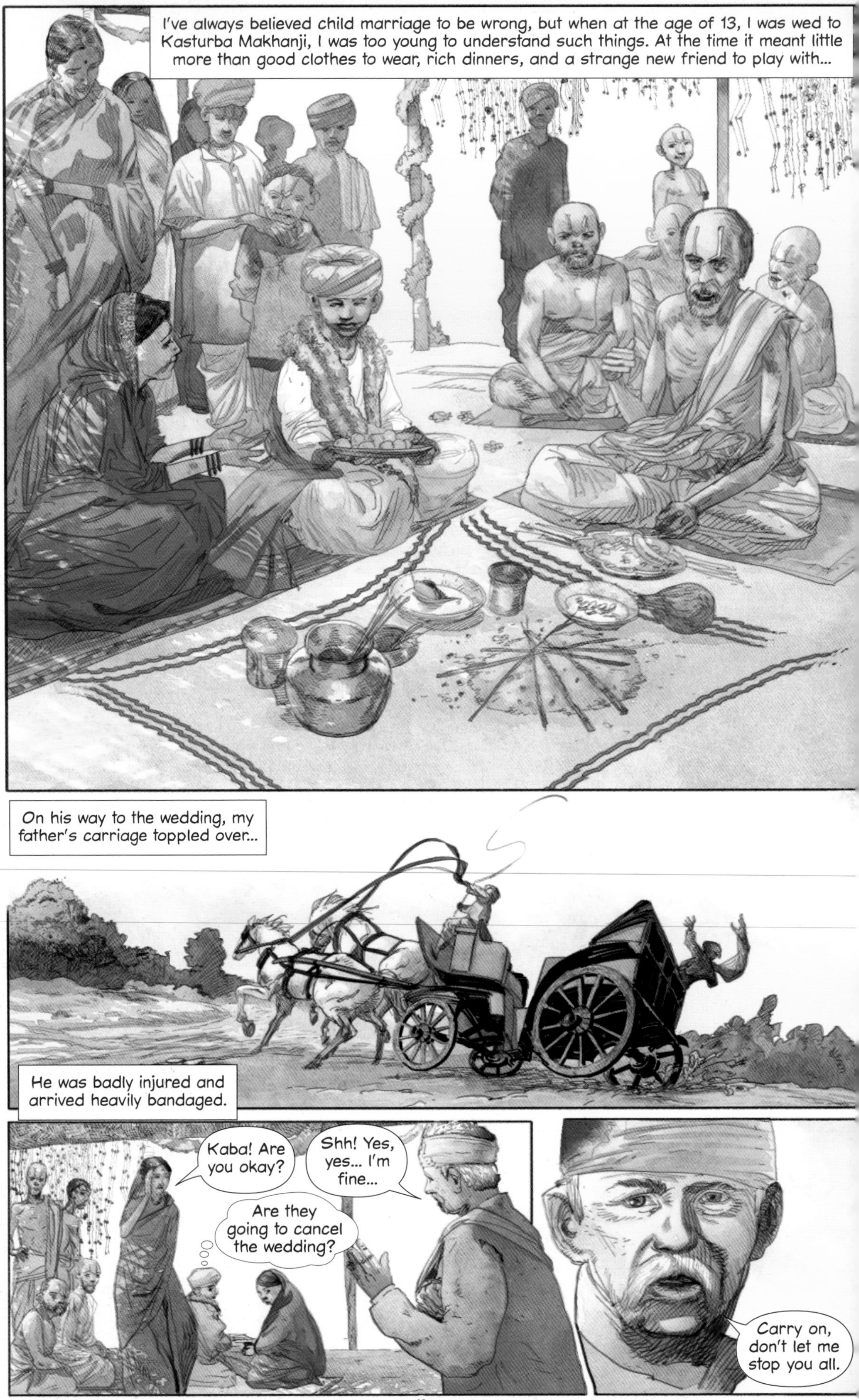
I've always believed child marriage to be wrong, but when at the age of 13, I was wed to Kasturba Makhanji, I was too young to understand such things. At the time it meant little more than good clothes to wear, rich dinners, and a strange new friend to play with...
On his way to the wedding, my father's carriage toppled over...
He was badly injured and arrived heavily bandaged.
Kaba! Are you okay?
Shh! Yes, yes... I'm fine...
Are they going to cancel the wedding?
Carry on, don't let me stop you all.

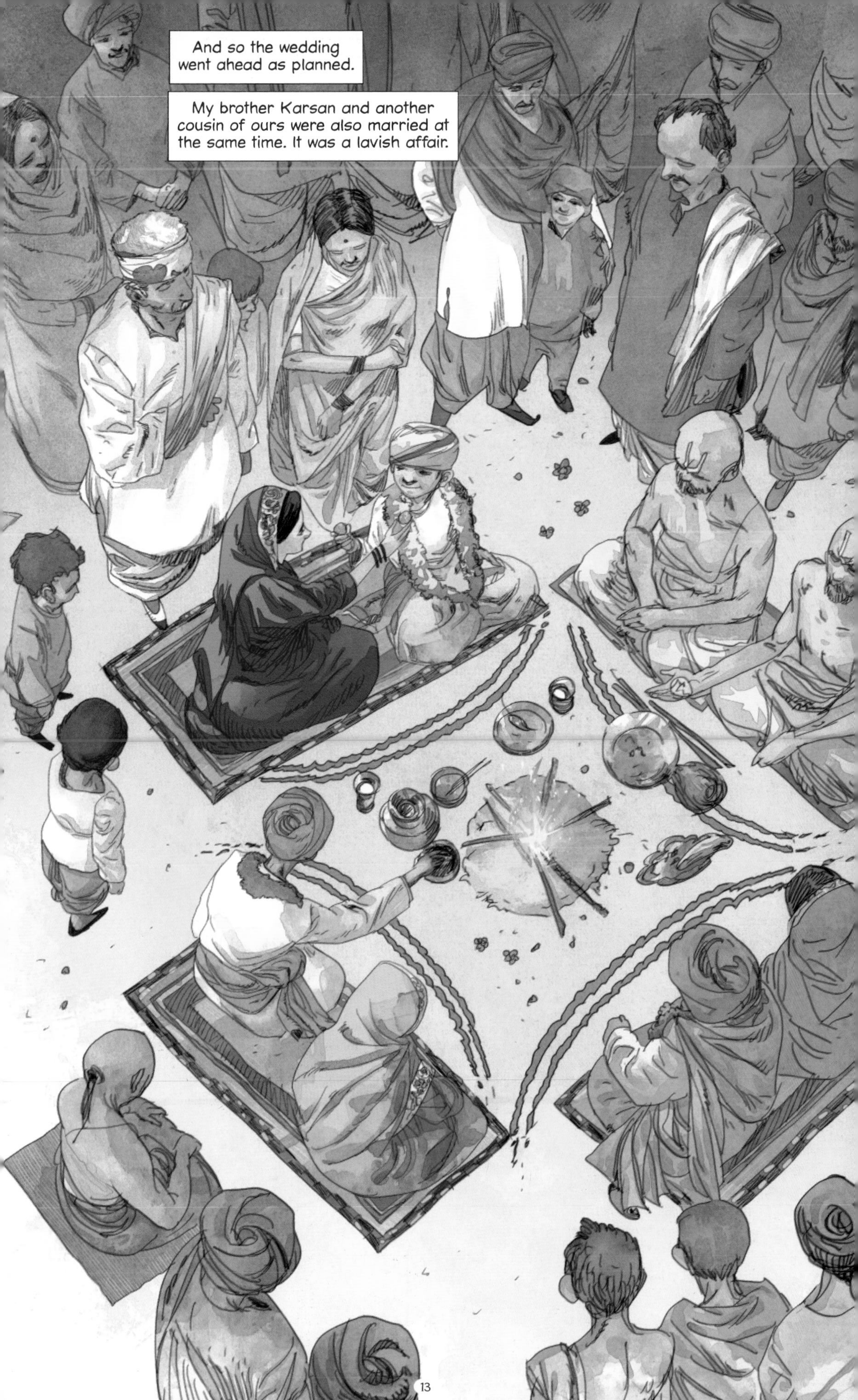
And so the wedding went ahead as planned.
My brother Karsan and another cousin of ours were also married at the same time. It was a lavish affair.

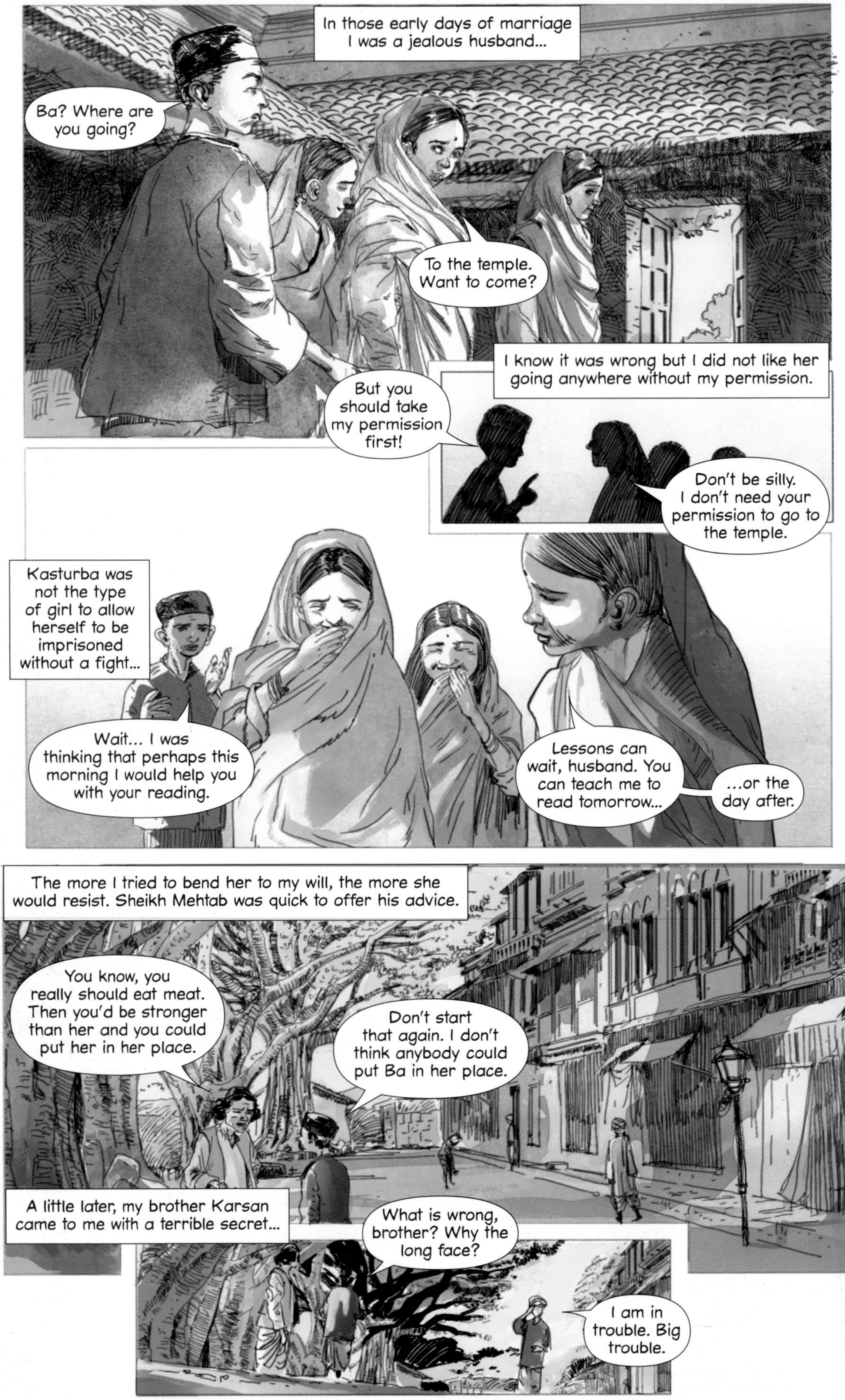

In those early days of marriage I was a jealous husband...
Ba? Where are you going?
To the temple. Want to come?
I know it was wrong but I did not like her going anywhere without my permission.
But you should take my permission first!
Don't be silly. I don't need your permission to go to the temple.
Kasturba was not the type of girl to allow herself to be imprisoned without a fight...
Wait... I was thinking that perhaps this morning I would help you with your reading.
Lessons can wait, husband. You can teach me to read tomorrow...
...or the day after.
The more I tried to bend her to my will, the more she would resist. Sheikh Mehtab was quick to offer his advice.
You know, you really should eat meat. Then you'd be stronger than her and you could put her in her place.
Don't start that again. I don't think anybody could put Ba in her place.
A little later, my brother Karsan came to me with a terrible secret...
What is wrong, brother? Why the long face?
I am in trouble. Big trouble.

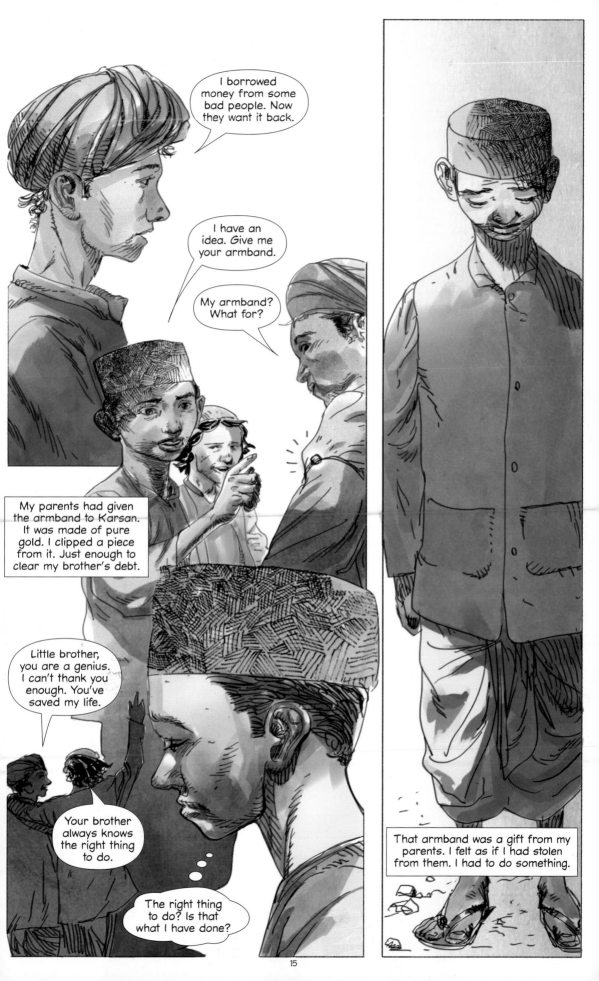

I borrowed money from some bad people. Now they want it back.

I have an idea. Give me your armband.

My armband? What for?

My parents had given the armband to Karsan. It was made of pure gold. I clipped a piece from it. Just enough to clear my brother's debt.

Little brother, you are a genius. I can't thank you enough. You've saved my life.

Your brother always knows the right thing to do.

The right thing to do? Is that what I have done?

That armband was a gift from my parents. I felt as if I had stolen from them. I had to do something.

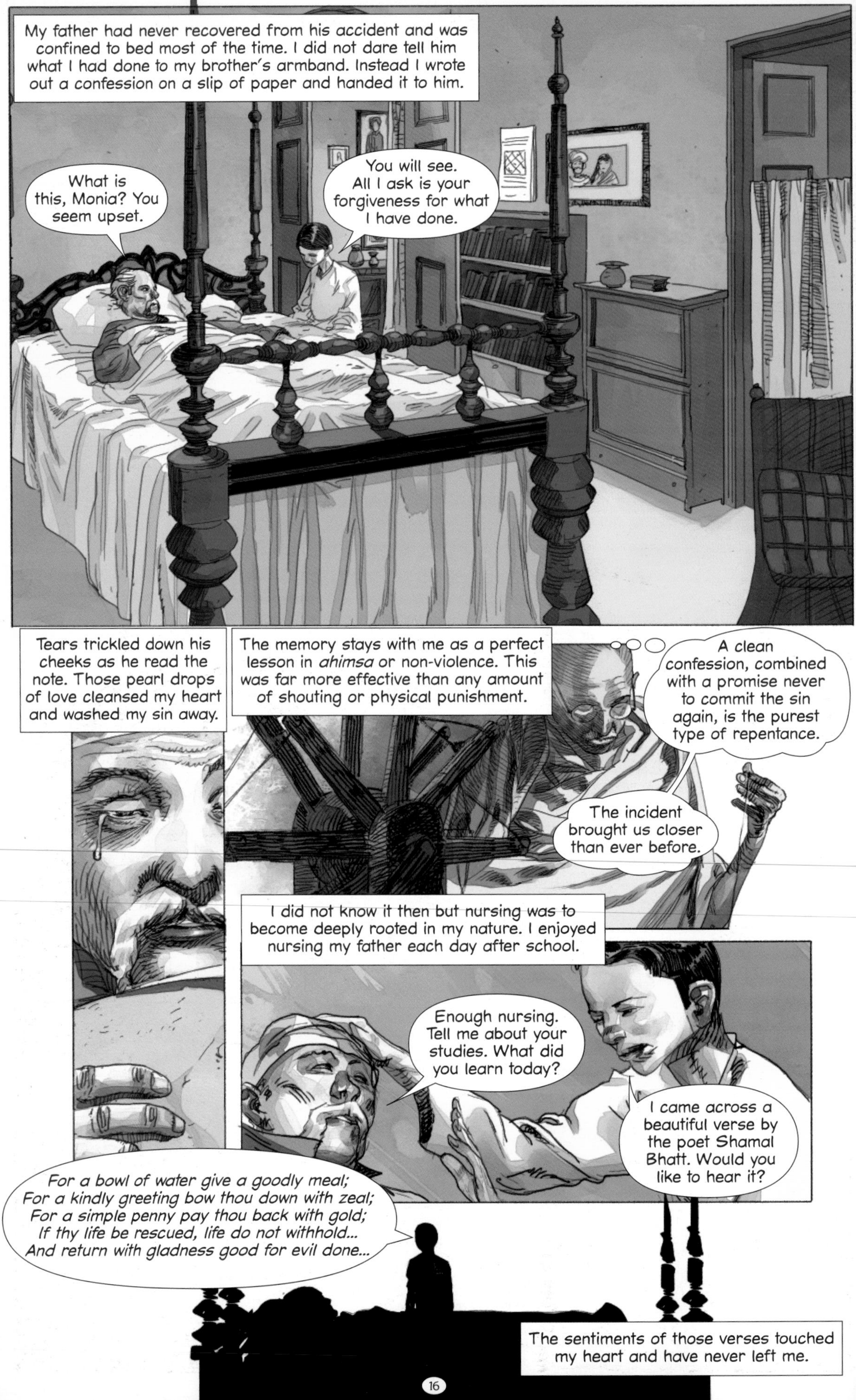
My father had never recovered from his accident and was confined to bed most of the time. I did not dare tell him what I had done to my brother's armband. Instead I wrote out a confession on a slip of paper and handed it to him.
What is this, Monia? You seem upset.
You will see. All I ask is your forgiveness for what I have done.
Tears trickled down his cheeks as he read the note. Those pearl drops of love cleansed my heart and washed my sin away.
The memory stays with me as a perfect lesson in *ahimsa* or non-violence. This was far more effective than any amount of shouting or physical punishment.
A clean confession, combined with a promise never to commit the sin again, is the purest type of repentance.
The incident brought us closer than ever before.
I did not know it then but nursing was to become deeply rooted in my nature. I enjoyed nursing my father each day after school.
Enough nursing. Tell me about your studies. What did you learn today?
I came across a beautiful verse by the poet Shamal Bhatt. Would you like to hear it?
For a bowl of water give a goodly meal;
For a kindly greeting bow thou down with zeal;
For a simple penny pay thou back with gold;
If thy life be rescued, life do not withhold...
And return with gladness good for evil done...
The sentiments of those verses touched my heart and have never left me.

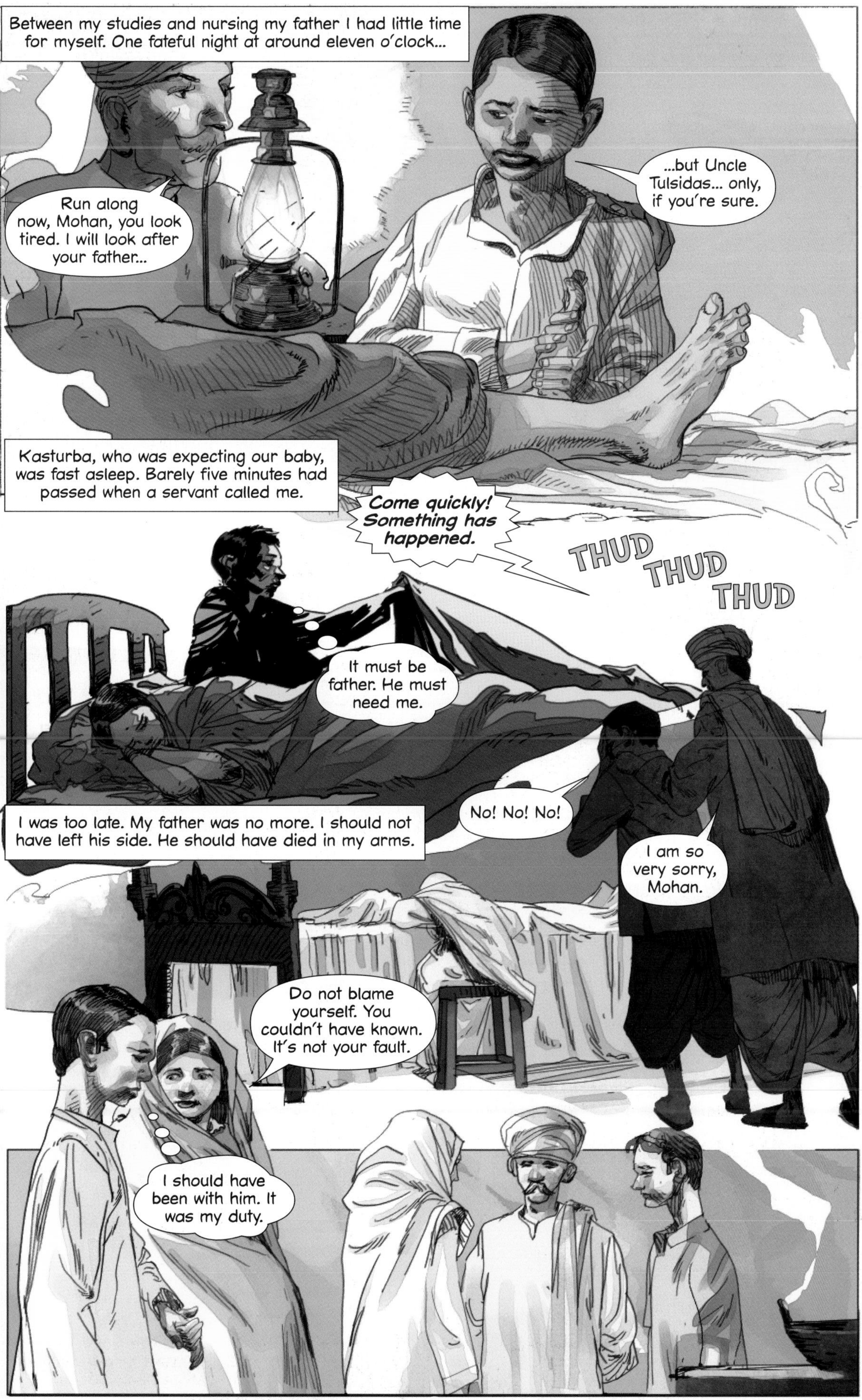

Between my studies and nursing my father I had little time for myself. One fateful night at around eleven o'clock...
Run along now, Mohan, you look tired. I will look after your father...
...but Uncle Tulsidas... only, if you're sure.
Kasturba, who was expecting our baby, was fast asleep. Barely five minutes had passed when a servant called me.
Come quickly! Something has happened.
THUD THUD THUD
It must be father. He must need me.
I was too late. My father was no more. I should not have left his side. He should have died in my arms.
No! No! No!
I am so very sorry, Mohan.
Do not blame yourself. You couldn't have known. It's not your fault.
I should have been with him. It was my duty.

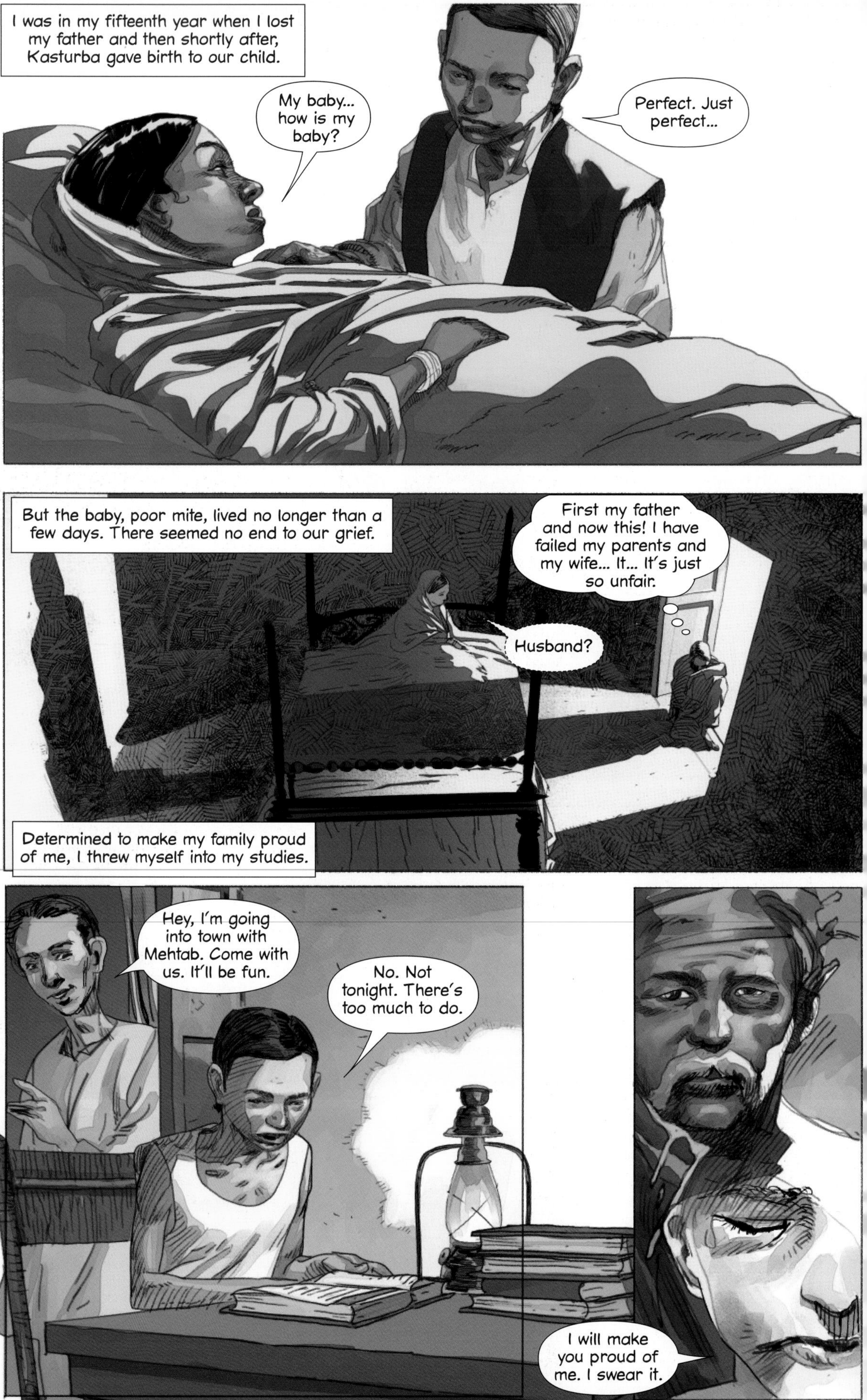
I was in my fifteenth year when I lost my father and then shortly after, Kasturba gave birth to our child.
My baby... how is my baby?
Perfect. Just perfect...
But the baby, poor mite, lived no longer than a few days. There seemed no end to our grief.
First my father and now this! I have failed my parents and my wife... It... It's just so unfair.
Husband?
Determined to make my family proud of me, I threw myself into my studies.
Hey, I'm going into town with Mehtab. Come with us. It'll be fun.
No. Not tonight. There's too much to do.
I will make you proud of me. I swear it.

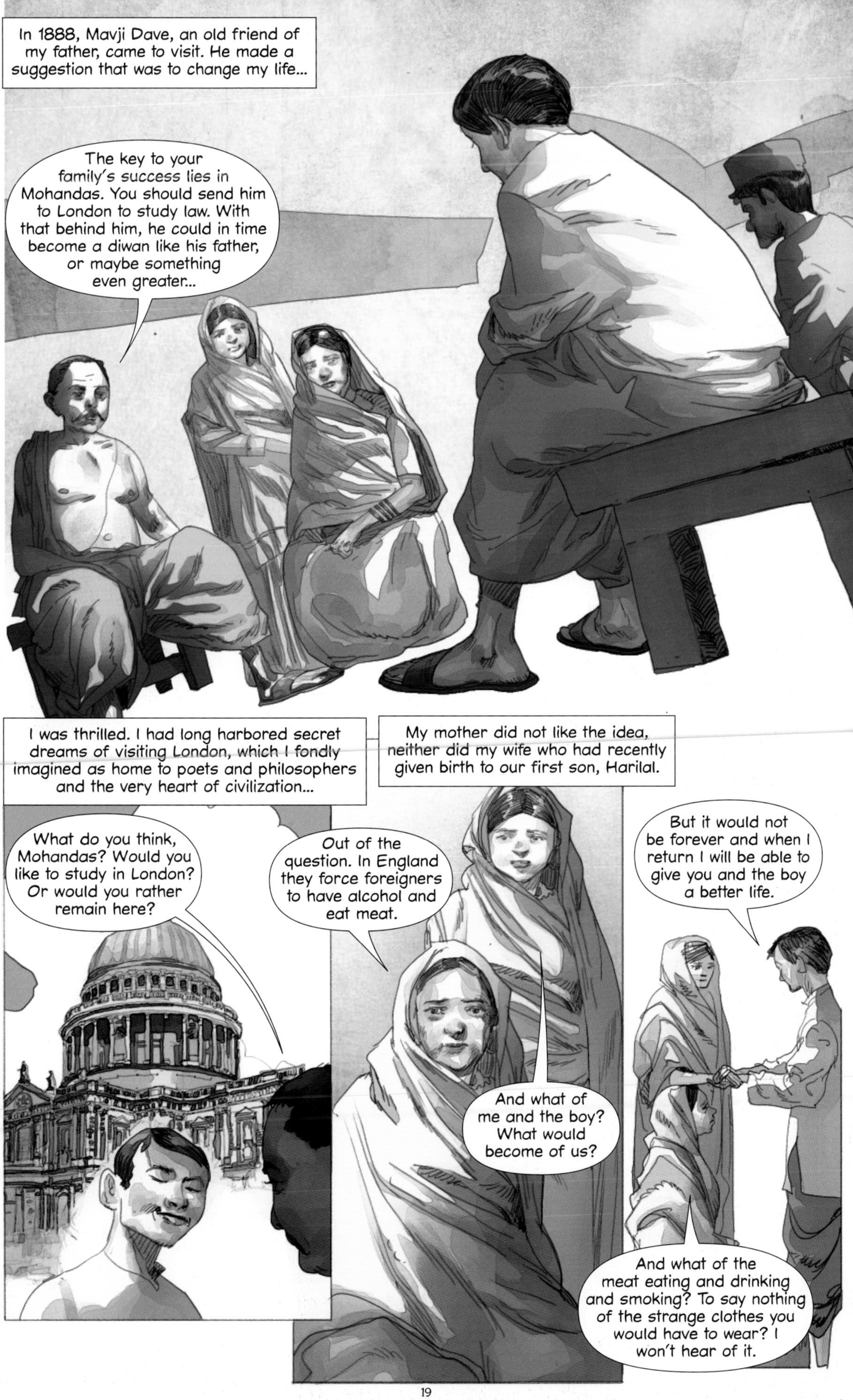

In 1888, Mavji Dave, an old friend of my father, came to visit. He made a suggestion that was to change my life...
The key to your family's success lies in Mohandas. You should send him to London to study law. With that behind him, he could in time become a diwan like his father, or maybe something even greater...
I was thrilled. I had long harbored secret dreams of visiting London, which I fondly imagined as home to poets and philosophers and the very heart of civilization...
What do you think, Mohandas? Would you like to study in London? Or would you rather remain here?
My mother did not like the idea, neither did my wife who had recently given birth to our first son, Harilal.
Out of the question. In England they force foreigners to have alcohol and eat meat.
And what of me and the boy? What would become of us?
But it would not be forever and when I return I will be able to give you and the boy a better life.
And what of the meat eating and drinking and smoking? To say nothing of the strange clothes you would have to wear? I won't hear of it.

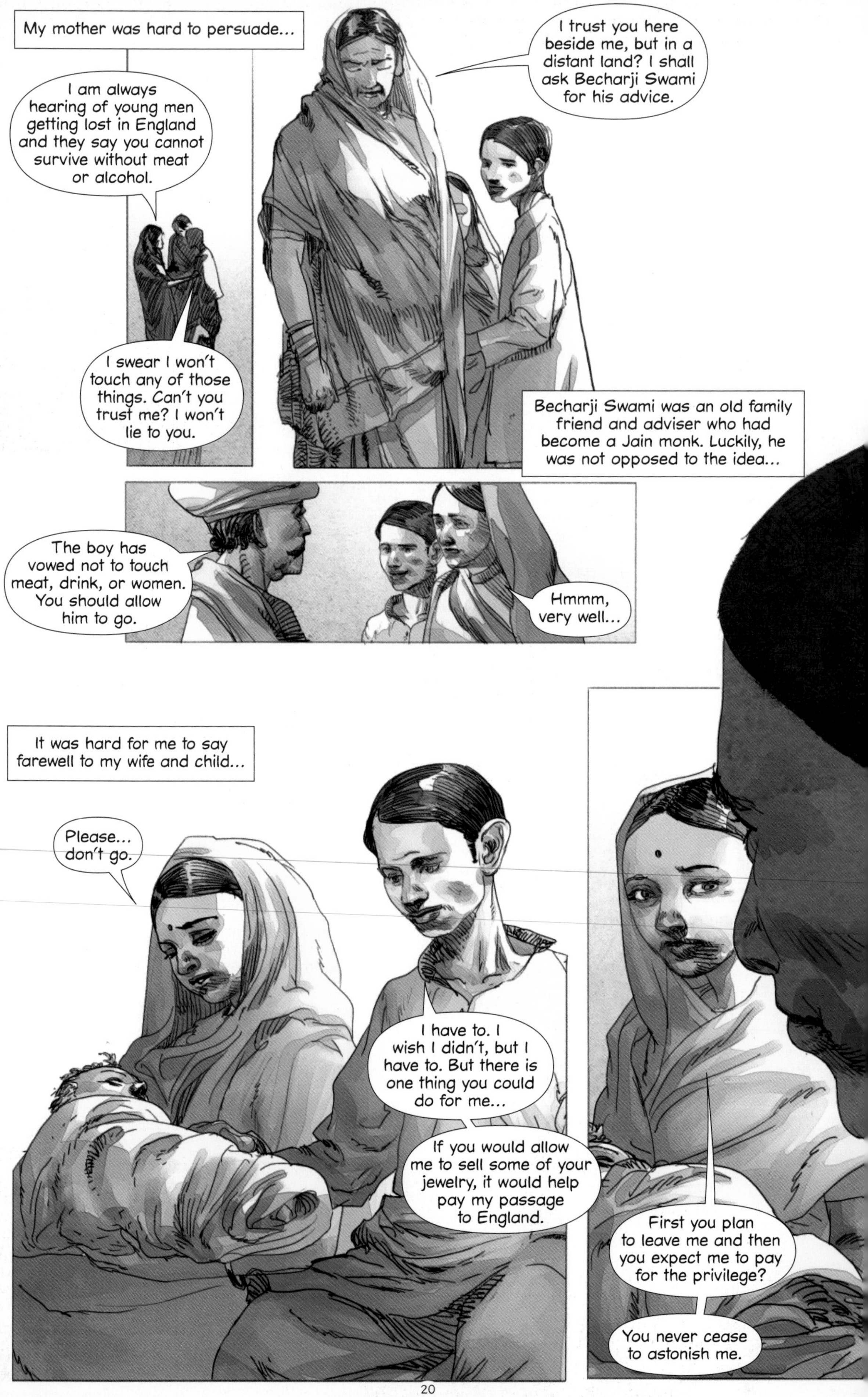
My mother was hard to persuade...
I am always hearing of young men getting lost in England and they say you cannot survive without meat or alcohol.
I trust you here beside me, but in a distant land? I shall ask Becharji Swami for his advice.
I swear I won't touch any of those things. Can't you trust me? I won't lie to you.
Becharji Swami was an old family friend and adviser who had become a Jain monk. Luckily, he was not opposed to the idea...
The boy has vowed not to touch meat, drink, or women. You should allow him to go.
Hmmm, very well...
It was hard for me to say farewell to my wife and child...
Please... don't go.
I have to. I wish I didn't, but I have to. But there is one thing you could do for me...
If you would allow me to sell some of your jewelry, it would help pay my passage to England.
First you plan to leave me and then you expect me to pay for the privilege?
You never cease to astonish me.

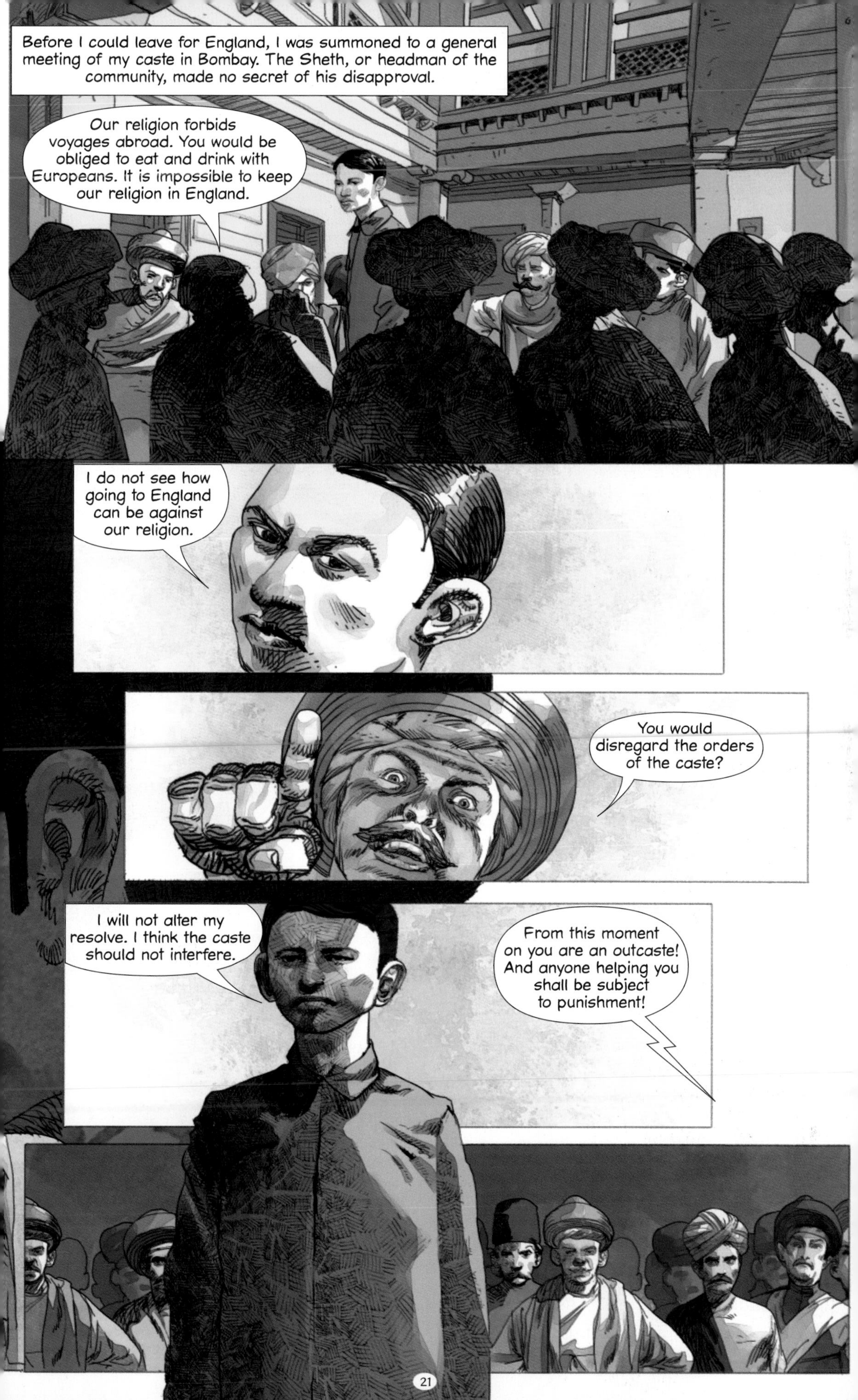

Before I could leave for England, I was summoned to a general meeting of my caste in Bombay. The Sheth, or headman of the community, made no secret of his disapproval.
Our religion forbids voyages abroad. You would be obliged to eat and drink with Europeans. It is impossible to keep our religion in England.
I do not see how going to England can be against our religion.
You would disregard the orders of the caste?
I will not alter my resolve. I think the caste should not interfere.
From this moment on you are an outcaste! And anyone helping you shall be subject to punishment!

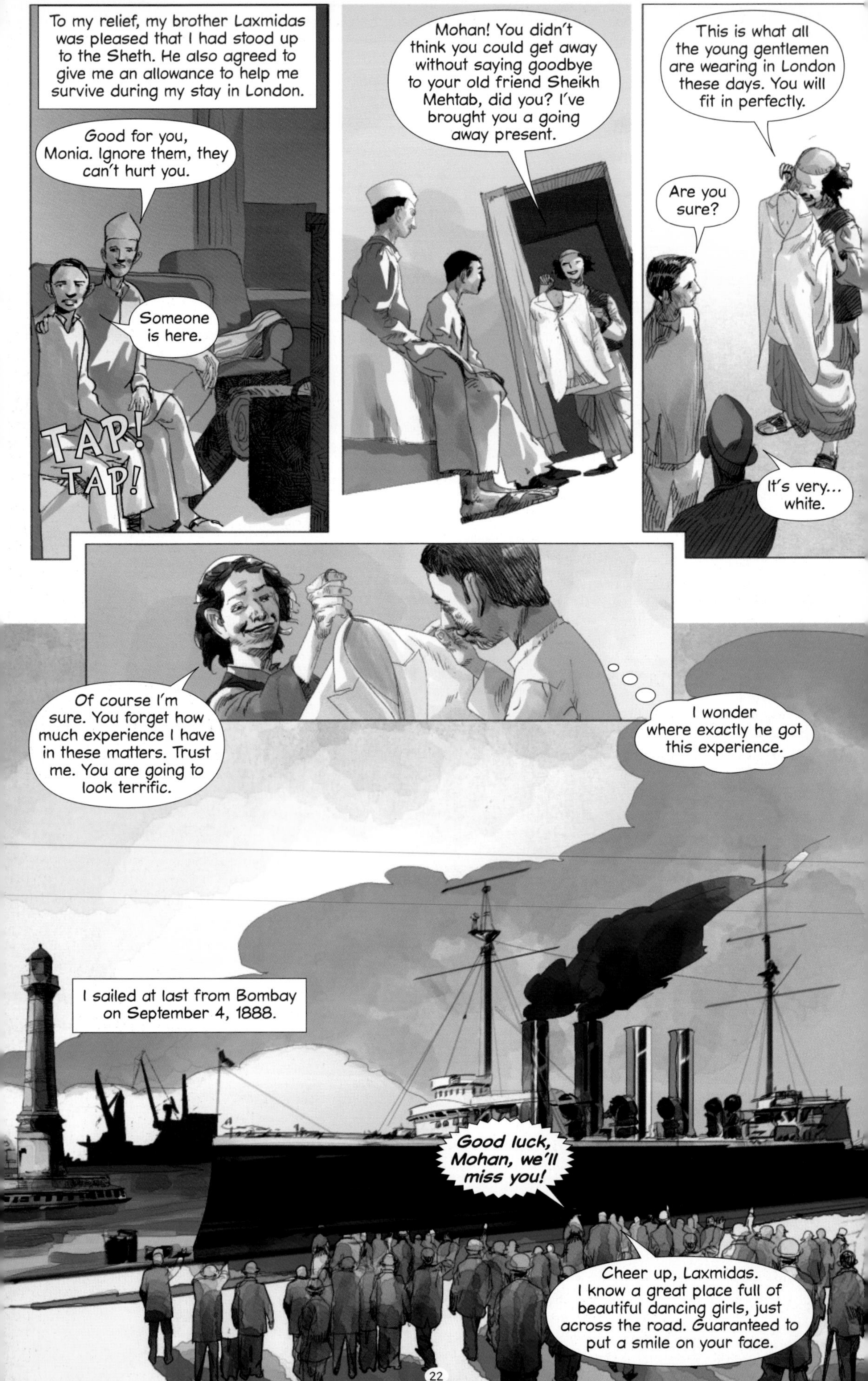

To my relief, my brother Laxmidas was pleased that I had stood up to the Sheth. He also agreed to give me an allowance to help me survive during my stay in London.
Good for you, Monia. Ignore them, they can't hurt you.
TAP! TAP!
Someone is here.
Mohan! You didn't think you could get away without saying goodbye to your old friend Sheikh Mehtab, did you? I've brought you a going away present.
This is what all the young gentlemen are wearing in London these days. You will fit in perfectly.
Are you sure?
It's very... white.
Of course I'm sure. You forget how much experience I have in these matters. Trust me. You are going to look terrific.
I wonder where exactly he got this experience.
I sailed at last from Bombay on September 4, 1888.
Good luck, Mohan, we'll miss you!
Cheer up, Laxmidas. I know a great place full of beautiful dancing girls, just across the road. Guaranteed to put a smile on your face.

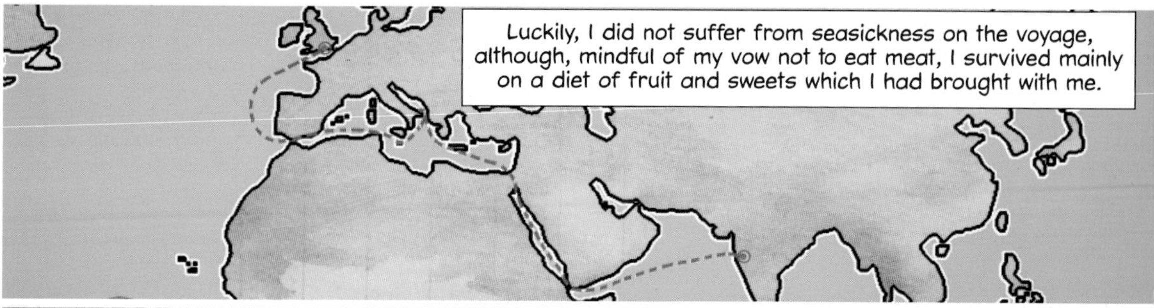
Luckily, I did not suffer from seasickness on the voyage, although, mindful of my vow not to eat meat, I survived mainly on a diet of fruit and sweets which I had brought with me.

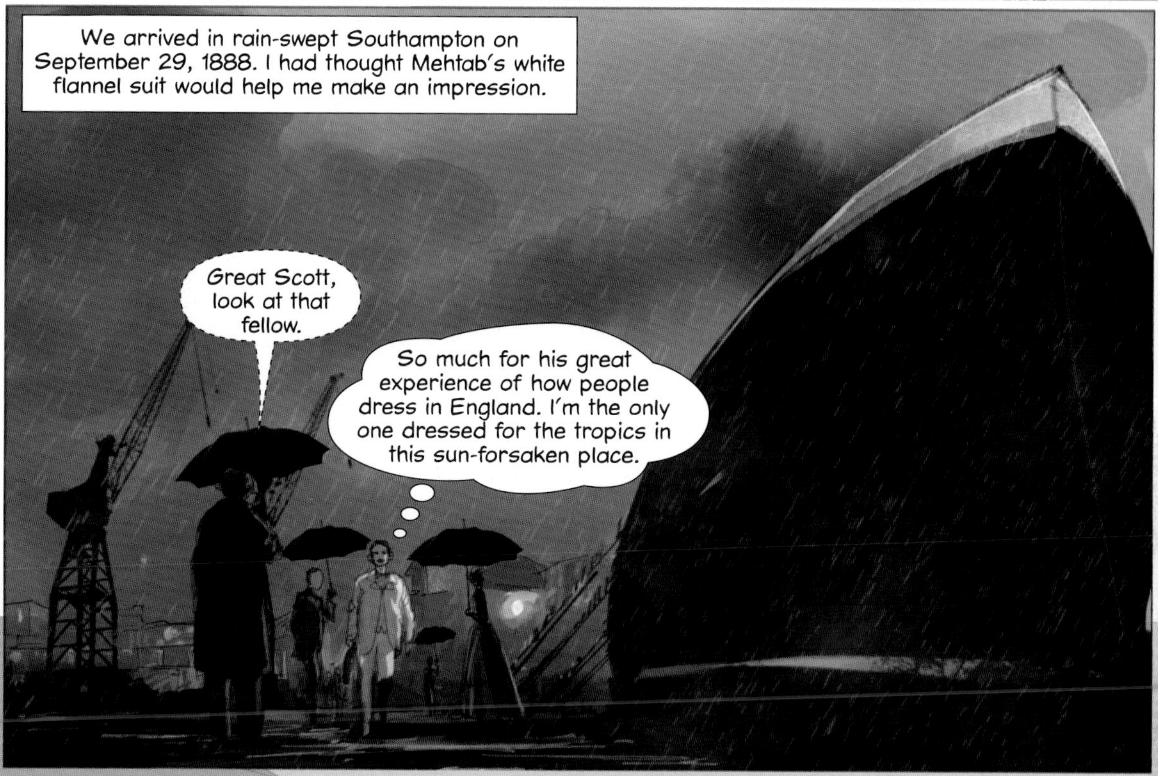
We arrived in rain-swept Southampton on September 29, 1888. I had thought Mehtab's white flannel suit would help me make an impression.
Great Scott, look at that fellow.
So much for his great experience of how people dress in England. I'm the only one dressed for the tropics in this sun-forsaken place.

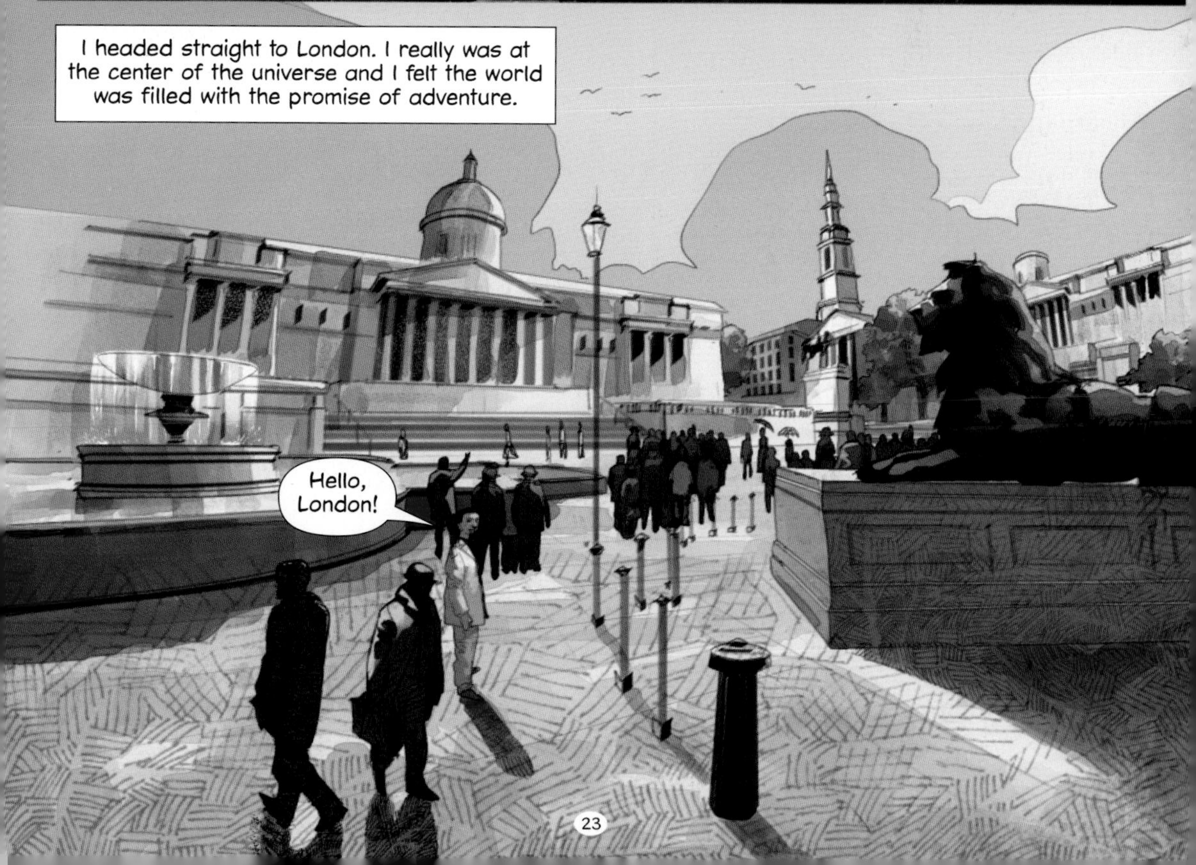
I headed straight to London. I really was at the center of the universe and I felt the world was filled with the promise of adventure.
Hello, London!

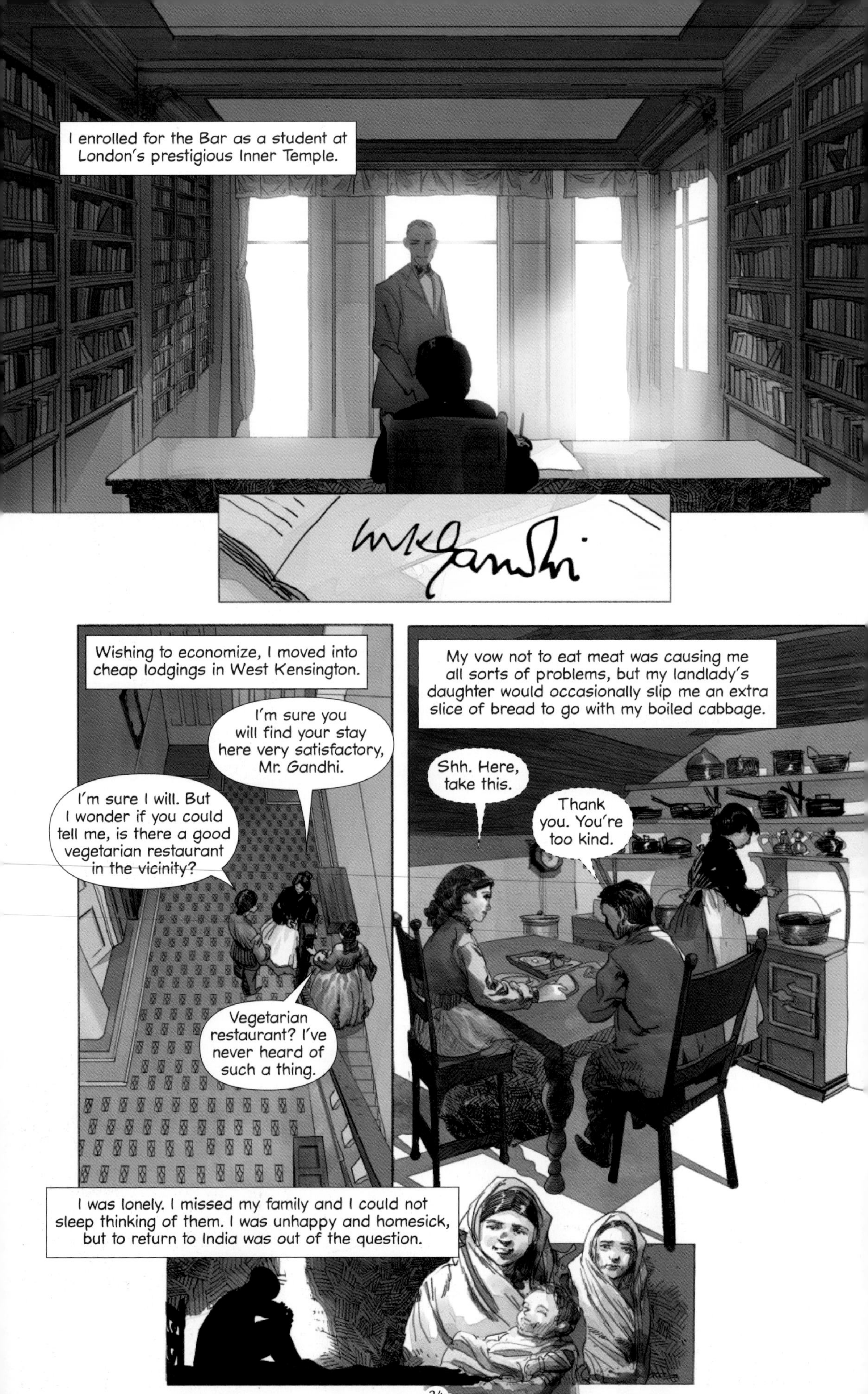
I enrolled for the Bar as a student at London's prestigious Inner Temple.
Wishing to economize, I moved into cheap lodgings in West Kensington.
I'm sure you will find your stay here very satisfactory, Mr. Gandhi.
I'm sure I will. But I wonder if you could tell me, is there a good vegetarian restaurant in the vicinity?
Vegetarian restaurant? I've never heard of such a thing.
My vow not to eat meat was causing me all sorts of problems, but my landlady's daughter would occasionally slip me an extra slice of bread to go with my boiled cabbage.
Shh. Here, take this.
Thank you. You're too kind.
I was lonely. I missed my family and I could not sleep thinking of them. I was unhappy and homesick, but to return to India was out of the question.

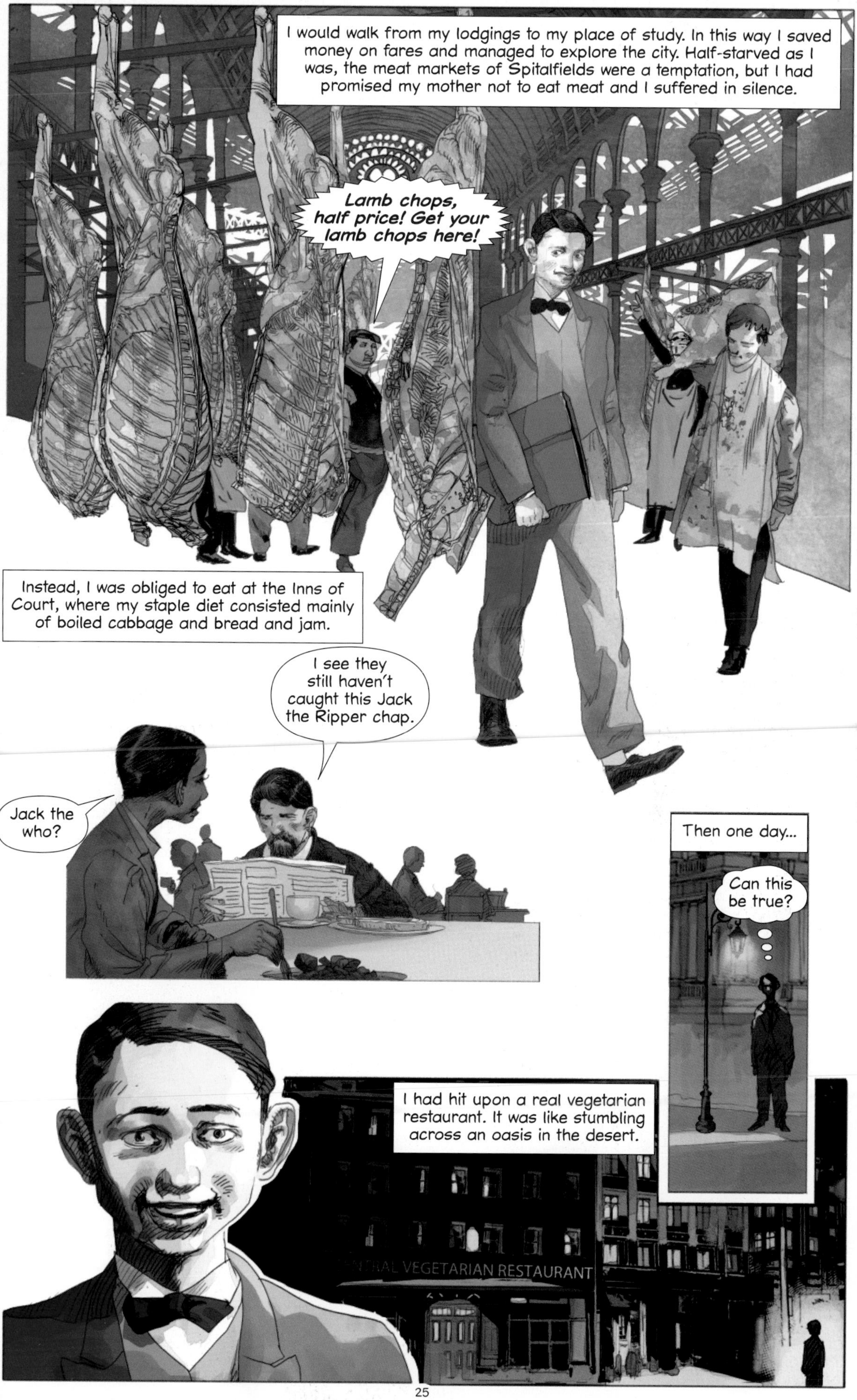
I would walk from my lodgings to my place of study. In this way I saved money on fares and managed to explore the city. Half-starved as I was, the meat markets of Spitalfields were a temptation, but I had promised my mother not to eat meat and I suffered in silence.
Lamb chops, half price! Get your lamb chops here!
Instead, I was obliged to eat at the Inns of Court, where my staple diet consisted mainly of boiled cabbage and bread and jam.
I see they still haven't caught this Jack the Ripper chap.
Jack the who?
Then one day...
Can this be true?
I had hit upon a real vegetarian restaurant. It was like stumbling across an oasis in the desert.
VEGETARIAN RESTAURANT

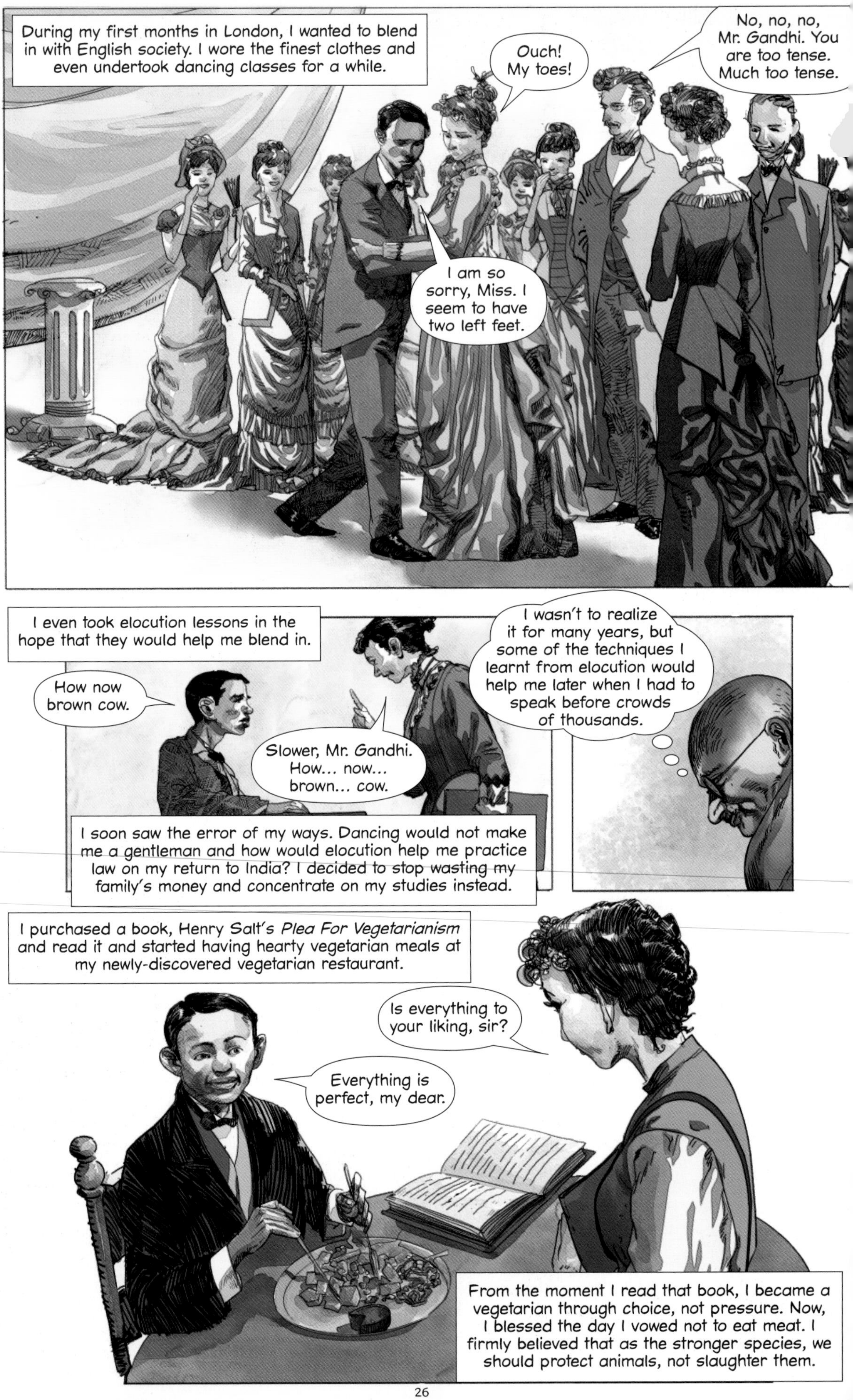
During my first months in London, I wanted to blend in with English society. I wore the finest clothes and even undertook dancing classes for a while.
Ouch! My toes!
No, no, no, Mr. Gandhi. You are too tense. Much too tense.
I am so sorry, Miss. I seem to have two left feet.
I even took elocution lessons in the hope that they would help me blend in.
How now brown cow.
Slower, Mr. Gandhi. How... now... brown... cow.
I wasn't to realize it for many years, but some of the techniques I learnt from elocution would help me later when I had to speak before crowds of thousands.
I soon saw the error of my ways. Dancing would not make me a gentleman and how would elocution help me practice law on my return to India? I decided to stop wasting my family's money and concentrate on my studies instead.
I purchased a book, Henry Salt's *Plea For Vegetarianism* and read it and started having hearty vegetarian meals at my newly-discovered vegetarian restaurant.
Is everything to your liking, sir?
Everything is perfect, my dear.
From the moment I read that book, I became a vegetarian through choice, not pressure. Now, I blessed the day I vowed not to eat meat. I firmly believed that as the stronger species, we should protect animals, not slaughter them.

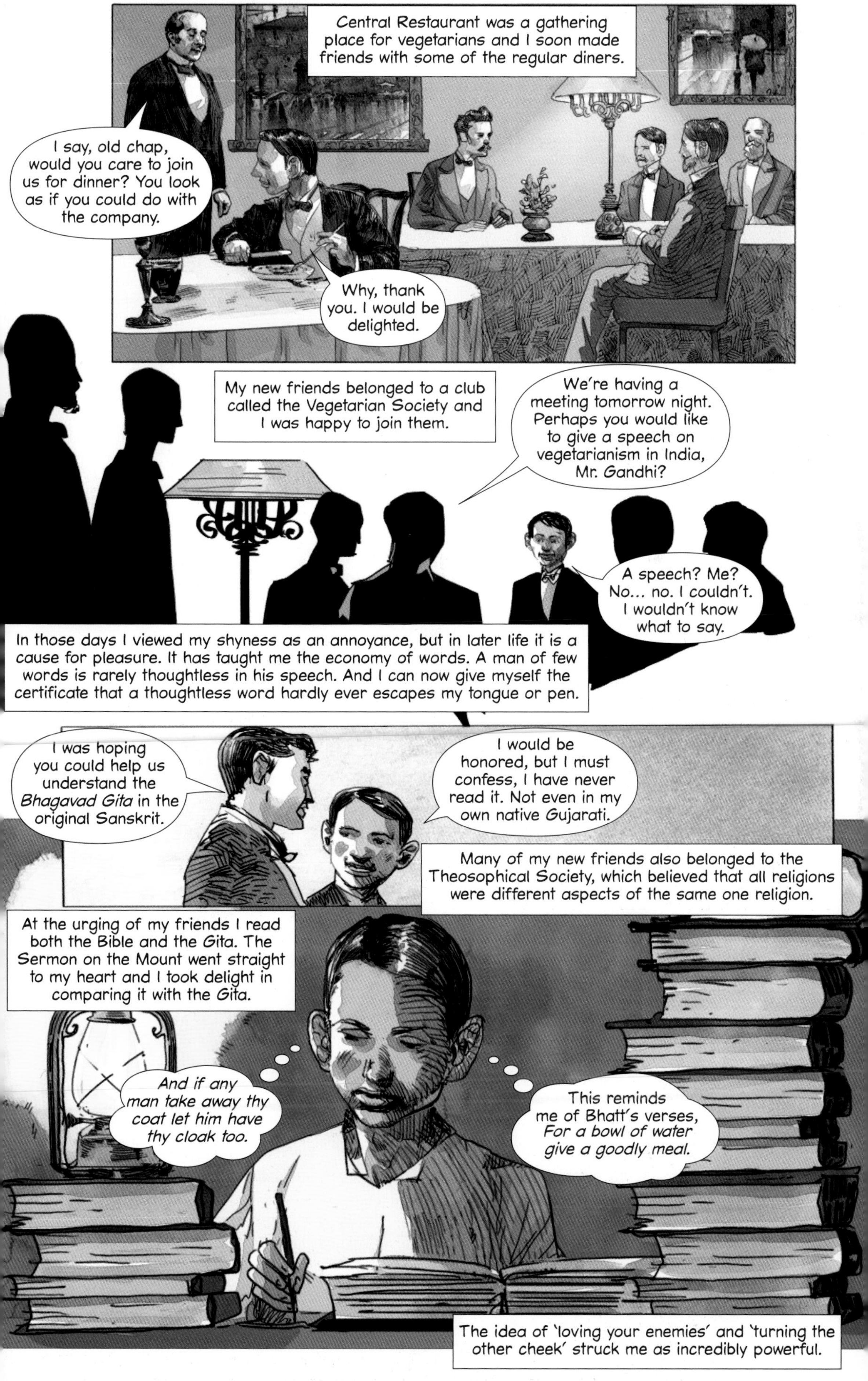
Central Restaurant was a gathering place for vegetarians and I soon made friends with some of the regular diners.
I say, old chap, would you care to join us for dinner? You look as if you could do with the company.
Why, thank you. I would be delighted.
My new friends belonged to a club called the Vegetarian Society and I was happy to join them.
We're having a meeting tomorrow night. Perhaps you would like to give a speech on vegetarianism in India, Mr. Gandhi?
A speech? Me? No... no. I couldn't. I wouldn't know what to say.
In those days I viewed my shyness as an annoyance, but in later life it is a cause for pleasure. It has taught me the economy of words. A man of few words is rarely thoughtless in his speech. And I can now give myself the certificate that a thoughtless word hardly ever escapes my tongue or pen.
I was hoping you could help us understand the *Bhagavad Gita* in the original Sanskrit.
I would be honored, but I must confess, I have never read it. Not even in my own native *Gujarati*.
Many of my new friends also belonged to the Theosophical Society, which believed that all religions were different aspects of the same one religion.
At the urging of my friends I read both the Bible and the Gita. The Sermon on the Mount went straight to my heart and I took delight in comparing it with the *Gita*.
And if any man take away thy coat let him have thy cloak too.
This reminds me of Bhatt's verses, *For a bowl of water give a goodly meal.*
The idea of 'loving your enemies' and 'turning the other cheek' struck me as incredibly powerful.

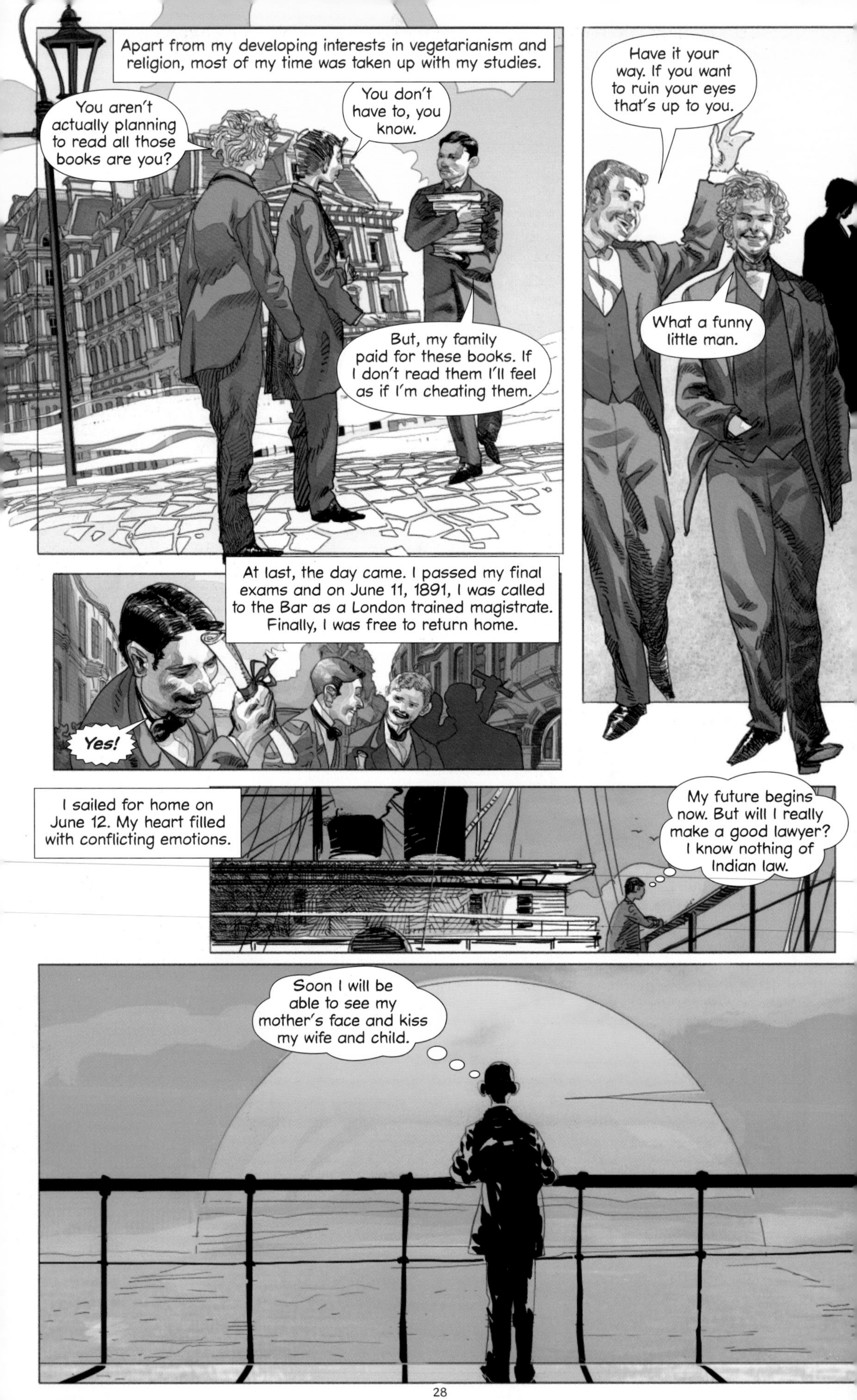
Apart from my developing interests in vegetarianism and religion, most of my time was taken up with my studies.
You aren't actually planning to read all those books are you?
You don't have to, you know.
But, my family paid for these books. If I don't read them I'll feel as if I'm cheating them.
Have it your way. If you want to ruin your eyes that's up to you.
What a funny little man.
At last, the day came. I passed my final exams and on June 11, 1891, I was called to the Bar as a London trained magistrate. Finally, I was free to return home.
Yes!
I sailed for home on June 12. My heart filled with conflicting emotions.
My future begins now. But will I really make a good lawyer? I know nothing of Indian law.
Soon I will be able to see my mother's face and kiss my wife and child.

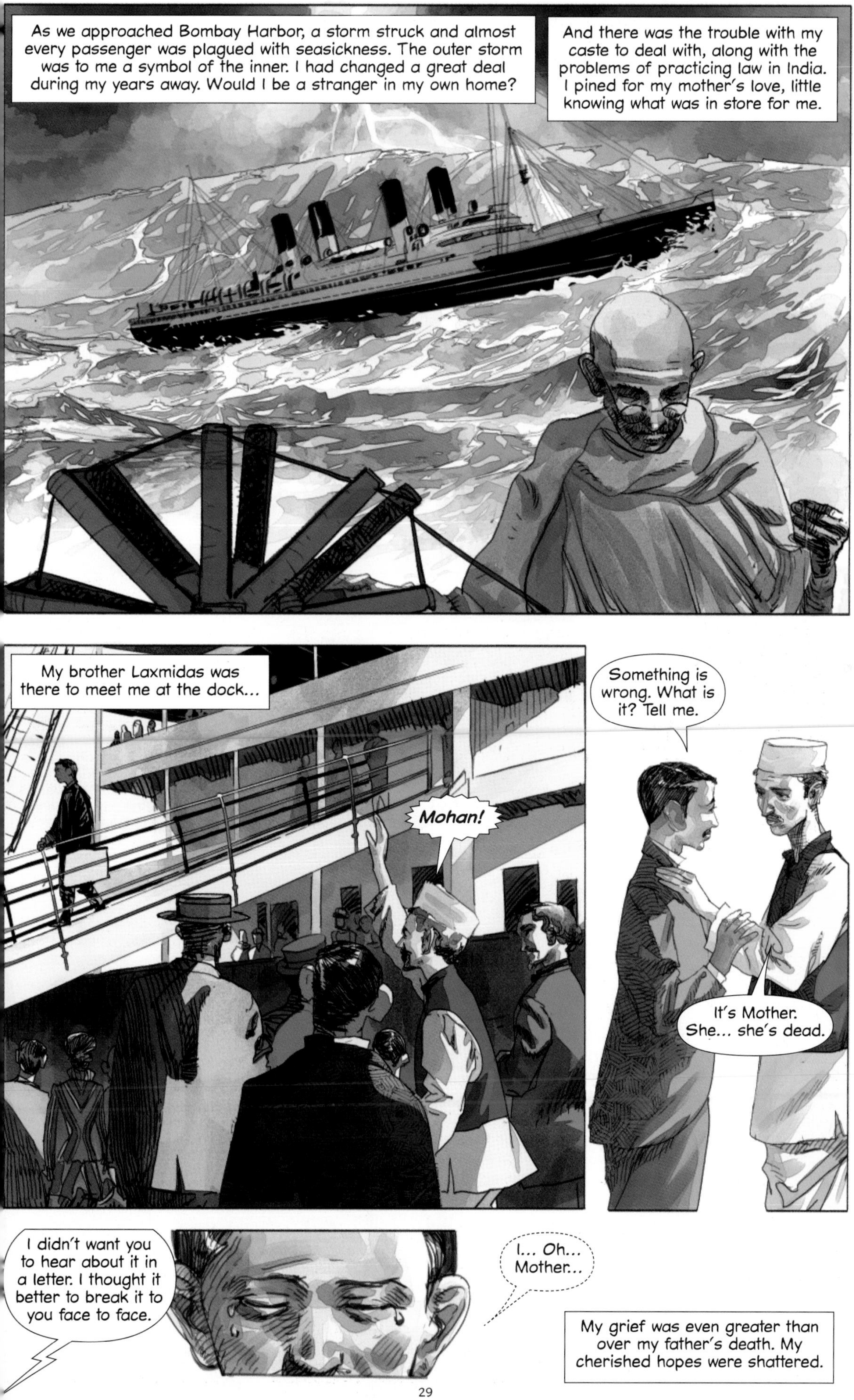
As we approached Bombay Harbor, a storm struck and almost every passenger was plagued with seasickness. The outer storm was to me a symbol of the inner. I had changed a great deal during my years away. Would I be a stranger in my own home?
And there was the trouble with my caste to deal with, along with the problems of practicing law in India. I pined for my mother's love, little knowing what was in store for me.
My brother Laxmidas was there to meet me at the dock...
Mohan!
Something is wrong. What is it? Tell me.
It's Mother. She... she's dead.
I didn't want you to hear about it in a letter. I thought it better to break it to you face to face.
I... Oh... Mother...
My grief was even greater than over my father's death. My cherished hopes were shattered.

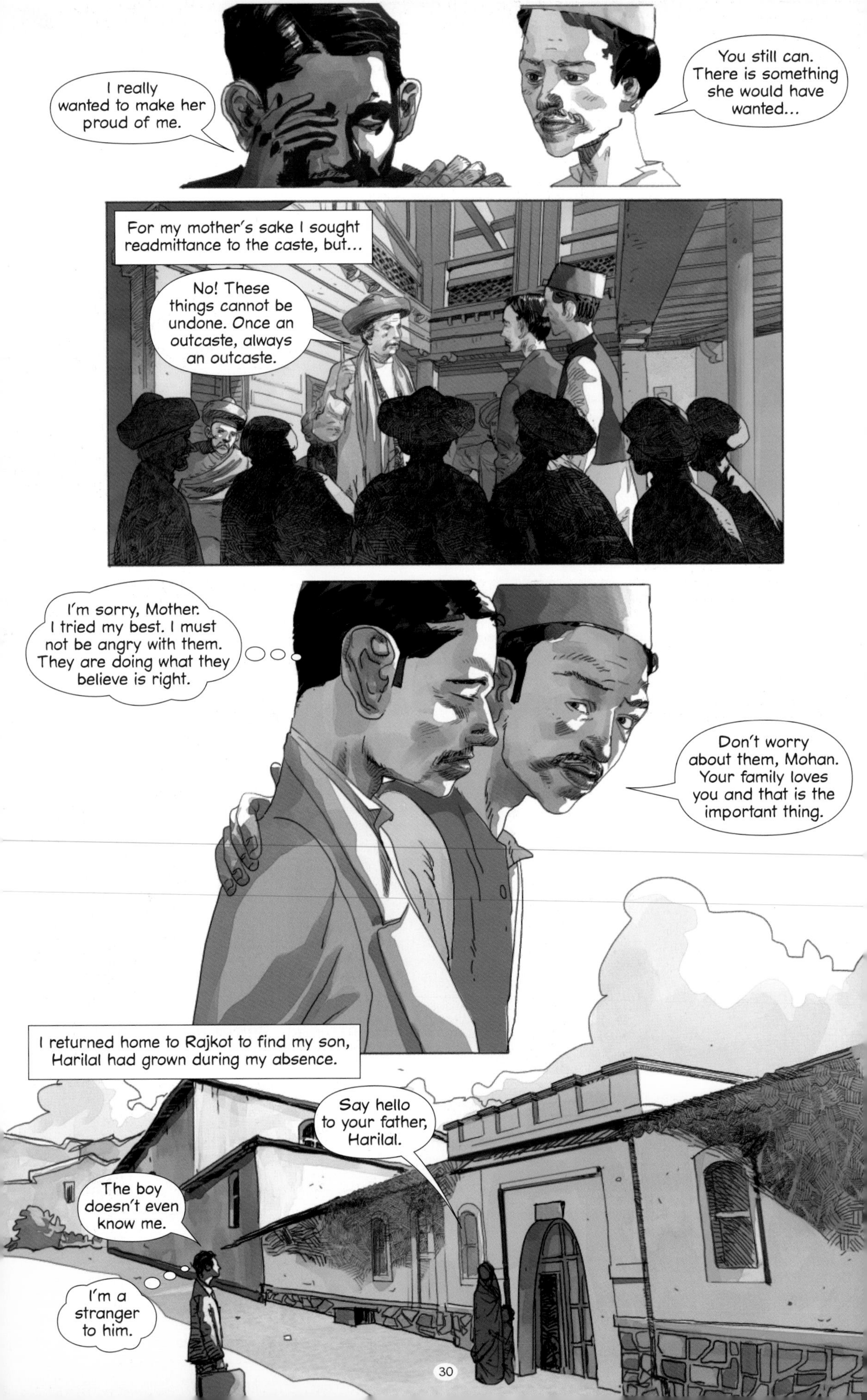
I really wanted to make her proud of me.
You still can. There is something she would have wanted...
For my mother's sake I sought readmittance to the caste, but...
No! These things cannot be undone. Once an outcaste, always an outcaste.
I'm sorry, Mother. I tried my best. I must not be angry with them. They are doing what they believe is right.
Don't worry about them, Mohan. Your family loves you and that is the important thing.
I returned home to Rajkot to find my son, Harilal had grown during my absence.
Say hello to your father, Harilal.
The boy doesn't even know me.
I'm a stranger to him.

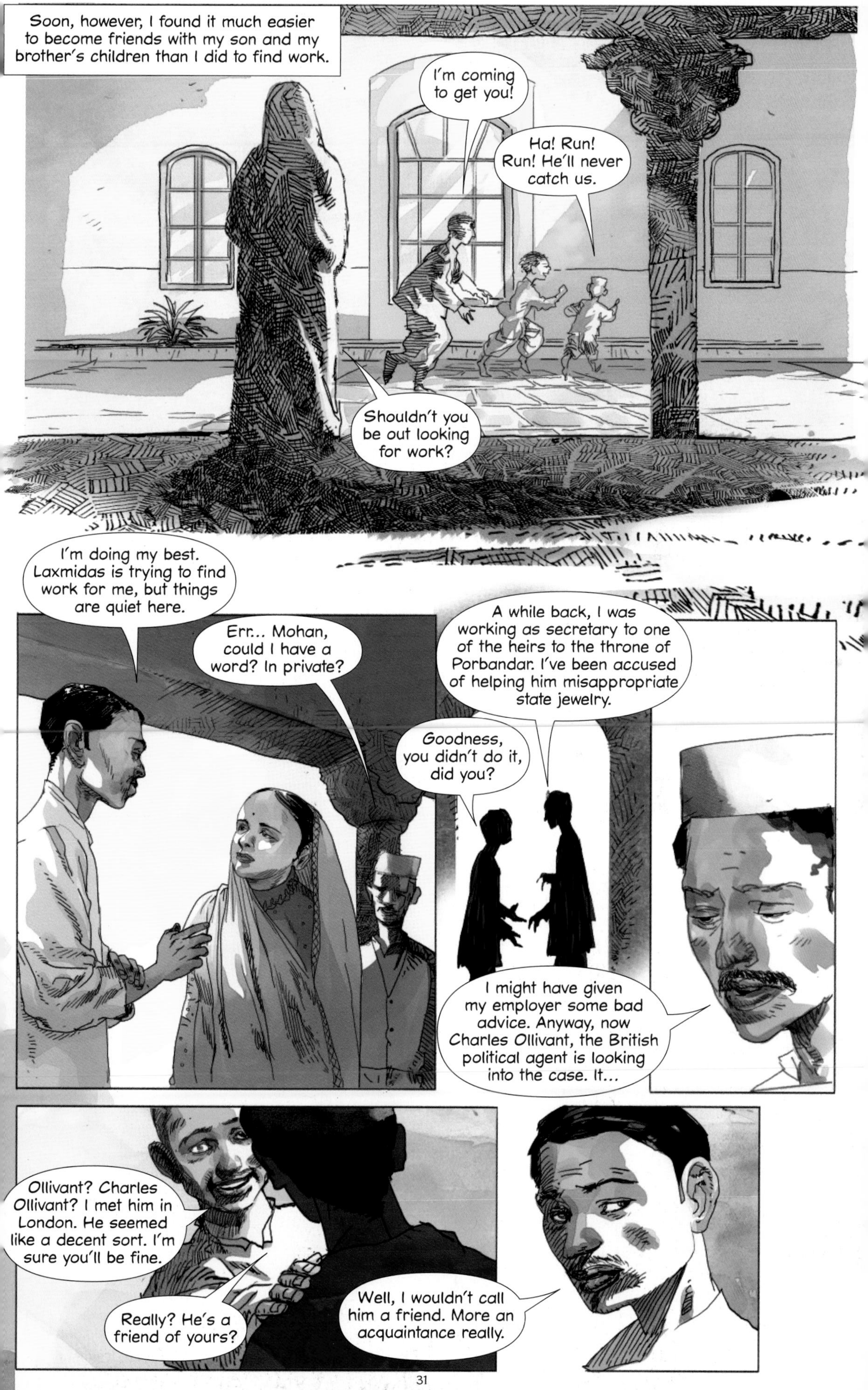
Soon, however, I found it much easier to become friends with my son and my brother's children than I did to find work.
I'm coming to get you!
Ha! Run! Run! He'll never catch us.
Shouldn't you be out looking for work?
I'm doing my best. Laxmidas is trying to find work for me, but things are quiet here.
Err... Mohan, could I have a word? In private?
A while back, I was working as secretary to one of the heirs to the throne of Porbandar. I've been accused of helping him misappropriate state jewelry.
Goodness, you didn't do it, did you?
I might have given my employer some bad advice. Anyway, now Charles Ollivant, the British political agent is looking into the case. It...
Ollivant? Charles Ollivant? I met him in London. He seemed like a decent sort. I'm sure you'll be fine.
Really? He's a friend of yours?
Well, I wouldn't call him a friend. More an acquaintance really.

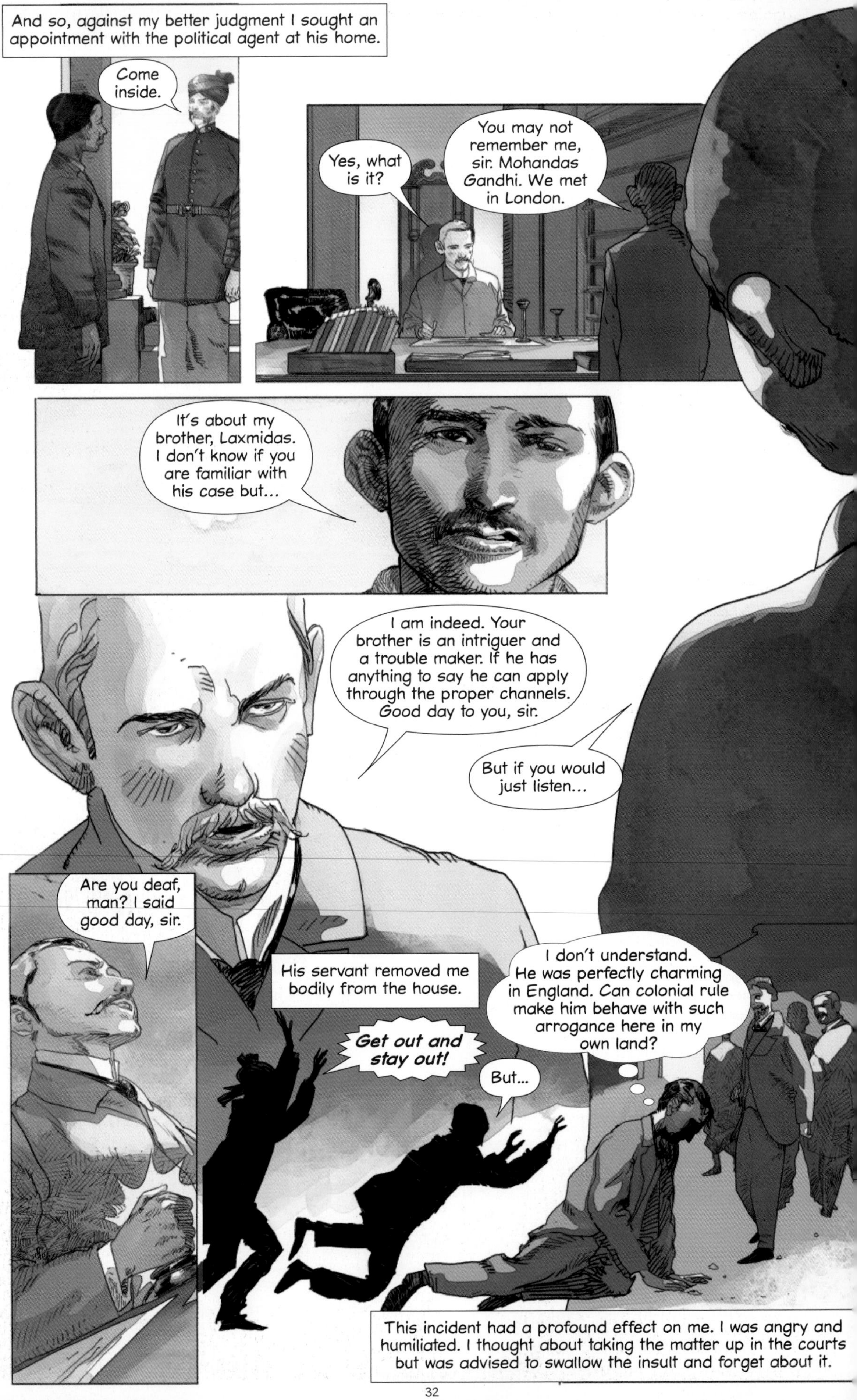
And so, against my better judgment I sought an appointment with the political agent at his home.
Come inside.
Yes, what is it?
You may not remember me, sir. Mohandas Gandhi. We met in London.
It's about my brother, Laxmidas. I don't know if you are familiar with his case but...
I am indeed. Your brother is an intriguer and a trouble maker. If he has anything to say he can apply through the proper channels. Good day to you, sir.
But if you would just listen...
Are you deaf, man? I said good day, sir.
His servant removed me bodily from the house.
Get out and stay out!
But...
I don't understand. He was perfectly charming in England. Can colonial rule make him behave with such arrogance here in my own land?
This incident had a profound effect on me. I was angry and humiliated. I thought about taking the matter up in the courts but was advised to swallow the insult and forget about it.

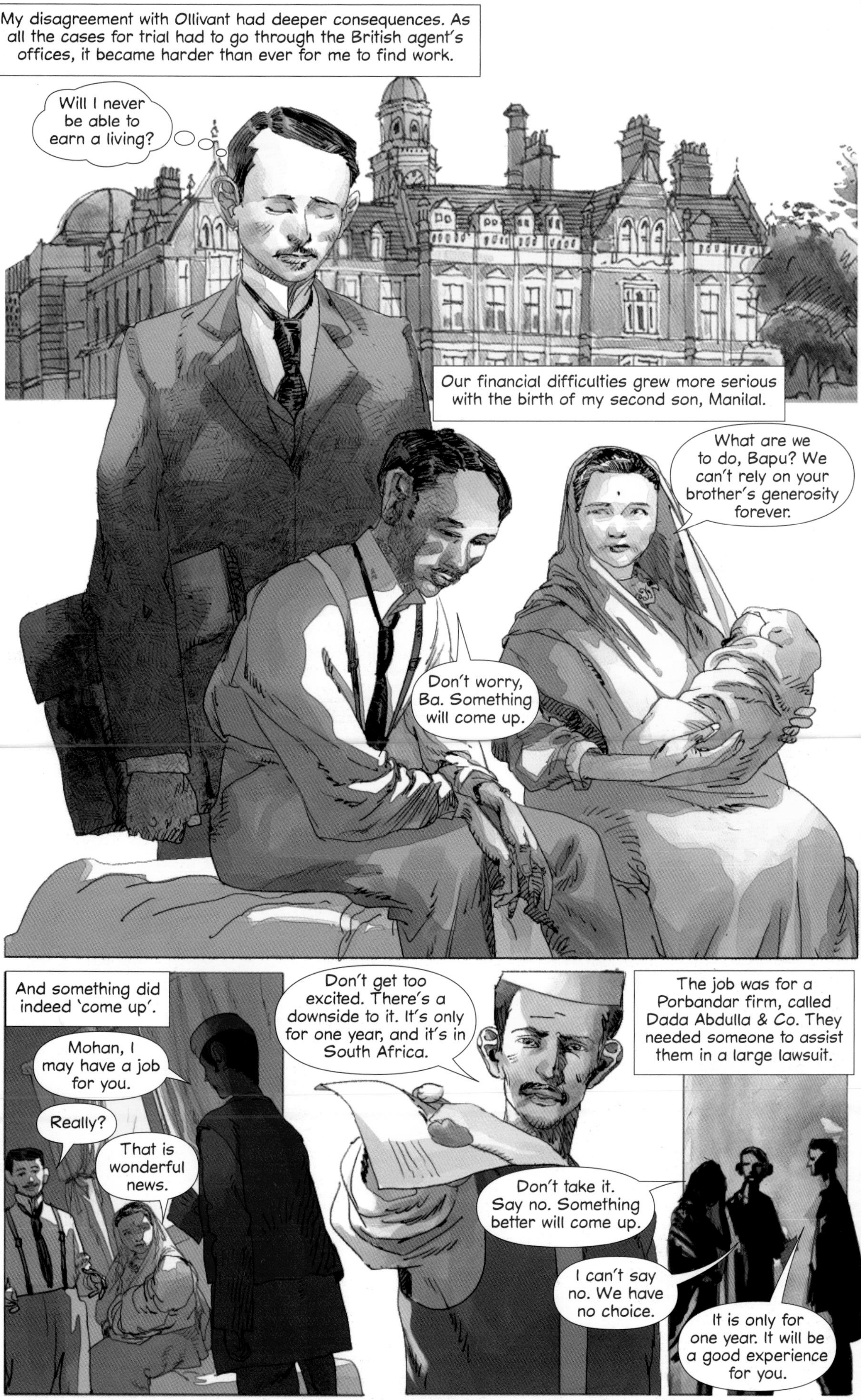

My disagreement with Ollivant had deeper consequences. As all the cases for trial had to go through the British agent's offices, it became harder than ever for me to find work.
Will I never be able to earn a living?
Our financial difficulties grew more serious with the birth of my second son, Manilal.
What are we to do, Bapu? We can't rely on your brother's generosity forever.
Don't worry, Ba. Something will come up.
And something did indeed 'come up'.
Mohan, I may have a job for you.
Really?
That is wonderful news.
Don't get too excited. There's a downside to it. It's only for one year, and it's in South Africa.
The job was for a Porbandar firm, called Dada Abdulla & Co. They needed someone to assist them in a large lawsuit.
Don't take it. Say no. Something better will come up.
I can't say no. We have no choice.
It is only for one year. It will be a good experience for you.

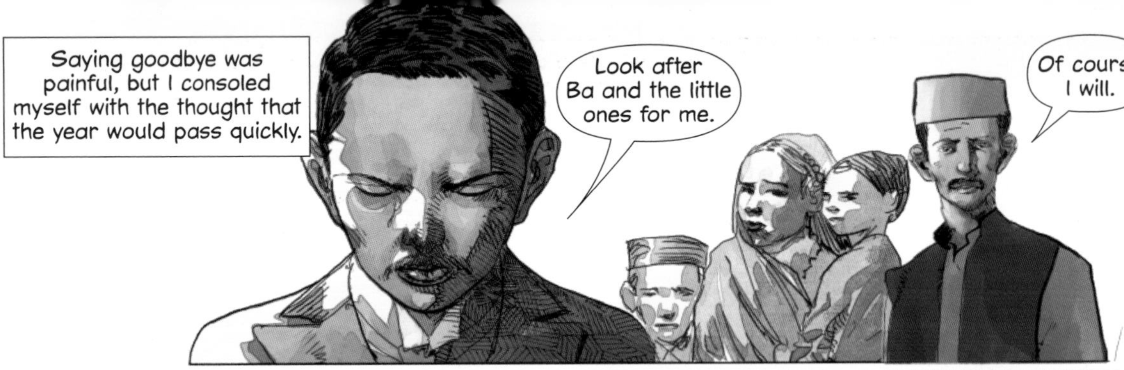
Saying goodbye was painful, but I consoled myself with the thought that the year would pass quickly.
Look after Ba and the little ones for me.
Of course I will.

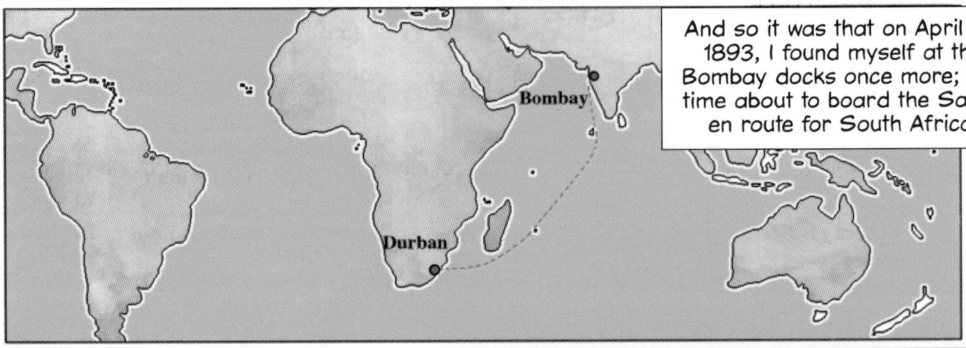
Bombay
Durban
And so it was that on April 19, 1893, I found myself at the Bombay docks once more; this time about to board the Safari en route for South Africa.

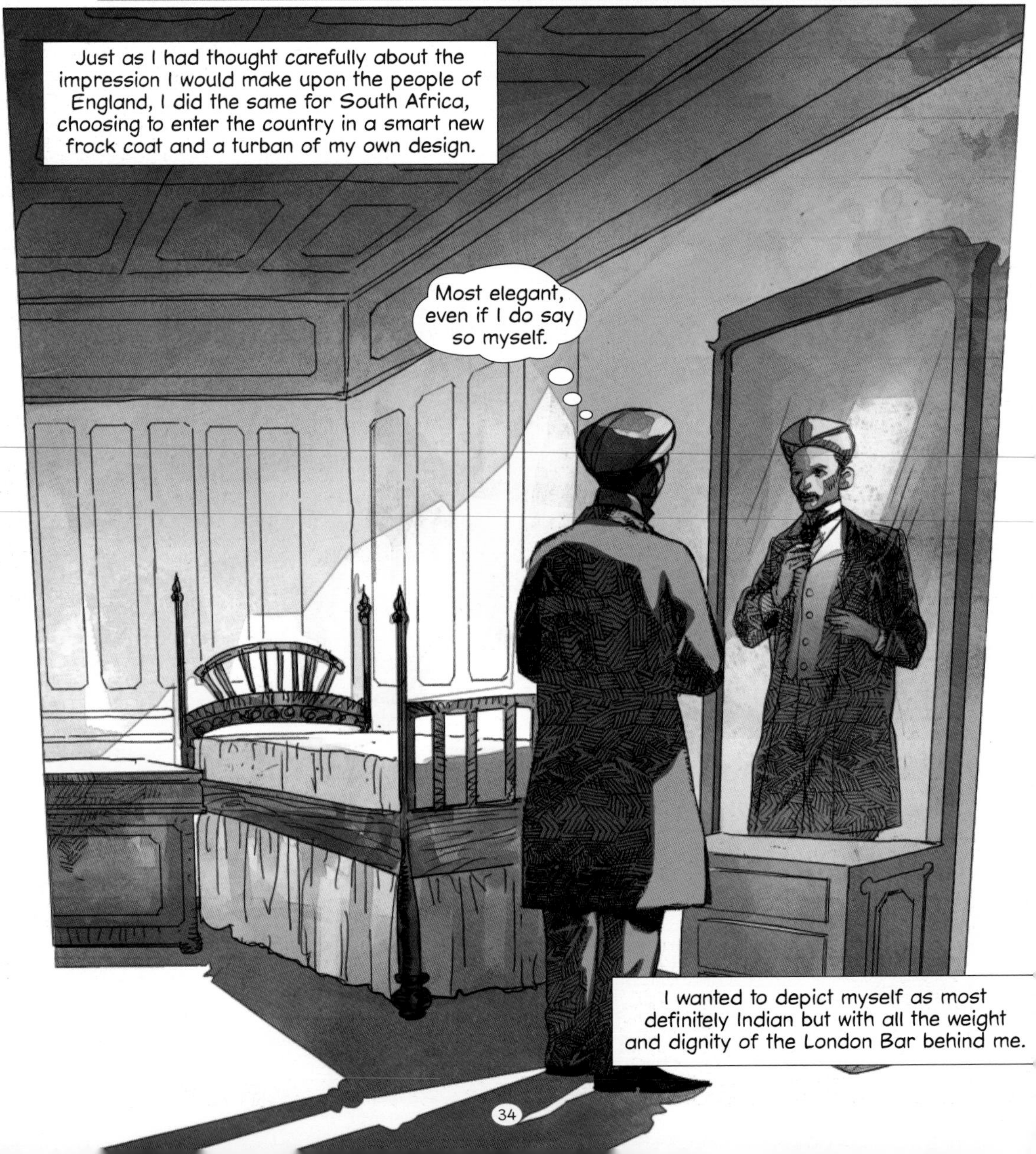
Just as I had thought carefully about the impression I would make upon the people of England, I did the same for South Africa, choosing to enter the country in a smart new frock coat and a turban of my own design.
Most elegant, even if I do say so myself.
I wanted to depict myself as most definitely Indian but with all the weight and dignity of the London Bar behind me.

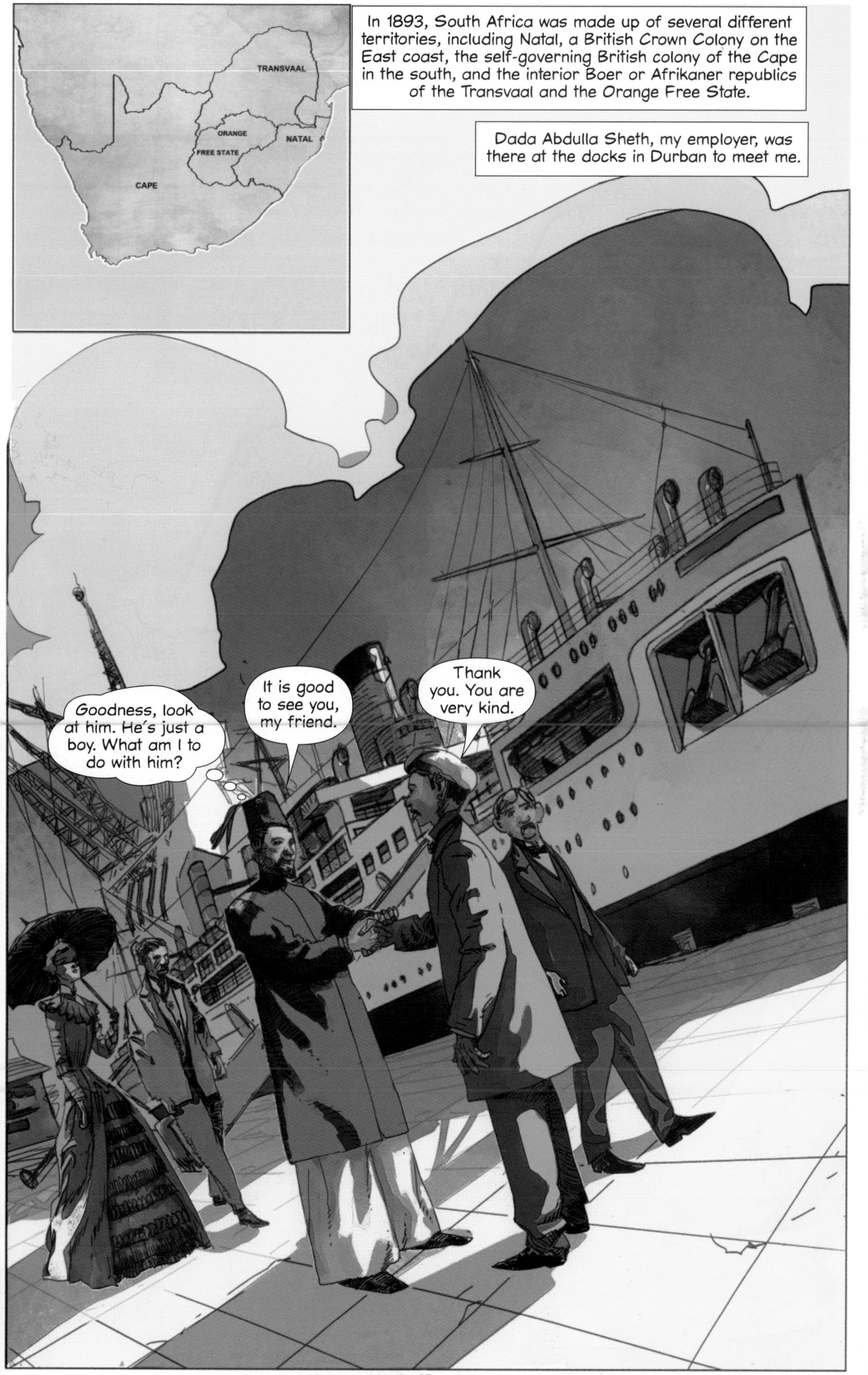
TRANSVAAL
ORANGE
FREE STATE
NATAL
CAPE
In 1893, South Africa was made up of several different territories, including Natal, a British Crown Colony on the East coast, the self-governing British colony of the Cape in the south, and the interior Boer or Afrikaner republics of the Transvaal and the Orange Free State.
Dada Abdulla Sheth, my employer, was there at the docks in Durban to meet me.
Goodness, look at him. He's just a boy. What am I to do with him?
It is good to see you, my friend.
Thank you. You are very kind.

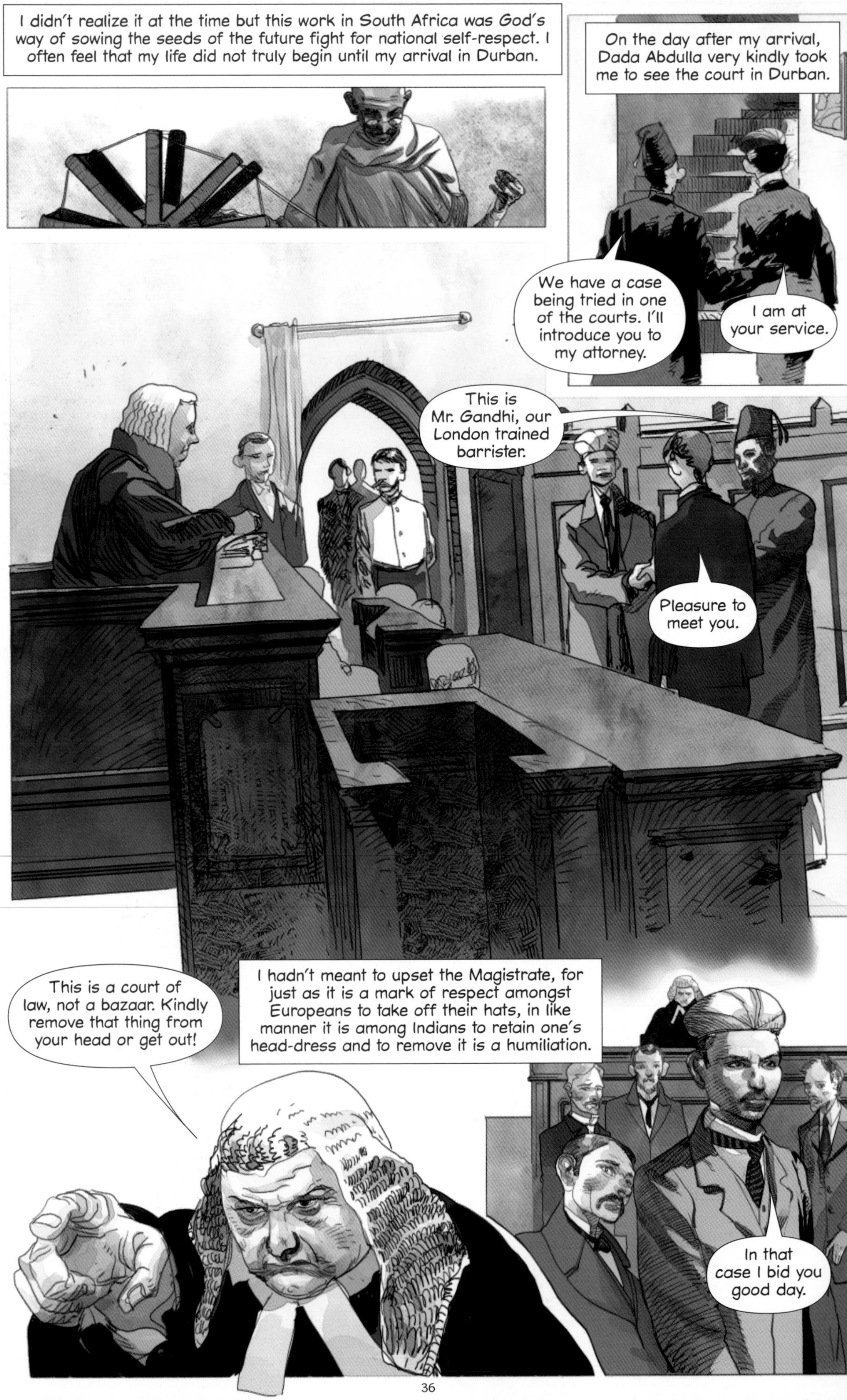
I didn't realize it at the time but this work in South Africa was God's way of sowing the seeds of the future fight for national self-respect. I often feel that my life did not truly begin until my arrival in Durban.
On the day after my arrival, Dada Abdulla very kindly took me to see the court in Durban.
We have a case being tried in one of the courts. I'll introduce you to my attorney.
I am at your service.
This is Mr. Gandhi, our London trained barrister.
Pleasure to meet you.
This is a court of law, not a bazaar. Kindly remove that thing from your head or get out!
I hadn't meant to upset the Magistrate, for just as it is a mark of respect amongst Europeans to take off their hats, in like manner it is among Indians to retain one's head-dress and to remove it is a humiliation.
In that case I bid you good day.

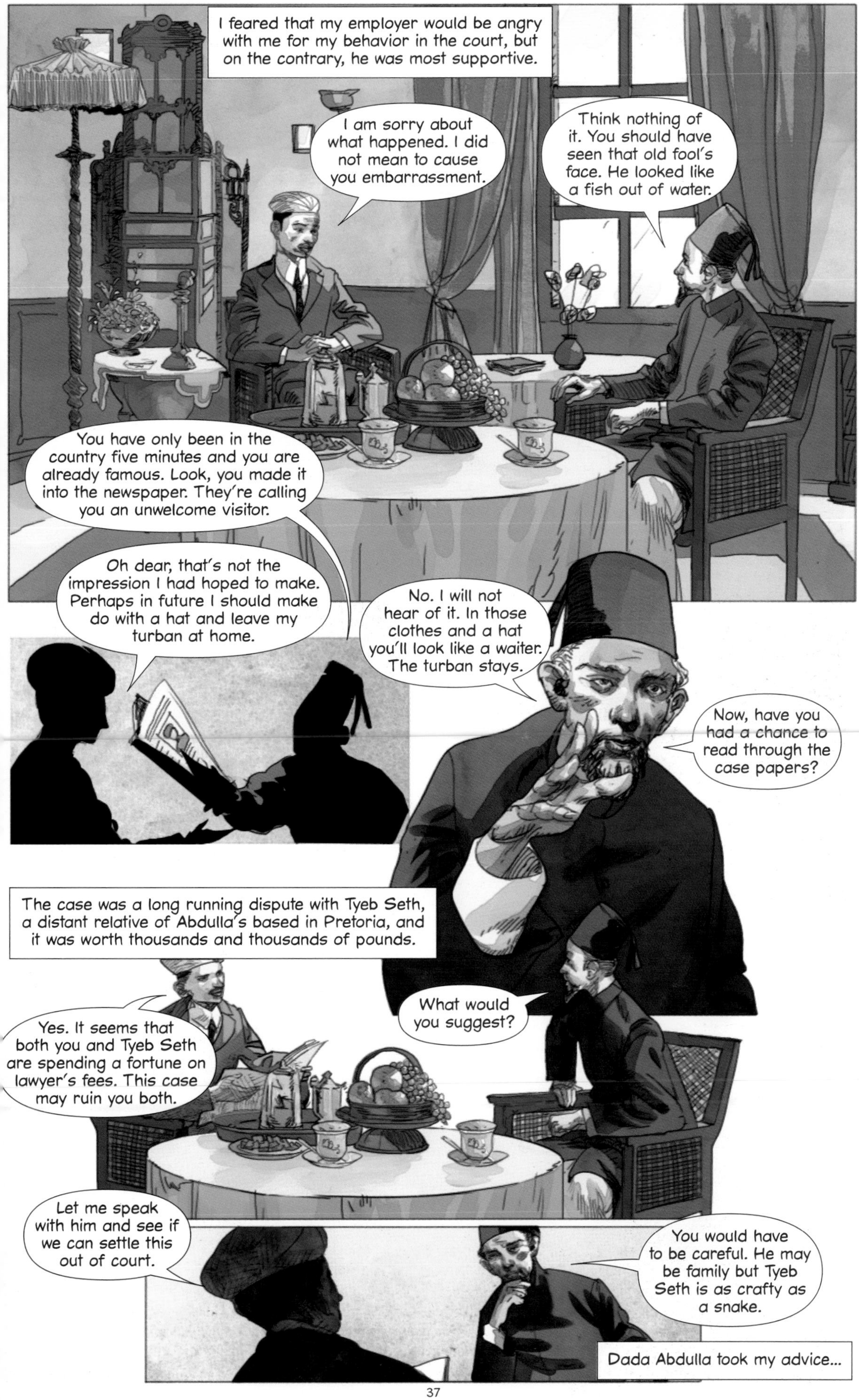
I feared that my employer would be angry with me for my behavior in the court, but on the contrary, he was most supportive.
I am sorry about what happened. I did not mean to cause you embarrassment.
Think nothing of it. You should have seen that old fool's face. He looked like a fish out of water.
You have only been in the country five minutes and you are already famous. Look, you made it into the newspaper. They're calling you an unwelcome visitor.
Oh dear, that's not the impression I had hoped to make. Perhaps in future I should make do with a hat and leave my turban at home.
No. I will not hear of it. In those clothes and a hat you'll look like a waiter. The turban stays.
Now, have you had a chance to read through the case papers?
The case was a long running dispute with Tyeb Seth, a distant relative of Abdulla's based in Pretoria, and it was worth thousands and thousands of pounds.
Yes. It seems that both you and Tyeb Seth are spending a fortune on lawyer's fees. This case may ruin you both.
What would you suggest?
Let me speak with him and see if we can settle this out of court.
You would have to be careful. He may be family but Tyeb Seth is as crafty as a snake.
Dada Abdulla took my advice...

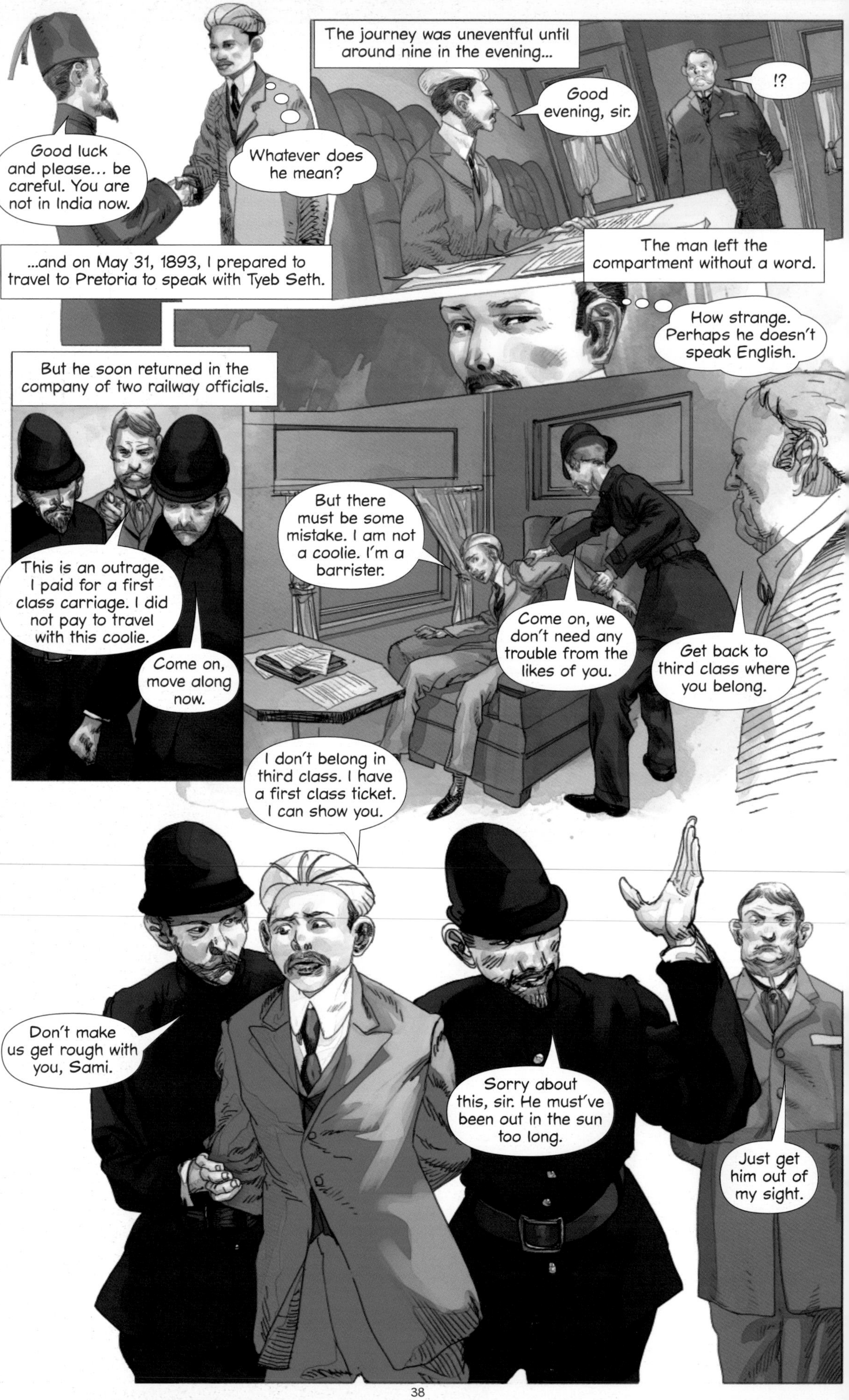
Good luck and please... be careful. You are not in India now.
Whatever does he mean?
...and on May 31, 1893, I prepared to travel to Pretoria to speak with Tyeb Seth.
The journey was uneventful until around nine in the evening...
Good evening, sir.
!?
The man left the compartment without a word.
How strange. Perhaps he doesn't speak English.
But he soon returned in the company of two railway officials.
This is an outrage. I paid for a first class carriage. I did not pay to travel with this coolie.
Come on, move along now.
But there must be some mistake. I am not a coolie. I'm a barrister.
Come on, we don't need any trouble from the likes of you.
Get back to third class where you belong.
I don't belong in third class. I have a first class ticket. I can show you.
Don't make us get rough with you, Sami.
Sorry about this, sir. He must've been out in the sun too long.
Just get him out of my sight.

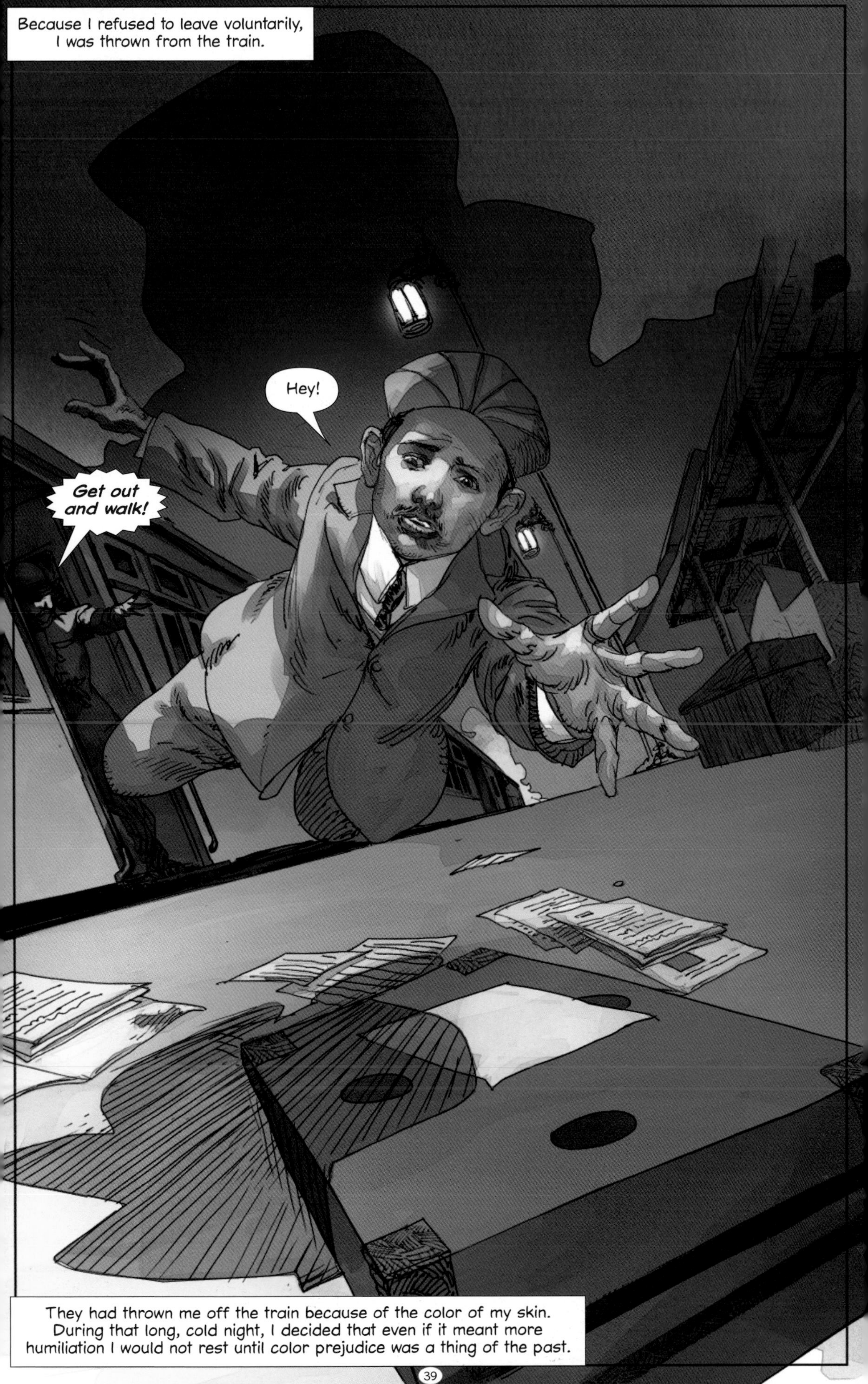
Because I refused to leave voluntarily, I was thrown from the train.
Hey!
Get out and walk!
They had thrown me off the train because of the color of my skin. During that long, cold night, I decided that even if it meant more humiliation I would not rest until color prejudice was a thing of the past.

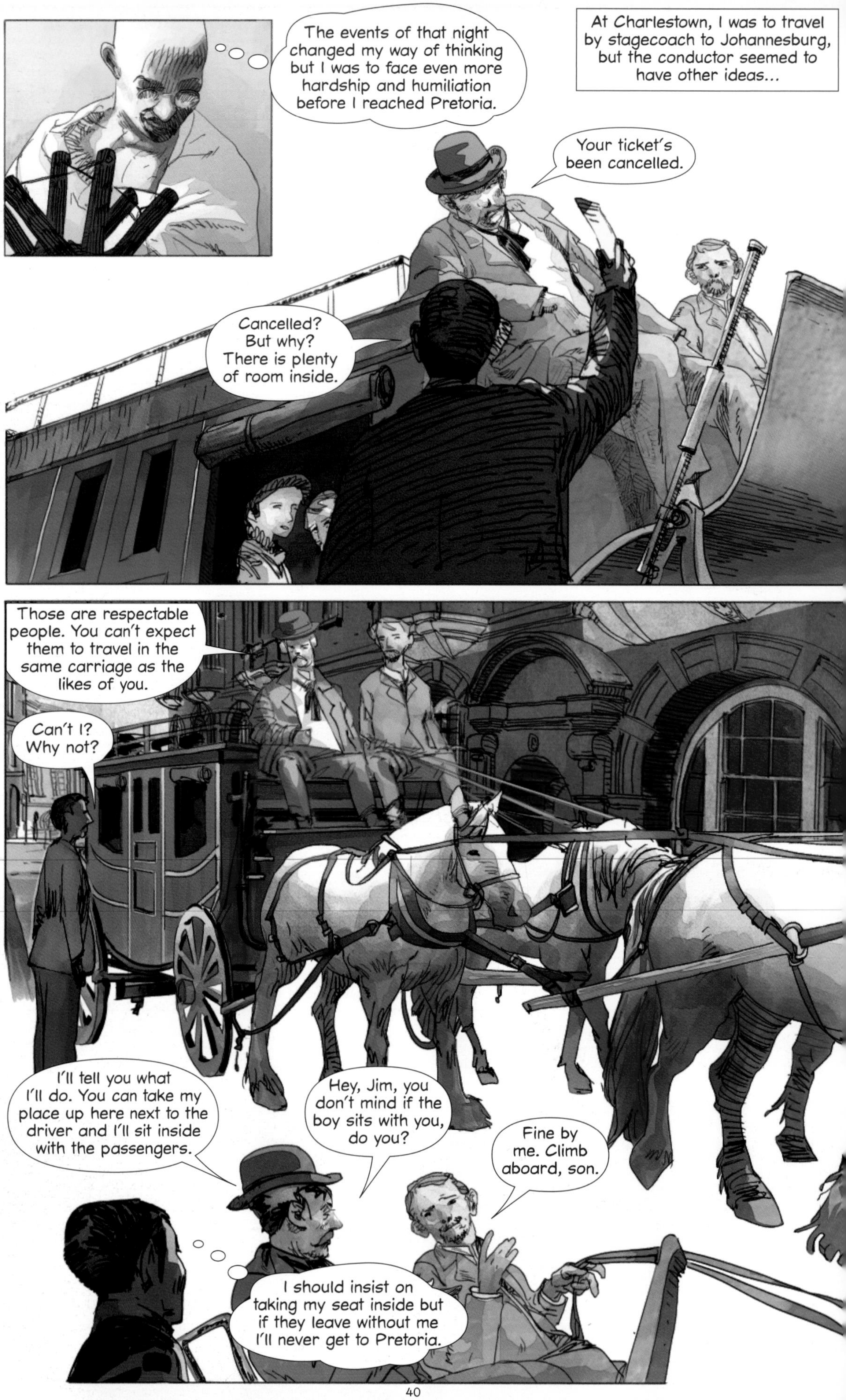
The events of that night changed my way of thinking but I was to face even more hardship and humiliation before I reached Pretoria.
At Charlestown, I was to travel by stagecoach to Johannesburg, but the conductor seemed to have other ideas...
Your ticket's been cancelled.
Cancelled? But why? There is plenty of room inside.
Those are respectable people. You can't expect them to travel in the same carriage as the likes of you.
Can't I? Why not?
I'll tell you what I'll do. You can take my place up here next to the driver and I'll sit inside with the passengers.
Hey, Jim, you don't mind if the boy sits with you, do you?
Fine by me. Climb aboard, son.
I should insist on taking my seat inside but if they leave without me I'll never get to Pretoria.

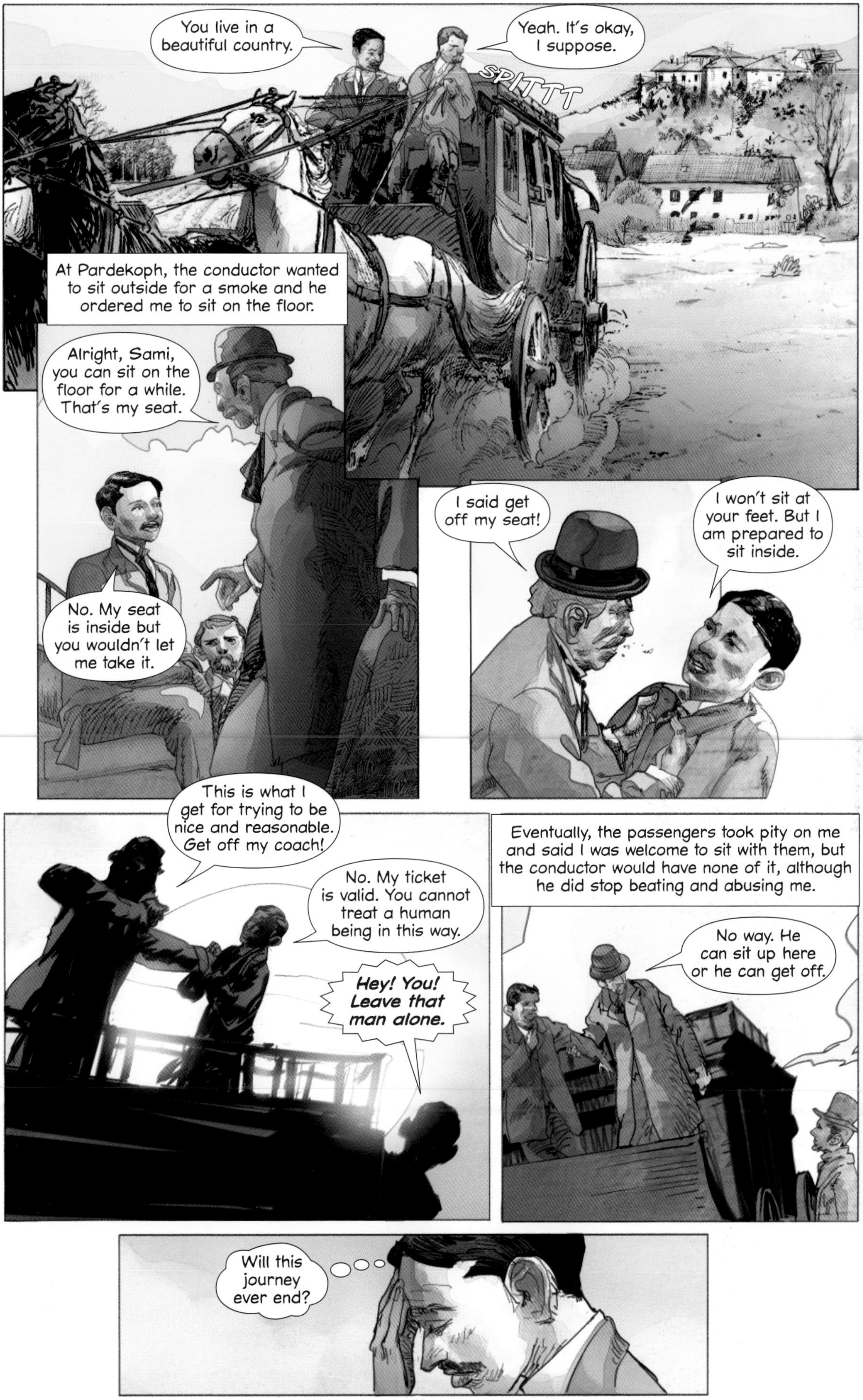
You live in a beautiful country.
Yeah. It's okay, I suppose.
SPITTT
At Pardekoph, the conductor wanted to sit outside for a smoke and he ordered me to sit on the floor.
Alright, Sami, you can sit on the floor for a while. That's my seat.
No. My seat is inside but you wouldn't let me take it.
I said get off my seat!
I won't sit at your feet. But I am prepared to sit inside.
This is what I get for trying to be nice and reasonable. Get off my coach!
No. My ticket is valid. You cannot treat a human being in this way.
Hey! You! Leave that man alone.
Eventually, the passengers took pity on me and said I was welcome to sit with them, but the conductor would have none of it, although he did stop beating and abusing me.
No way. He can sit up here or he can get off.
Will this journey ever end?

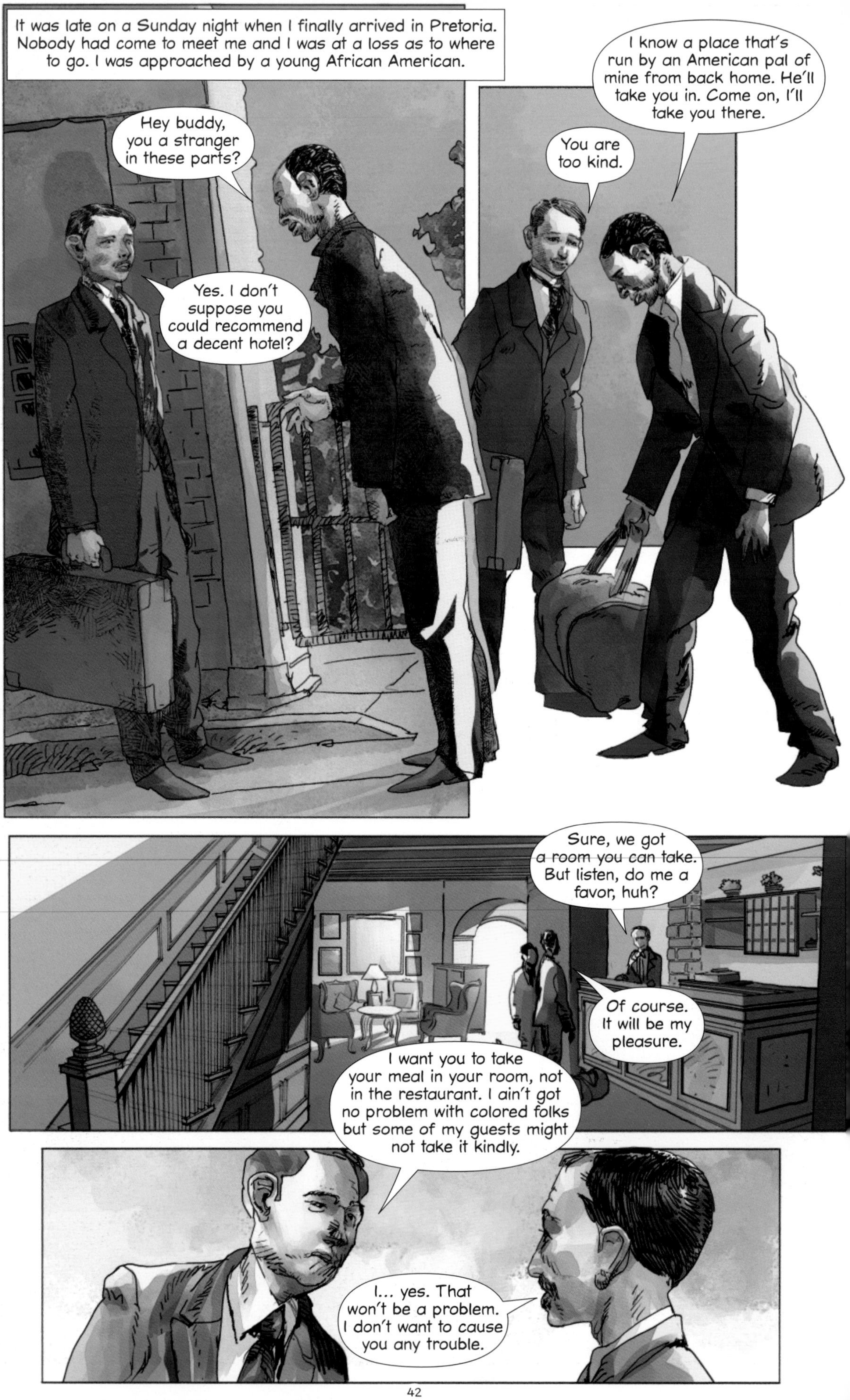

It was late on a Sunday night when I finally arrived in Pretoria. Nobody had come to meet me and I was at a loss as to where to go. I was approached by a young African American.
Hey buddy, you a stranger in these parts?
Yes. I don't suppose you could recommend a decent hotel?
I know a place that's run by an American pal of mine from back home. He'll take you in. Come on, I'll take you there.
You are too kind.
Sure, we got a room you can take. But listen, do me a favor, huh?
Of course. It will be my pleasure.
I want you to take your meal in your room, not in the restaurant. I ain't got no problem with colored folks but some of my guests might not take it kindly.
I... yes. That won't be a problem. I don't want to cause you any trouble.

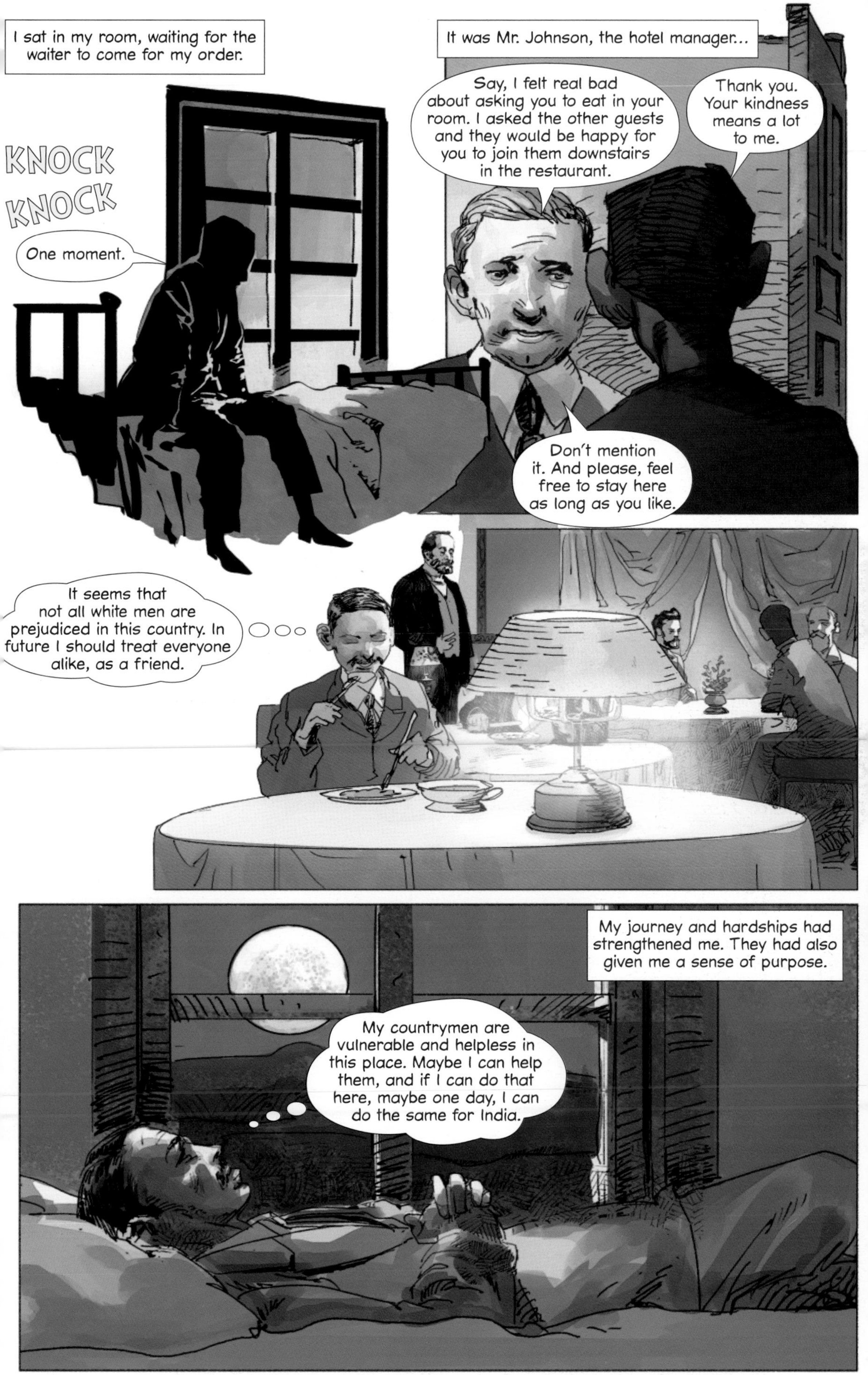
I sat in my room, waiting for the waiter to come for my order.
KNOCK KNOCK
One moment.
It was Mr. Johnson, the hotel manager...
Say, I felt real bad about asking you to eat in your room. I asked the other guests and they would be happy for you to join them downstairs in the restaurant.
Thank you. Your kindness means a lot to me.
Don't mention it. And please, feel free to stay here as long as you like.
It seems that not all white men are prejudiced in this country. In future I should treat everyone alike, as a friend.
My journey and hardships had strengthened me. They had also given me a sense of purpose.
My countrymen are vulnerable and helpless in this place. Maybe I can help them, and if I can do that here, maybe one day, I can do the same for India.

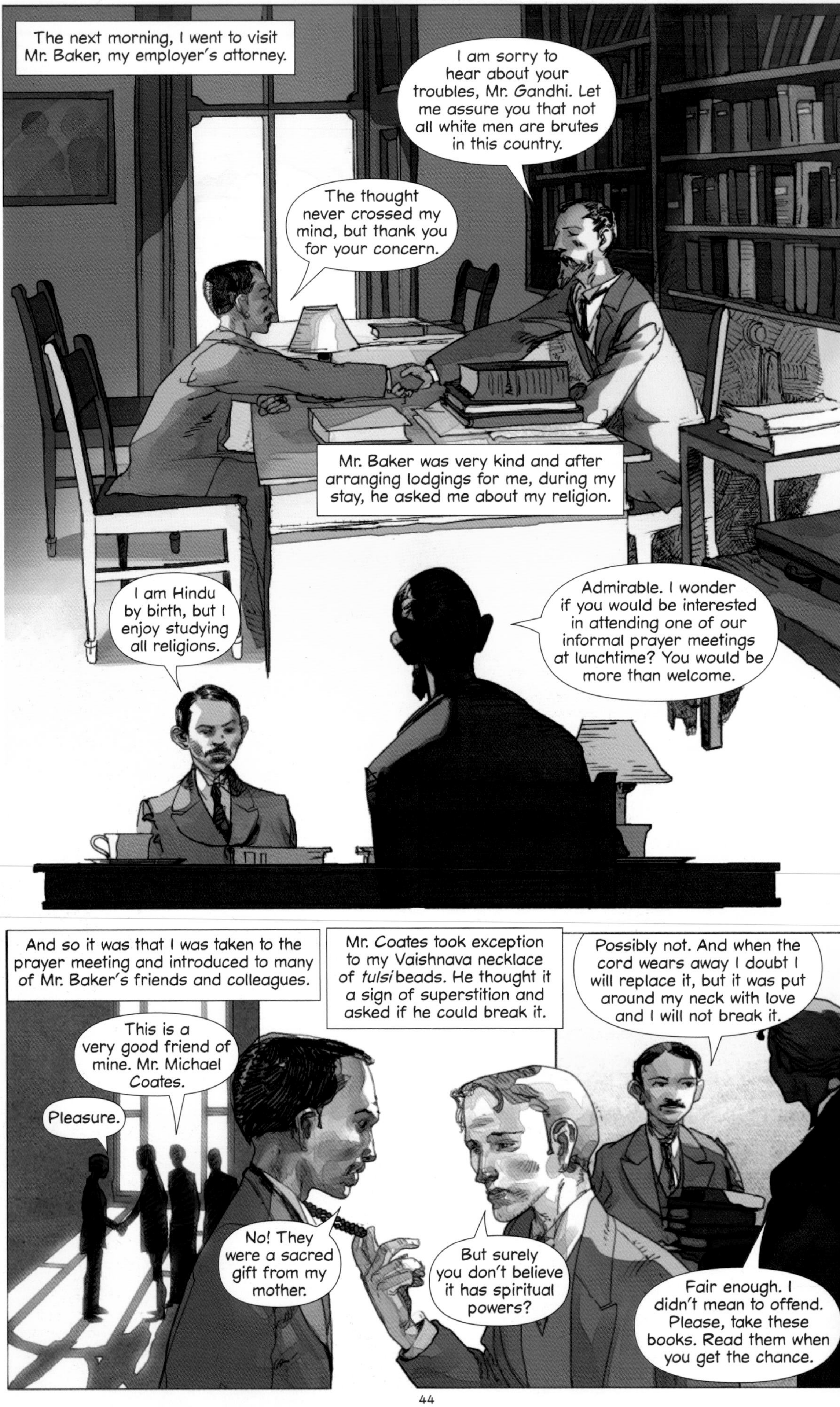
The next morning, I went to visit Mr. Baker, my employer's attorney.
I am sorry to hear about your troubles, Mr. Gandhi. Let me assure you that not all white men are brutes in this country.
The thought never crossed my mind, but thank you for your concern.
Mr. Baker was very kind and after arranging lodgings for me, during my stay, he asked me about my religion.
I am Hindu by birth, but I enjoy studying all religions.
Admirable. I wonder if you would be interested in attending one of our informal prayer meetings at lunchtime? You would be more than welcome.
And so it was that I was taken to the prayer meeting and introduced to many of Mr. Baker's friends and colleagues.
This is a very good friend of mine. Mr. Michael Coates.
Pleasure.
Mr. Coates took exception to my Vaishnava necklace of *tulsi* beads. He thought it a sign of superstition and asked if he could break it.
No! They were a sacred gift from my mother.
But surely you don't believe it has spiritual powers?
Possibly not. And when the cord wears away I doubt I will replace it, but it was put around my neck with love and I will not break it.
Fair enough. I didn't mean to offend. Please, take these books. Read them when you get the chance.

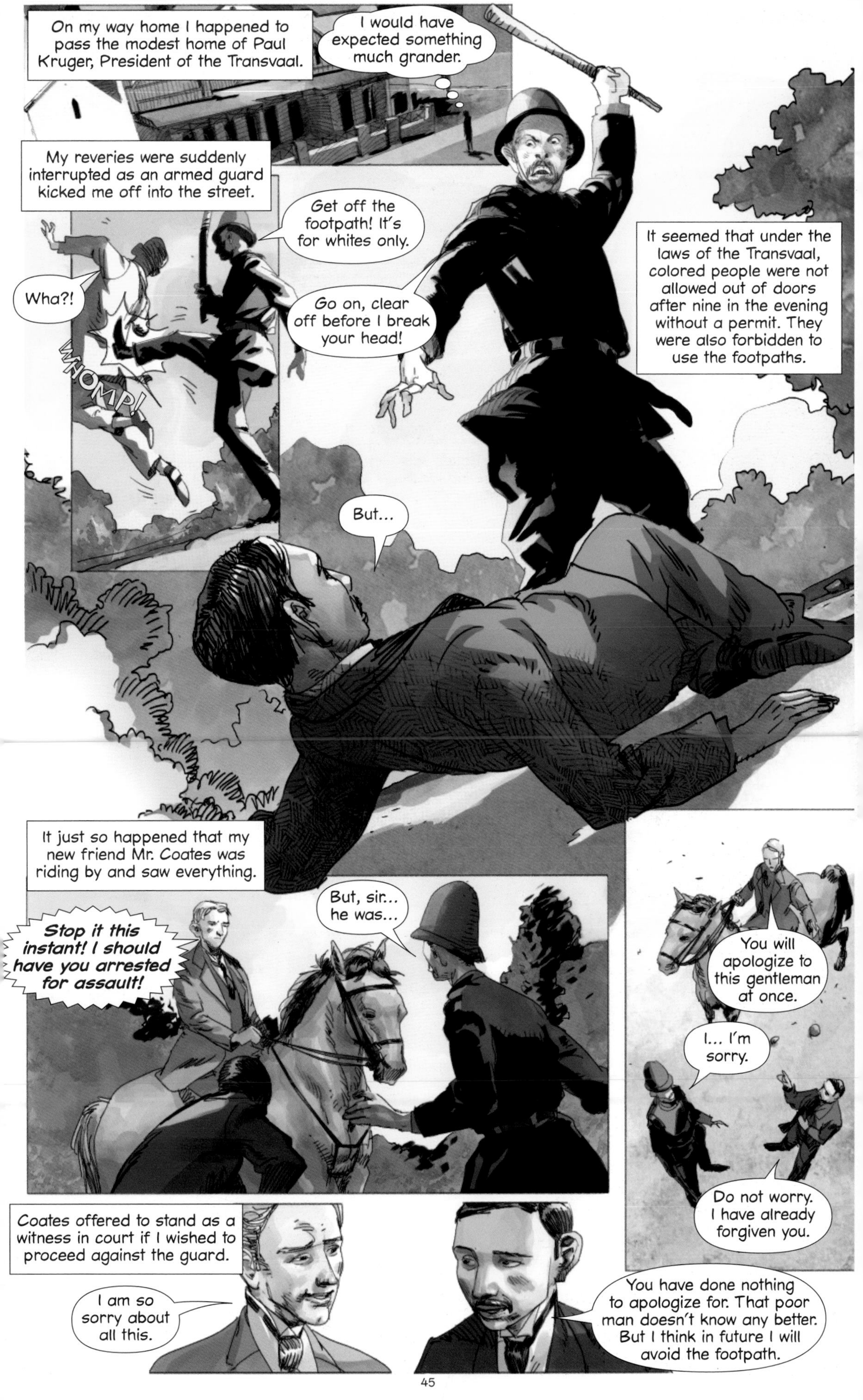

On my way home I happened to pass the modest home of Paul Kruger, President of the Transvaal.
I would have expected something much grander.
My reveries were suddenly interrupted as an armed guard kicked me off into the street.
Get off the footpath! It's for whites only.
Wha?!
WHOMP!
Go on, clear off before I break your head!
It seemed that under the laws of the Transvaal, colored people were not allowed out of doors after nine in the evening without a permit. They were also forbidden to use the footpaths.
But...
It just so happened that my new friend Mr. Coates was riding by and saw everything.
Stop it this instant! I should have you arrested for assault!
But, sir... he was...
You will apologize to this gentleman at once.
I... I'm sorry.
Do not worry. I have already forgiven you.
Coates offered to stand as a witness in court if I wished to proceed against the guard.
I am so sorry about all this.
You have done nothing to apologize for. That poor man doesn't know any better. But I think in future I will avoid the footpath.

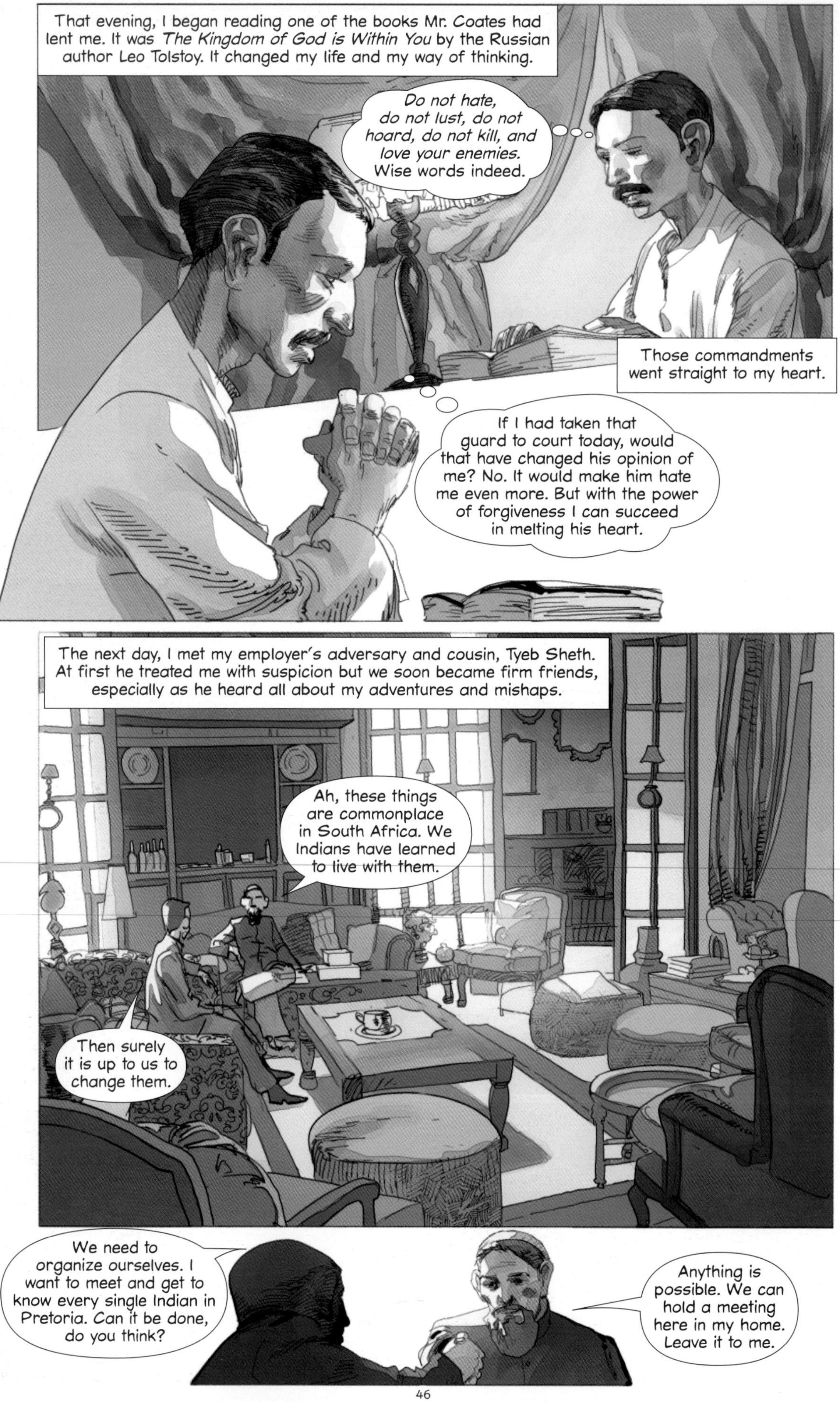
That evening, I began reading one of the books Mr. Coates had lent me. It was *The Kingdom of God is Within You* by the Russian author Leo Tolstoy. It changed my life and my way of thinking.
Do not hate, do not lust, do not hoard, do not kill, and love your enemies. Wise words indeed.
Those commandments went straight to my heart.
If I had taken that guard to court today, would that have changed his opinion of me? No. It would make him hate me even more. But with the power of forgiveness I can succeed in melting his heart.
The next day, I met my employer's adversary and cousin, Tyeb Sheth. At first he treated me with suspicion but we soon became firm friends, especially as he heard all about my adventures and mishaps.
Ah, these things are commonplace in South Africa. We Indians have learned to live with them.
Then surely it is up to us to change them.
We need to organize ourselves. I want to meet and get to know every single Indian in Pretoria. Can it be done, do you think?
Anything is possible. We can hold a meeting here in my home. Leave it to me.

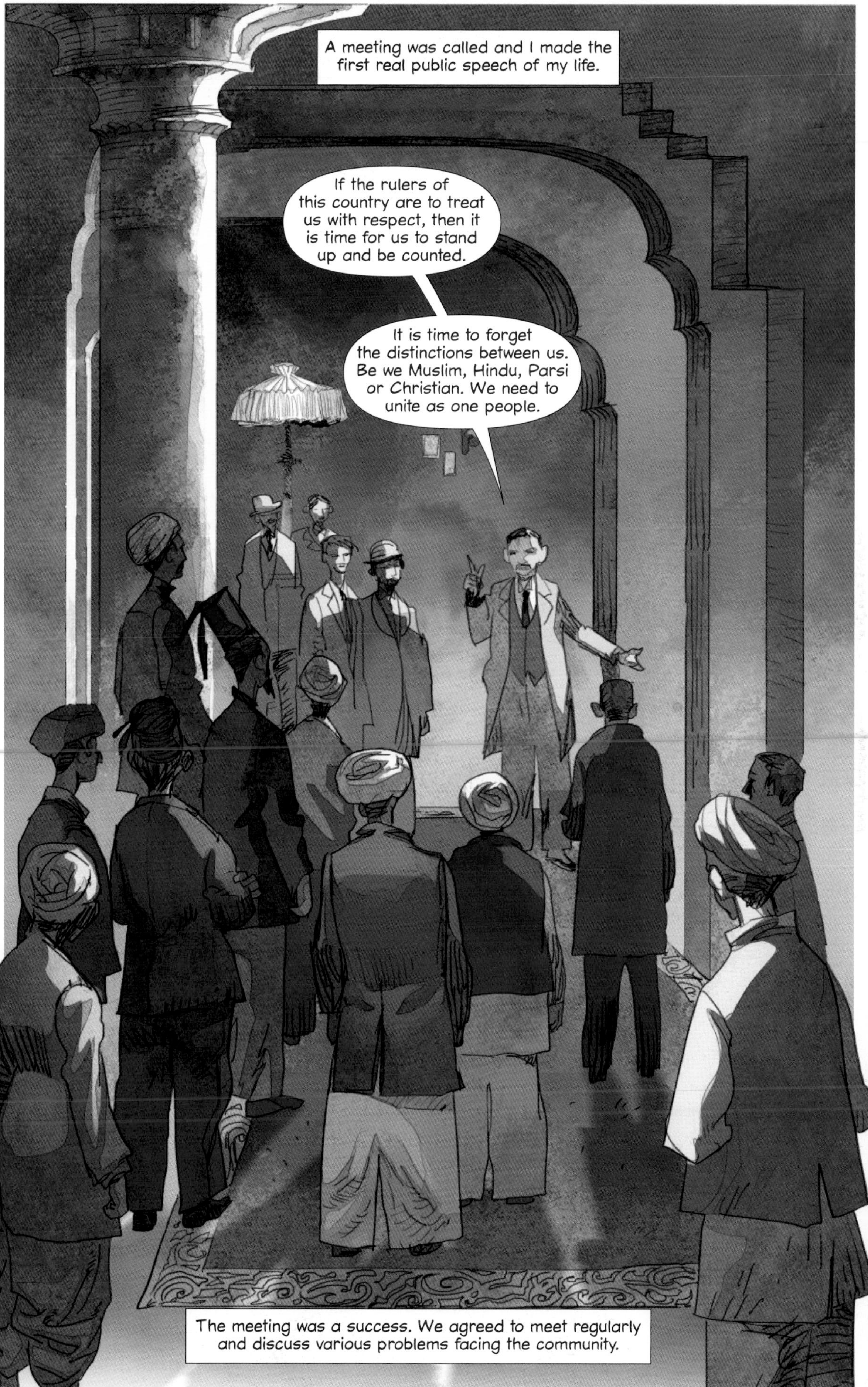
A meeting was called and I made the first real public speech of my life.
If the rulers of this country are to treat us with respect, then it is time for us to stand up and be counted.
It is time to forget the distinctions between us. Be we Muslim, Hindu, Parsi or Christian. We need to unite as one people.
The meeting was a success. We agreed to meet regularly and discuss various problems facing the community.

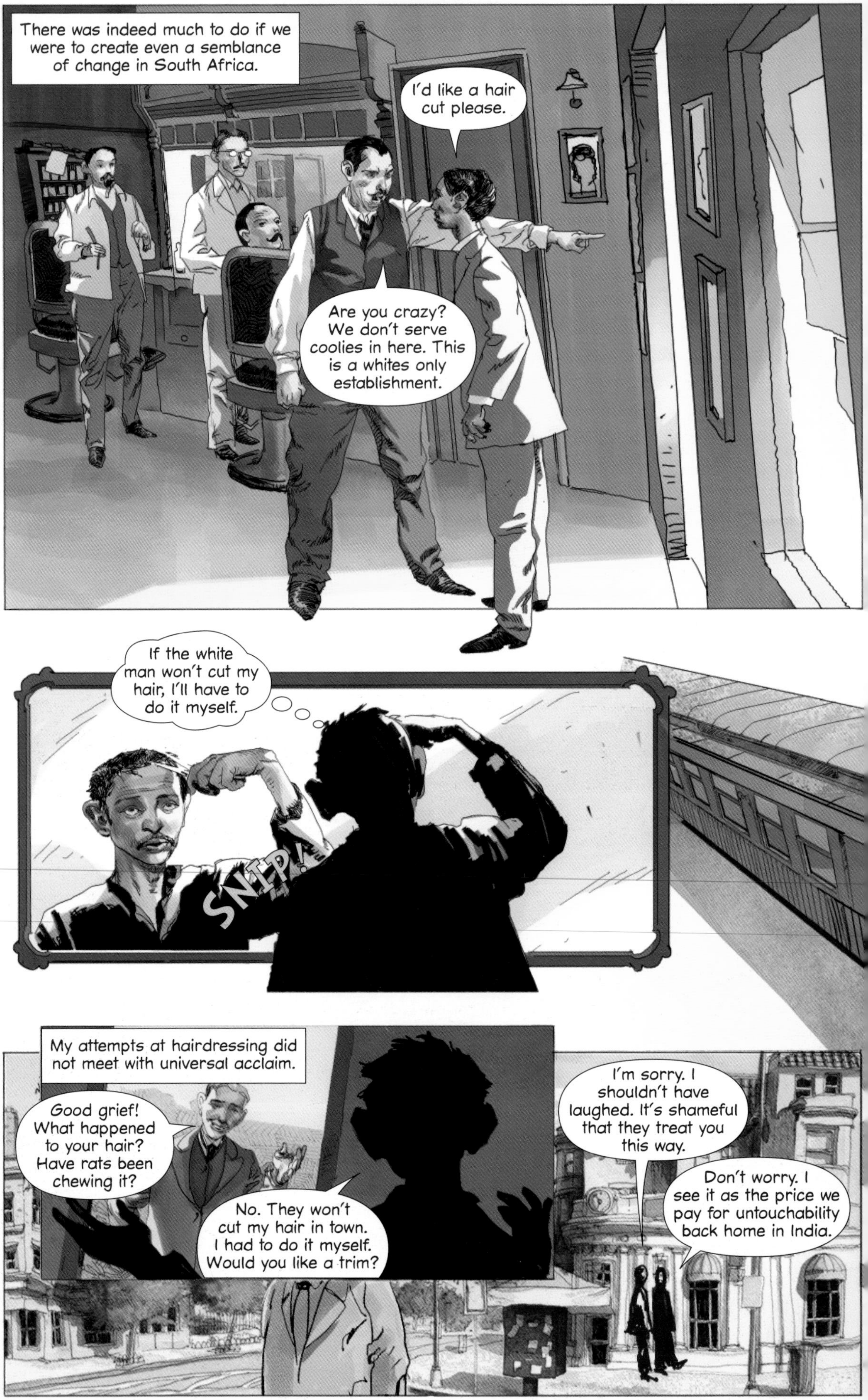

There was indeed much to do if we were to create even a semblance of change in South Africa.
I'd like a hair cut please.
Are you crazy? We don't serve coolies in here. This is a whites only establishment.
If the white man won't cut my hair, I'll have to do it myself.
SNIP!
My attempts at hairdressing did not meet with universal acclaim.
Good grief! What happened to your hair? Have rats been chewing it?
No. They won't cut my hair in town. I had to do it myself. Would you like a trim?
I'm sorry. I shouldn't have laughed. It's shameful that they treat you this way.
Don't worry. I see it as the price we pay for untouchability back home in India.

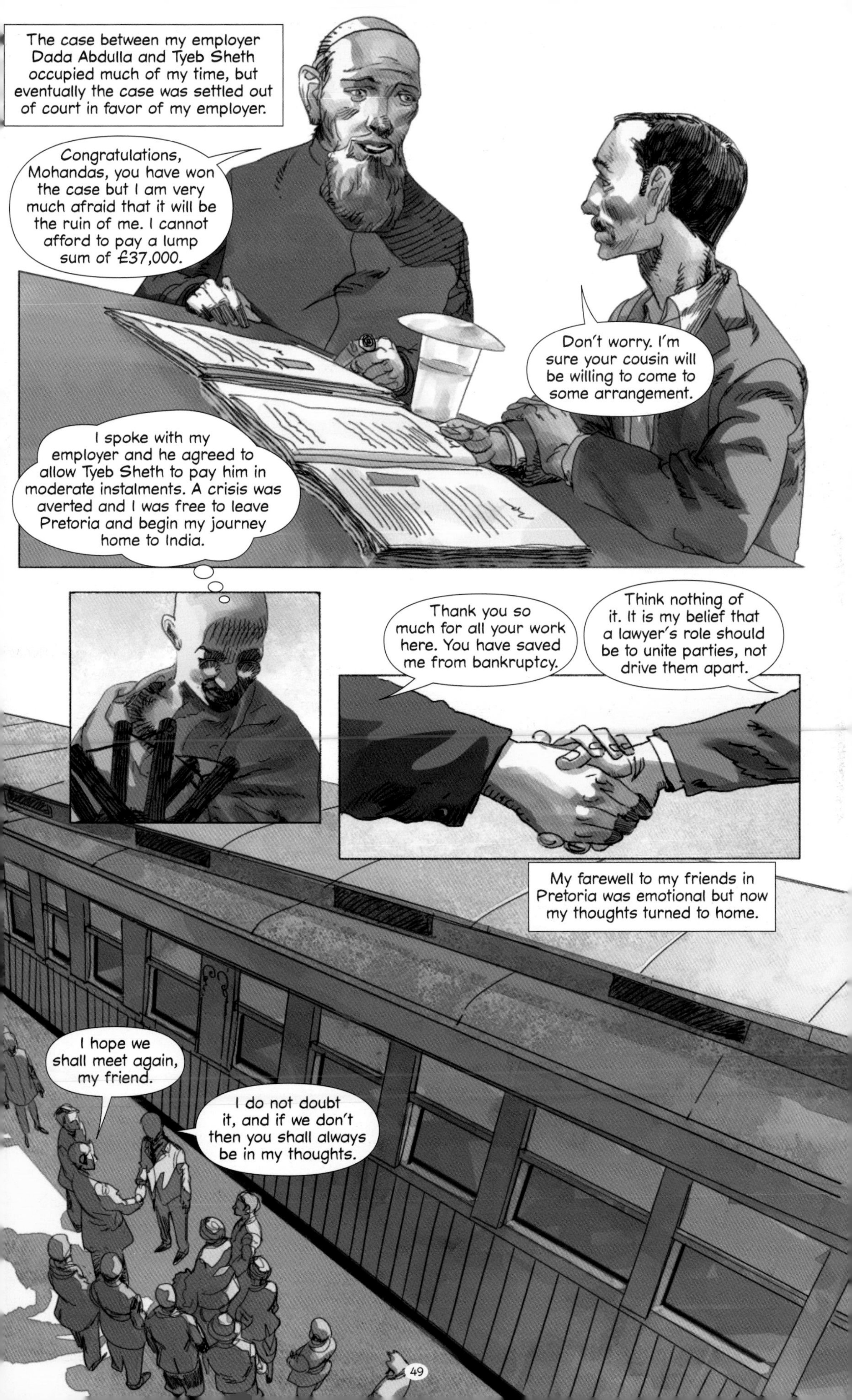
The case between my employer Dada Abdulla and Tyeb Sheth occupied much of my time, but eventually the case was settled out of court in favor of my employer.
Congratulations, Mohandas, you have won the case but I am very much afraid that it will be the ruin of me. I cannot afford to pay a lump sum of £37,000.
Don't worry. I'm sure your cousin will be willing to come to some arrangement.
I spoke with my employer and he agreed to allow Tyeb Sheth to pay him in moderate instalments. A crisis was averted and I was free to leave Pretoria and begin my journey home to India.
Thank you so much for all your work here. You have saved me from bankruptcy.
Think nothing of it. It is my belief that a lawyer's role should be to unite parties, not drive them apart.
My farewell to my friends in Pretoria was emotional but now my thoughts turned to home.
I hope we shall meet again, my friend.
I do not doubt it, and if we don't then you shall always be in my thoughts.

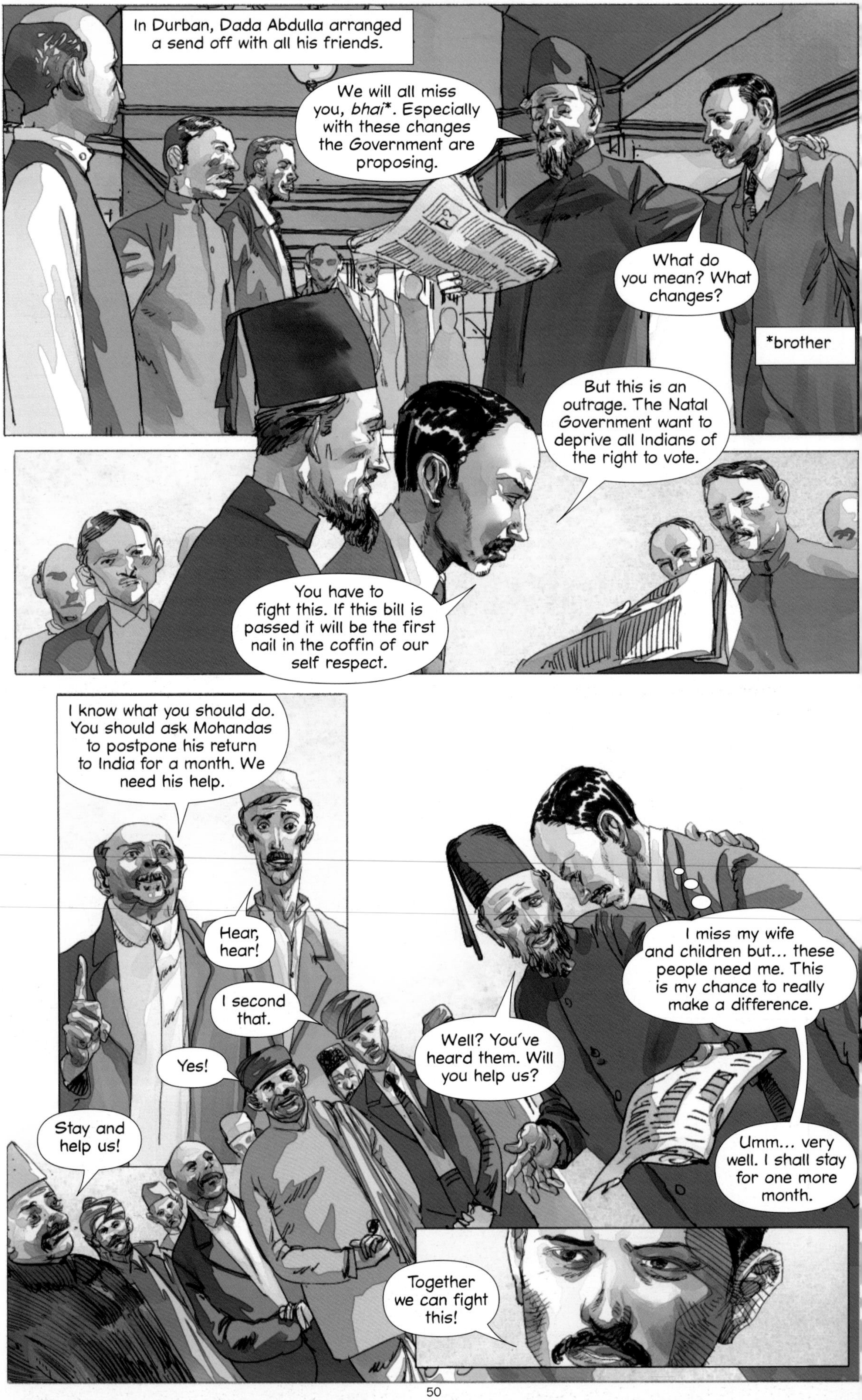

In Durban, Dada Abdulla arranged a send off with all his friends.
We will all miss you, bhai*. Especially with these changes the Government are proposing.
What do you mean? What changes?
*brother
But this is an outrage. The Natal Government want to deprive all Indians of the right to vote.
You have to fight this. If this bill is passed it will be the first nail in the coffin of our self respect.
I know what you should do. You should ask Mohandas to postpone his return to India for a month. We need his help.
Hear, hear!
I second that.
Yes!
Stay and help us!
Well? You've heard them. Will you help us?
I miss my wife and children but... these people need me. This is my chance to really make a difference.
Umm... very well. I shall stay for one more month.
Together we can fight this!

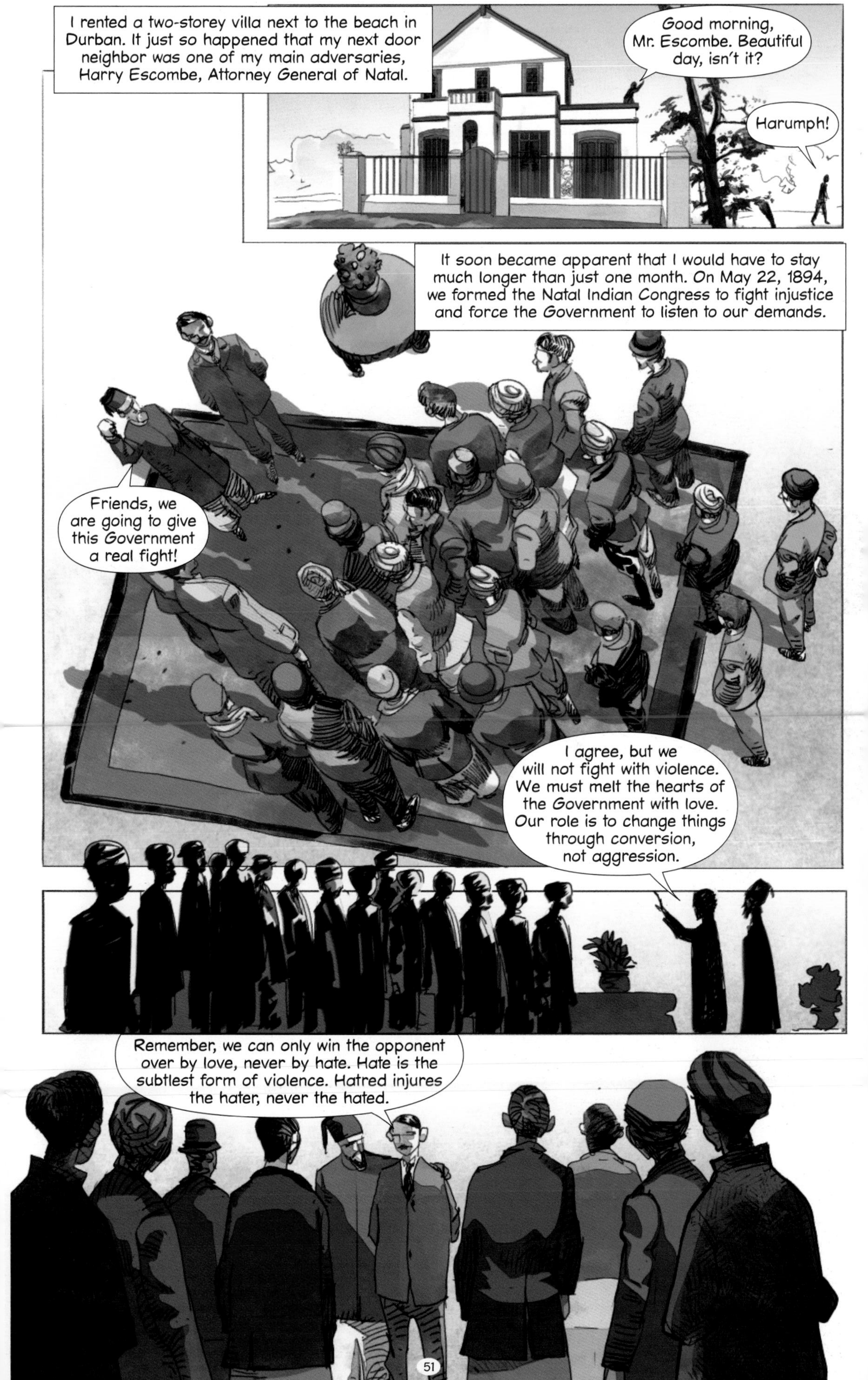
I rented a two-storey villa next to the beach in Durban. It just so happened that my next door neighbor was one of my main adversaries, Harry Escombe, Attorney General of Natal.
Good morning, Mr. Escombe. Beautiful day, isn't it?
Harumph!
It soon became apparent that I would have to stay much longer than just one month. On May 22, 1894, we formed the Natal Indian Congress to fight injustice and force the Government to listen to our demands.
Friends, we are going to give this Government a real fight!
I agree, but we will not fight with violence. We must melt the hearts of the Government with love. Our role is to change things through conversion, not aggression.
Remember, we can only win the opponent over by love, never by hate. Hate is the subtlest form of violence. Hatred injures the hater, never the hated.

One of the greatest evils in South Africa was that of indentured labor. These indentured laborers made up a large part of the Indian community.

These workers were little more than slaves, who had signed up to work in South Africa for five years, for low pay, and few if any rights. At the end of their term of employment they would either sign up for another five years or face deportation back to India.

One morning, not long after the formation of the Natal Indian Congress, one such indentured laborer came to see me. He was in a terrible state.

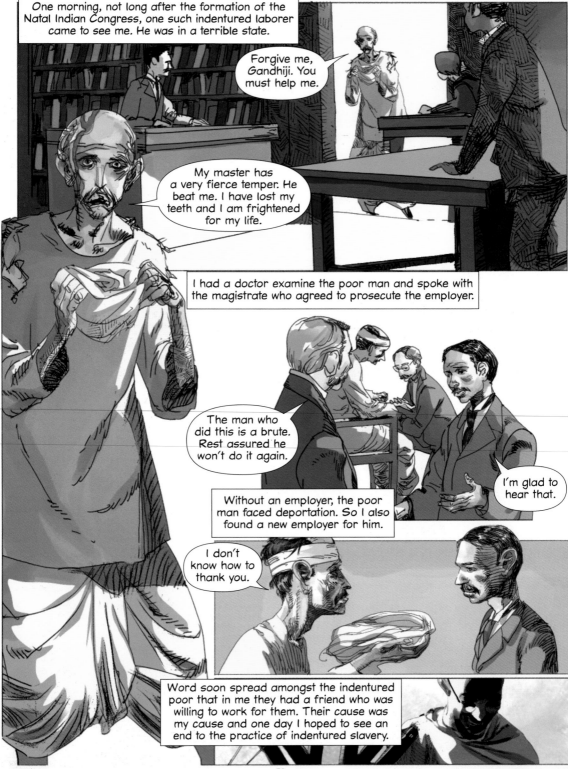

Forgive me, Gandhiji. You must help me.

My master has a very fierce temper. He beat me. I have lost my teeth and I am frightened for my life.

I had a doctor examine the poor man and spoke with the magistrate who agreed to prosecute the employer.

The man who did this is a brute. Rest assured he won't do it again.

I'm glad to hear that.

Without an employer, the poor man faced deportation. So I also found a new employer for him.

I don't know how to thank you.

Word soon spread amongst the indentured poor that in me they had a friend who was willing to work for them. Their cause was my cause and one day I hoped to see an end to the practice of indentured slavery.

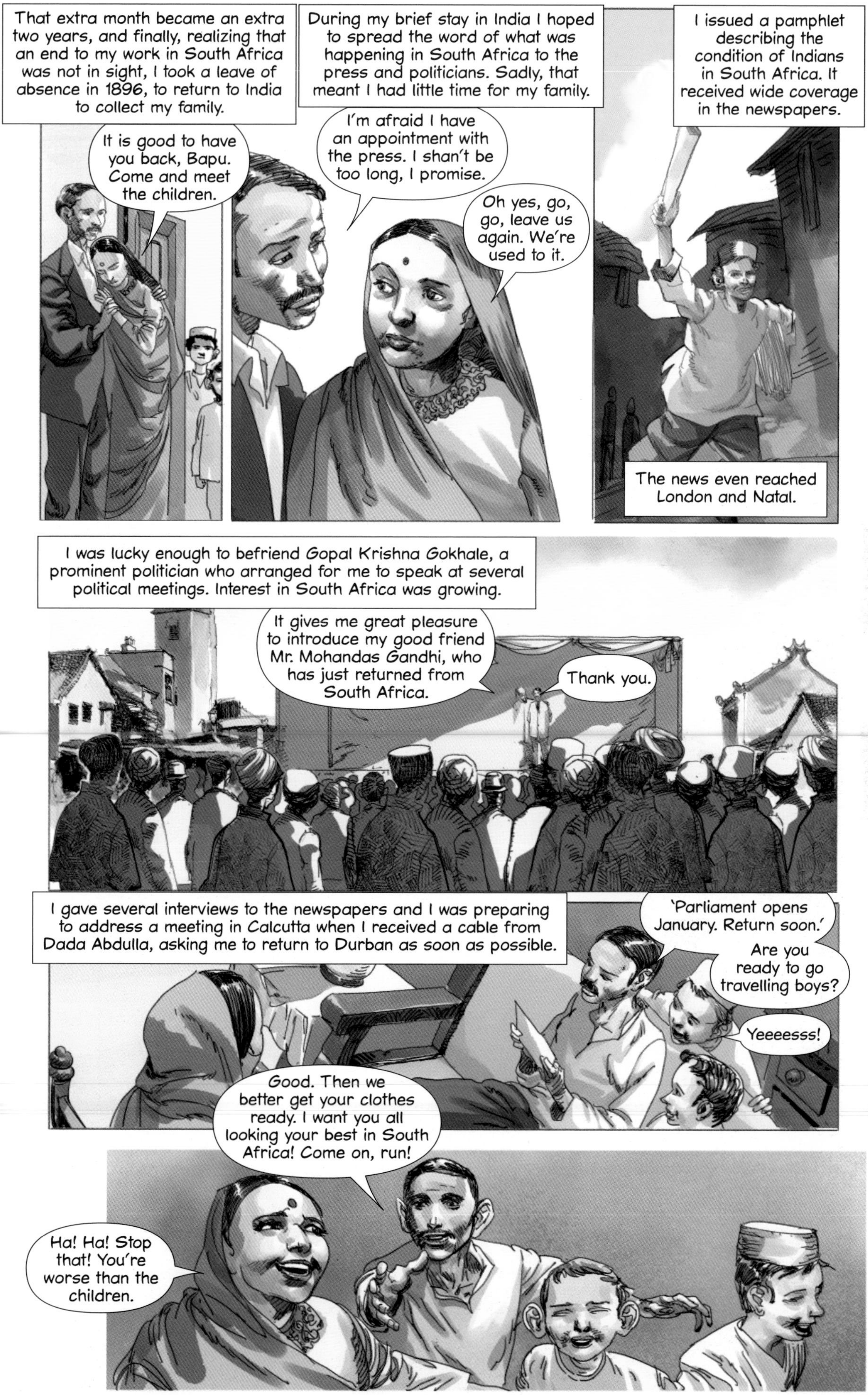
That extra month became an extra two years, and finally, realizing that an end to my work in South Africa was not in sight, I took a leave of absence in 1896, to return to India to collect my family.
It is good to have you back, Bapu. Come and meet the children.
During my brief stay in India I hoped to spread the word of what was happening in South Africa to the press and politicians. Sadly, that meant I had little time for my family.
I'm afraid I have an appointment with the press. I shan't be too long, I promise.
Oh yes, go, go, leave us again. We're used to it.
I issued a pamphlet describing the condition of Indians in South Africa. It received wide coverage in the newspapers.
The news even reached London and Natal.
I was lucky enough to befriend Gopal Krishna Gokhale, a prominent politician who arranged for me to speak at several political meetings. Interest in South Africa was growing.
It gives me great pleasure to introduce my good friend Mr. Mohandas Gandhi, who has just returned from South Africa.
Thank you.
I gave several interviews to the newspapers and I was preparing to address a meeting in Calcutta when I received a cable from Dada Abdulla, asking me to return to Durban as soon as possible.
'Parliament opens January. Return soon.'
Are you ready to go travelling boys?
Yeeeesss!
Good. Then we better get your clothes ready. I want you all looking your best in South Africa! Come on, run!
Ha! Ha! Stop that! You're worse than the children.

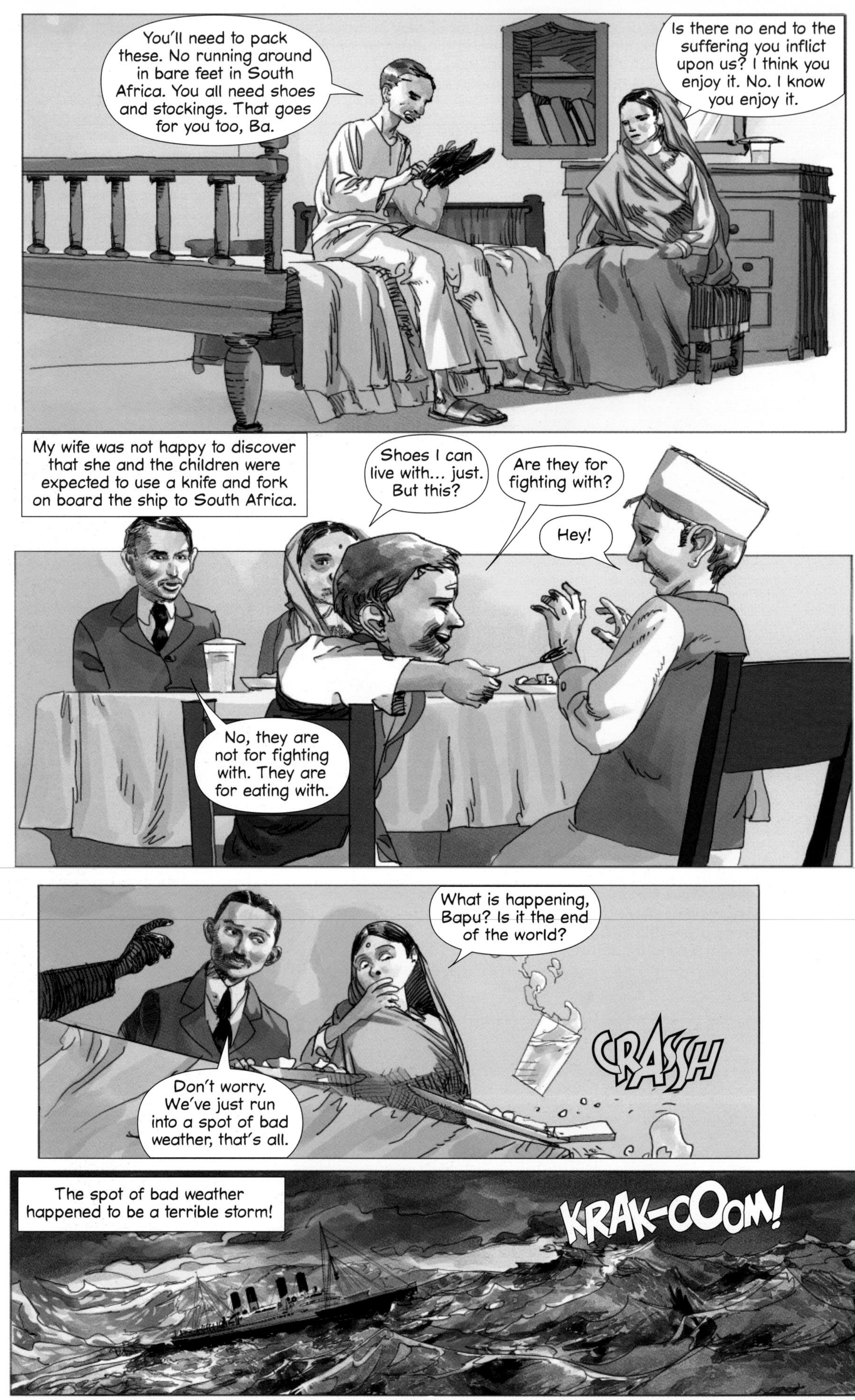

You'll need to pack these. No running around in bare feet in South Africa. You all need shoes and stockings. That goes for you too, Ba.
Is there no end to the suffering you inflict upon us? I think you enjoy it. No. I know you enjoy it.
My wife was not happy to discover that she and the children were expected to use a knife and fork on board the ship to South Africa.
Shoes I can live with... just. But this?
Are they for fighting with?
Hey!
No, they are not for fighting with. They are for eating with.
What is happening, Bapu? Is it the end of the world?
Don't worry. We've just run into a spot of bad weather, that's all.
CRASSH
The spot of bad weather happened to be a terrible storm!
KRAK-COOM!

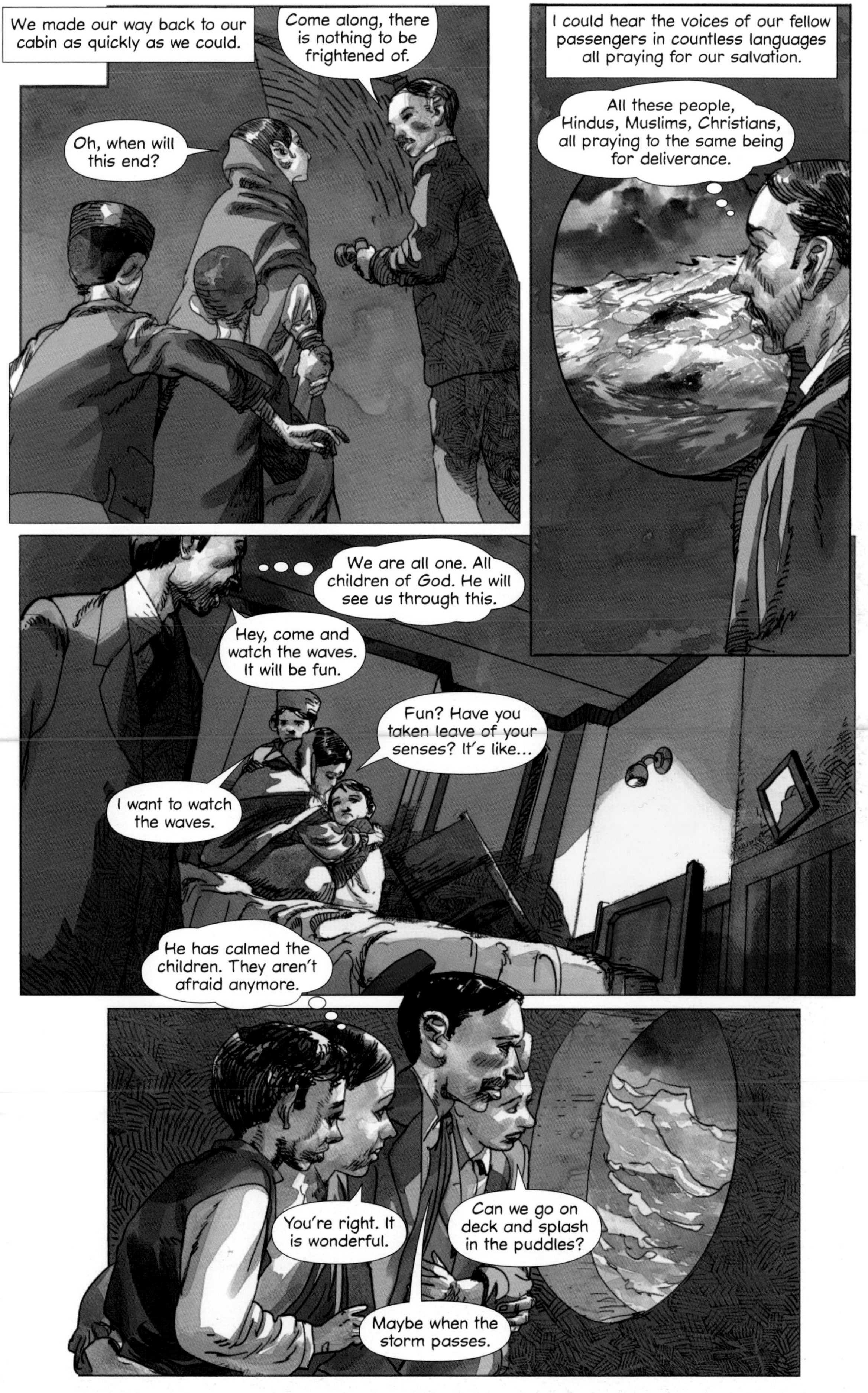
We made our way back to our cabin as quickly as we could.
Come along, there is nothing to be frightened of.
Oh, when will this end?
I could hear the voices of our fellow passengers in countless languages all praying for our salvation.
All these people, Hindus, Muslims, Christians, all praying to the same being for deliverance.
We are all one. All children of God. He will see us through this.
Hey, come and watch the waves. It will be fun.
Fun? Have you taken leave of your senses? It's like...
I want to watch the waves.
He has calmed the children. They aren't afraid anymore.
You're right. It is wonderful.
Can we go on deck and splash in the puddles?
Maybe when the storm passes.

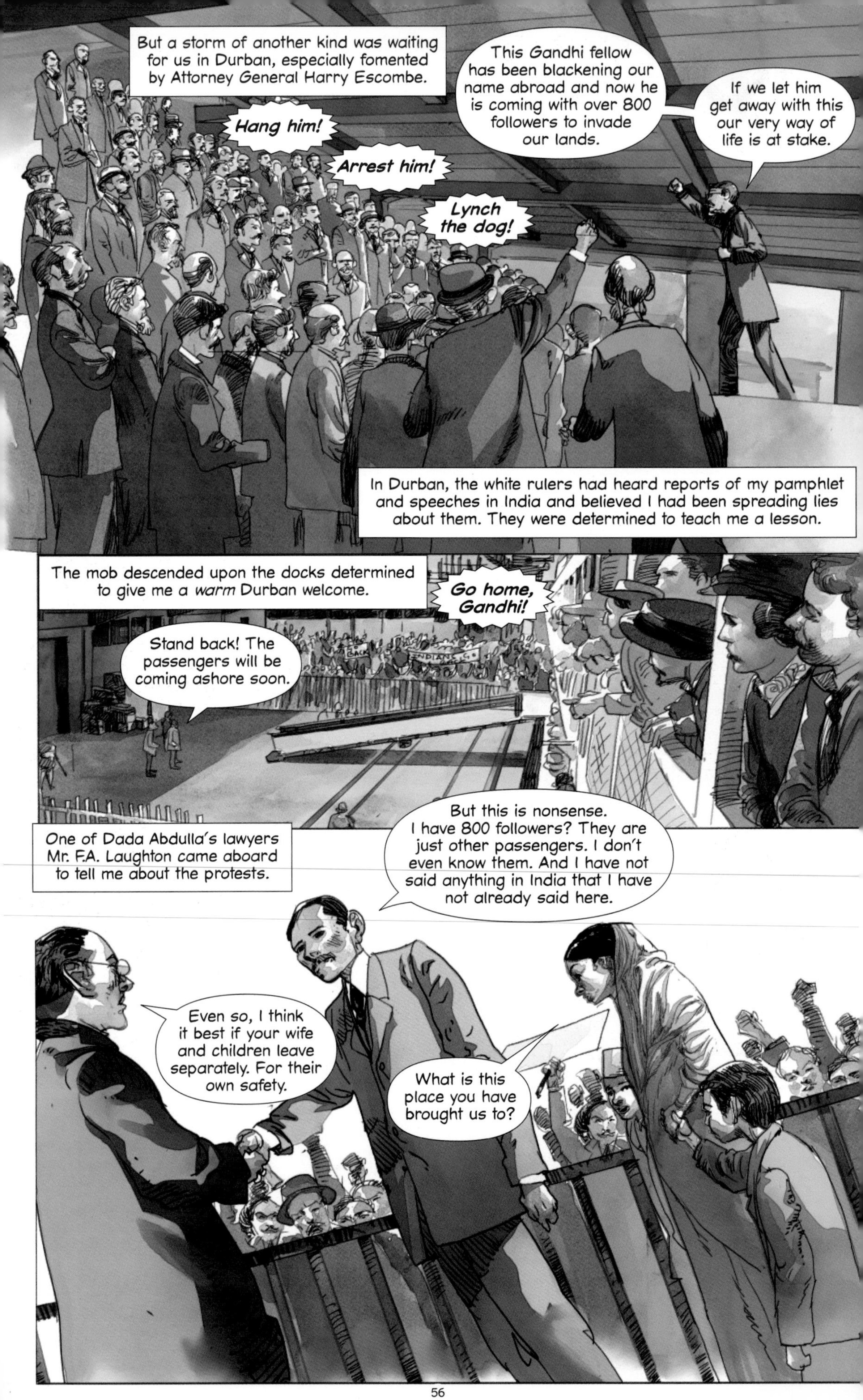
But a storm of another kind was waiting for us in Durban, especially fomented by Attorney General Harry Escombe.
Hang him!
Arrest him!
Lynch the dog!
This Gandhi fellow has been blackening our name abroad and now he is coming with over 800 followers to invade our lands.
If we let him get away with this our very way of life is at stake.
In Durban, the white rulers had heard reports of my pamphlet and speeches in India and believed I had been spreading lies about them. They were determined to teach me a lesson.
The mob descended upon the docks determined to give me a *warm* Durban welcome.
Go home, Gandhi!
Stand back! The passengers will be coming ashore soon.
One of Dada Abdulla's lawyers Mr. F.A. Laughton came aboard to tell me about the protests.
But this is nonsense. I have 800 followers? They are just other passengers. I don't even know them. And I have not said anything in India that I have not already said here.
Even so, I think it best if your wife and children leave separately. For their own safety.
What is this place you have brought us to?

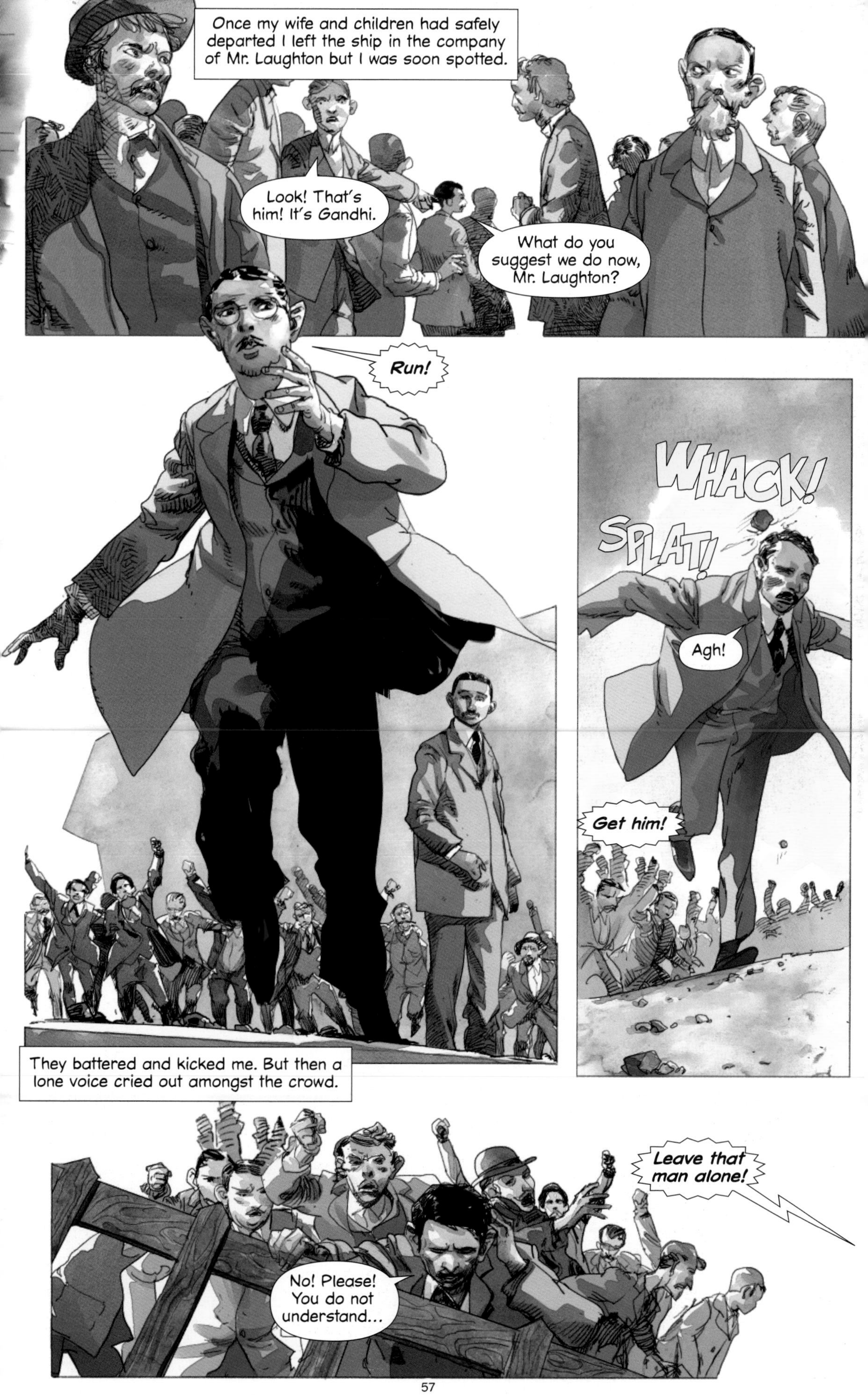
Once my wife and children had safely departed I left the ship in the company of Mr. Laughton but I was soon spotted.
Look! That's him! It's Gandhi.
What do you suggest we do now, Mr. Laughton?
Run!
WHACK!
SPLAT!
Agh!
Get him!
They battered and kicked me. But then a lone voice cried out amongst the crowd.
Leave that man alone!
No! Please! You do not understand...

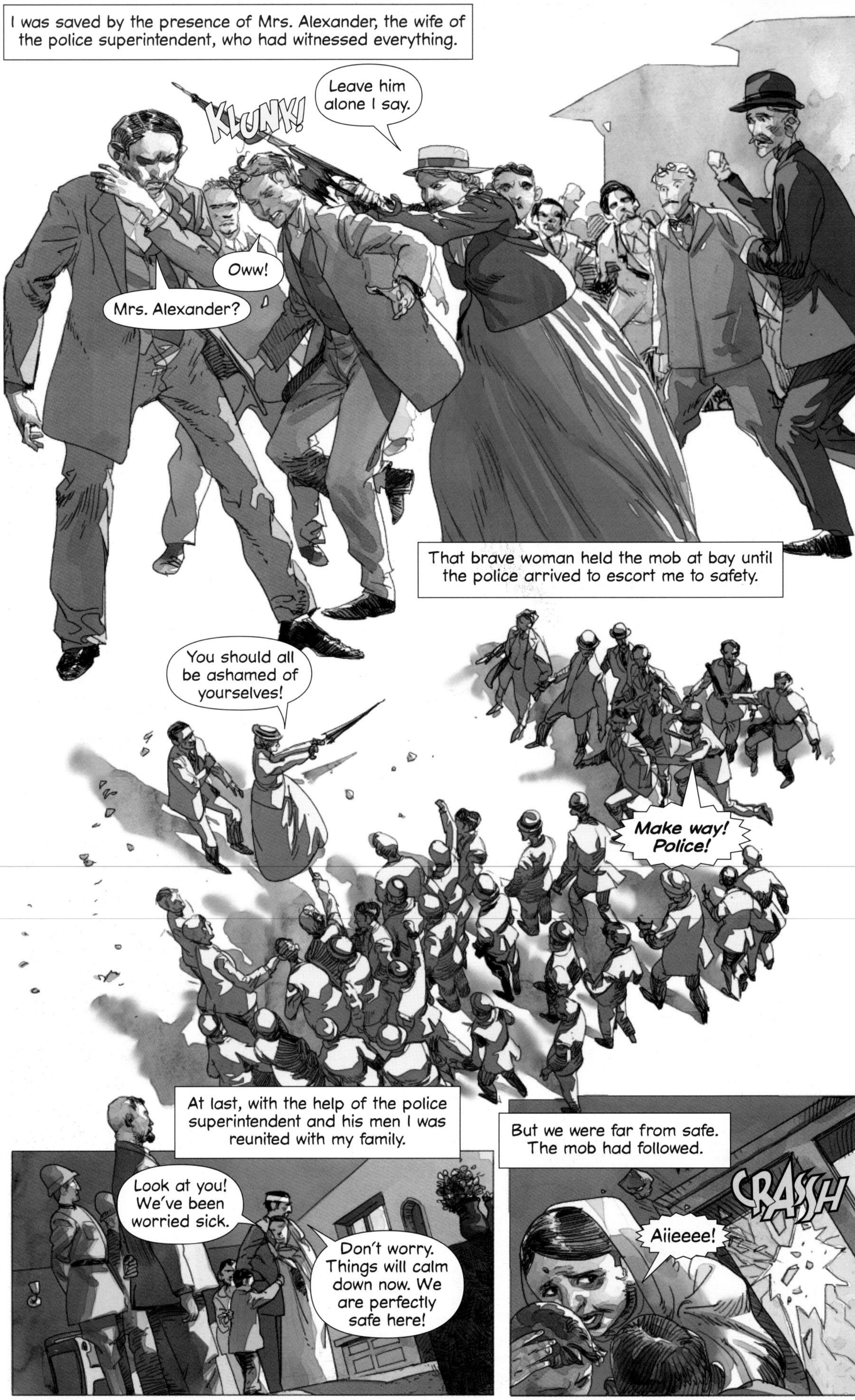

I was saved by the presence of Mrs. Alexander, the wife of the police superintendent, who had witnessed everything.
KLUNK!
Leave him alone I say.
Oww!
Mrs. Alexander?
That brave woman held the mob at bay until the police arrived to escort me to safety.
You should all be ashamed of yourselves!
Make way! Police!
At last, with the help of the police superintendent and his men I was reunited with my family.
Look at you! We've been worried sick.
Don't worry. Things will calm down now. We are perfectly safe here!
But we were far from safe. The mob had followed.
CRASSH
Aiieeee!

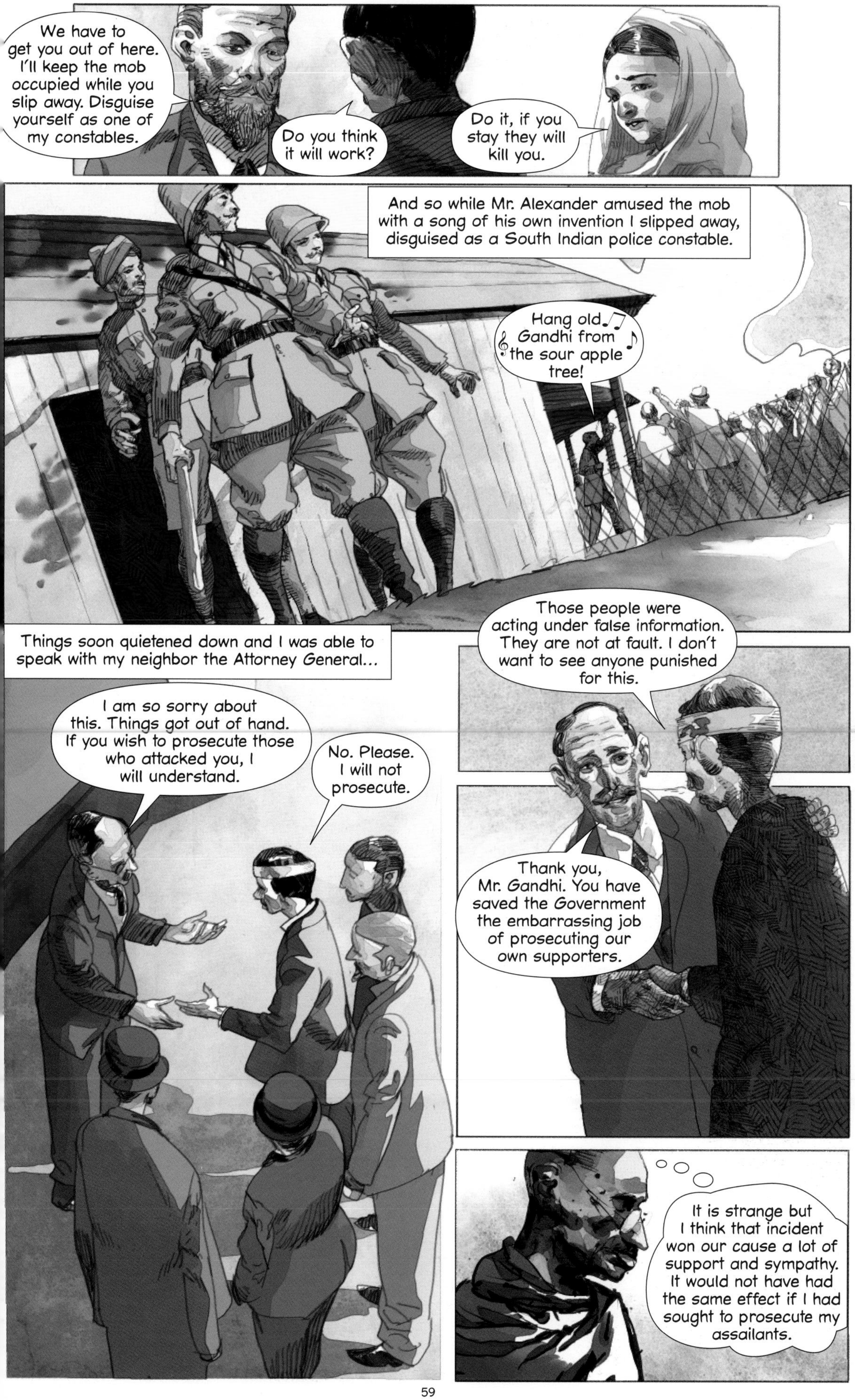
We have to get you out of here. I'll keep the mob occupied while you slip away. Disguise yourself as one of my constables.
Do you think it will work?
Do it, if you stay they will kill you.
And so while Mr. Alexander amused the mob with a song of his own invention I slipped away, disguised as a South Indian police constable.
Hang old Gandhi from the sour apple tree!
Things soon quietened down and I was able to speak with my neighbor the Attorney General...
I am so sorry about this. Things got out of hand. If you wish to prosecute those who attacked you, I will understand.
No. Please. I will not prosecute.
Those people were acting under false information. They are not at fault. I don't want to see anyone punished for this.
Thank you, Mr. Gandhi. You have saved the Government the embarrassing job of prosecuting our own supporters.
It is strange but I think that incident won our cause a lot of support and sympathy. It would not have had the same effect if I had sought to prosecute my assailants.

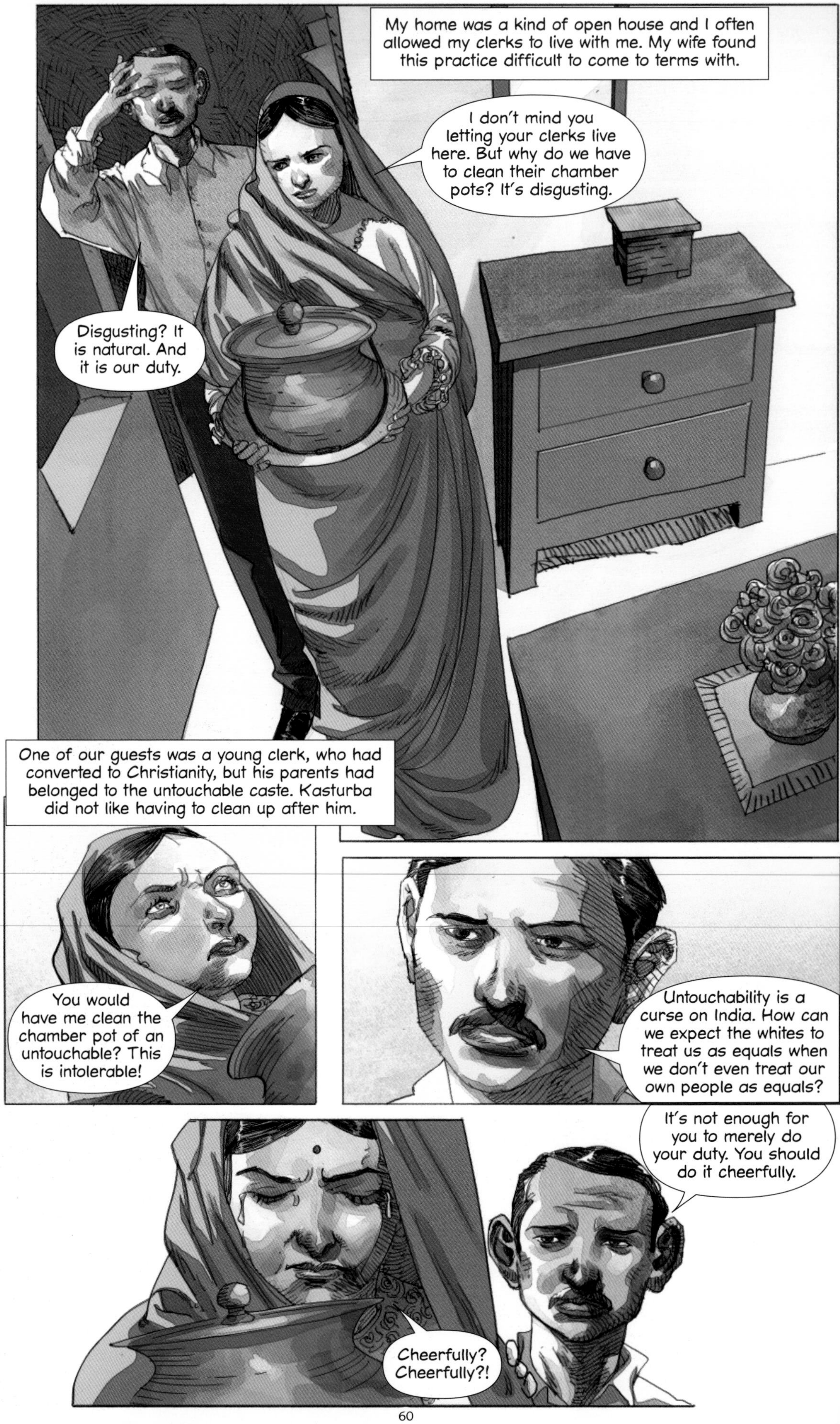
My home was a kind of open house and I often allowed my clerks to live with me. My wife found this practice difficult to come to terms with.
I don't mind you letting your clerks live here. But why do we have to clean their chamber pots? It's disgusting.
Disgusting? It is natural. And it is our duty.
One of our guests was a young clerk, who had converted to Christianity, but his parents had belonged to the untouchable caste. Kasturba did not like having to clean up after him.
You would have me clean the chamber pot of an untouchable? This is intolerable!
Untouchability is a curse on India. How can we expect the whites to treat us as equals when we don't even treat our own people as equals?
It's not enough for you to merely do your duty. You should do it cheerfully.
Cheerfully? Cheerfully?!

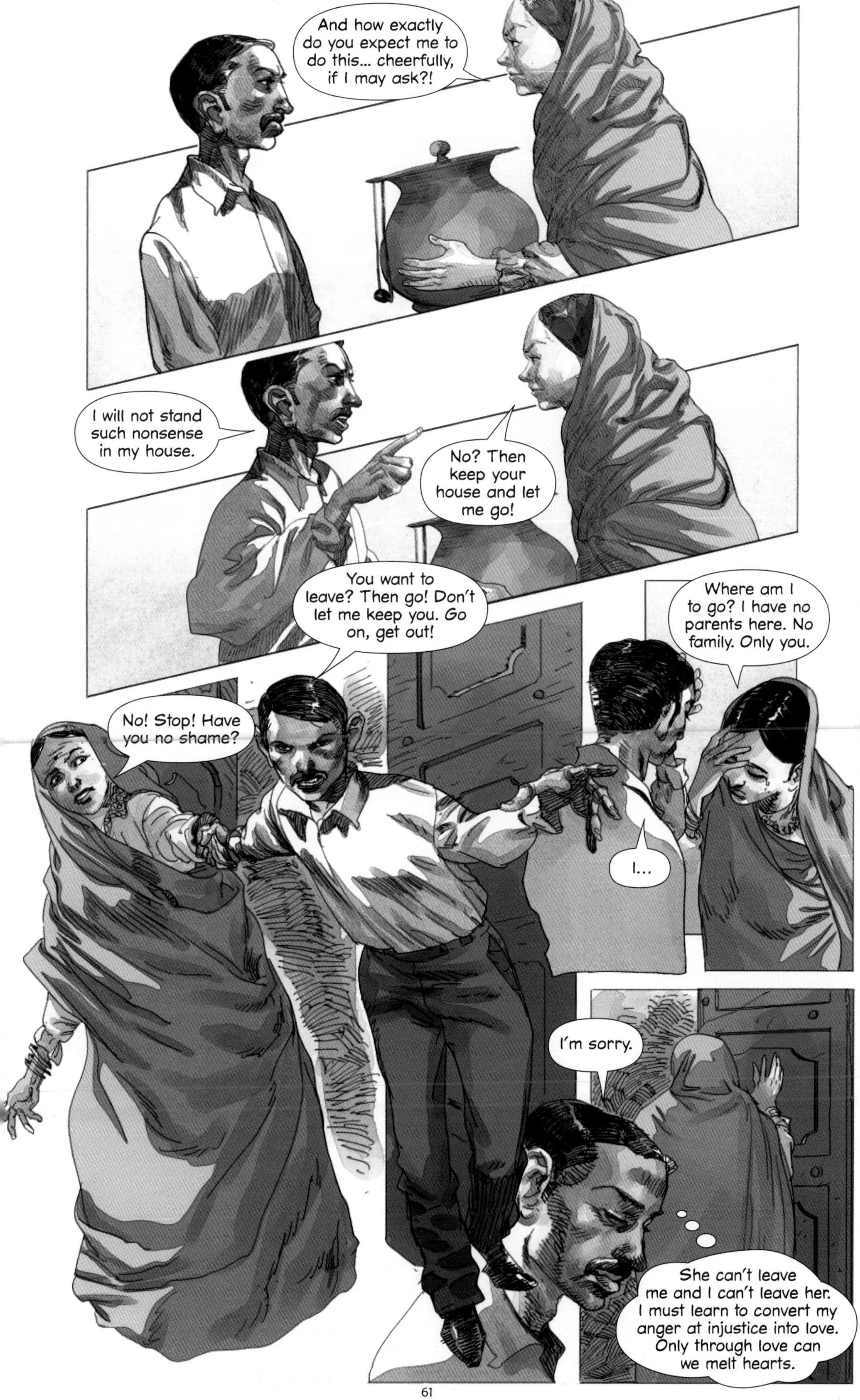
And how exactly do you expect me to do this... cheerfully, if I may ask?!
I will not stand such nonsense in my house.
No? Then keep your house and let me go!
You want to leave? Then go! Don't let me keep you. Go on, get out!
No! Stop! Have you no shame?
Where am I to go? I have no parents here. No family. Only you.
I...
I'm sorry.
She can't leave me and I can't leave her. I must learn to convert my anger at injustice into love. Only through love can we melt hearts.

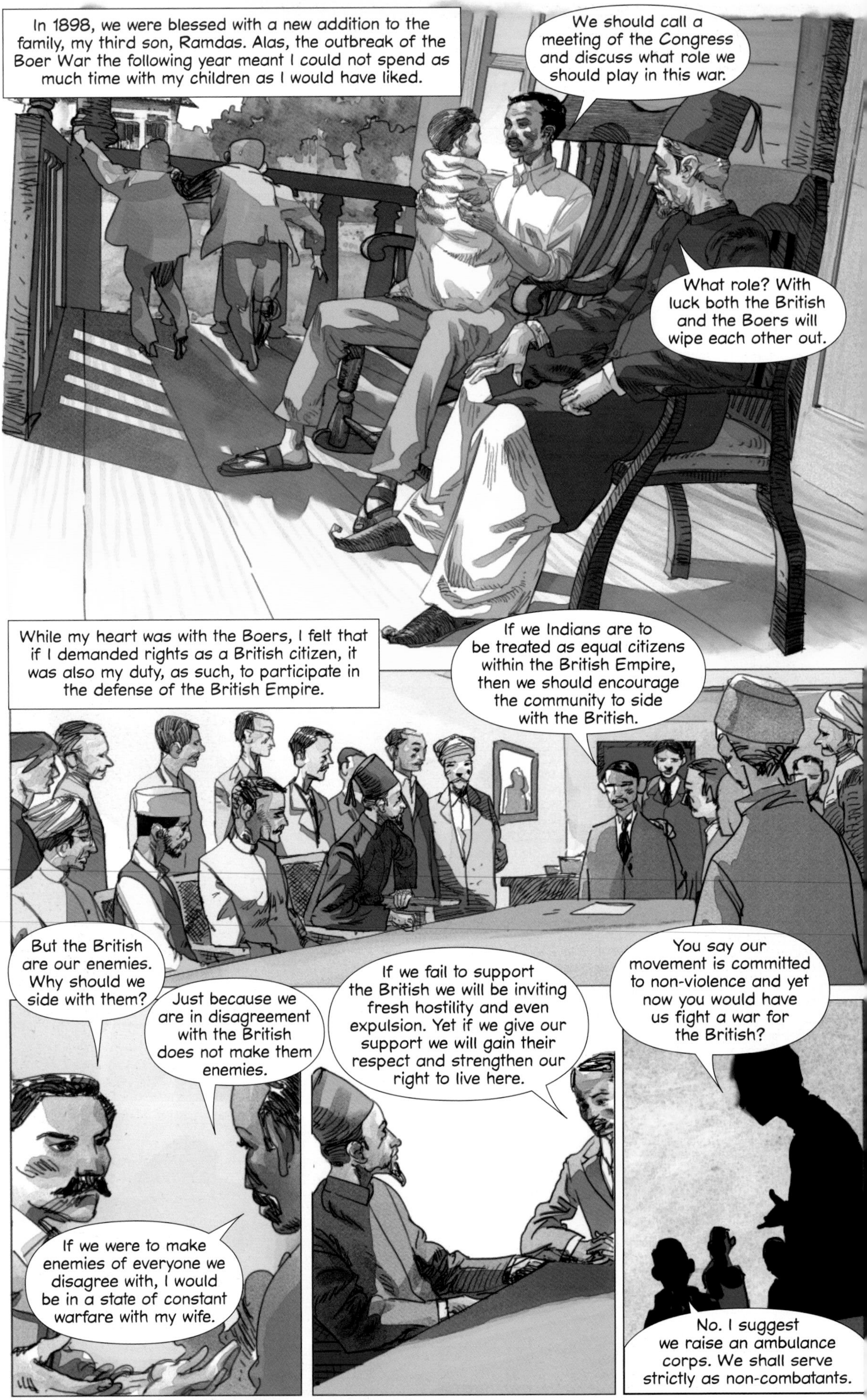
In 1898, we were blessed with a new addition to the family, my third son, Ramdas. Alas, the outbreak of the Boer War the following year meant I could not spend as much time with my children as I would have liked.
We should call a meeting of the Congress and discuss what role we should play in this war.
What role? With luck both the British and the Boers will wipe each other out.
While my heart was with the Boers, I felt that if I demanded rights as a British citizen, it was also my duty, as such, to participate in the defense of the British Empire.
If we Indians are to be treated as equal citizens within the British Empire, then we should encourage the community to side with the British.
But the British are our enemies. Why should we side with them?
Just because we are in disagreement with the British does not make them enemies.
If we were to make enemies of everyone we disagree with, I would be in a state of constant warfare with my wife.
If we fail to support the British we will be inviting fresh hostility and even expulsion. Yet if we give our support we will gain their respect and strengthen our right to live here.
You say our movement is committed to non-violence and yet now you would have us fight a war for the British?
No. I suggest we raise an ambulance corps. We shall serve strictly as non-combatants.

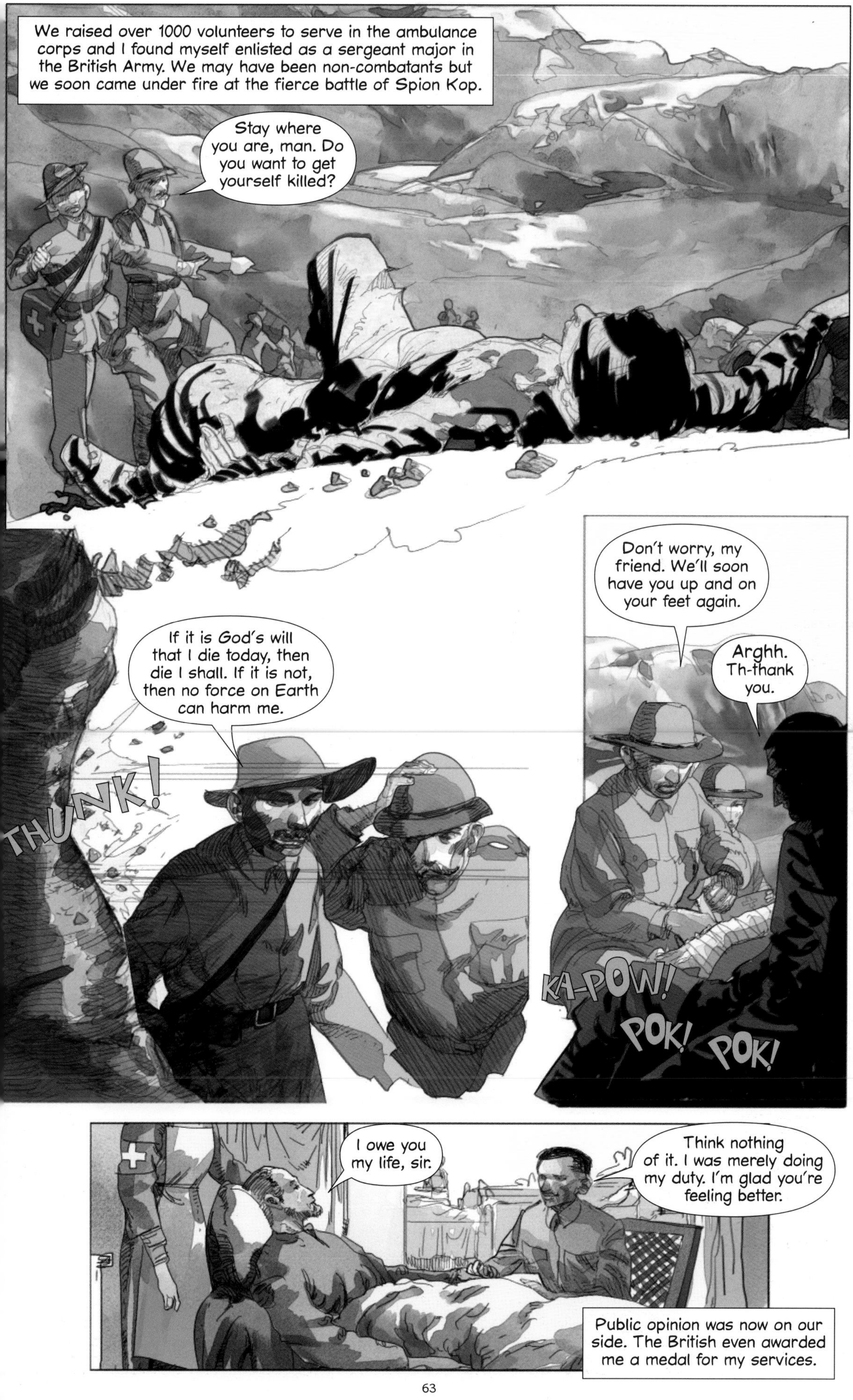
We raised over 1000 volunteers to serve in the ambulance corps and I found myself enlisted as a sergeant major in the British Army. We may have been non-combatants but we soon came under fire at the fierce battle of Spion Kop.
Stay where you are, man. Do you want to get yourself killed?
If it is God's will that I die today, then die I shall. If it is not, then no force on Earth can harm me.
THUNK!
Don't worry, my friend. We'll soon have you up and on your feet again.
Arghh. Th-thank you.
KA-POW!
POK! POK!
I owe you my life, sir.
Think nothing of it. I was merely doing my duty. I'm glad you're feeling better.
Public opinion was now on our side. The British even awarded me a medal for my services.

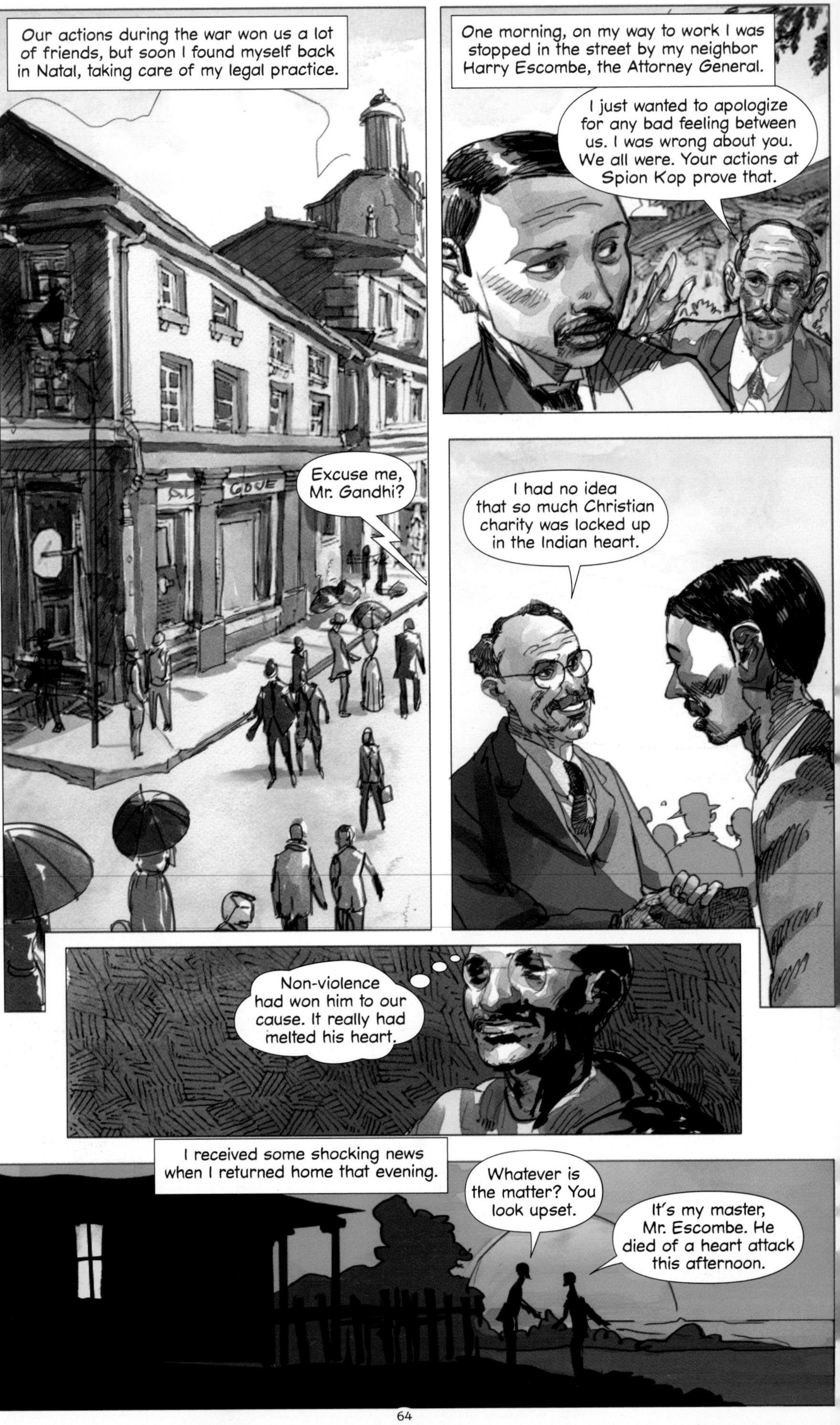
Our actions during the war won us a lot of friends, but soon I found myself back in Natal, taking care of my legal practice.
Excuse me, Mr. Gandhi?
One morning, on my way to work I was stopped in the street by my neighbor Harry Escombe, the Attorney General.
I just wanted to apologize for any bad feeling between us. I was wrong about you. We all were. Your actions at Spion Kop prove that.
I had no idea that so much Christian charity was locked up in the Indian heart.
Non-violence had won him to our cause. It really had melted his heart.
I received some shocking news when I returned home that evening.
Whatever is the matter? You look upset.
It's my master, Mr. Escombe. He died of a heart attack this afternoon.

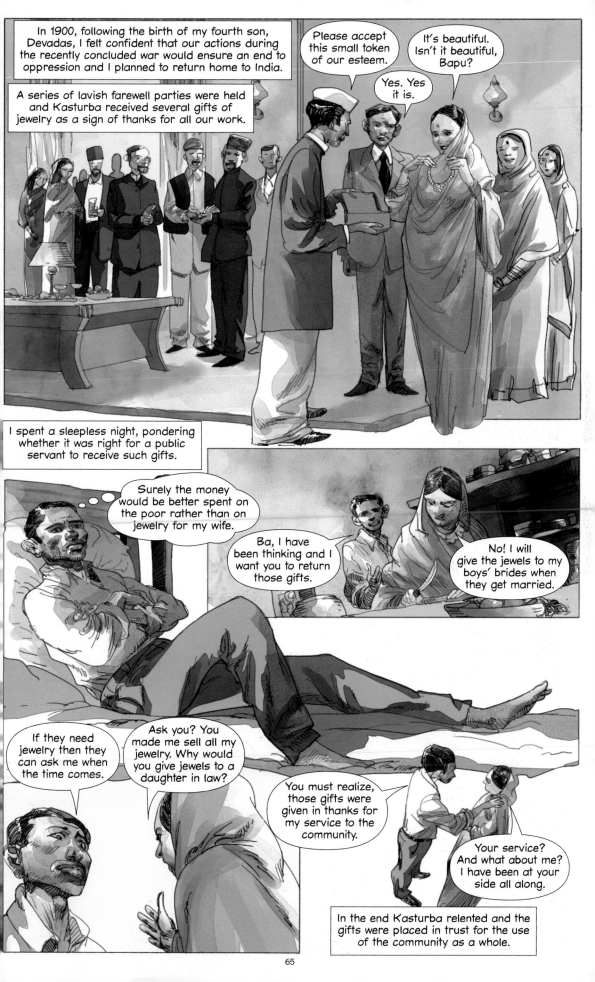

In 1900, following the birth of my fourth son, Devadas, I felt confident that our actions during the recently concluded war would ensure an end to oppression and I planned to return home to India.

Please accept this small token of our esteem.

It's beautiful. Isn't it beautiful, Bapu?

Yes. Yes it is.

A series of lavish farewell parties were held and Kasturba received several gifts of jewelry as a sign of thanks for all our work.

I spent a sleepless night, pondering whether it was right for a public servant to receive such gifts.

Surely the money would be better spent on the poor rather than on jewelry for my wife.

Ba, I have been thinking and I want you to return those gifts.

No! I will give the jewels to my boys' brides when they get married.

If they need jewelry then they can ask me when the time comes.

Ask you? You made me sell all my jewelry. Why would you give jewels to a daughter in law?

You must realize, those gifts were given in thanks for my service to the community.

Your service? And what about me? I have been at your side all along.

In the end Kasturba relented and the gifts were placed in trust for the use of the community as a whole.

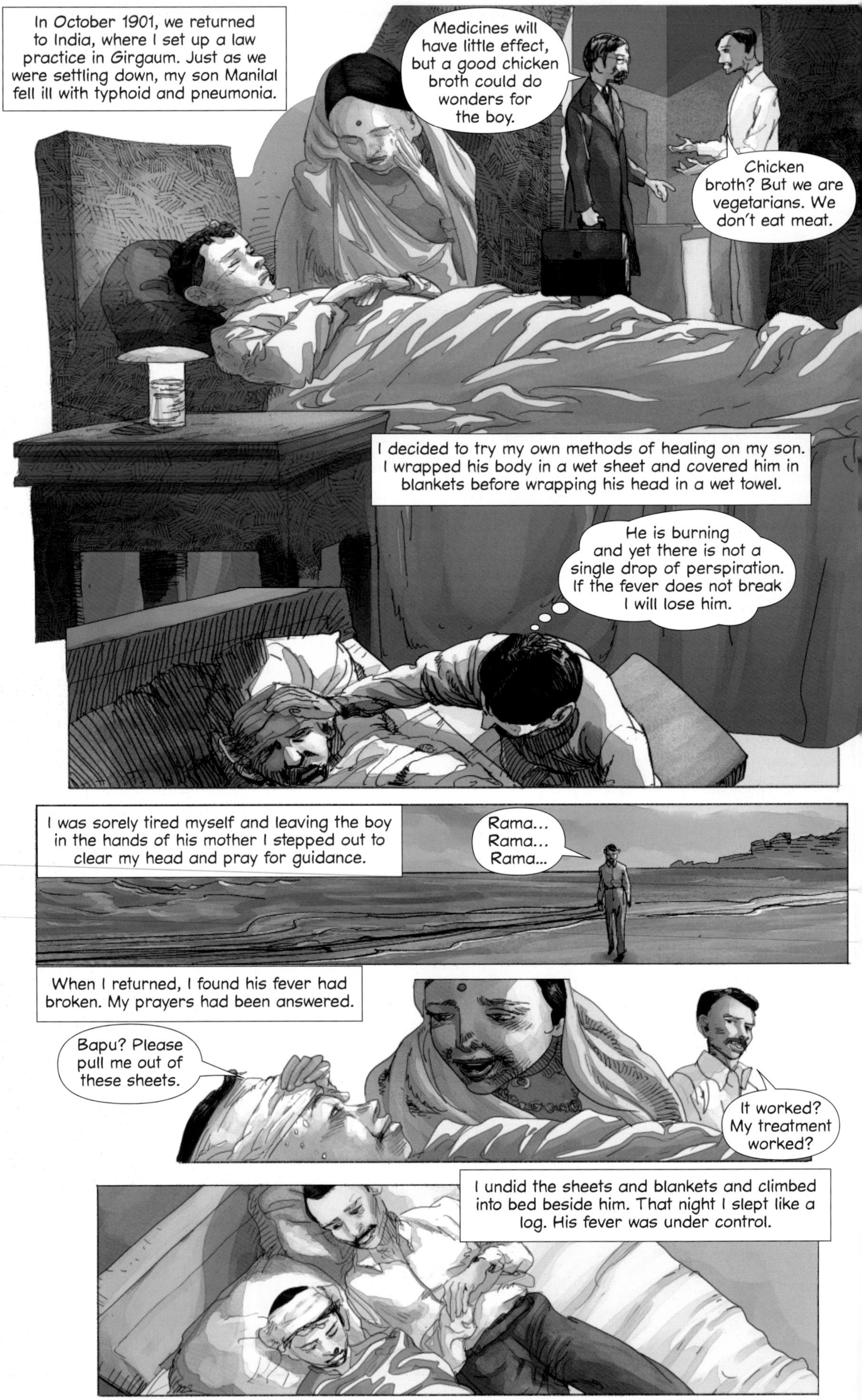
In October 1901, we returned to India, where I set up a law practice in Girgaum. Just as we were settling down, my son Manilal fell ill with typhoid and pneumonia.
Medicines will have little effect, but a good chicken broth could do wonders for the boy.
Chicken broth? But we are vegetarians. We don't eat meat.
I decided to try my own methods of healing on my son. I wrapped his body in a wet sheet and covered him in blankets before wrapping his head in a wet towel.
He is burning and yet there is not a single drop of perspiration. If the fever does not break I will lose him.
I was sorely tired myself and leaving the boy in the hands of his mother I stepped out to clear my head and pray for guidance.
Rama... Rama... Rama...
When I returned, I found his fever had broken. My prayers had been answered.
Bapu? Please pull me out of these sheets.
It worked? My treatment worked?
I undid the sheets and blankets and climbed into bed beside him. That night I slept like a log. His fever was under control.

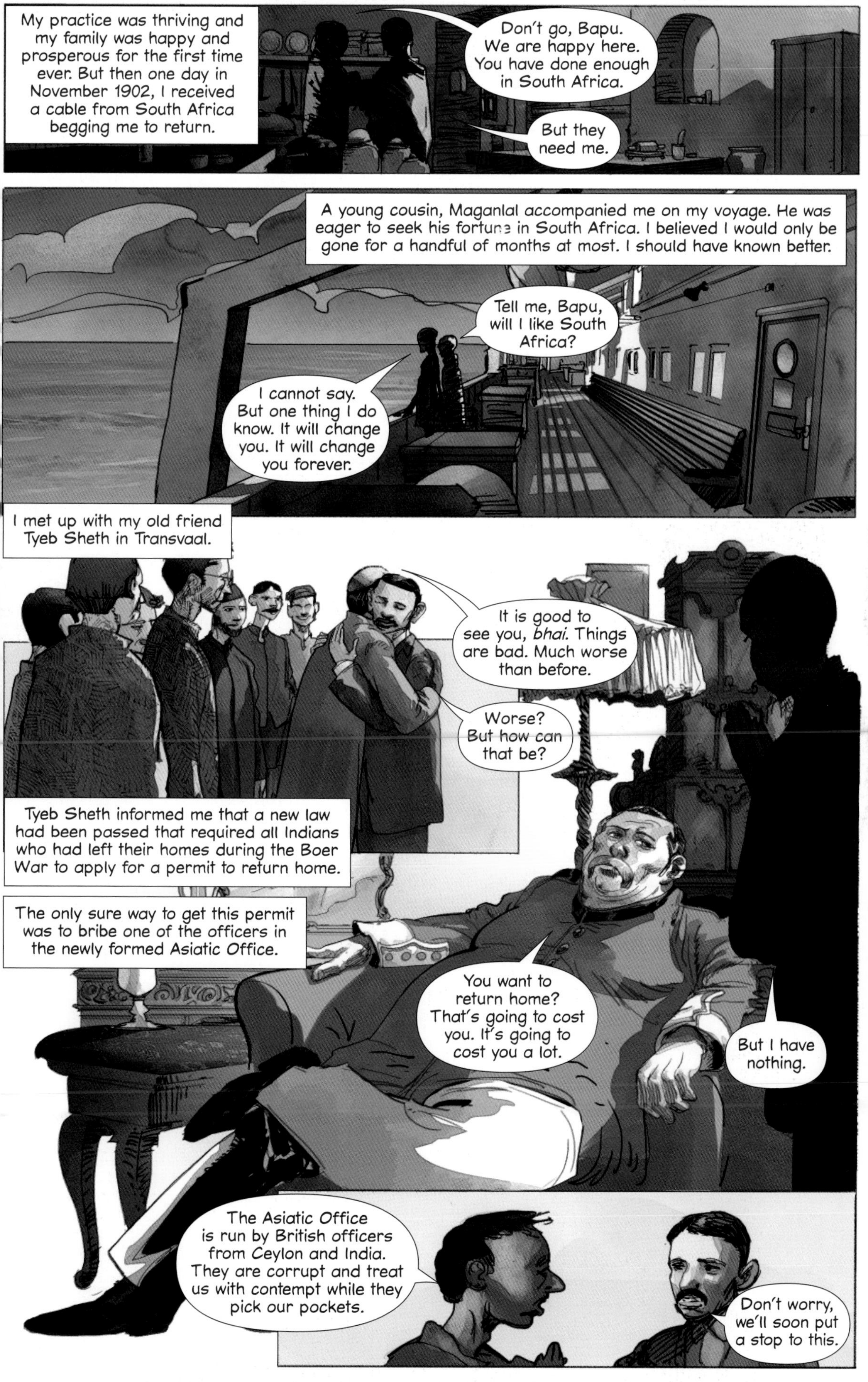
My practice was thriving and my family was happy and prosperous for the first time ever. But then one day in November 1902, I received a cable from South Africa begging me to return.
Don't go, Bapu. We are happy here. You have done enough in South Africa.
But they need me.
A young cousin, Maganlal accompanied me on my voyage. He was eager to seek his fortune in South Africa. I believed I would only be gone for a handful of months at most. I should have known better.
Tell me, Bapu, will I like South Africa?
I cannot say. But one thing I do know. It will change you. It will change you forever.
I met up with my old friend Tyeb Sheth in Transvaal.
It is good to see you, *bhai*. Things are bad. Much worse than before.
Worse? But how can that be?
Tyeb Sheth informed me that a new law had been passed that required all Indians who had left their homes during the Boer War to apply for a permit to return home.
The only sure way to get this permit was to bribe one of the officers in the newly formed Asiatic Office.
You want to return home? That's going to cost you. It's going to cost you a lot.
But I have nothing.
The Asiatic Office is run by British officers from Ceylon and India. They are corrupt and treat us with contempt while they pick our pockets.
Don't worry, we'll soon put a stop to this.

It did not take me long to compile evidence against two of the worst offenders in the Asiatic Office. I took it straight to the police in Johannesburg.

These men will certainly stand trial but I should warn you, no jury in South Africa will convict a white man on evidence supplied by non-whites.

I cannot help that, but I must see them brought to account.

The police commissioner's prediction proved correct...

Not guilty!

The jury found them not guilty, but in spite of their acquittal, their guilt was so clear that they were forced to give up their positions and leave the Asiatic Office.

One of those men has asked me if you would stand in his way were he to seek employment with another department in the city.

Of course not. I hate the wrongs they did but not them personally.

Following this small victory, in 1903 I agreed to finance *Indian Opinion*, a newspaper aimed at giving the Indian community in South Africa a voice. I also agreed to supply the paper with at least one article a week.

THE
INDIAN • OPINION.

ENGLISH.   GUJARATI.   PUBLISHED IN   TAMIL.   HINDE.

Vol. I.   (12 Pages with Supplement)   Durban, June 4th, 1903   No. 1.

હેમાન ગૌરડન એન્ડ કું

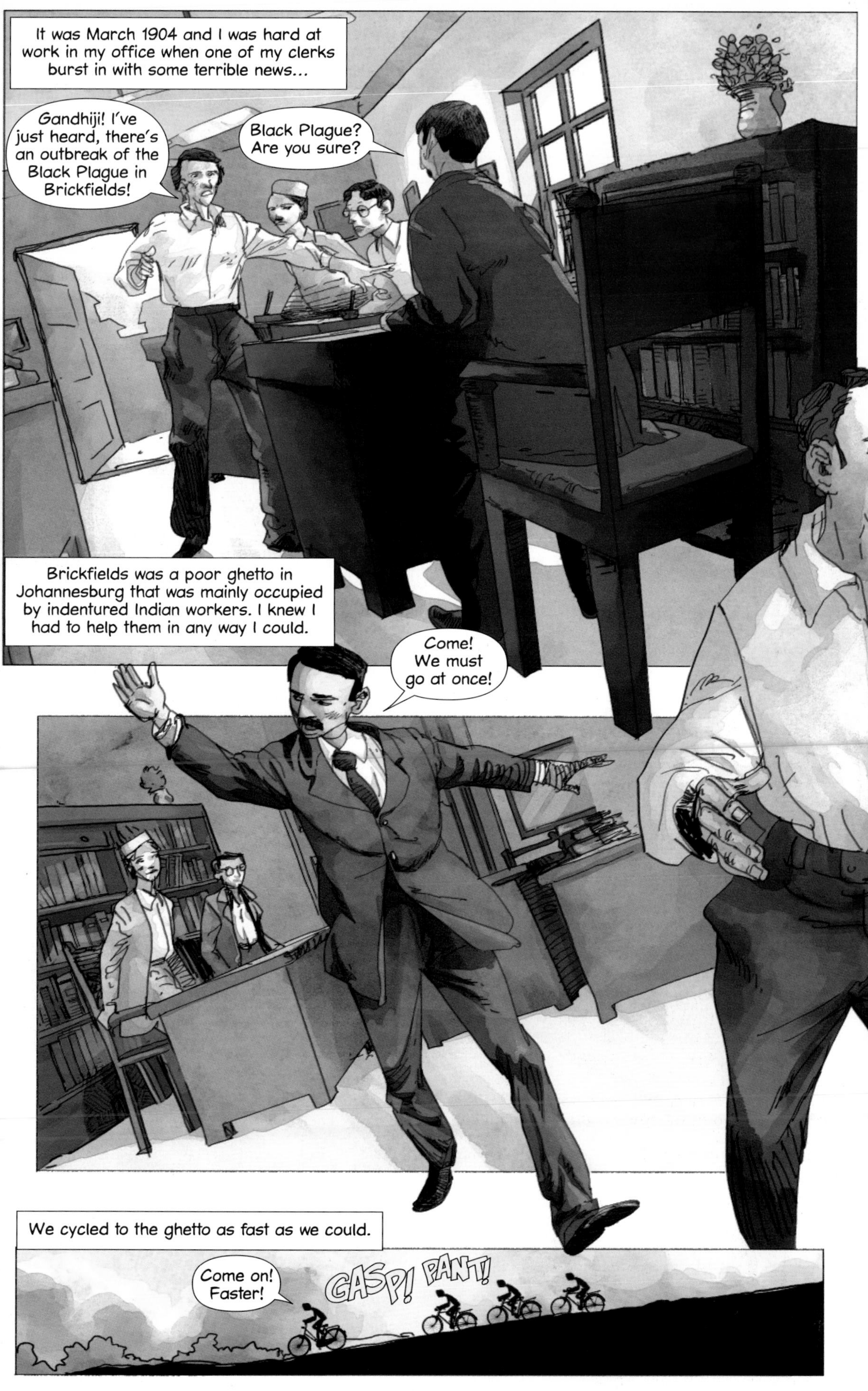
It was March 1904 and I was hard at work in my office when one of my clerks burst in with some terrible news...
Gandhiji! I've just heard, there's an outbreak of the Black Plague in Brickfields!
Black Plague? Are you sure?
Brickfields was a poor ghetto in Johannesburg that was mainly occupied by indentured Indian workers. I knew I had to help them in any way I could.
Come! We must go at once!
We cycled to the ghetto as fast as we could.
Come on! Faster!
GASP! PANT!

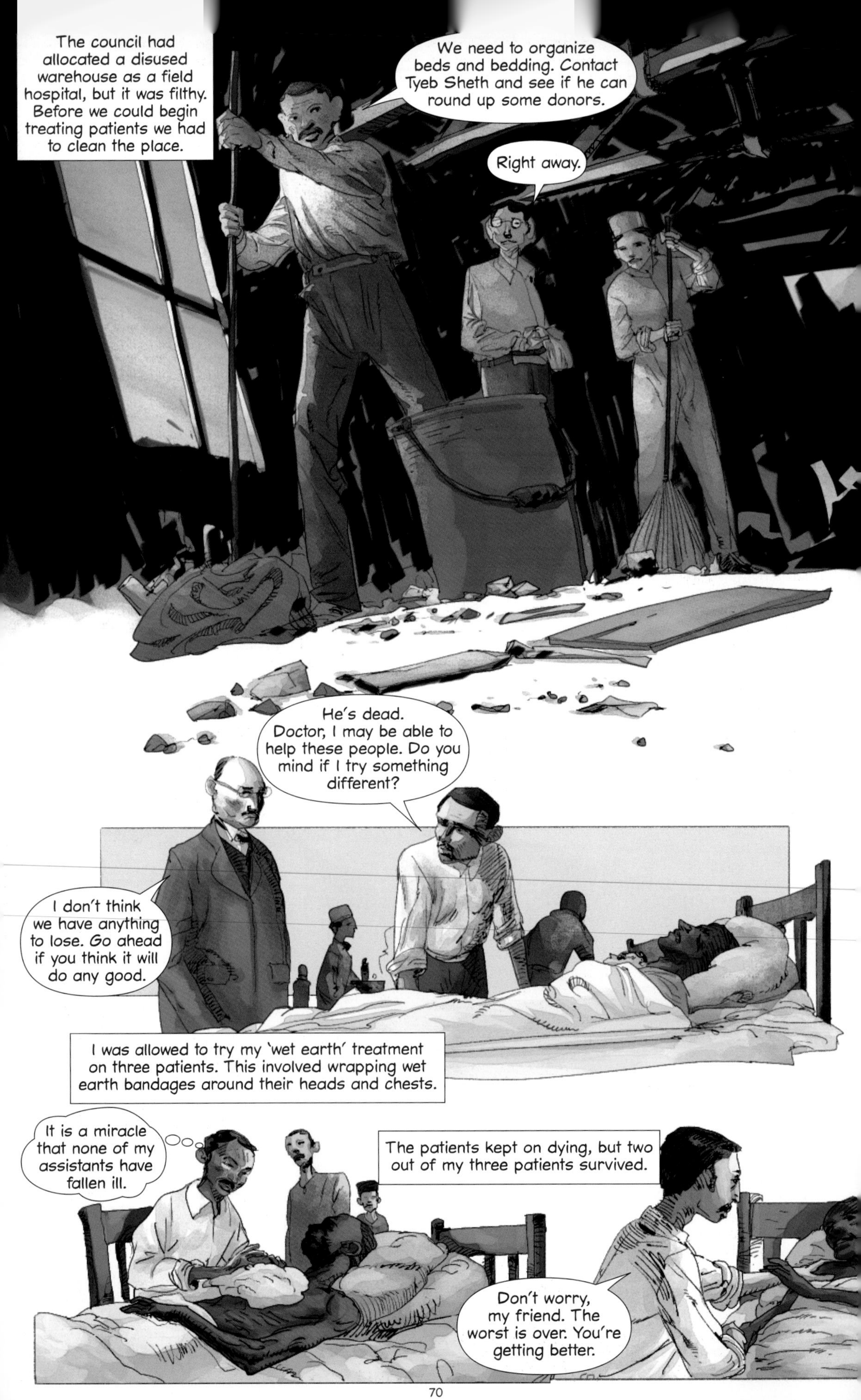

The council had allocated a disused warehouse as a field hospital, but it was filthy. Before we could begin treating patients we had to clean the place.
We need to organize beds and bedding. Contact Tyeb Sheth and see if he can round up some donors.
Right away.
He's dead. Doctor, I may be able to help these people. Do you mind if I try something different?
I don't think we have anything to lose. Go ahead if you think it will do any good.
I was allowed to try my 'wet earth' treatment on three patients. This involved wrapping wet earth bandages around their heads and chests.
It is a miracle that none of my assistants have fallen ill.
The patients kept on dying, but two out of my three patients survived.
Don't worry, my friend. The worst is over. You're getting better.

One of my European friends, Henry Polak had lent me a book. It was John Ruskin's *Unto This Last*. Inspired by its ideas of social equality and the celebration of the simple life, I decided to buy a farm close to Phoenix Station... I invited Maganlal, his brother Chhaganlal, and Polak to come and stay on the farm with me.

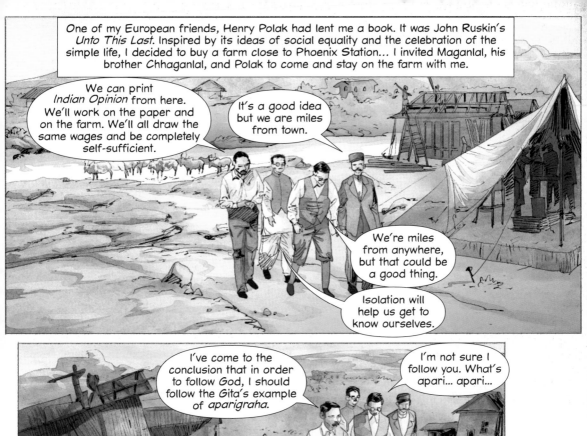

We can print *Indian Opinion* from here. We'll work on the paper and on the farm. We'll all draw the same wages and be completely self-sufficient.

It's a good idea but we are miles from town.

We're miles from anywhere, but that could be a good thing.

Isolation will help us get to know ourselves.

I've come to the conclusion that in order to follow God, I should follow the *Gita*'s example of *aparigraha*.

I'm not sure I follow you. What's apari... apari...

It means non-possession. The renunciation of worldly goods.

Yes, I have decided to give up my life insurance policy – Oh, be careful of this snake, this is his home too.

But what if something should happen to you? What would become of your family?

If I die, God will look after my family. That is what happens to the countless number of impoverished people. Why should I be any different? Why should I rob my children of their right to self reliance?

Well, when you put it that way it does sound perfectly reasonable.

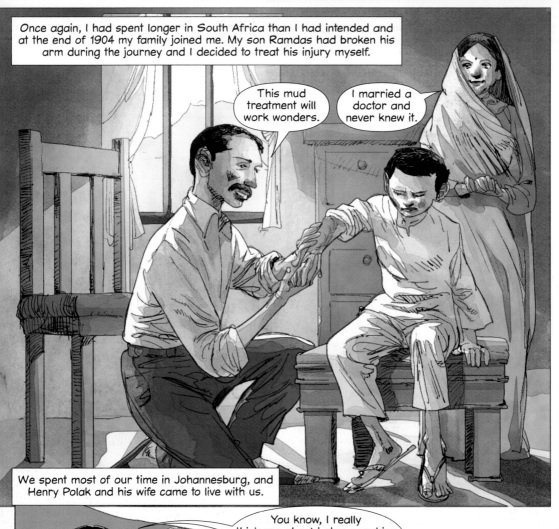

Once again, I had spent longer in South Africa than I had intended and at the end of 1904 my family joined me. My son Ramdas had broken his arm during the journey and I decided to treat his injury myself.

This mud treatment will work wonders.

I married a doctor and never knew it.

We spent most of our time in Johannesburg, and Henry Polak and his wife came to live with us.

You know, I really think you should stop speaking to your children in Gujarati. English would be much more helpful for them.

Why? They can learn English from you. If they cannot speak Gujarati they will seem like foreigners to their own people.

A German friend of mine, Hermann Kallenbach invited me to visit a Trappist monastery with him.

Tell me, why do so many of your monks take this vow of silence?

The reason is apparent, my son. We do not know often what we say. If we want to listen to the still small voice that is always speaking within us, it will not be heard if we continually speak.

Of course. Silence can help us listen to the small voice within.

In 1906, the newspapers were full of reports about the Zulu Rebellion that was supposedly sweeping through South Africa. It seemed as if the British Empire was under threat and once again I raised volunteers to serve in the ambulance corps.

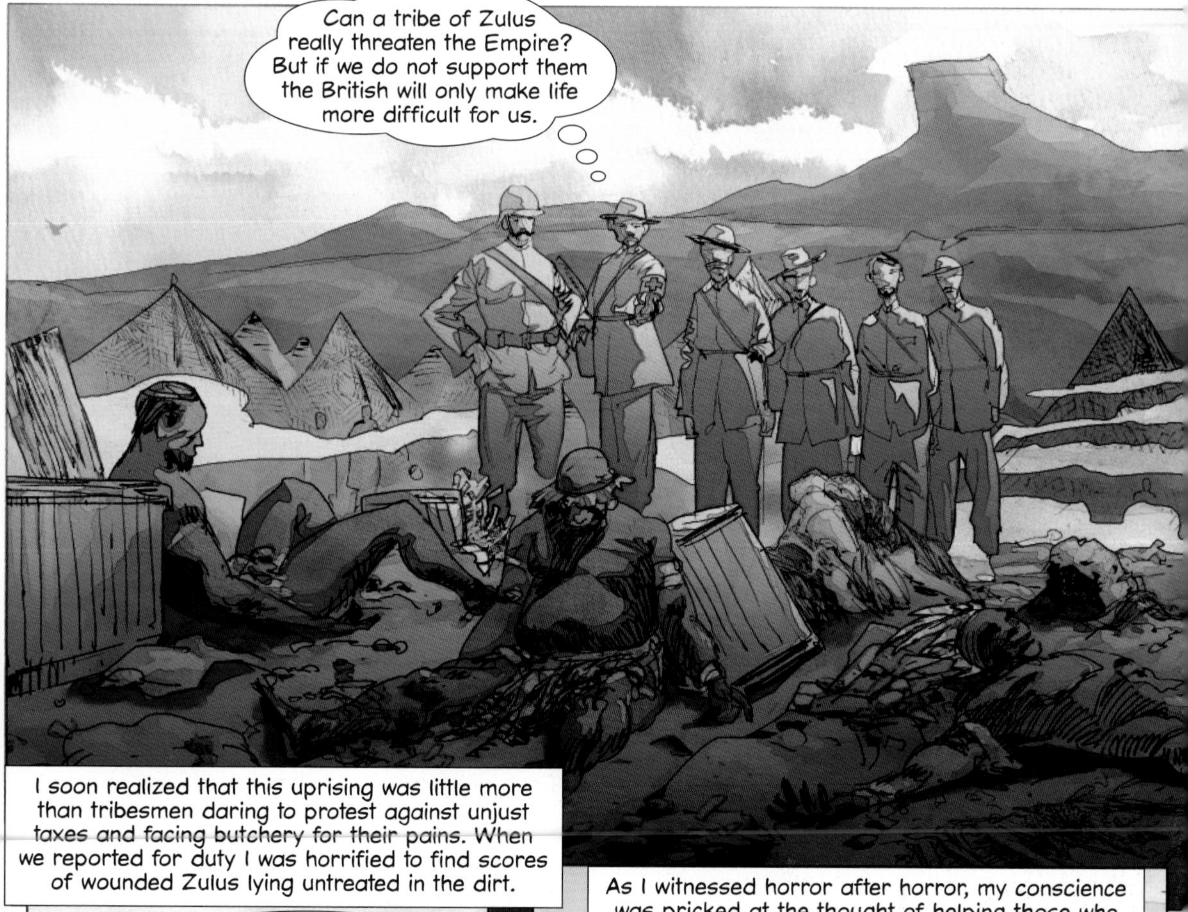
Can a tribe of Zulus really threaten the Empire? But if we do not support them the British will only make life more difficult for us.
I soon realized that this uprising was little more than tribesmen daring to protest against unjust taxes and facing butchery for their pains. When we reported for duty I was horrified to find scores of wounded Zulus lying untreated in the dirt.

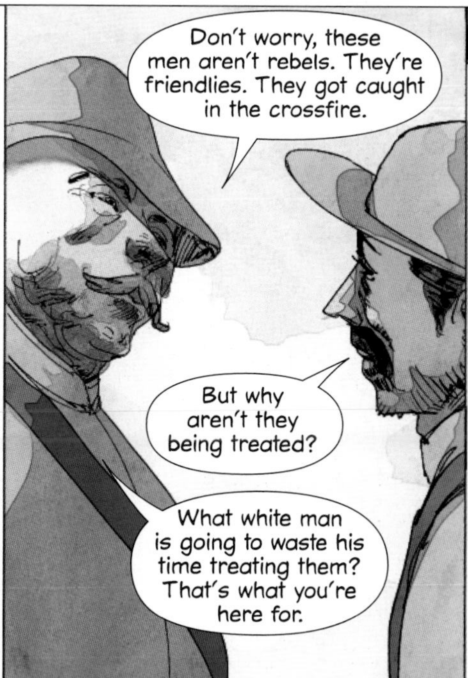
Don't worry, these men aren't rebels. They're friendlies. They got caught in the crossfire.
But why aren't they being treated?
What white man is going to waste his time treating them? That's what you're here for.

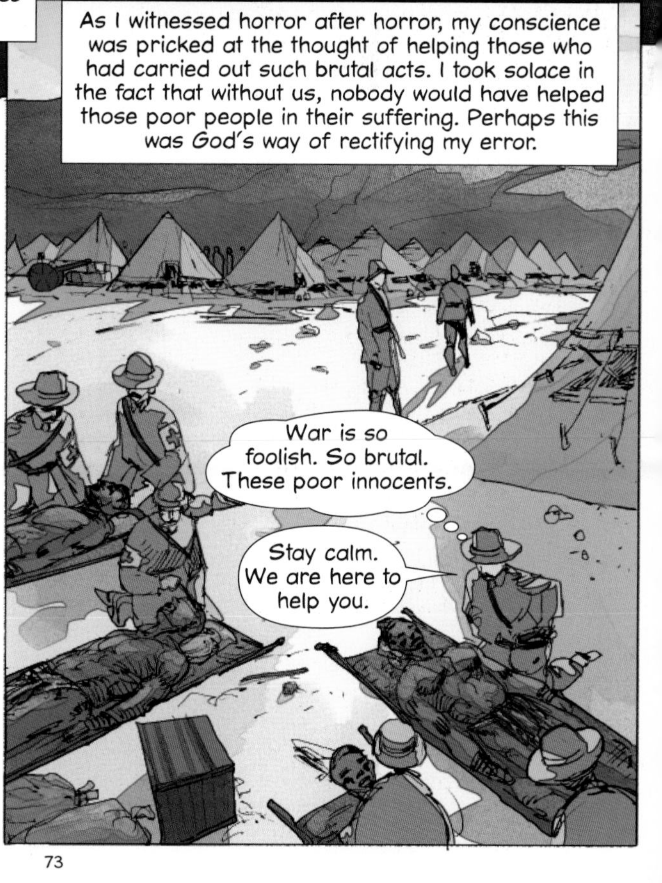
As I witnessed horror after horror, my conscience was pricked at the thought of helping those who had carried out such brutal acts. I took solace in the fact that without us, nobody would have helped those poor people in their suffering. Perhaps this was God's way of rectifying my error.
War is so foolish. So brutal. These poor innocents.
Stay calm. We are here to help you.

Not long after my return to Johannesburg, I learnt of a new government bill, one that came to be known as the Black Act. This act required all Asians over the age of eight to be fingerprinted and registered with the authorities.

I called for a mass meeting at the Empire Theatre in Johannesburg to discuss what options were open to us...

Fingerprinting is for catching criminals. Are the authorities saying we are criminals?

I am calling for full scale passive resistance to this act.

We need to unite and resist registration.

We should be prepared to face imprisonment rather than comply with this attack on our honor and dignity.

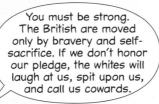

You must be strong. The British are moved only by bravery and self-sacrifice. If we don't honor our pledge, the whites will laugh at us, spit upon us, and call us cowards.

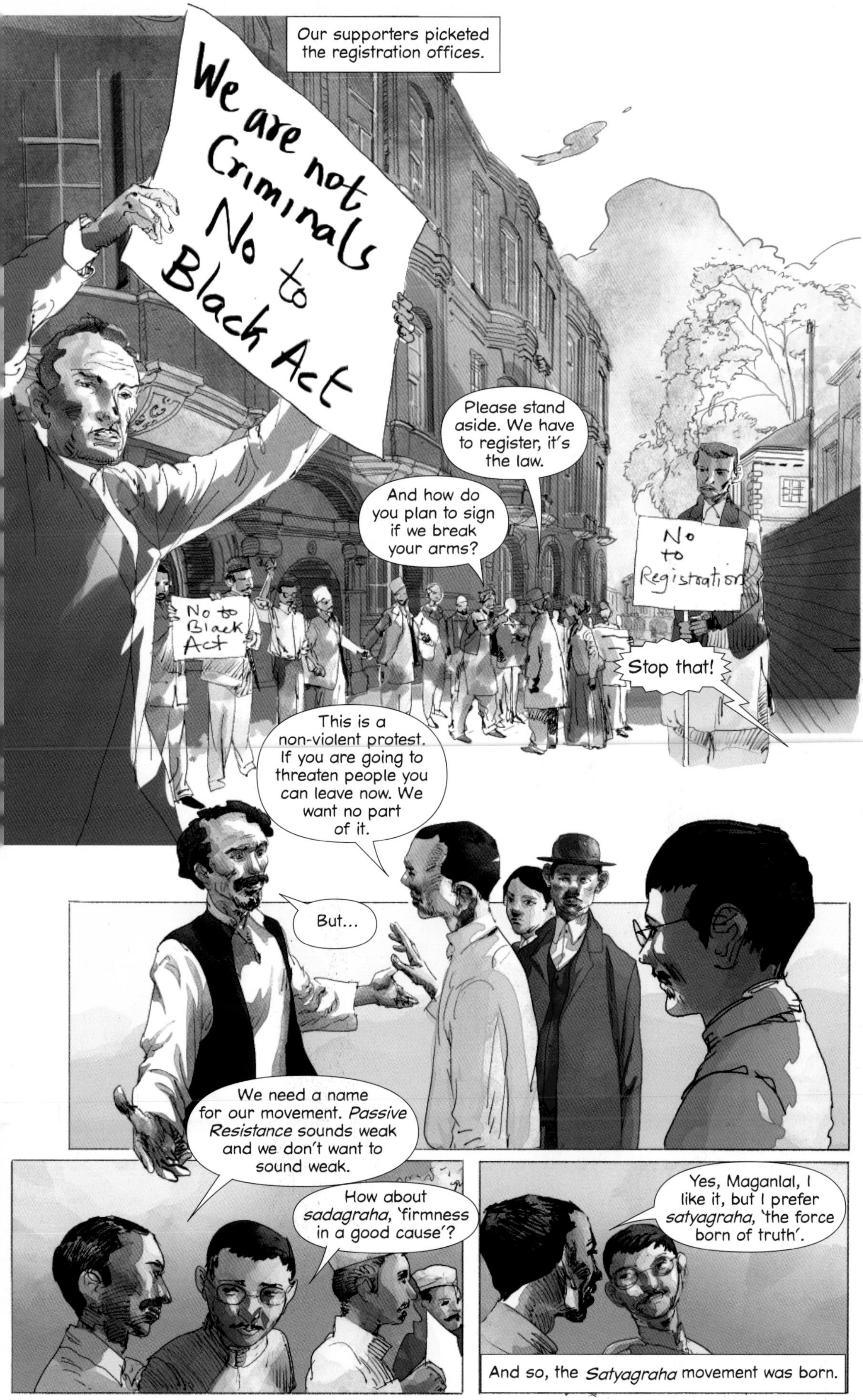
Our supporters picketed the registration offices.
We are not Criminals No to Black Act
Please stand aside. We have to register, it's the law.
And how do you plan to sign if we break your arms?
No to Black Act
No to Registration
Stop that!
This is a non-violent protest. If you are going to threaten people you can leave now. We want no part of it.
But...
We need a name for our movement. *Passive Resistance* sounds weak and we don't want to sound weak.
How about *sadagraha*, 'firmness in a good cause'?
Yes, Maganlal, I like it, but I prefer *satyagraha*, 'the force born of truth'.
And so, the *Satyagraha* movement was born.

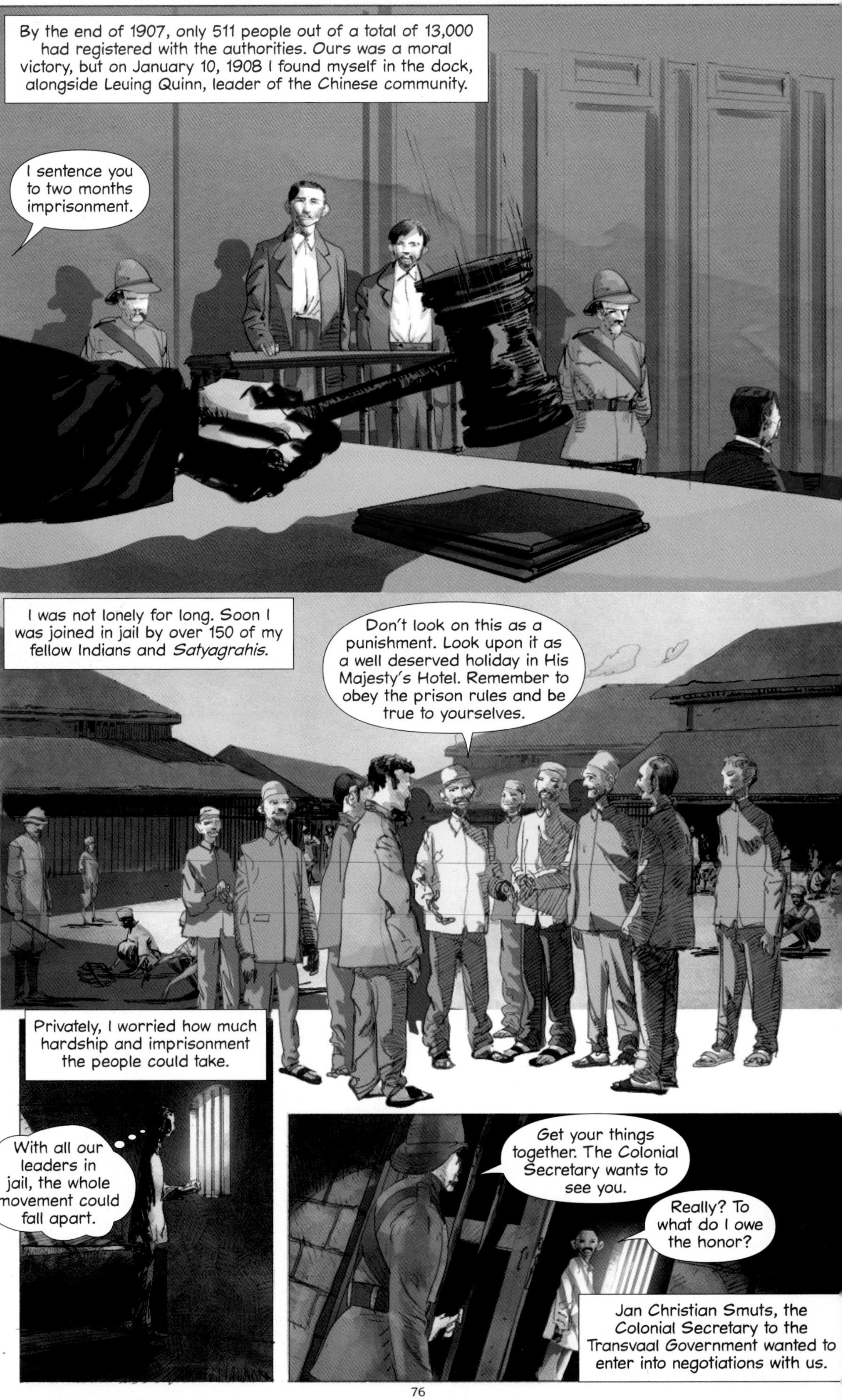
By the end of 1907, only 511 people out of a total of 13,000 had registered with the authorities. Ours was a moral victory, but on January 10, 1908 I found myself in the dock, alongside Leuing Quinn, leader of the Chinese community.
I sentence you to two months imprisonment.
I was not lonely for long. Soon I was joined in jail by over 150 of my fellow Indians and *Satyagrahis*.
Don't look on this as a punishment. Look upon it as a well deserved holiday in His Majesty's Hotel. Remember to obey the prison rules and be true to yourselves.
Privately, I worried how much hardship and imprisonment the people could take.
With all our leaders in jail, the whole movement could fall apart.
Get your things together. The Colonial Secretary wants to see you.
Really? To what do I owe the honor?
Jan Christian Smuts, the Colonial Secretary to the Transvaal Government wanted to enter into negotiations with us.

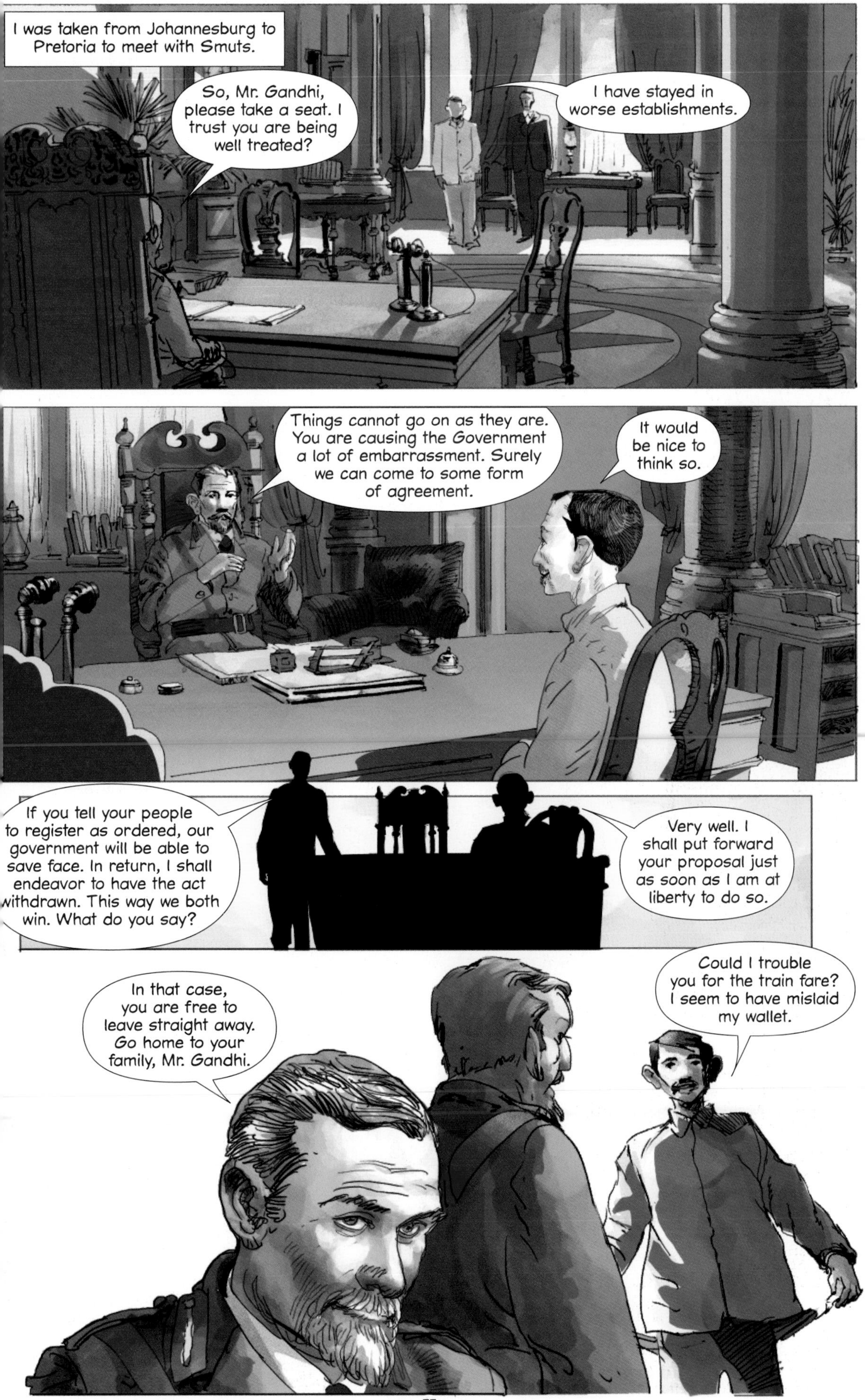
I was taken from Johannesburg to Pretoria to meet with Smuts.
So, Mr. Gandhi, please take a seat. I trust you are being well treated?
I have stayed in worse establishments.
Things cannot go on as they are. You are causing the Government a lot of embarrassment. Surely we can come to some form of agreement.
It would be nice to think so.
If you tell your people to register as ordered, our government will be able to save face. In return, I shall endeavor to have the act withdrawn. This way we both win. What do you say?
Very well. I shall put forward your proposal just as soon as I am at liberty to do so.
In that case, you are free to leave straight away. Go home to your family, Mr. Gandhi.
Could I trouble you for the train fare? I seem to have mislaid my wallet.

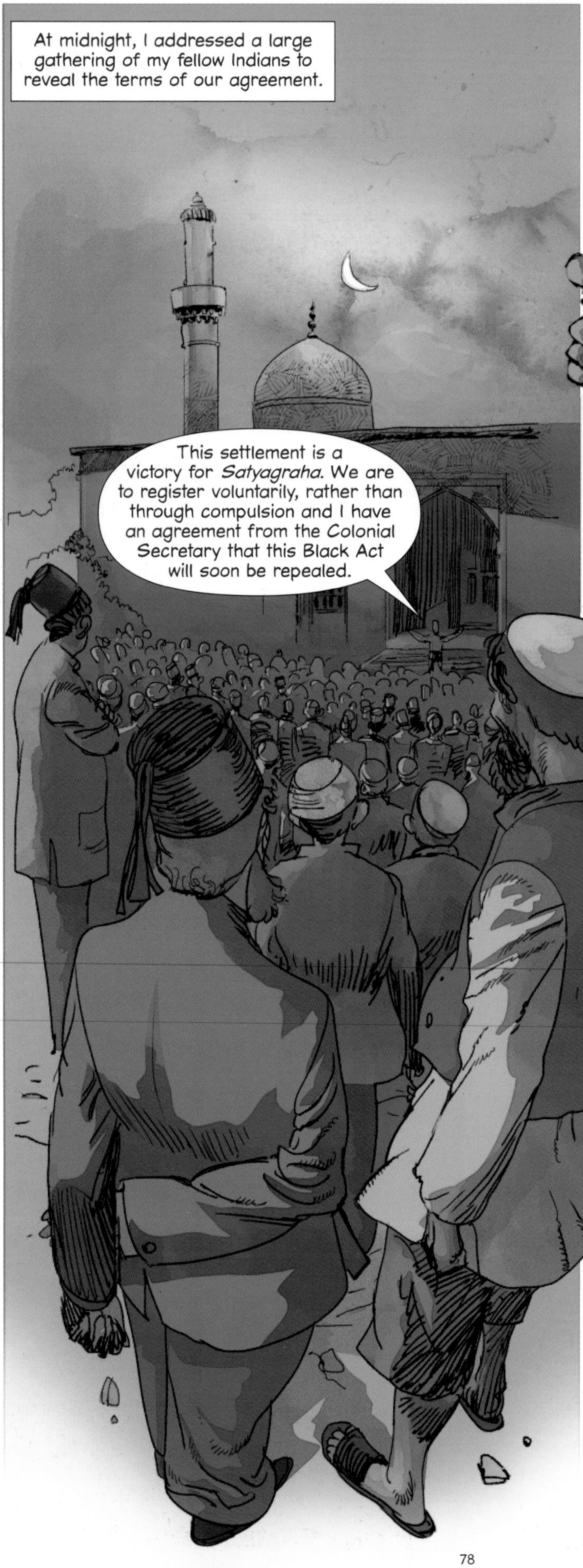
At midnight, I addressed a large gathering of my fellow Indians to reveal the terms of our agreement.
This settlement is a victory for *Satyagraha.* We are to register voluntarily, rather than through compulsion and I have an agreement from the Colonial Secretary that this Black Act will soon be repealed.

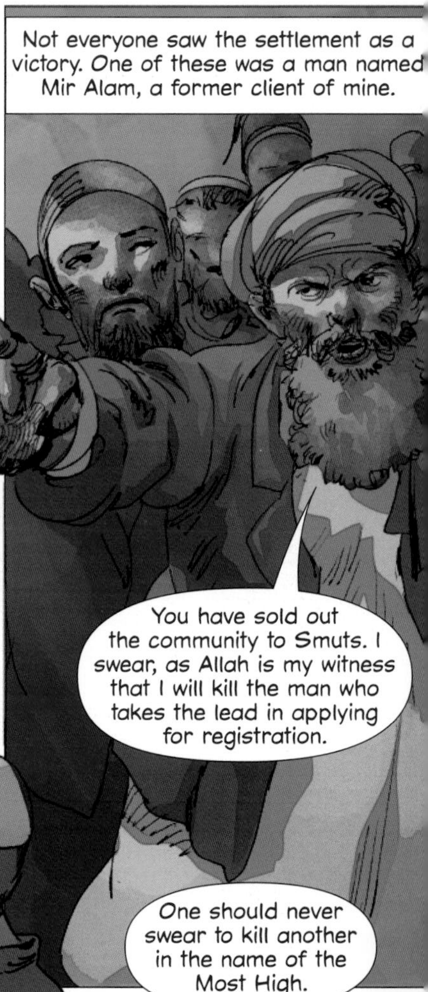
Not everyone saw the settlement as a victory. One of these was a man named Mir Alam, a former client of mine.
You have sold out the community to Smuts. I swear, as Allah is my witness that I will kill the man who takes the lead in applying for registration.

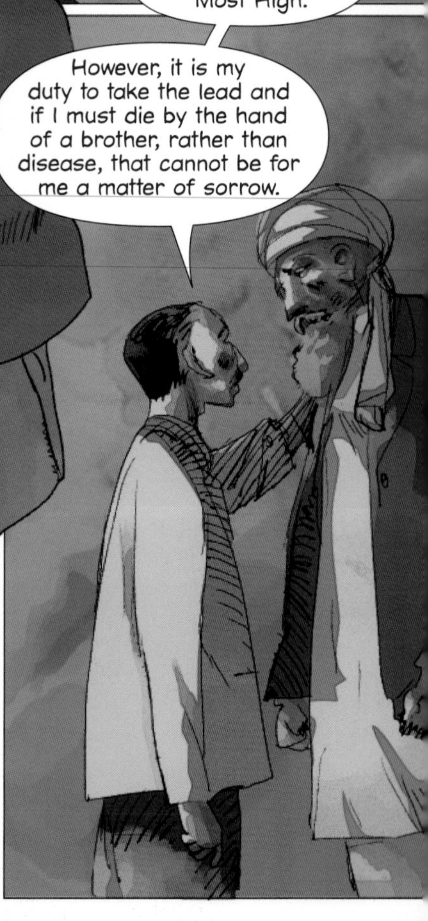
One should never swear to kill another in the name of the Most High.
However, it is my duty to take the lead and if I must die by the hand of a brother, rather than disease, that cannot be for me a matter of sorrow.

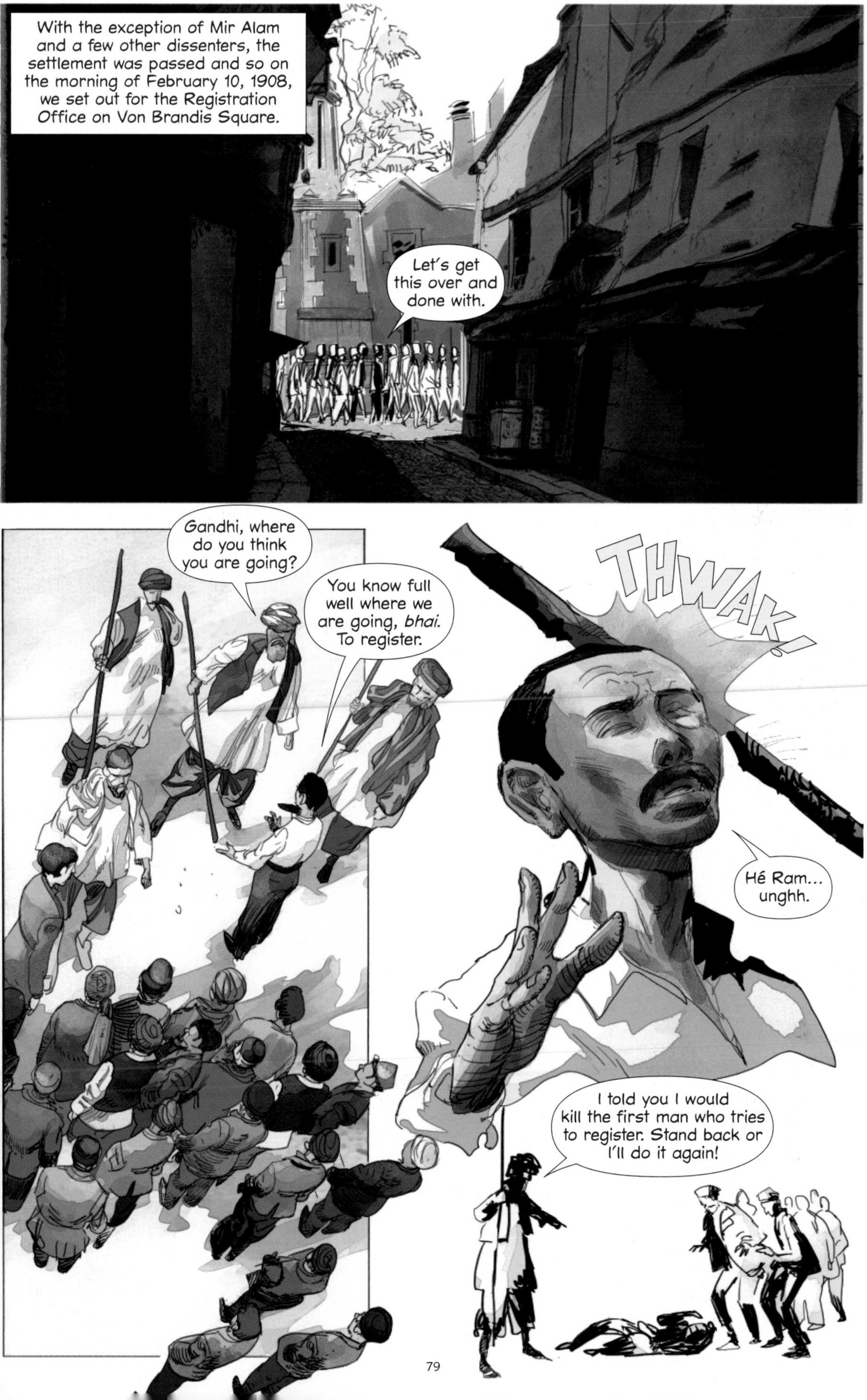

With the exception of Mir Alam and a few other dissenters, the settlement was passed and so on the morning of February 10, 1908, we set out for the Registration Office on Von Brandis Square.
Let's get this over and done with.
Gandhi, where do you think you are going?
You know full well where we are going, *bhai*. To register.
THWAK!
Hé Ram... unghh.
I told you I would kill the first man who tries to register. Stand back or I'll do it again!

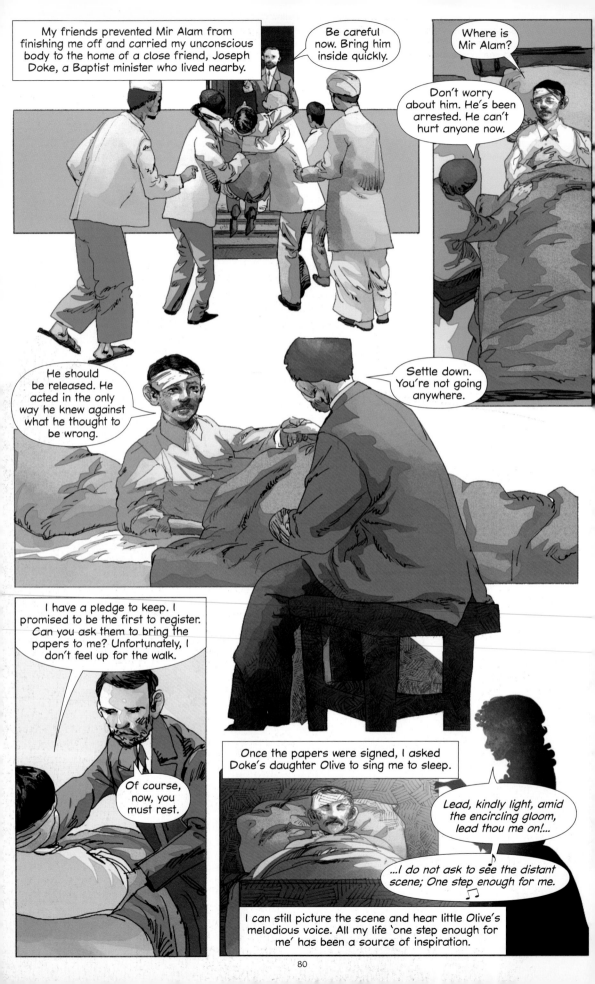

My friends prevented Mir Alam from finishing me off and carried my unconscious body to the home of a close friend, Joseph Doke, a Baptist minister who lived nearby.

Be careful now. Bring him inside quickly.

Where is Mir Alam?

Don't worry about him. He's been arrested. He can't hurt anyone now.

He should be released. He acted in the only way he knew against what he thought to be wrong.

Settle down. You're not going anywhere.

I have a pledge to keep. I promised to be the first to register. Can you ask them to bring the papers to me? Unfortunately, I don't feel up for the walk.

Of course, now, you must rest.

Once the papers were signed, I asked Doke's daughter Olive to sing me to sleep.

Lead, kindly light, amid the encircling gloom, lead thou me on!...

...I do not ask to see the distant scene; One step enough for me.

I can still picture the scene and hear little Olive's melodious voice. All my life 'one step enough for me' has been a source of inspiration.

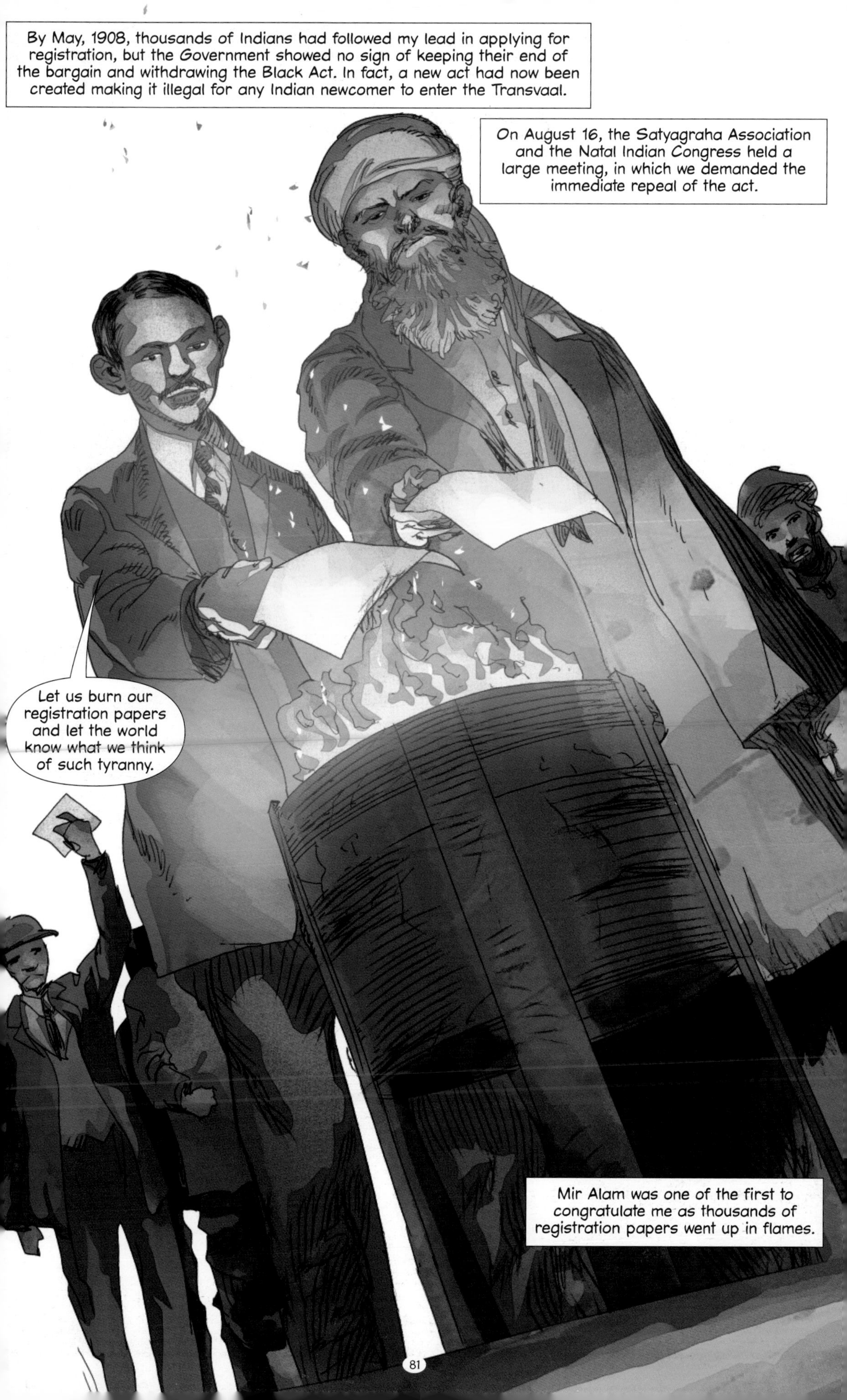
By May, 1908, thousands of Indians had followed my lead in applying for registration, but the Government showed no sign of keeping their end of the bargain and withdrawing the Black Act. In fact, a new act had now been created making it illegal for any Indian newcomer to enter the Transvaal.
On August 16, the Satyagraha Association and the Natal Indian Congress held a large meeting, in which we demanded the immediate repeal of the act.
Let us burn our registration papers and let the world know what we think of such tyranny.
Mir Alam was one of the first to congratulate me as thousands of registration papers went up in flames.

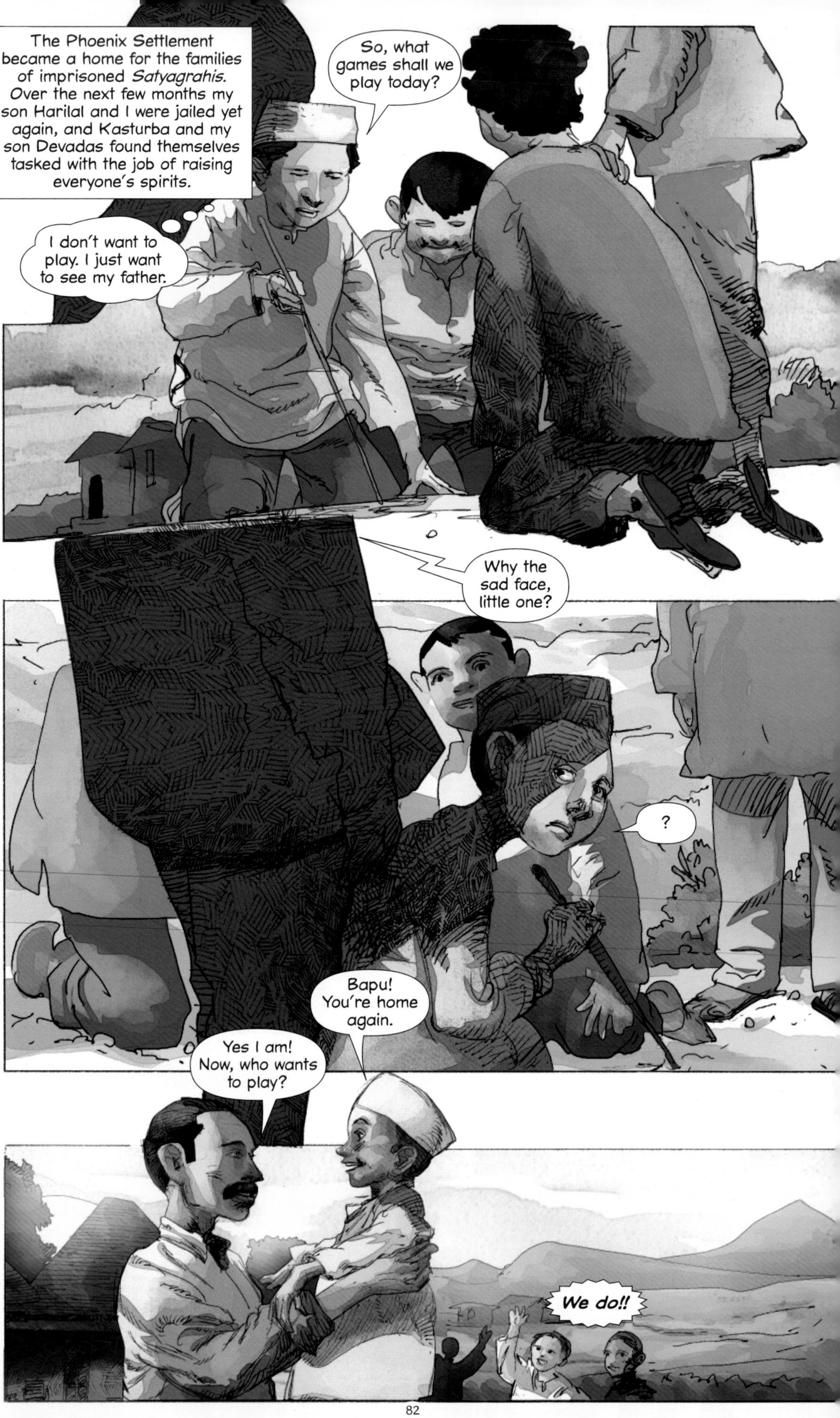

The Phoenix Settlement became a home for the families of imprisoned *Satyagrahis.* Over the next few months my son Harilal and I were jailed yet again, and Kasturba and my son Devadas found themselves tasked with the job of raising everyone's spirits.
So, what games shall we play today?
I don't want to play. I just want to see my father.
Why the sad face, little one?
?
Bapu! You're home again.
Yes I am! Now, who wants to play?
We do!!

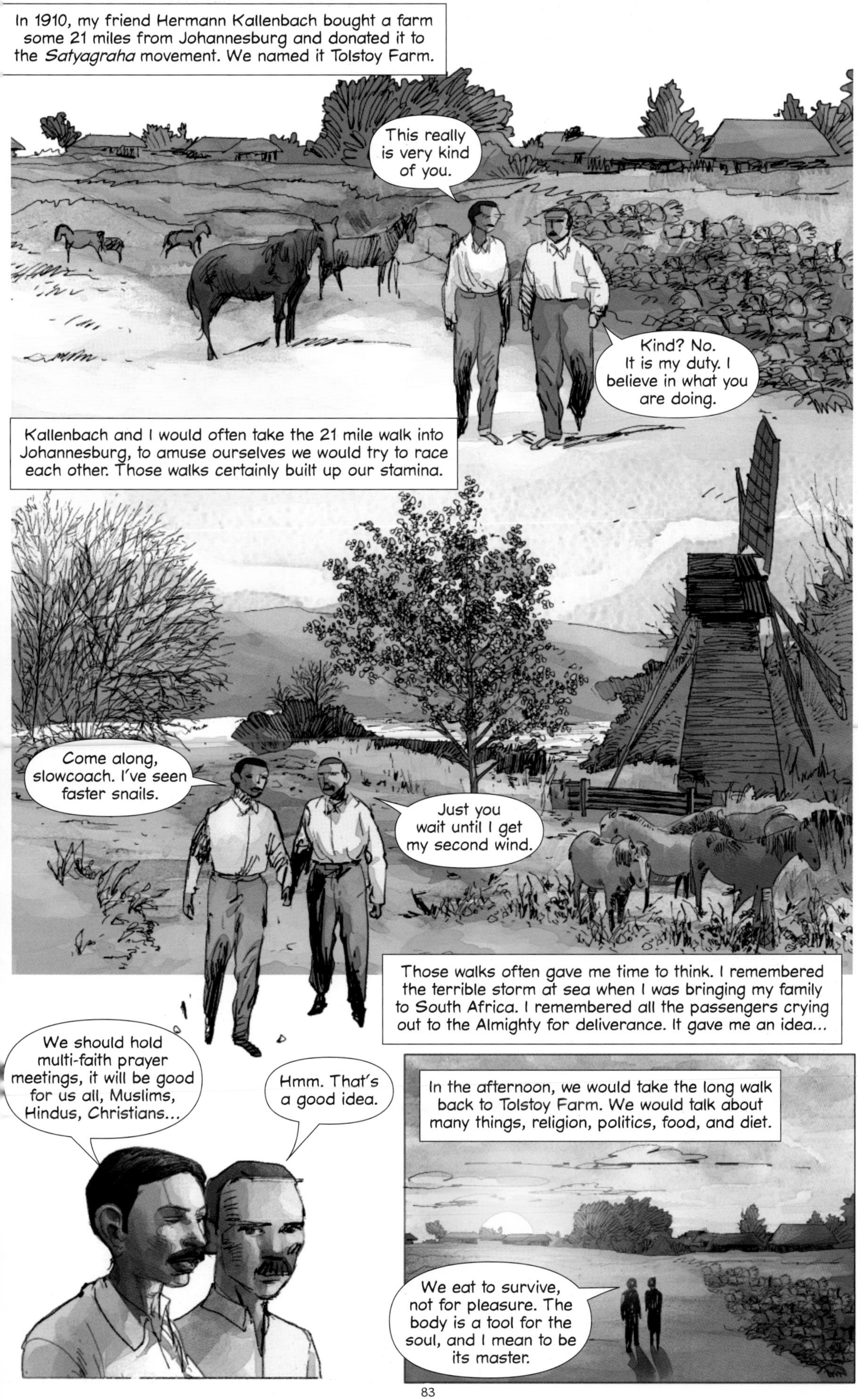
In 1910, my friend Hermann Kallenbach bought a farm some 21 miles from Johannesburg and donated it to the *Satyagraha* movement. We named it Tolstoy Farm.
This really is very kind of you.
Kind? No. It is my duty. I believe in what you are doing.
Kallenbach and I would often take the 21 mile walk into Johannesburg, to amuse ourselves we would try to race each other. Those walks certainly built up our stamina.
Come along, slowcoach. I've seen faster snails.
Just you wait until I get my second wind.
Those walks often gave me time to think. I remembered the terrible storm at sea when I was bringing my family to South Africa. I remembered all the passengers crying out to the Almighty for deliverance. It gave me an idea...
We should hold multi-faith prayer meetings, it will be good for us all, Muslims, Hindus, Christians...
Hmm. That's a good idea.
In the afternoon, we would take the long walk back to Tolstoy Farm. We would talk about many things, religion, politics, food, and diet.
We eat to survive, not for pleasure. The body is a tool for the soul, and I mean to be its master.

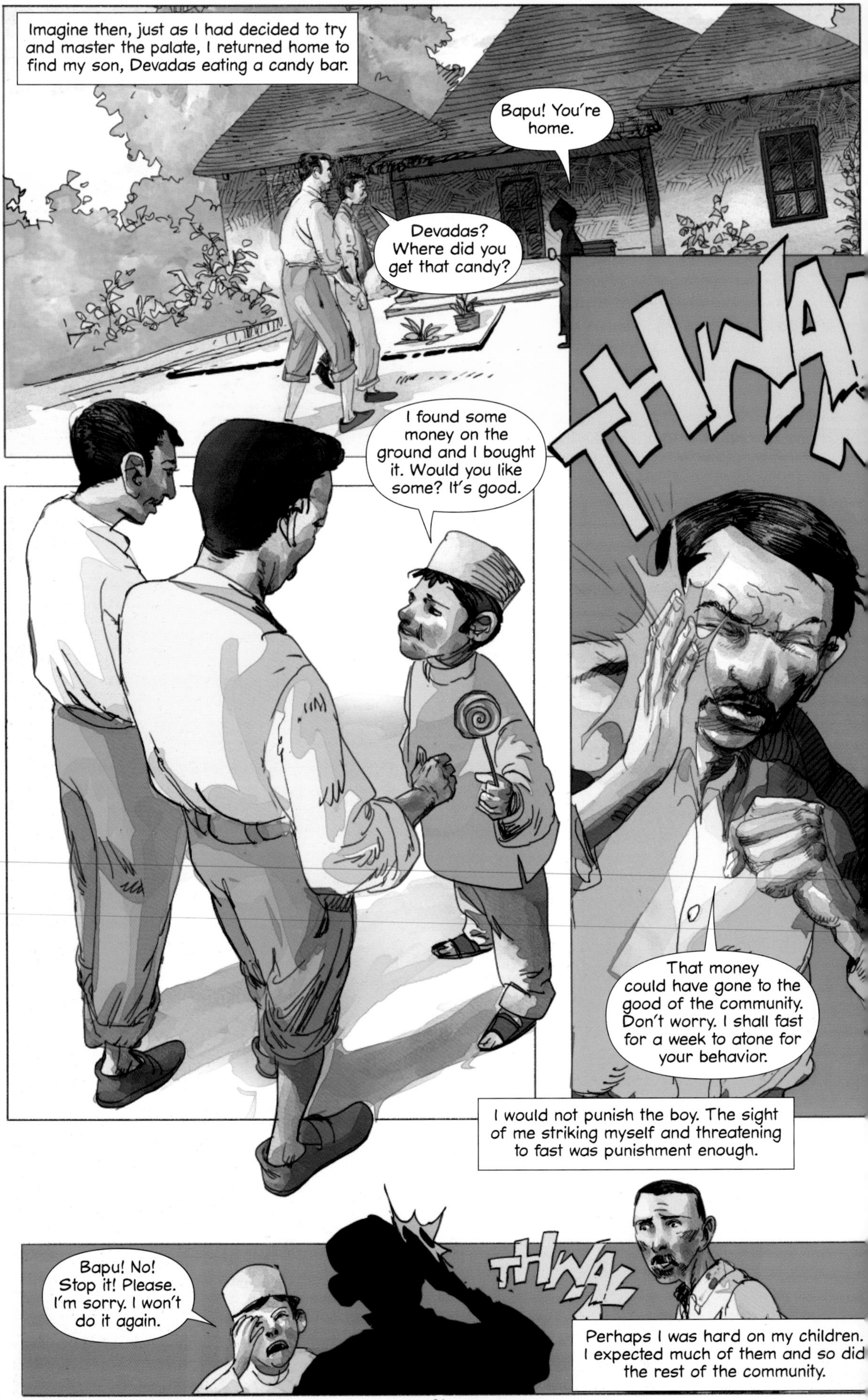
Imagine then, just as I had decided to try and master the palate, I returned home to find my son, Devadas eating a candy bar.
Bapu! You're home.
Devadas? Where did you get that candy?
I found some money on the ground and I bought it. Would you like some? It's good.
THWAK
That money could have gone to the good of the community. Don't worry. I shall fast for a week to atone for your behavior.
I would not punish the boy. The sight of me striking myself and threatening to fast was punishment enough.
Bapu! No! Stop it! Please. I'm sorry. I won't do it again.
THWAK
Perhaps I was hard on my children. I expected much of them and so did the rest of the community.

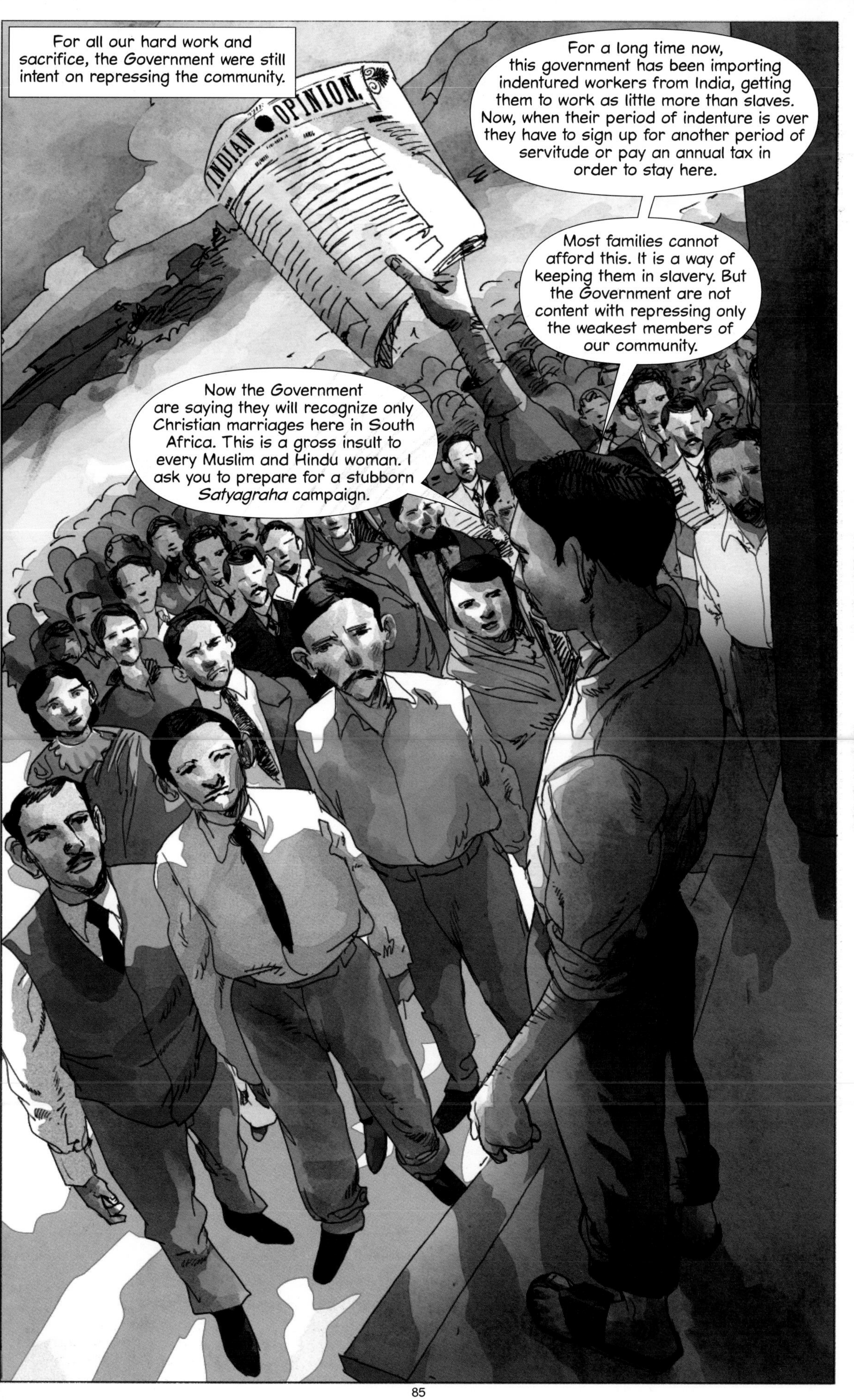
For all our hard work and sacrifice, the Government were still intent on repressing the community.
INDIAN OPINION.
For a long time now, this government has been importing indentured workers from India, getting them to work as little more than slaves. Now, when their period of indenture is over they have to sign up for another period of servitude or pay an annual tax in order to stay here.
Most families cannot afford this. It is a way of keeping them in slavery. But the Government are not content with repressing only the weakest members of our community.
Now the Government are saying they will recognize only Christian marriages here in South Africa. This is a gross insult to every Muslim and Hindu woman. I ask you to prepare for a stubborn *Satyagraha* campaign.

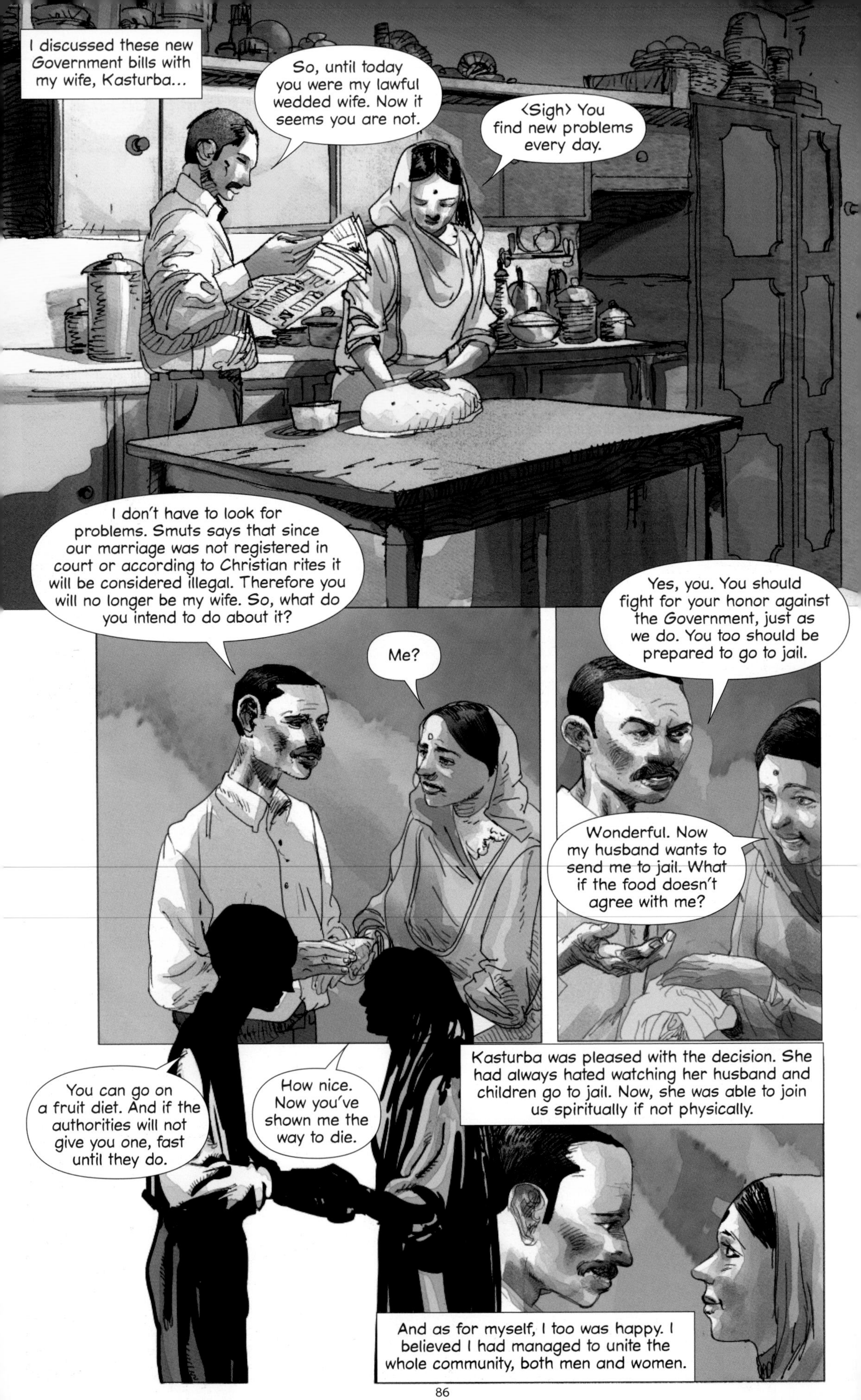
I discussed these new Government bills with my wife, Kasturba...
So, until today you were my lawful wedded wife. Now it seems you are not.
<Sigh> You find new problems every day.
I don't have to look for problems. Smuts says that since our marriage was not registered in court or according to Christian rites it will be considered illegal. Therefore you will no longer be my wife. So, what do you intend to do about it?
Me?
Yes, you. You should fight for your honor against the Government, just as we do. You too should be prepared to go to jail.
Wonderful. Now my husband wants to send me to jail. What if the food doesn't agree with me?
You can go on a fruit diet. And if the authorities will not give you one, fast until they do.
How nice. Now you've shown me the way to die.
Kasturba was pleased with the decision. She had always hated watching her husband and children go to jail. Now, she was able to join us spiritually if not physically.
And as for myself, I too was happy. I believed I had managed to unite the whole community, both men and women.

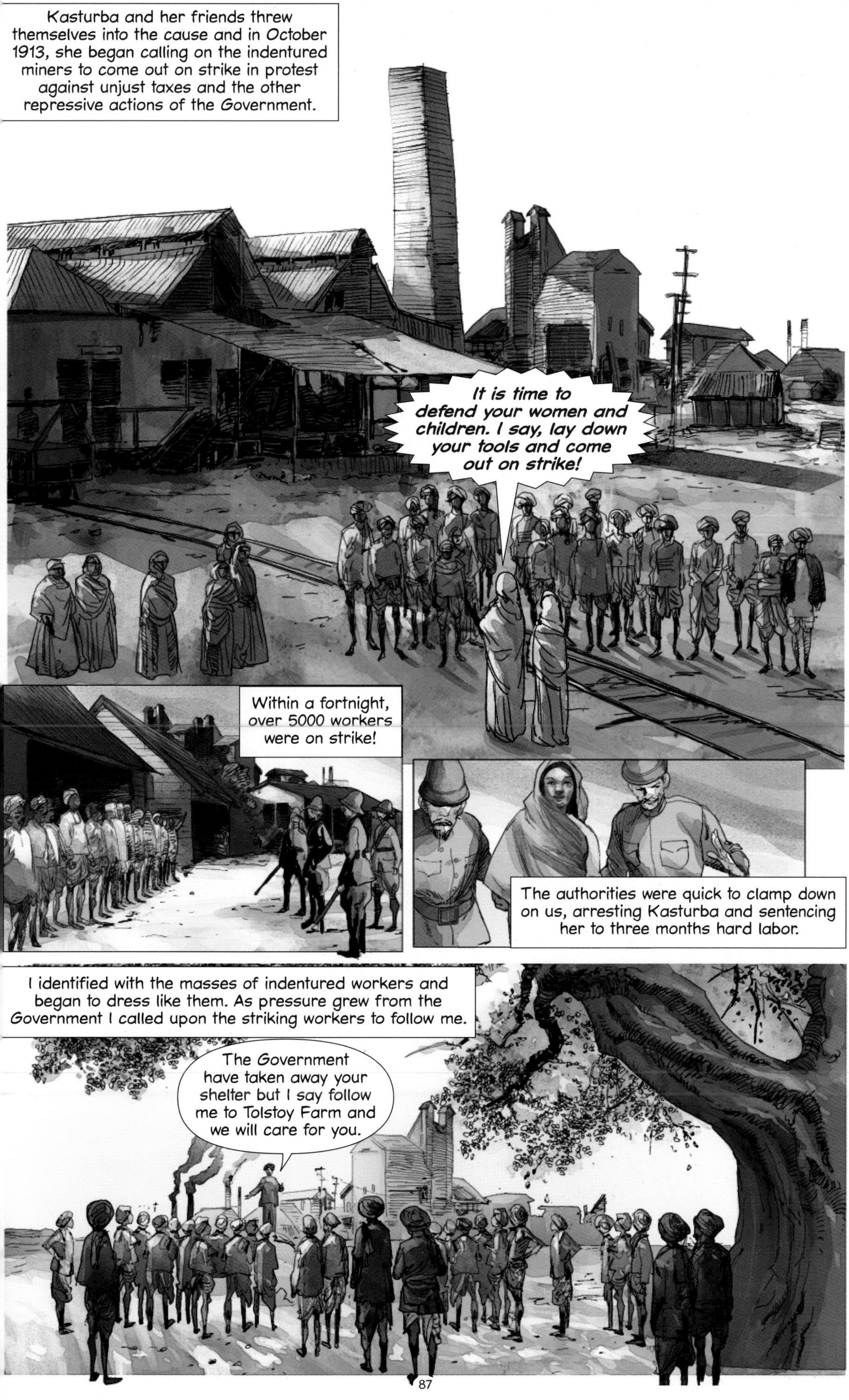
Kasturba and her friends threw themselves into the cause and in October 1913, she began calling on the indentured miners to come out on strike in protest against unjust taxes and the other repressive actions of the Government.
It is time to defend your women and children. I say, lay down your tools and come out on strike!
Within a fortnight, over 5000 workers were on strike!
The authorities were quick to clamp down on us, arresting Kasturba and sentencing her to three months hard labor.
I identified with the masses of indentured workers and began to dress like them. As pressure grew from the Government I called upon the striking workers to follow me.
The Government have taken away your shelter but I say follow me to Tolstoy Farm and we will care for you.

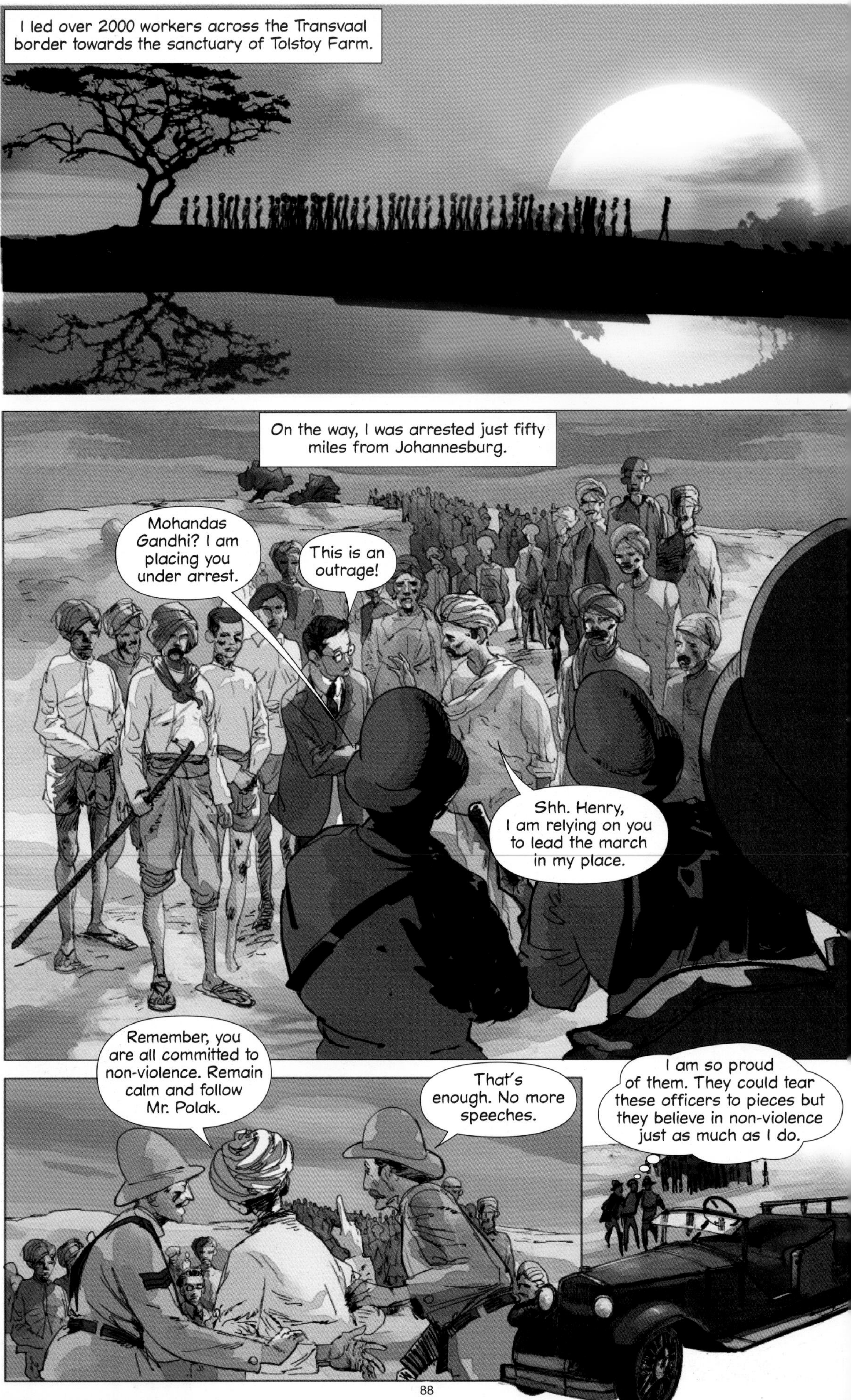
I led over 2000 workers across the Transvaal border towards the sanctuary of Tolstoy Farm.
On the way, I was arrested just fifty miles from Johannesburg.
Mohandas Gandhi? I am placing you under arrest.
This is an outrage!
Shh. Henry, I am relying on you to lead the march in my place.
Remember, you are all committed to non-violence. Remain calm and follow Mr. Polak.
That's enough. No more speeches.
I am so proud of them. They could tear these officers to pieces but they believe in non-violence just as much as I do.

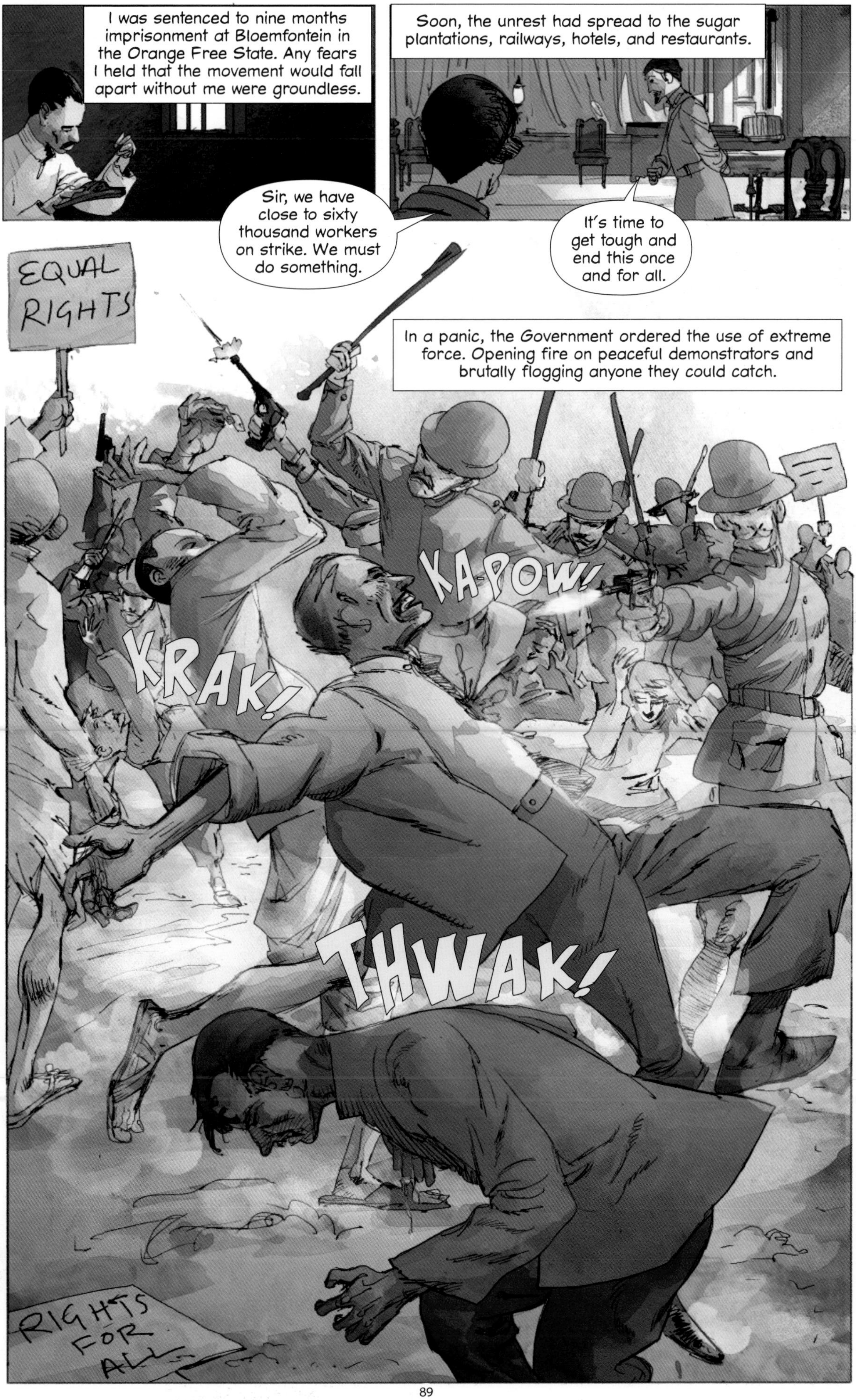
I was sentenced to nine months imprisonment at Bloemfontein in the Orange Free State. Any fears I held that the movement would fall apart without me were groundless.
Soon, the unrest had spread to the sugar plantations, railways, hotels, and restaurants.
Sir, we have close to sixty thousand workers on strike. We must do something.
It's time to get tough and end this once and for all.
EQUAL RIGHTS
In a panic, the Government ordered the use of extreme force. Opening fire on peaceful demonstrators and brutally flogging anyone they could catch.
KA-POW!
KRAK!
THWAK!
RIGHTS FOR ALL

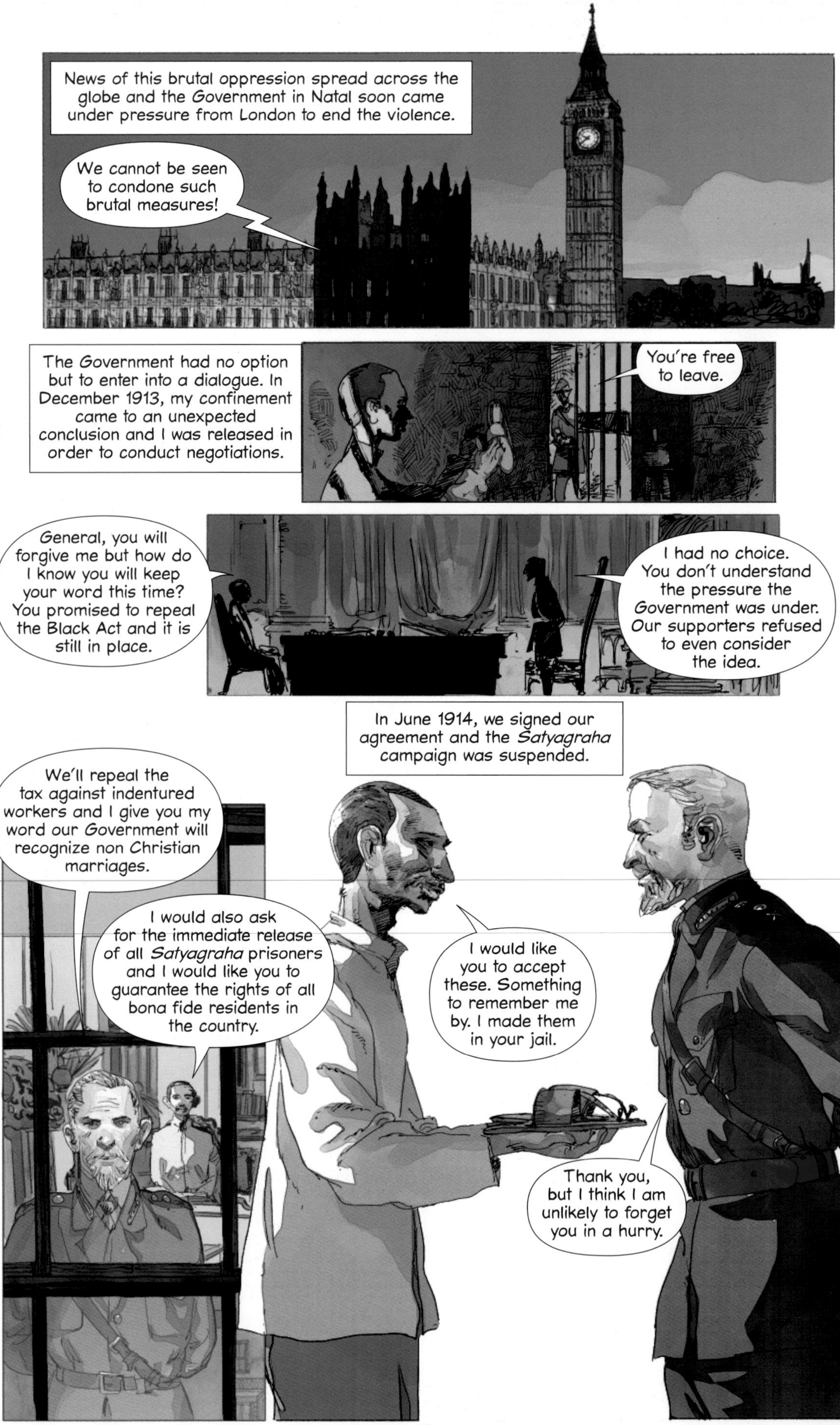
News of this brutal oppression spread across the globe and the Government in Natal soon came under pressure from London to end the violence.
We cannot be seen to condone such brutal measures!
The Government had no option but to enter into a dialogue. In December 1913, my confinement came to an unexpected conclusion and I was released in order to conduct negotiations.
You're free to leave.
General, you will forgive me but how do I know you will keep your word this time? You promised to repeal the Black Act and it is still in place.
I had no choice. You don't understand the pressure the Government was under. Our supporters refused to even consider the idea.
In June 1914, we signed our agreement and the *Satyagraha* campaign was suspended.
We'll repeal the tax against indentured workers and I give you my word our Government will recognize non Christian marriages.
I would also ask for the immediate release of all *Satyagraha* prisoners and I would like you to guarantee the rights of all bona fide residents in the country.
I would like you to accept these. Something to remember me by. I made them in your jail.
Thank you, but I think I am unlikely to forget you in a hurry.

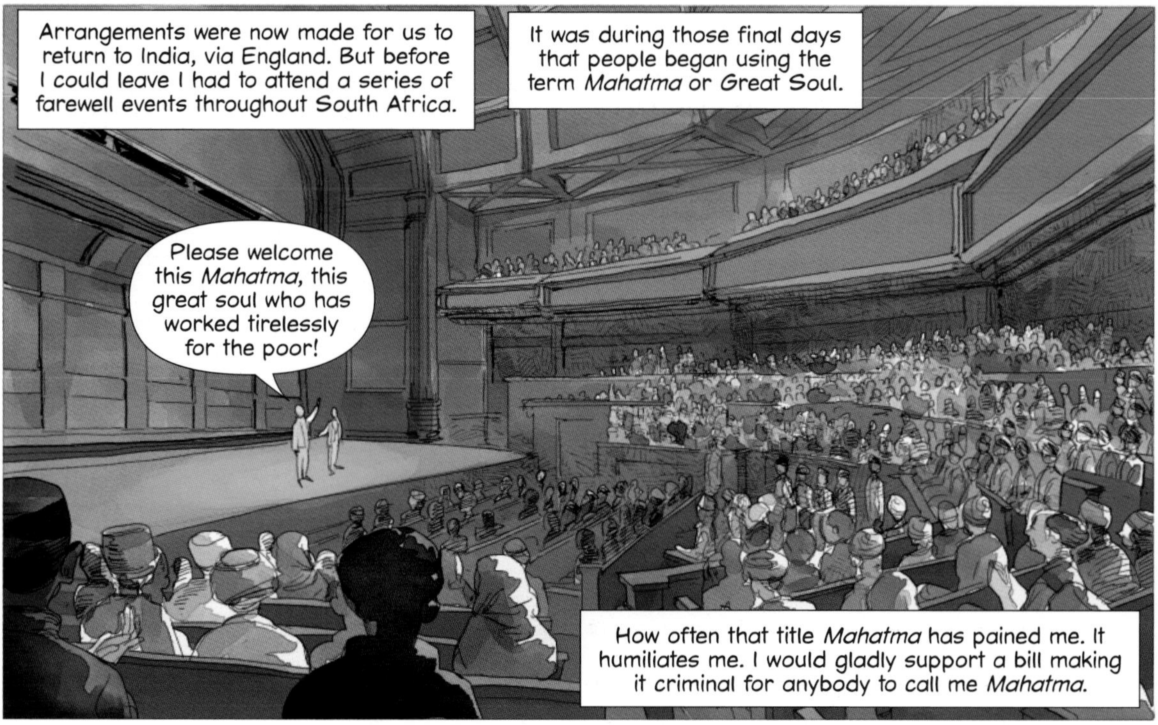
Arrangements were now made for us to return to India, via England. But before I could leave I had to attend a series of farewell events throughout South Africa.
It was during those final days that people began using the term *Mahatma* or Great Soul.
Please welcome this *Mahatma*, this great soul who has worked tirelessly for the poor!
How often that title *Mahatma* has pained me. It humiliates me. I would gladly support a bill making it criminal for anybody to call me *Mahatma*.

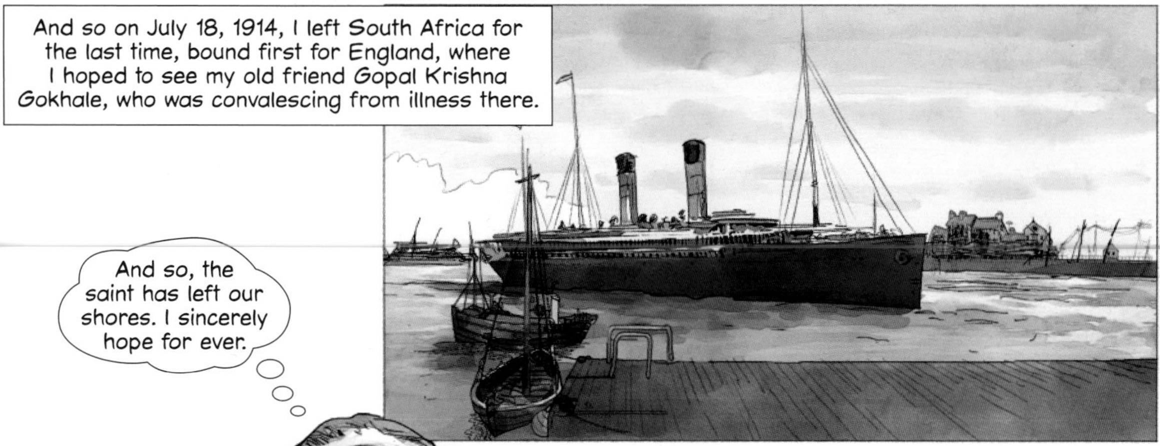
And so on July 18, 1914, I left South Africa for the last time, bound first for England, where I hoped to see my old friend Gopal Krishna Gokhale, who was convalescing from illness there.

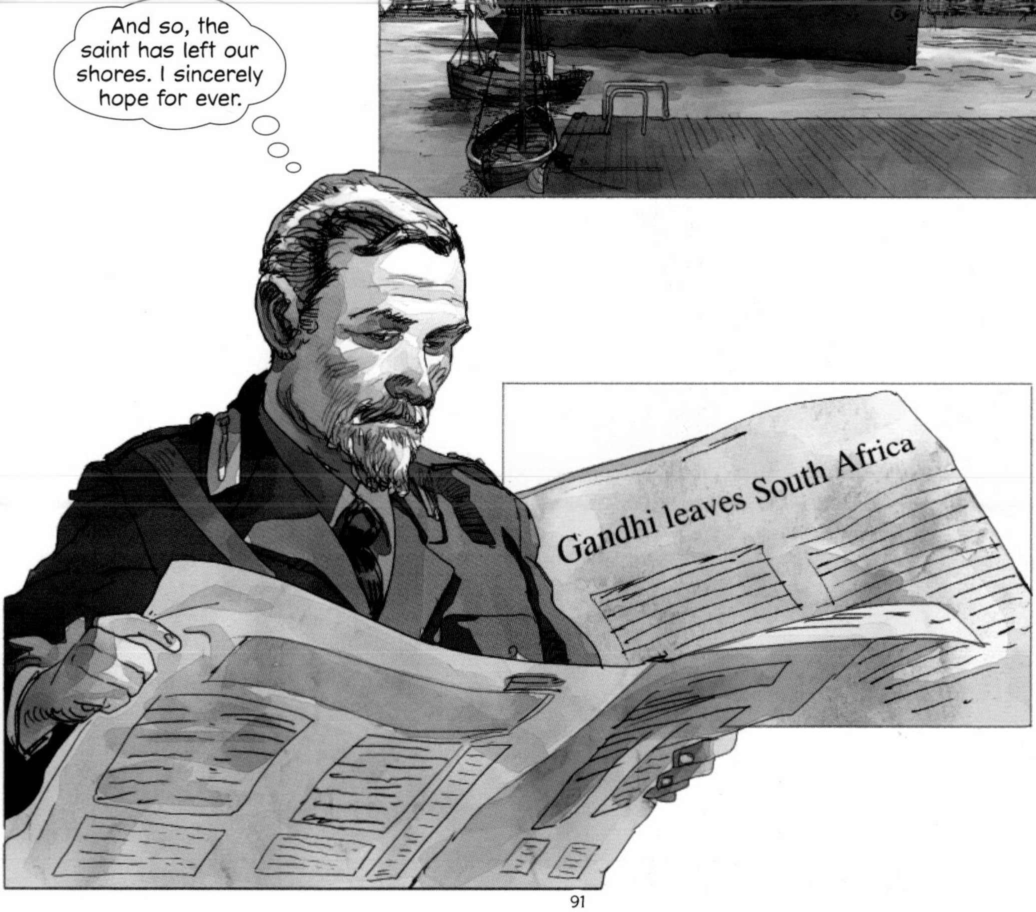
And so, the saint has left our shores. I sincerely hope for ever.
Gandhi leaves South Africa

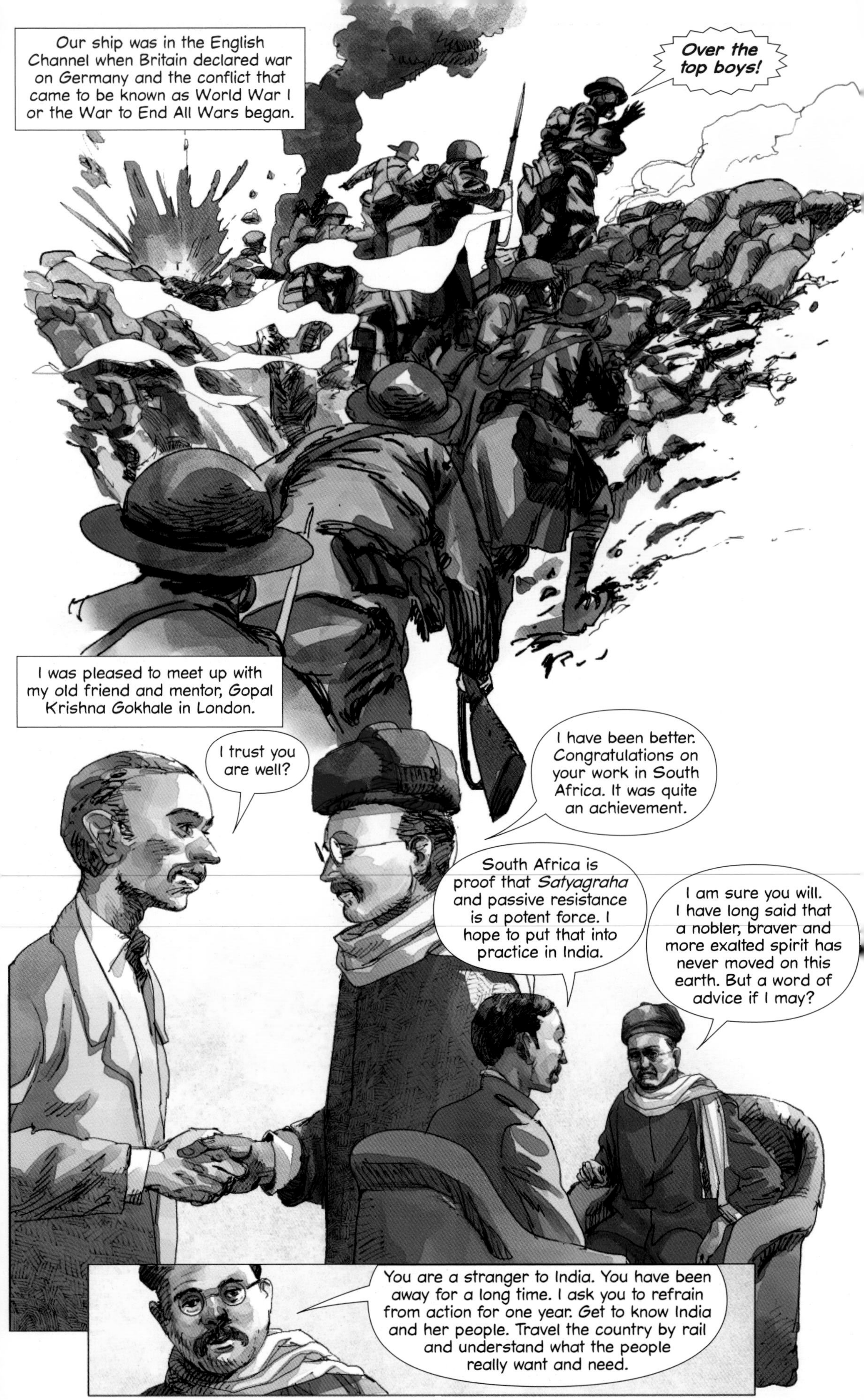
Our ship was in the English Channel when Britain declared war on Germany and the conflict that came to be known as World War I or the War to End All Wars began.
Over the top boys!
I was pleased to meet up with my old friend and mentor, Gopal Krishna Gokhale in London.
I trust you are well?
I have been better. Congratulations on your work in South Africa. It was quite an achievement.
South Africa is proof that *Satyagraha* and passive resistance is a potent force. I hope to put that into practice in India.
I am sure you will. I have long said that a nobler, braver and more exalted spirit has never moved on this earth. But a word of advice if I may?
You are a stranger to India. You have been away for a long time. I ask you to refrain from action for one year. Get to know India and her people. Travel the country by rail and understand what the people really want and need.

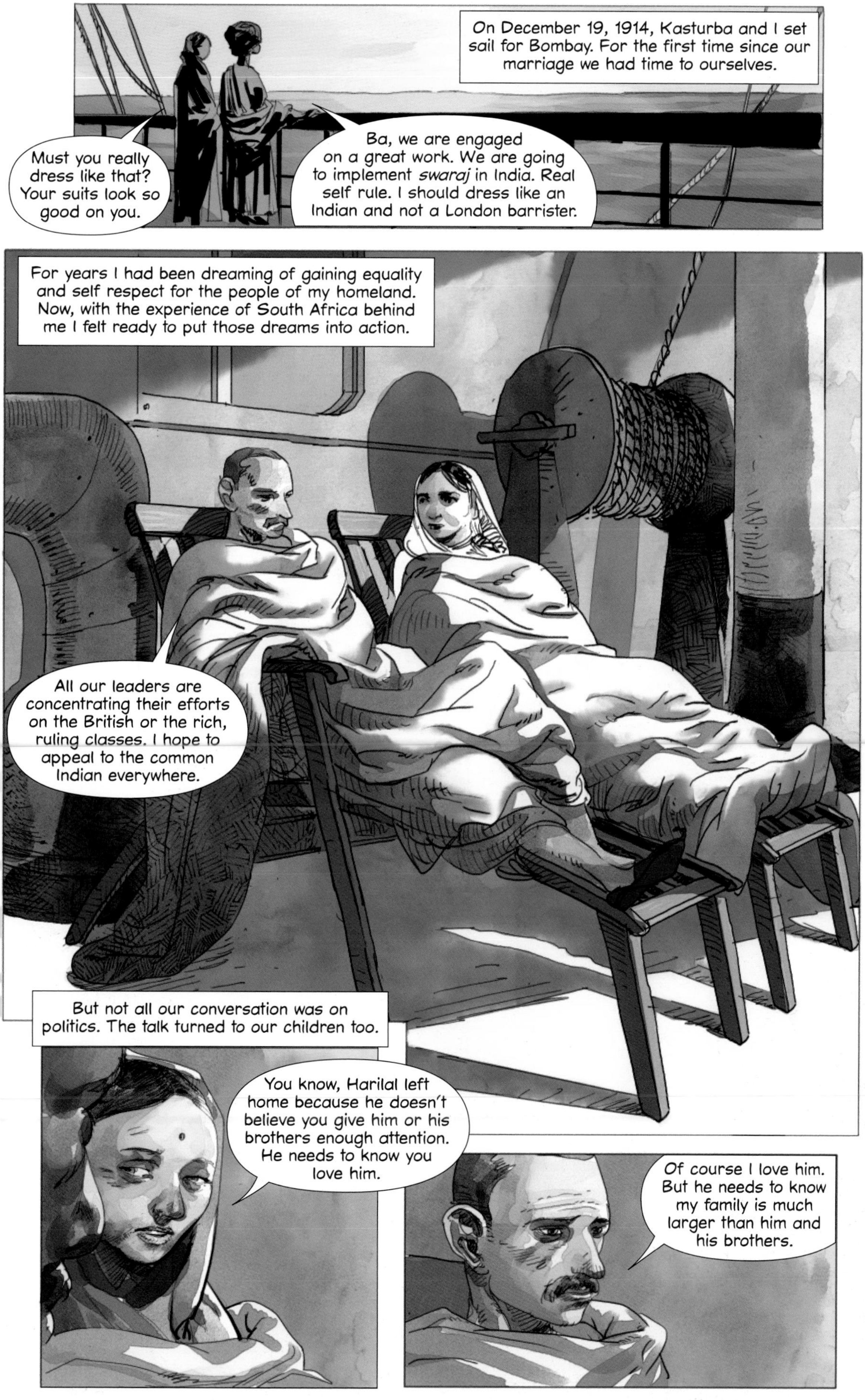
On December 19, 1914, Kasturba and I set sail for Bombay. For the first time since our marriage we had time to ourselves.
Must you really dress like that? Your suits look so good on you.
Ba, we are engaged on a great work. We are going to implement *swaraj* in India. Real self rule. I should dress like an Indian and not a London barrister.
For years I had been dreaming of gaining equality and self respect for the people of my homeland. Now, with the experience of South Africa behind me I felt ready to put those dreams into action.
All our leaders are concentrating their efforts on the British or the rich, ruling classes. I hope to appeal to the common Indian everywhere.
But not all our conversation was on politics. The talk turned to our children too.
You know, Harilal left home because he doesn't believe you give him or his brothers enough attention. He needs to know you love him.
Of course I love him. But he needs to know my family is much larger than him and his brothers.

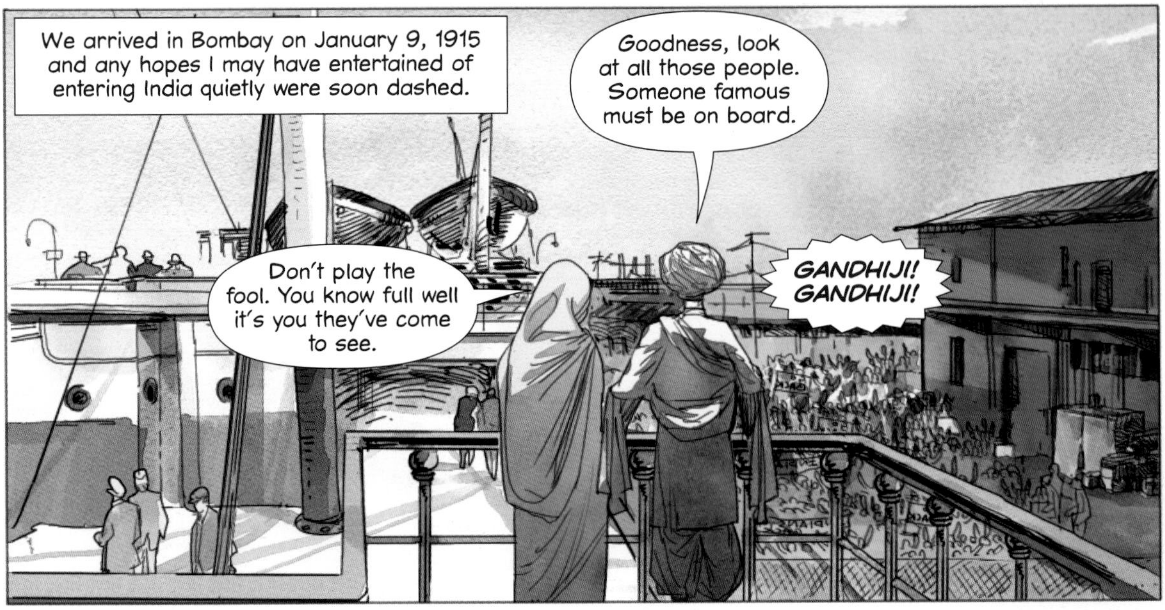
We arrived in Bombay on January 9, 1915 and any hopes I may have entertained of entering India quietly were soon dashed.
Goodness, look at all those people. Someone famous must be on board.
Don't play the fool. You know full well it's you they've come to see.
GANDHIJI! GANDHIJI!

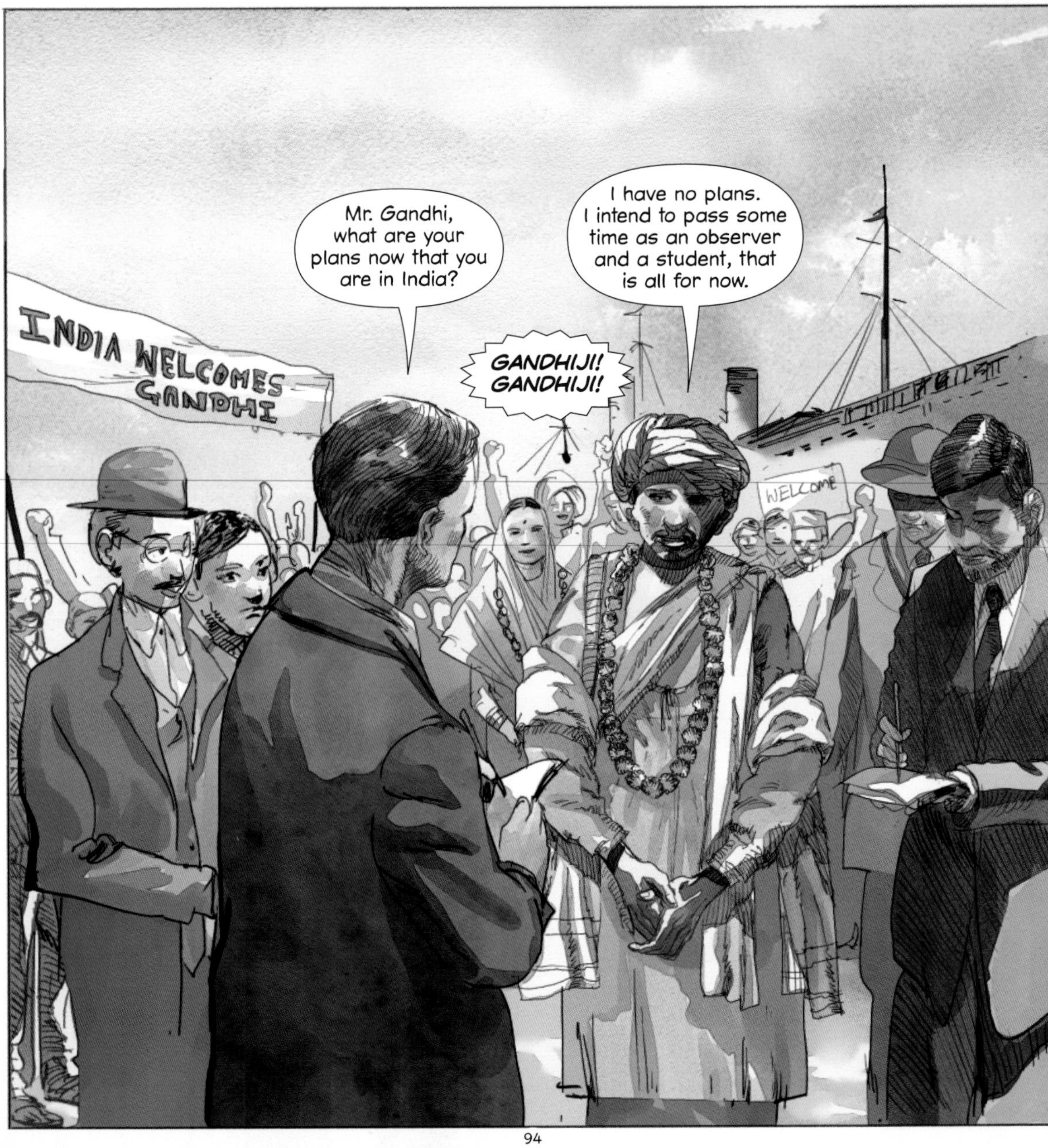
INDIA WELCOMES GANDHI
Mr. Gandhi, what are your plans now that you are in India?
GANDHIJI! GANDHIJI!
I have no plans. I intend to pass some time as an observer and a student, that is all for now.
WELCOME

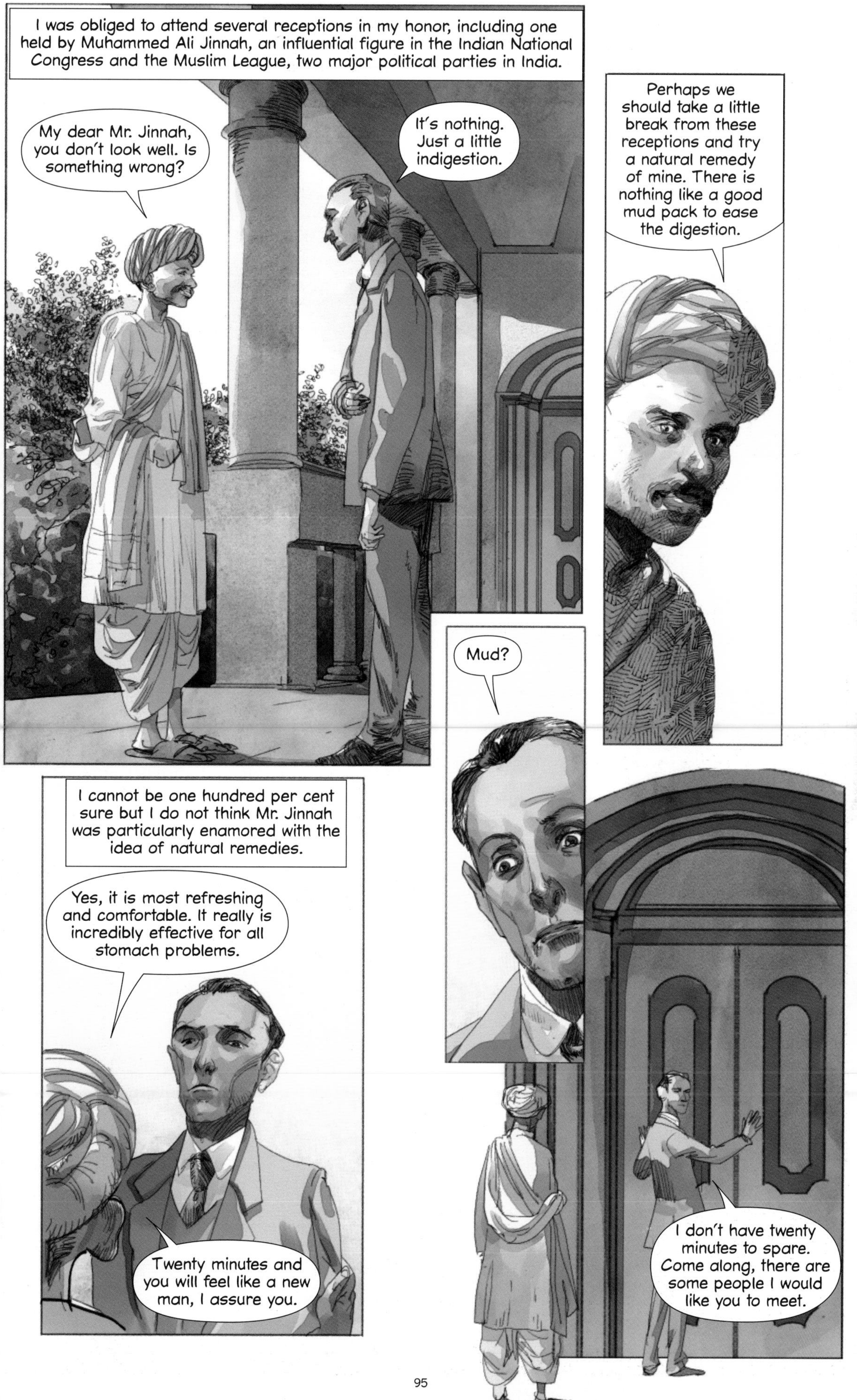

I was obliged to attend several receptions in my honor, including one held by Muhammed Ali Jinnah, an influential figure in the Indian National Congress and the Muslim League, two major political parties in India.
My dear Mr. Jinnah, you don't look well. Is something wrong?
It's nothing. Just a little indigestion.
Perhaps we should take a little break from these receptions and try a natural remedy of mine. There is nothing like a good mud pack to ease the digestion.
Mud?
I cannot be one hundred per cent sure but I do not think Mr. Jinnah was particularly enamored with the idea of natural remedies.
Yes, it is most refreshing and comfortable. It really is incredibly effective for all stomach problems.
Twenty minutes and you will feel like a new man, I assure you.
I don't have twenty minutes to spare. Come along, there are some people I would like you to meet.

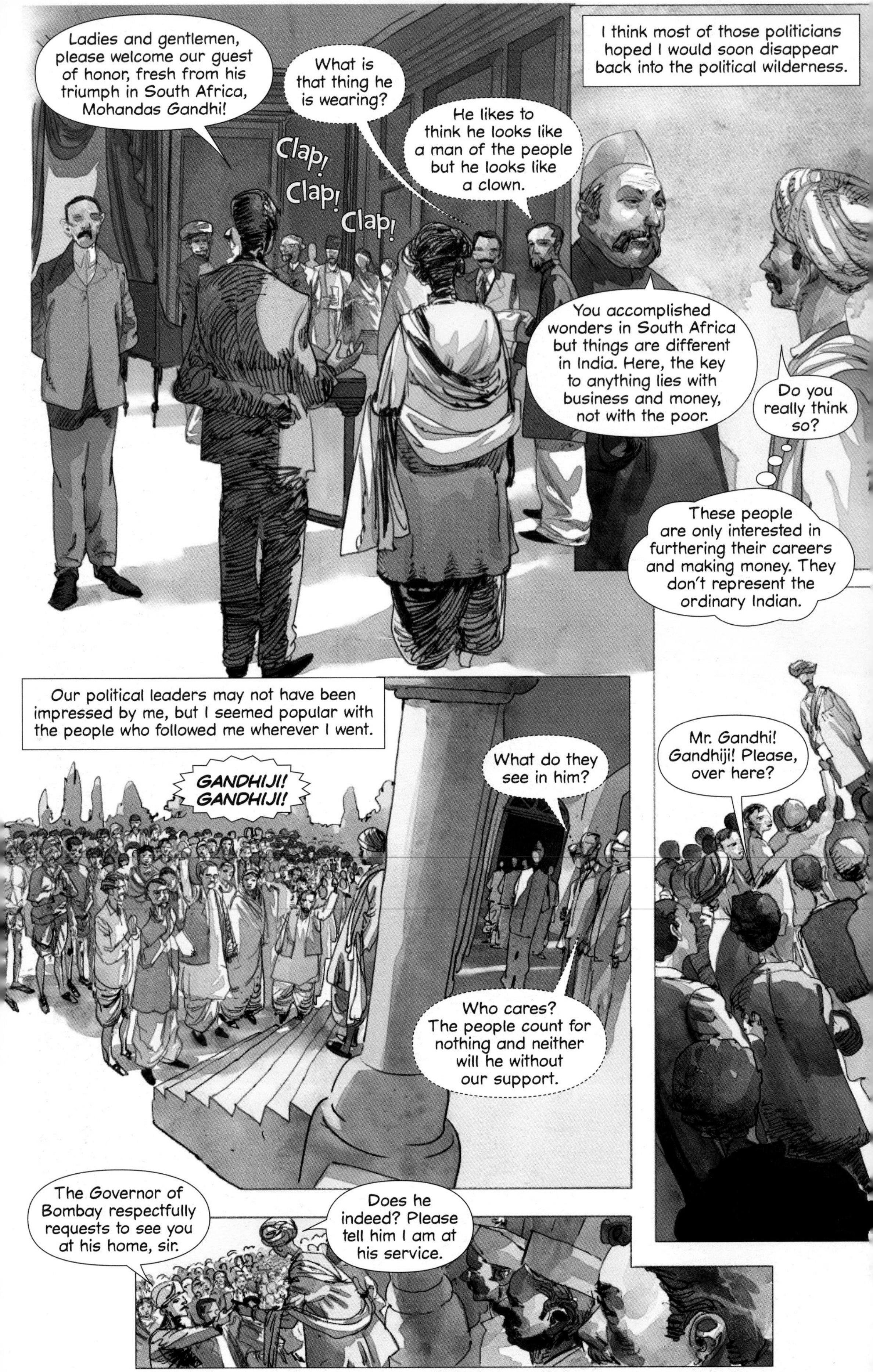
Ladies and gentlemen, please welcome our guest of honor, fresh from his triumph in South Africa, Mohandas Gandhi!
What is that thing he is wearing?
He likes to think he looks like a man of the people but he looks like a clown.
Clap! Clap! Clap!
I think most of those politicians hoped I would soon disappear back into the political wilderness.
You accomplished wonders in South Africa but things are different in India. Here, the key to anything lies with business and money, not with the poor.
Do you really think so?
These people are only interested in furthering their careers and making money. They don't represent the ordinary Indian.
Our political leaders may not have been impressed by me, but I seemed popular with the people who followed me wherever I went.
GANDHIJI! GANDHIJI!
What do they see in him?
Who cares? The people count for nothing and neither will he without our support.
Mr. Gandhi! Gandhiji! Please, over here?
The Governor of Bombay respectfully requests to see you at his home, sir.
Does he indeed? Please tell him I am at his service.

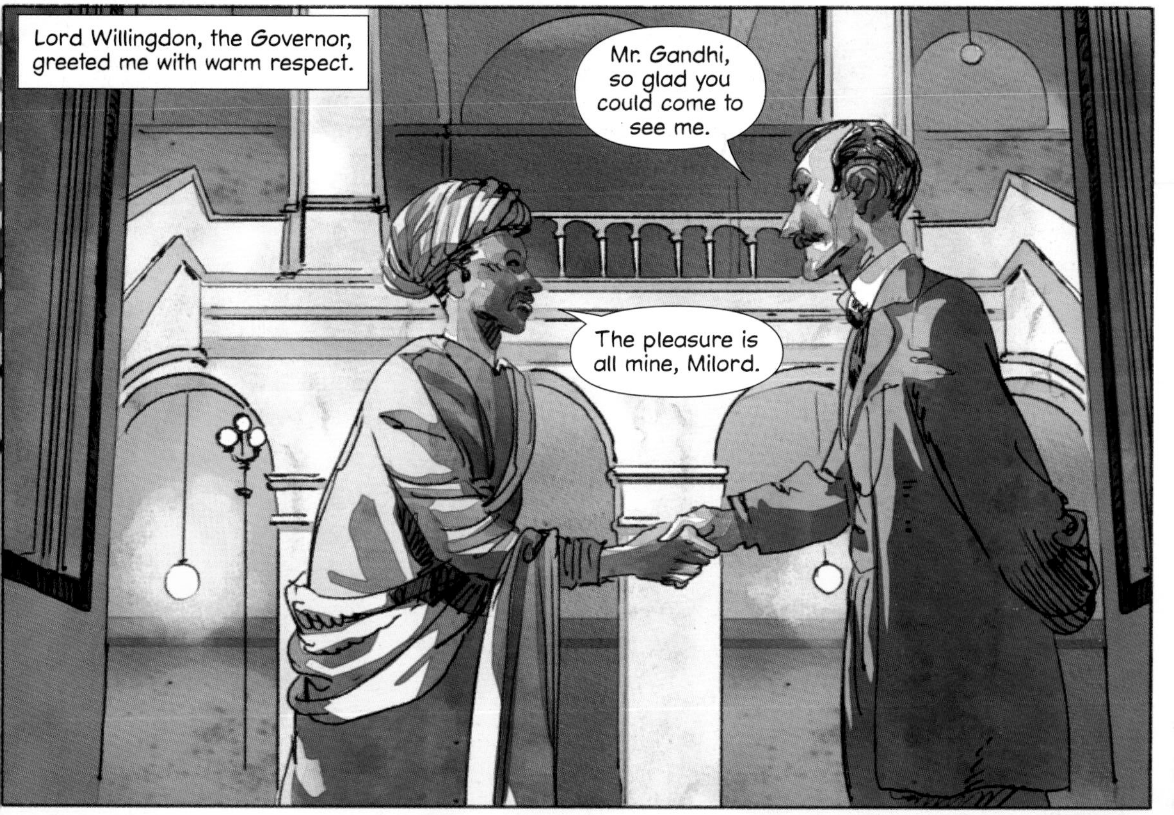
Lord Willingdon, the Governor, greeted me with warm respect.
Mr. Gandhi, so glad you could come to see me.
The pleasure is all mine, Milord.

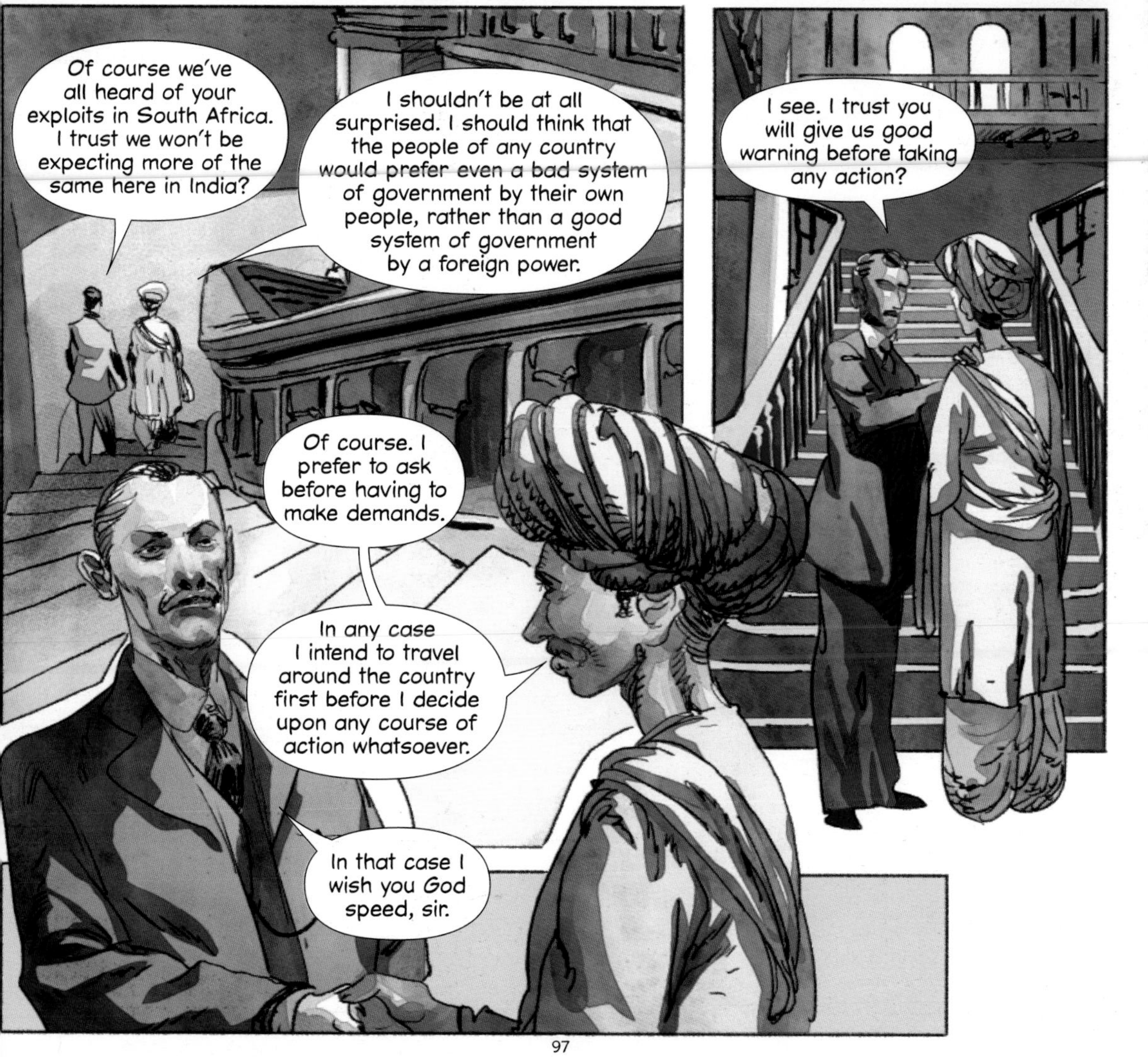
Of course we've all heard of your exploits in South Africa. I trust we won't be expecting more of the same here in India?
I shouldn't be at all surprised. I should think that the people of any country would prefer even a bad system of government by their own people, rather than a good system of government by a foreign power.
I see. I trust you will give us good warning before taking any action?
Of course. I prefer to ask before having to make demands.
In any case I intend to travel around the country first before I decide upon any course of action whatsoever.
In that case I wish you God speed, sir.

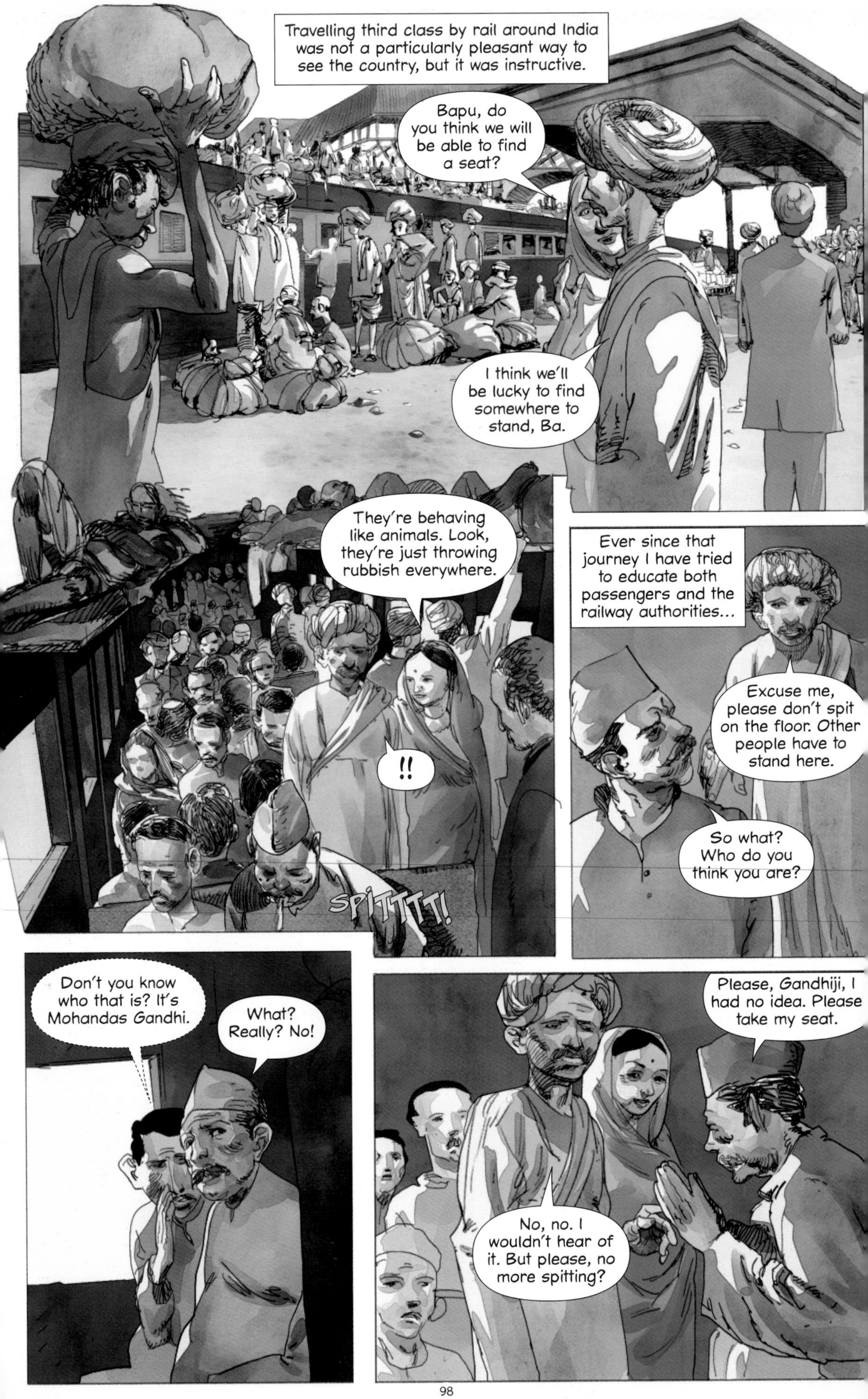
Travelling third class by rail around India was not a particularly pleasant way to see the country, but it was instructive.
Bapu, do you think we will be able to find a seat?
I think we'll be lucky to find somewhere to stand, Ba.
They're behaving like animals. Look, they're just throwing rubbish everywhere.
!!
SPITTTT!
Ever since that journey I have tried to educate both passengers and the railway authorities...
Excuse me, please don't spit on the floor. Other people have to stand here.
So what? Who do you think you are?
Don't you know who that is? It's Mohandas Gandhi.
What? Really? No!
Please, Gandhiji, I had no idea. Please take my seat.
No, no. I wouldn't hear of it. But please, no more spitting?

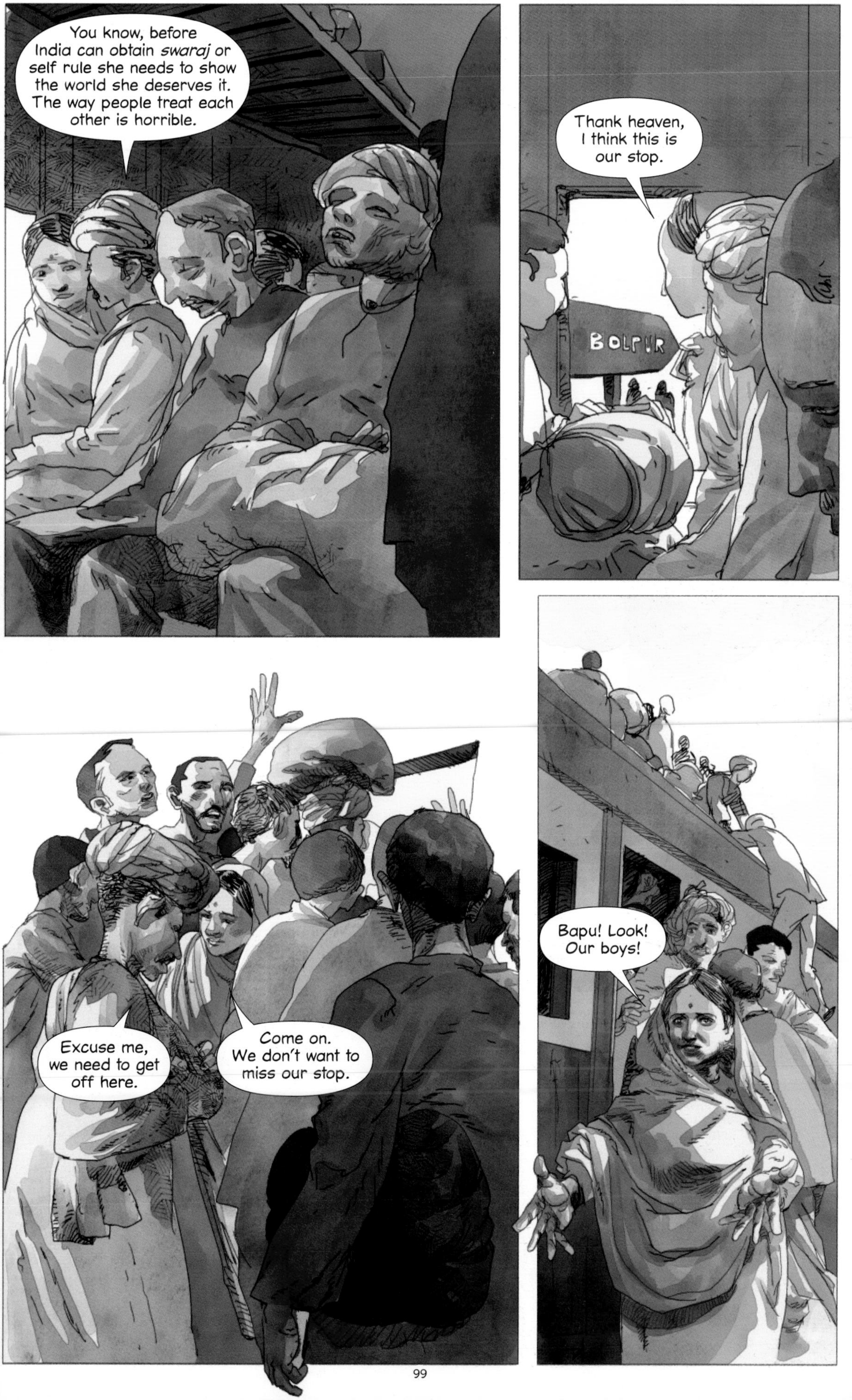
You know, before India can obtain *swaraj* or self rule she needs to show the world she deserves it. The way people treat each other is horrible.
Thank heaven, I think this is our stop.
BOLPUR
Excuse me, we need to get off here.
Come on. We don't want to miss our stop.
Bapu! Look! Our boys!

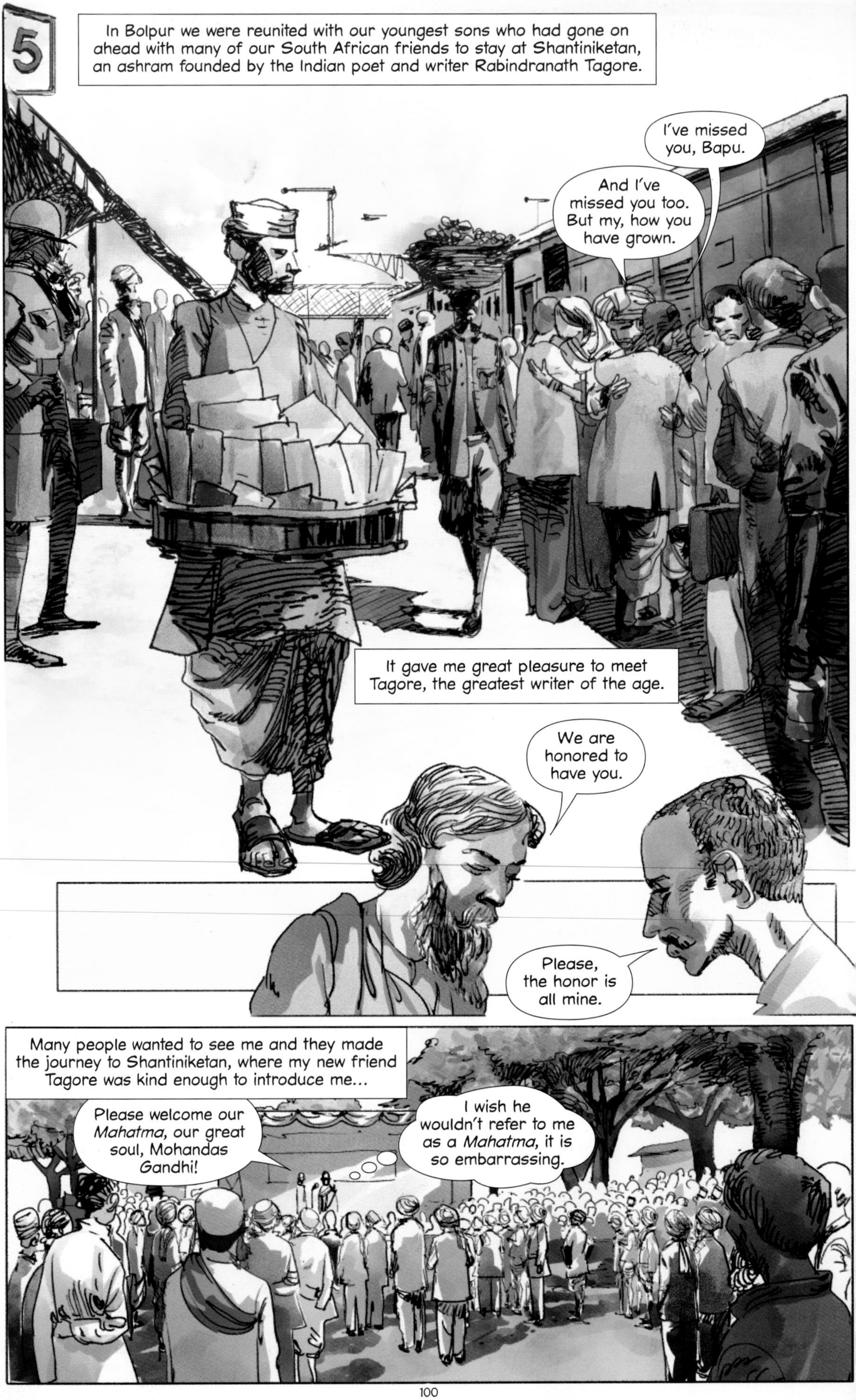
5
In Bolpur we were reunited with our youngest sons who had gone on ahead with many of our South African friends to stay at Shantiniketan, an ashram founded by the Indian poet and writer Rabindranath Tagore.
I've missed you, Bapu.
And I've missed you too. But my, how you have grown.
It gave me great pleasure to meet Tagore, the greatest writer of the age.
We are honored to have you.
Please, the honor is all mine.
Many people wanted to see me and they made the journey to Shantiniketan, where my new friend Tagore was kind enough to introduce me...
Please welcome our *Mahatma*, our great soul, Mohandas Gandhi!
I wish he wouldn't refer to me as a *Mahatma*, it is so embarrassing.

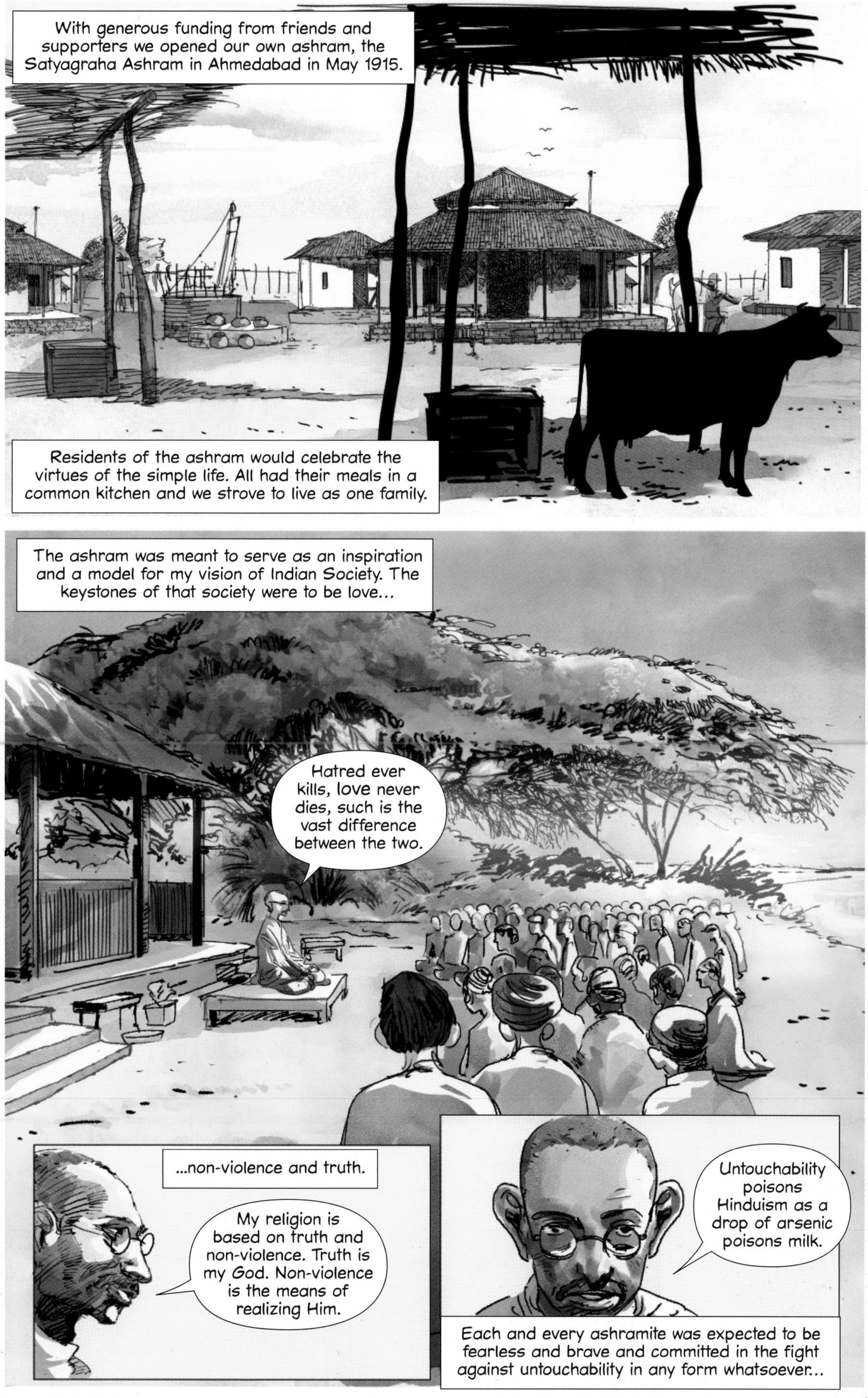
With generous funding from friends and supporters we opened our own ashram, the Satyagraha Ashram in Ahmedabad in May 1915.
Residents of the ashram would celebrate the virtues of the simple life. All had their meals in a common kitchen and we strove to live as one family.
The ashram was meant to serve as an inspiration and a model for my vision of Indian Society. The keystones of that society were to be love...
Hatred ever kills, love never dies, such is the vast difference between the two.
...non-violence and truth.
My religion is based on truth and non-violence. Truth is my God. Non-violence is the means of realizing Him.
Untouchability poisons Hinduism as a drop of arsenic poisons milk.
Each and every ashramite was expected to be fearless and brave and committed in the fight against untouchability in any form whatsoever...

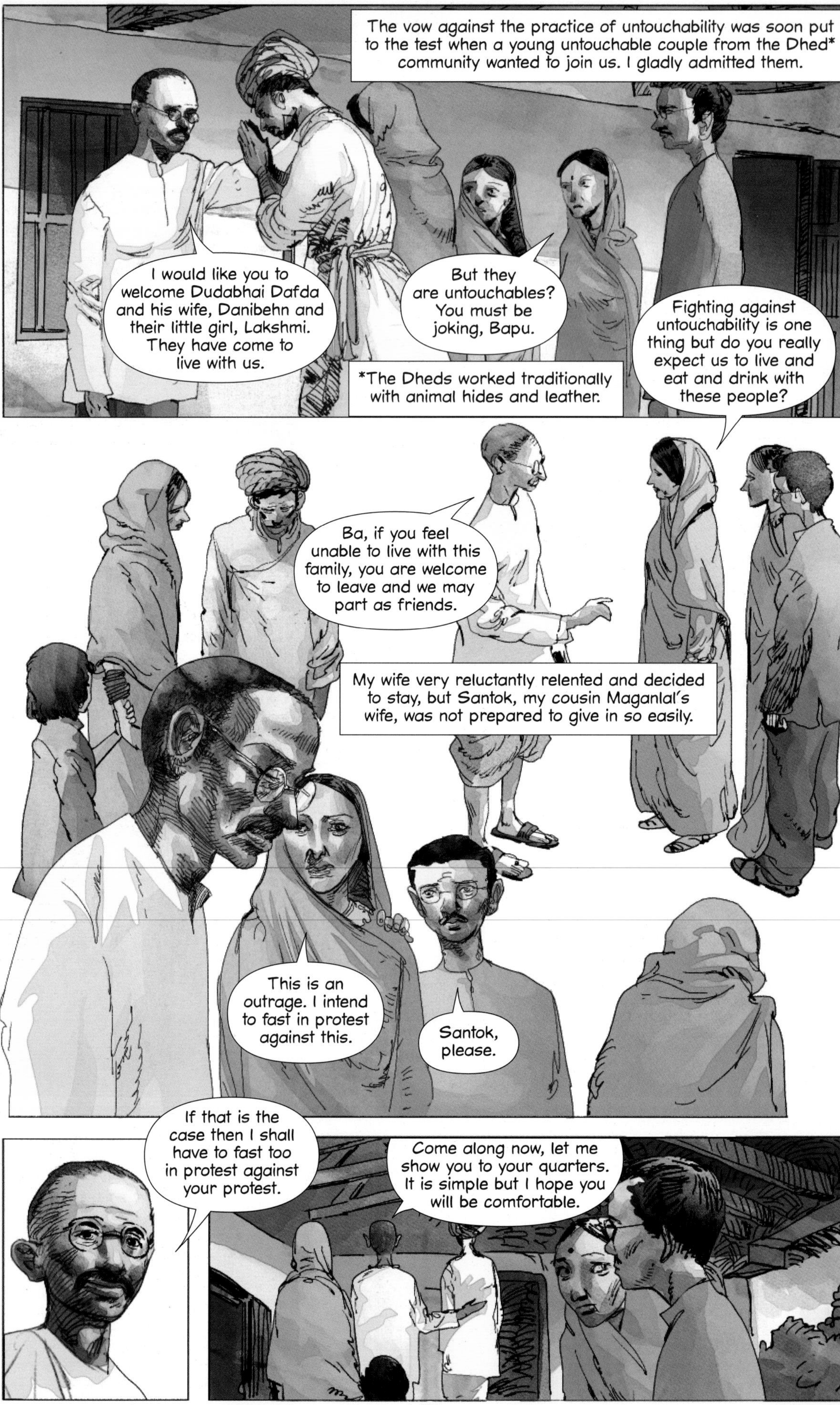
The vow against the practice of untouchability was soon put to the test when a young untouchable couple from the Dhed* community wanted to join us. I gladly admitted them.
I would like you to welcome Dudabhai Dafda and his wife, Danibehn and their little girl, Lakshmi. They have come to live with us.
But they are untouchables? You must be joking, Bapu.
*The Dheds worked traditionally with animal hides and leather.
Fighting against untouchability is one thing but do you really expect us to live and eat and drink with these people?
Ba, if you feel unable to live with this family, you are welcome to leave and we may part as friends.
My wife very reluctantly relented and decided to stay, but Santok, my cousin Maganlal's wife, was not prepared to give in so easily.
This is an outrage. I intend to fast in protest against this.
Santok, please.
If that is the case then I shall have to fast too in protest against your protest.
Come along now, let me show you to your quarters. It is simple but I hope you will be comfortable.

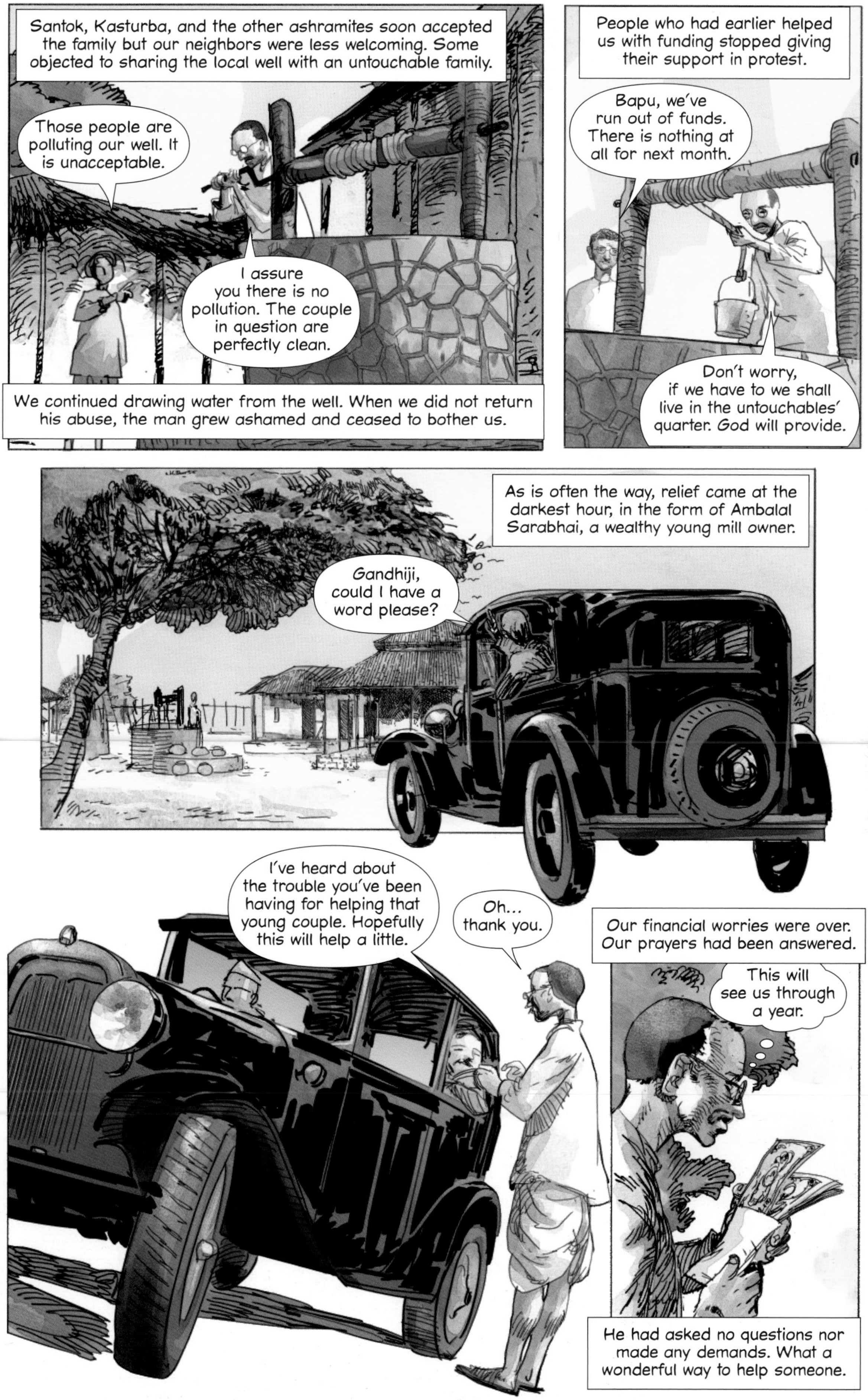
Santok, Kasturba, and the other ashramites soon accepted the family but our neighbors were less welcoming. Some objected to sharing the local well with an untouchable family.
Those people are polluting our well. It is unacceptable.
I assure you there is no pollution. The couple in question are perfectly clean.
We continued drawing water from the well. When we did not return his abuse, the man grew ashamed and ceased to bother us.
People who had earlier helped us with funding stopped giving their support in protest.
Bapu, we've run out of funds. There is nothing at all for next month.
Don't worry, if we have to we shall live in the untouchables' quarter. God will provide.
As is often the way, relief came at the darkest hour, in the form of Ambalal Sarabhai, a wealthy young mill owner.
Gandhiji, could I have a word please?
I've heard about the trouble you've been having for helping that young couple. Hopefully this will help a little.
Oh... thank you.
Our financial worries were over. Our prayers had been answered.
This will see us through a year.
He had asked no questions nor made any demands. What a wonderful way to help someone.

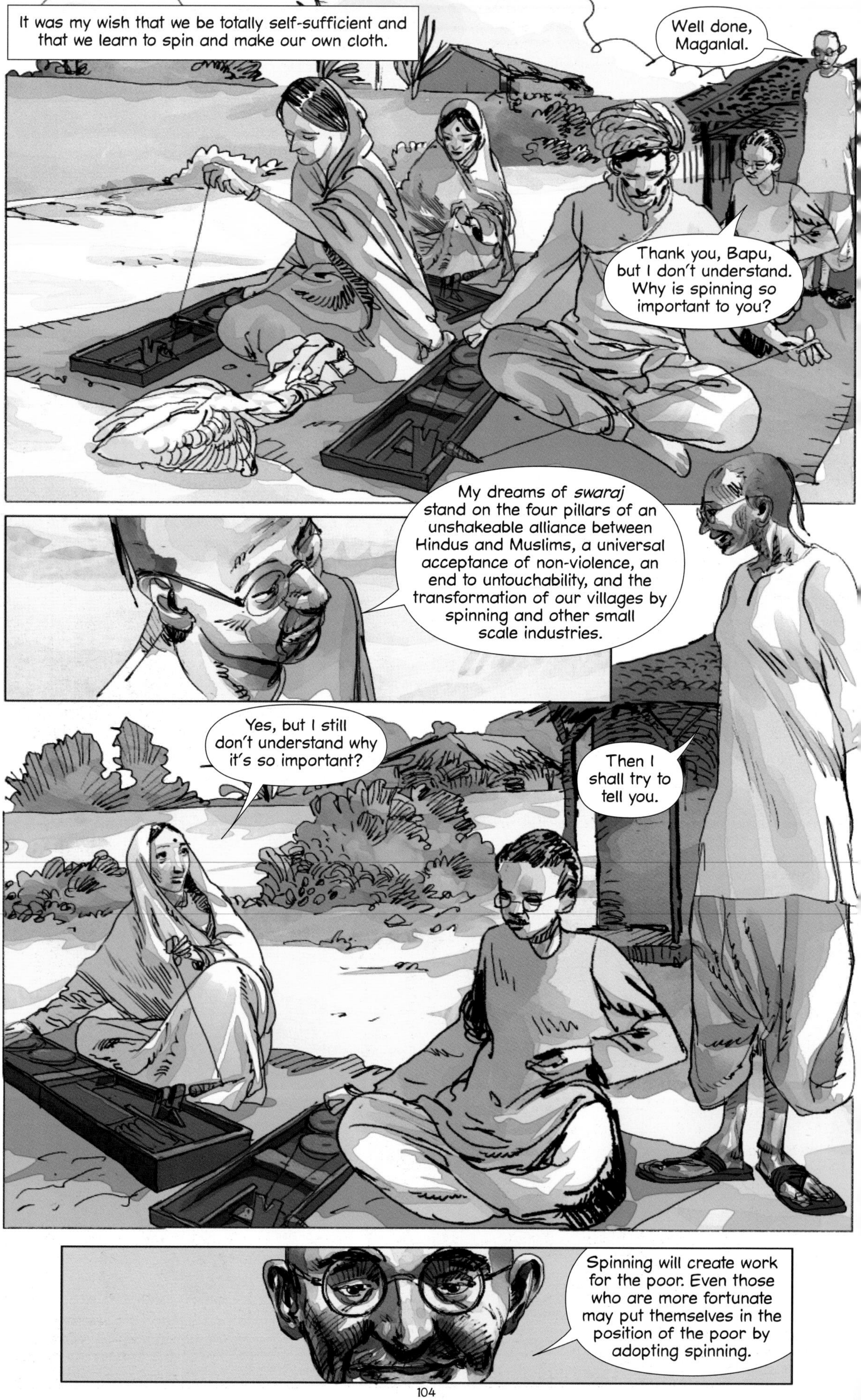
It was my wish that we be totally self-sufficient and that we learn to spin and make our own cloth.
Well done, Maganlal.
Thank you, Bapu, but I don't understand. Why is spinning so important to you?
My dreams of *swaraj* stand on the four pillars of an unshakeable alliance between Hindus and Muslims, a universal acceptance of non-violence, an end to untouchability, and the transformation of our villages by spinning and other small scale industries.
Yes, but I still don't understand why it's so important?
Then I shall try to tell you.
Spinning will create work for the poor. Even those who are more fortunate may put themselves in the position of the poor by adopting spinning.

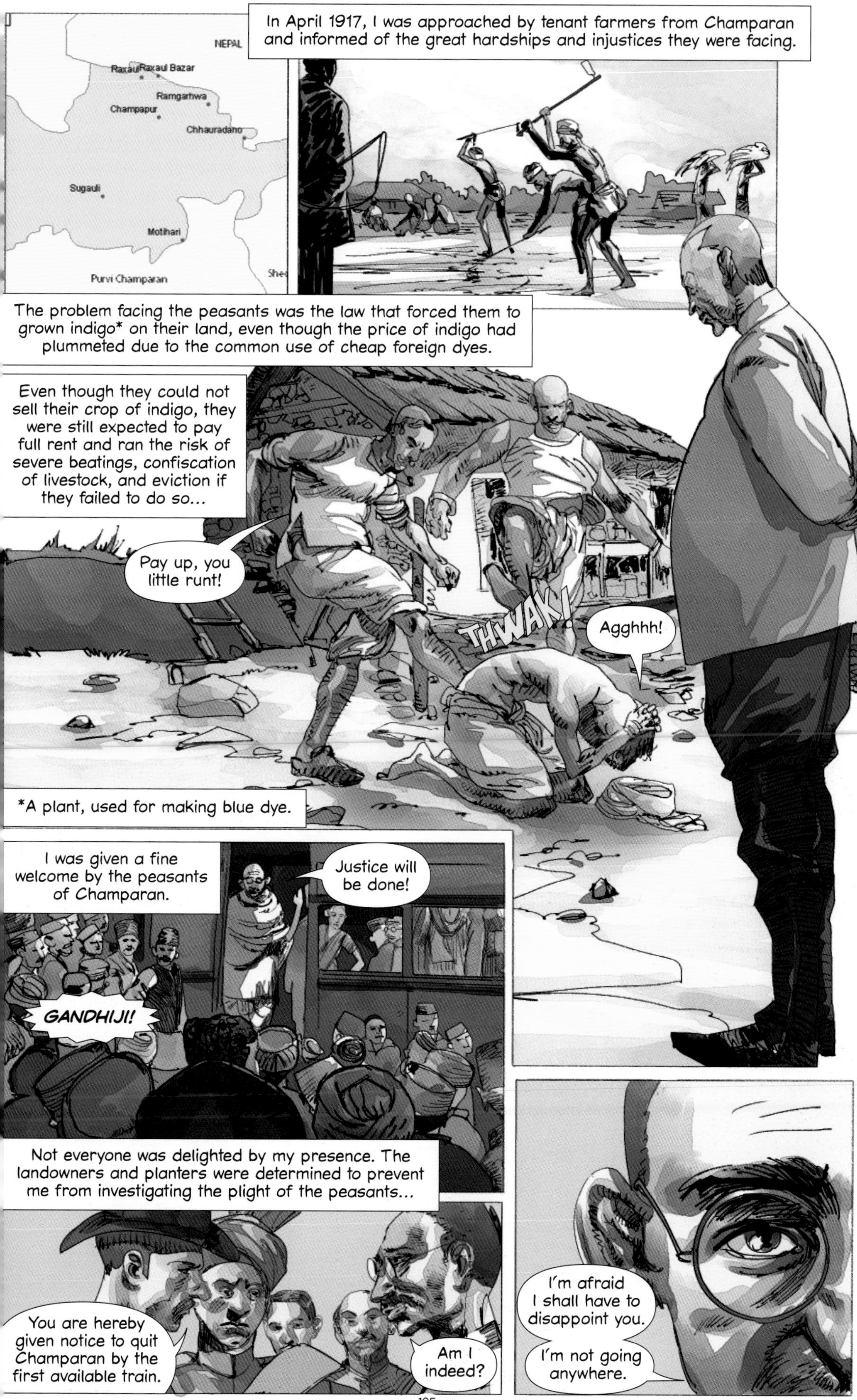
In April 1917, I was approached by tenant farmers from Champaran and informed of the great hardships and injustices they were facing.
NEPAL
Raxaul
Raxaul Bazar
Ramgarhwa
Champapur
Chhauradano
Sugauli
Motihari
Purvi Champaran
The problem facing the peasants was the law that forced them to grown indigo* on their land, even though the price of indigo had plummeted due to the common use of cheap foreign dyes.
Even though they could not sell their crop of indigo, they were still expected to pay full rent and ran the risk of severe beatings, confiscation of livestock, and eviction if they failed to do so...
Pay up, you little runt!
THWAK!
Agghhh!
*A plant, used for making blue dye.
I was given a fine welcome by the peasants of Champaran.
Justice will be done!
GANDHIJI!
Not everyone was delighted by my presence. The landowners and planters were determined to prevent me from investigating the plight of the peasants...
You are hereby given notice to quit Champaran by the first available train.
Am I indeed?
I'm afraid I shall have to disappoint you.
I'm not going anywhere.

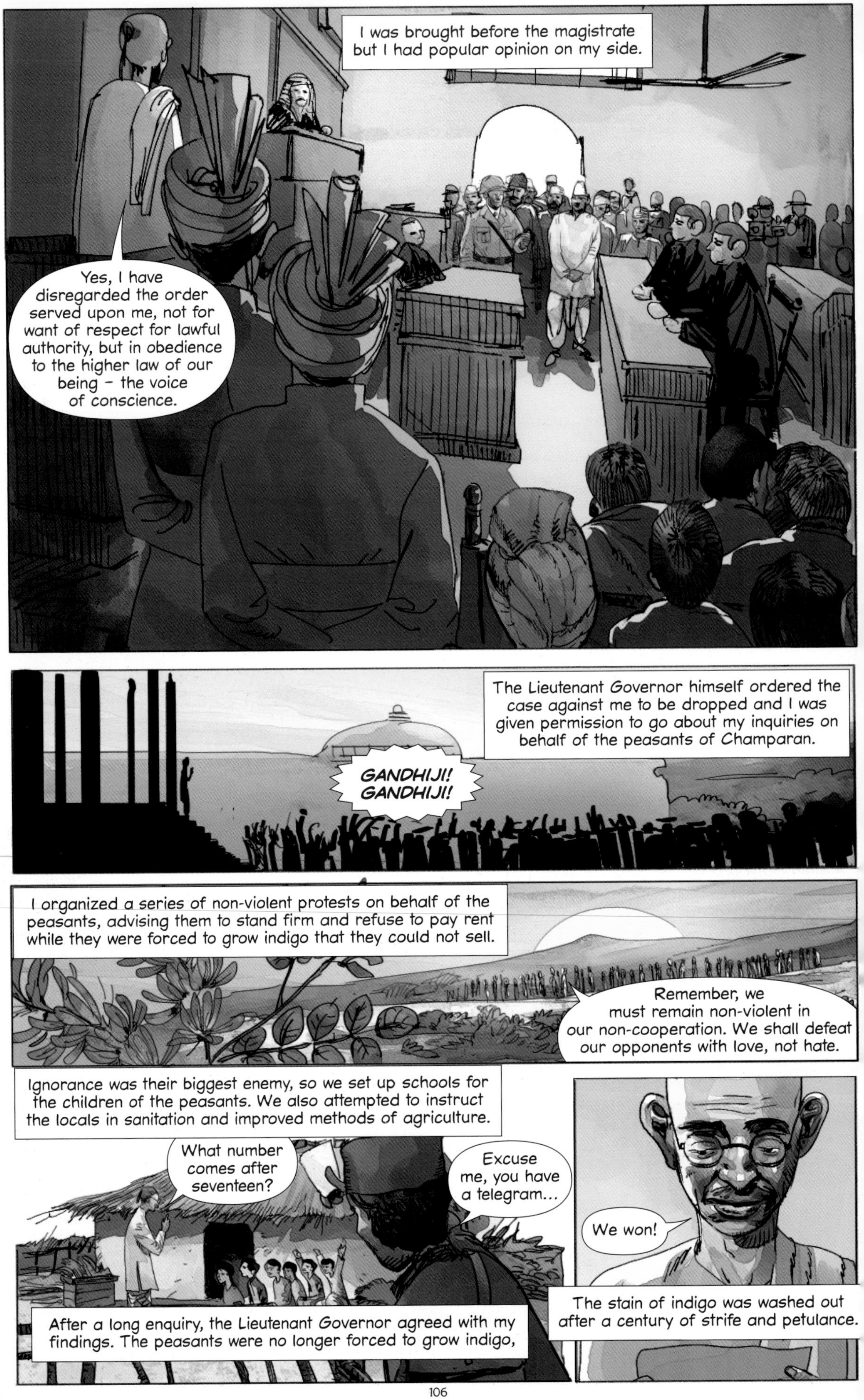
I was brought before the magistrate but I had popular opinion on my side.
Yes, I have disregarded the order served upon me, not for want of respect for lawful authority, but in obedience to the higher law of our being – the voice of conscience.
The Lieutenant Governor himself ordered the case against me to be dropped and I was given permission to go about my inquiries on behalf of the peasants of Champaran.
GANDHIJI! GANDHIJI!
I organized a series of non-violent protests on behalf of the peasants, advising them to stand firm and refuse to pay rent while they were forced to grow indigo that they could not sell.
Remember, we must remain non-violent in our non-cooperation. We shall defeat our opponents with love, not hate.
Ignorance was their biggest enemy, so we set up schools for the children of the peasants. We also attempted to instruct the locals in sanitation and improved methods of agriculture.
What number comes after seventeen?
Excuse me, you have a telegram...
After a long enquiry, the Lieutenant Governor agreed with my findings. The peasants were no longer forced to grow indigo,
We won!
The stain of indigo was washed out after a century of strife and petulance.

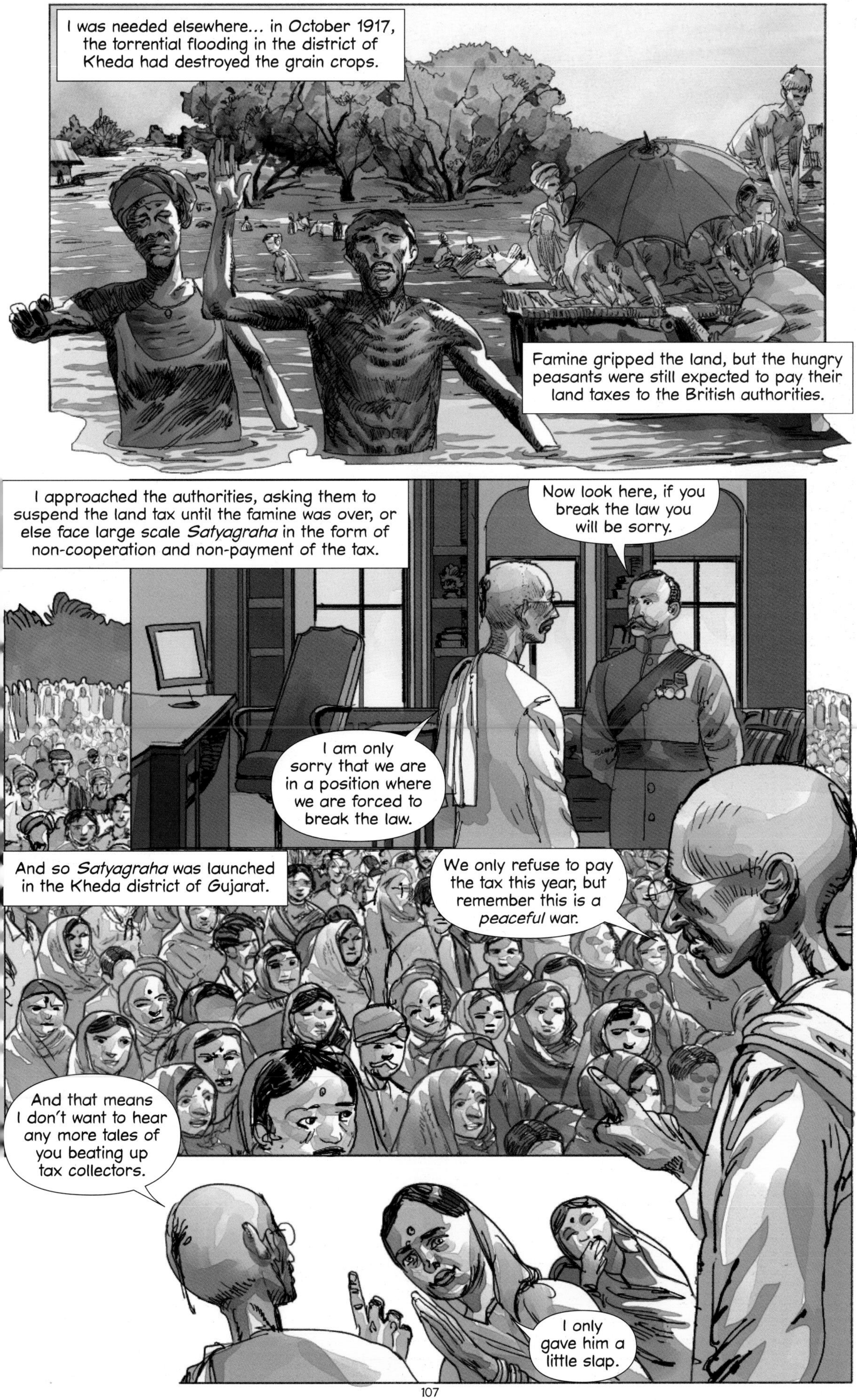

I was needed elsewhere... in October 1917, the torrential flooding in the district of Kheda had destroyed the grain crops.
Famine gripped the land, but the hungry peasants were still expected to pay their land taxes to the British authorities.
I approached the authorities, asking them to suspend the land tax until the famine was over, or else face large scale *Satyagraha* in the form of non-cooperation and non-payment of the tax.
Now look here, if you break the law you will be sorry.
I am only sorry that we are in a position where we are forced to break the law.
And so *Satyagraha* was launched in the Kheda district of Gujarat.
We only refuse to pay the tax this year, but remember this is a *peaceful* war.
And that means I don't want to hear any more tales of you beating up tax collectors.
I only gave him a little slap.

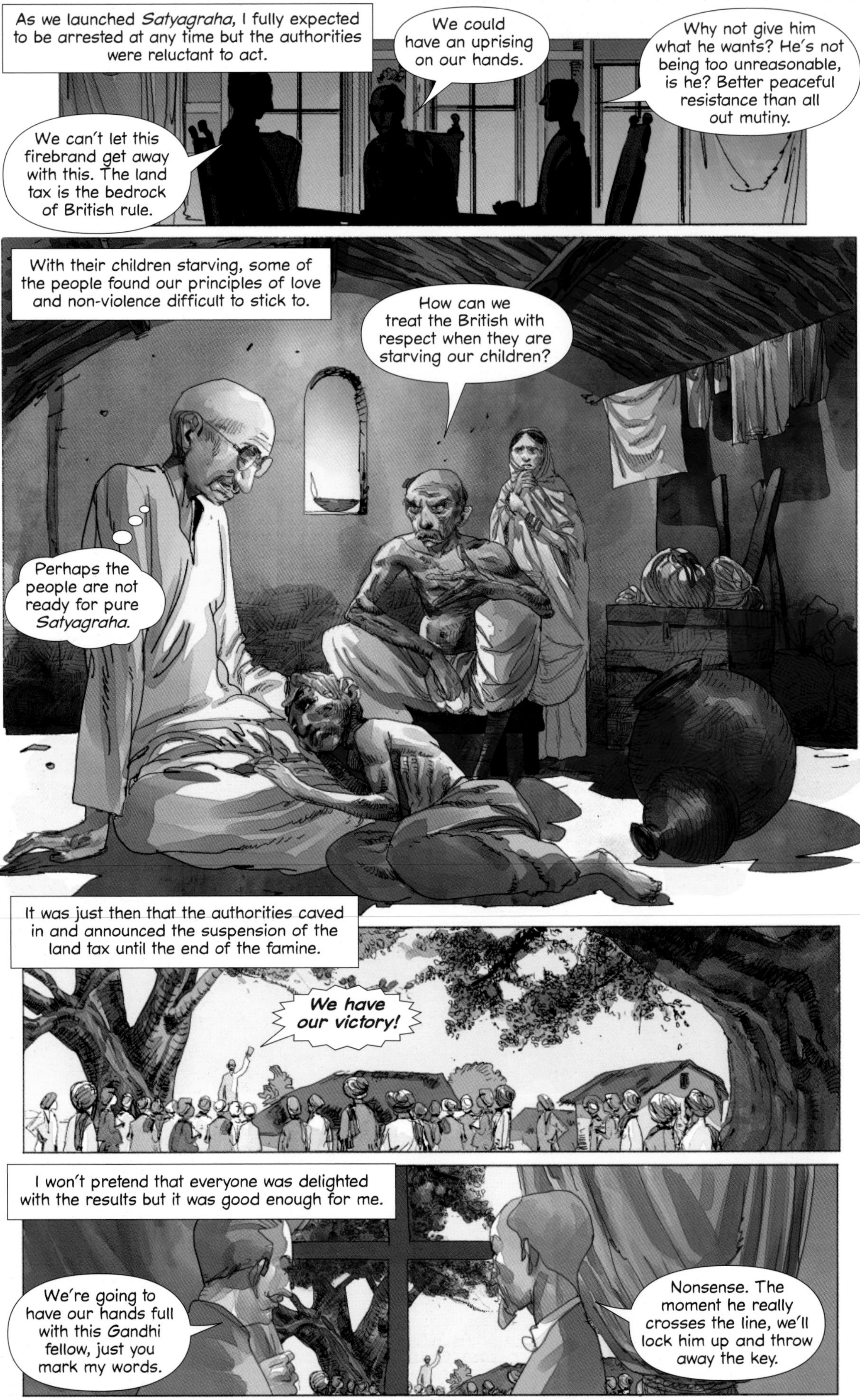

As we launched *Satyagraha*, I fully expected to be arrested at any time but the authorities were reluctant to act.
We can't let this firebrand get away with this. The land tax is the bedrock of British rule.
We could have an uprising on our hands.
Why not give him what he wants? He's not being too unreasonable, is he? Better peaceful resistance than all out mutiny.
With their children starving, some of the people found our principles of love and non-violence difficult to stick to.
How can we treat the British with respect when they are starving our children?
Perhaps the people are not ready for pure *Satyagraha*.
It was just then that the authorities caved in and announced the suspension of the land tax until the end of the famine.
We have our victory!
I won't pretend that everyone was delighted with the results but it was good enough for me.
We're going to have our hands full with this Gandhi fellow, just you mark my words.
Nonsense. The moment he really crosses the line, we'll lock him up and throw away the key.

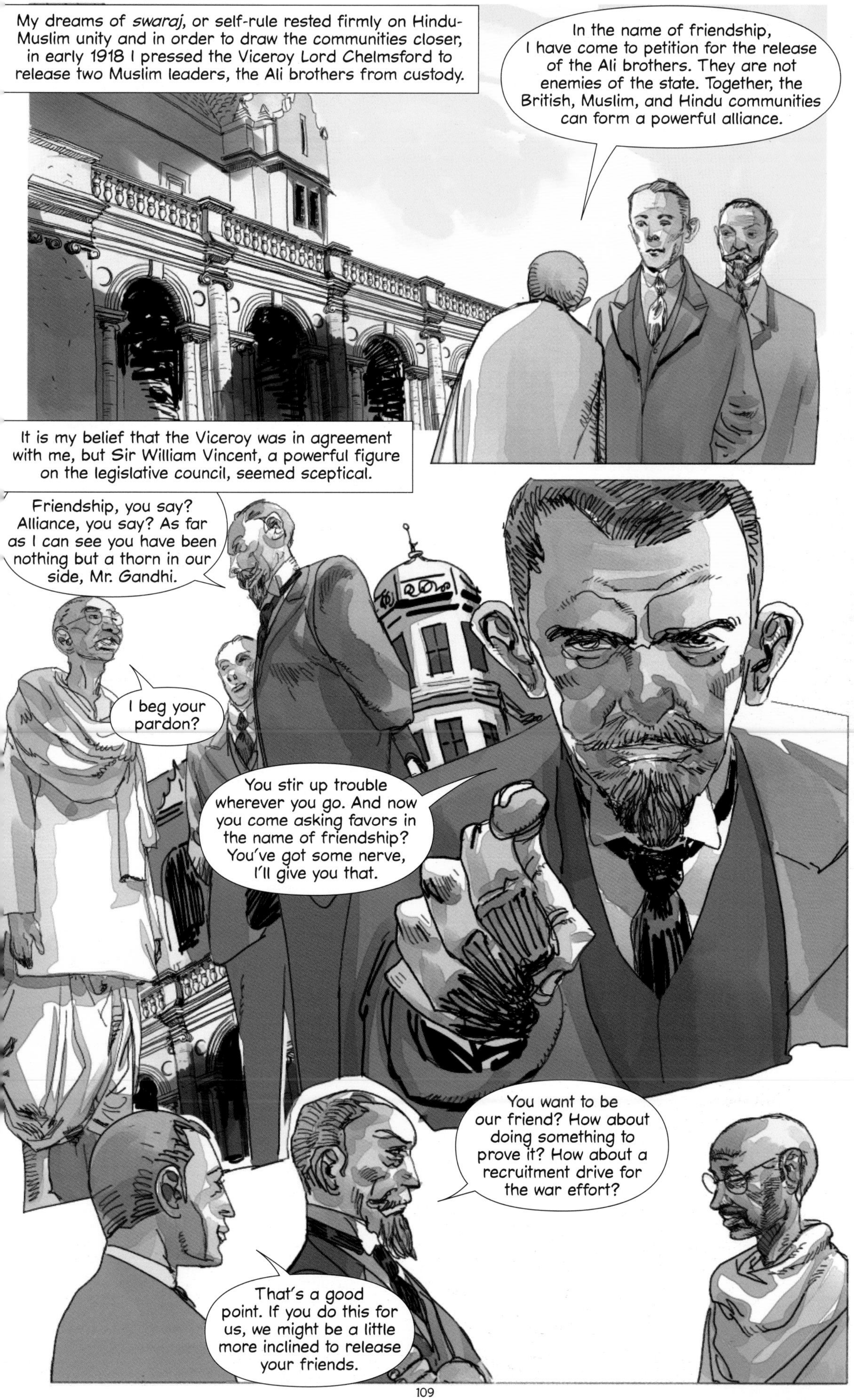

My dreams of *swaraj*, or self-rule rested firmly on Hindu-Muslim unity and in order to draw the communities closer, in early 1918 I pressed the Viceroy Lord Chelmsford to release two Muslim leaders, the Ali brothers from custody.
In the name of friendship, I have come to petition for the release of the Ali brothers. They are not enemies of the state. Together, the British, Muslim, and Hindu communities can form a powerful alliance.
It is my belief that the Viceroy was in agreement with me, but Sir William Vincent, a powerful figure on the legislative council, seemed sceptical.
Friendship, you say? Alliance, you say? As far as I can see you have been nothing but a thorn in our side, Mr. Gandhi.
I beg your pardon?
You stir up trouble wherever you go. And now you come asking favors in the name of friendship? You've got some nerve, I'll give you that.
You want to be our friend? How about doing something to prove it? How about a recruitment drive for the war effort?
That's a good point. If you do this for us, we might be a little more inclined to release your friends.

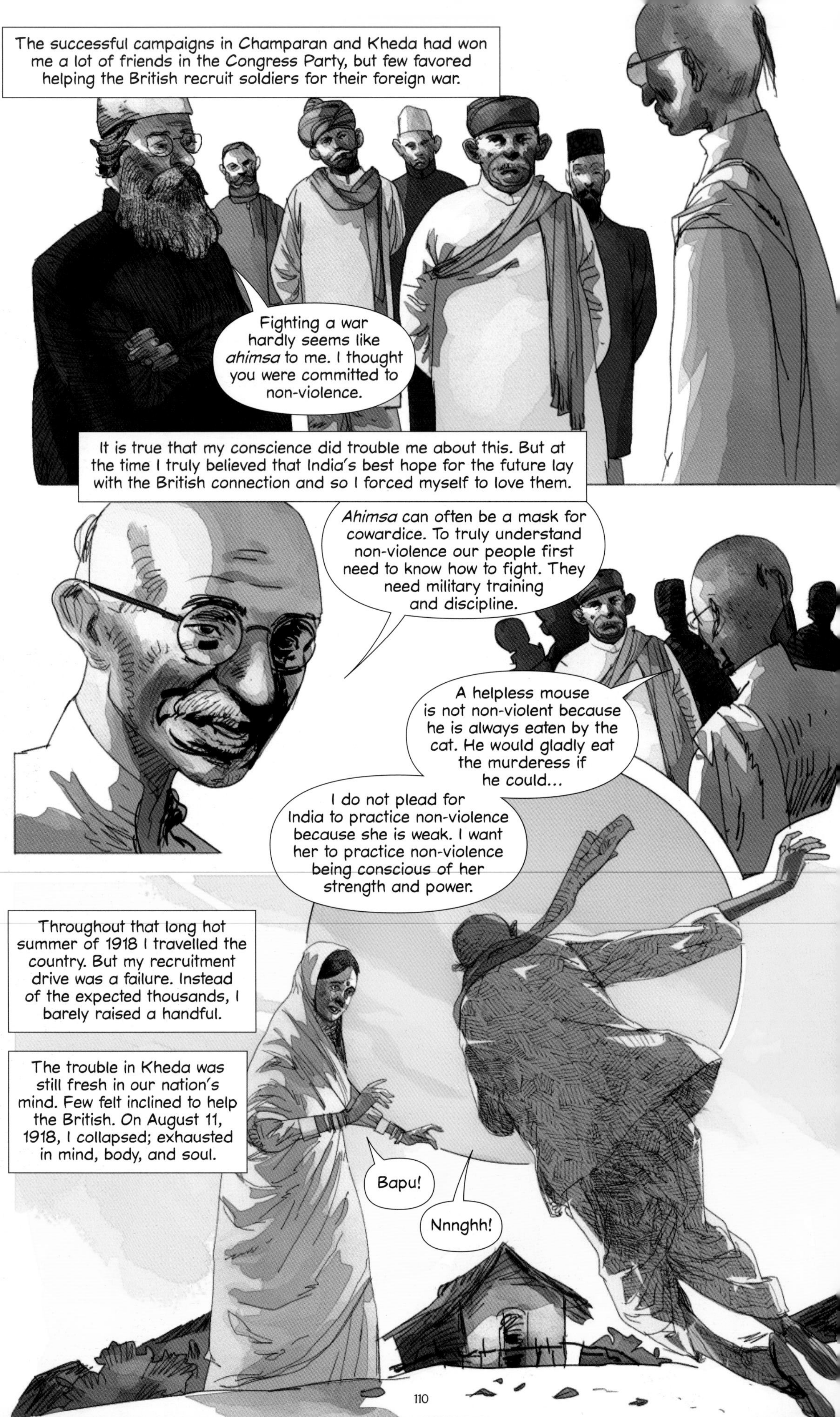
The successful campaigns in Champaran and Kheda had won me a lot of friends in the Congress Party, but few favored helping the British recruit soldiers for their foreign war.
Fighting a war hardly seems like *ahimsa* to me. I thought you were committed to non-violence.
It is true that my conscience did trouble me about this. But at the time I truly believed that India's best hope for the future lay with the British connection and so I forced myself to love them.
Ahimsa can often be a mask for cowardice. To truly understand non-violence our people first need to know how to fight. They need military training and discipline.
A helpless mouse is not non-violent because he is always eaten by the cat. He would gladly eat the murderess if he could...
I do not plead for India to practice non-violence because she is weak. I want her to practice non-violence being conscious of her strength and power.
Throughout that long hot summer of 1918 I travelled the country. But my recruitment drive was a failure. Instead of the expected thousands, I barely raised a handful.
The trouble in Kheda was still fresh in our nation's mind. Few felt inclined to help the British. On August 11, 1918, I collapsed; exhausted in mind, body, and soul.
Bapu!
Nnnghh!

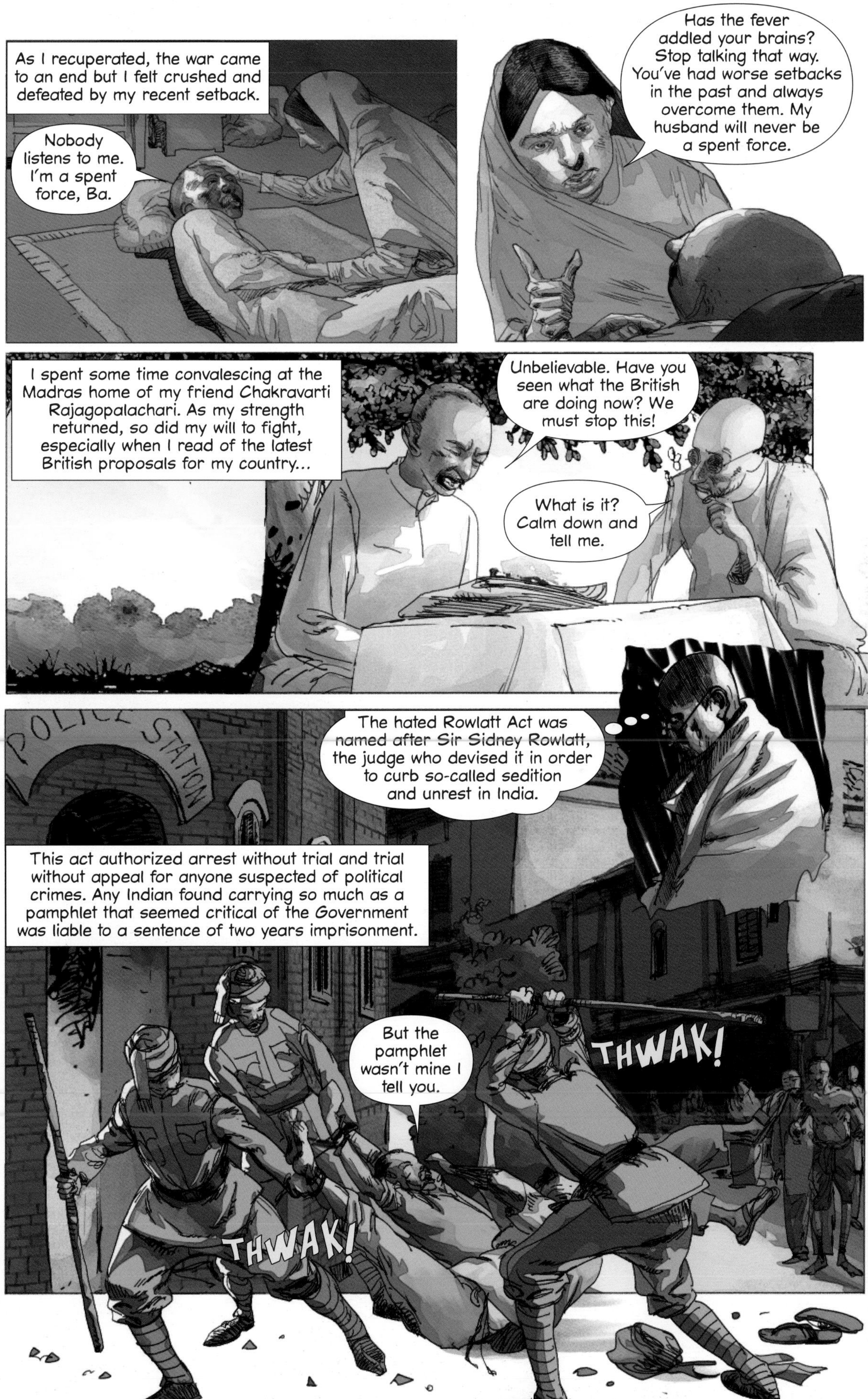
As I recuperated, the war came to an end but I felt crushed and defeated by my recent setback.
Nobody listens to me. I'm a spent force, Ba.
Has the fever addled your brains? Stop talking that way. You've had worse setbacks in the past and always overcome them. My husband will never be a spent force.
I spent some time convalescing at the Madras home of my friend Chakravarti Rajagopalachari. As my strength returned, so did my will to fight, especially when I read of the latest British proposals for my country...
Unbelievable. Have you seen what the British are doing now? We must stop this!
What is it? Calm down and tell me.
POLICE STATION
The hated Rowlatt Act was named after Sir Sidney Rowlatt, the judge who devised it in order to curb so-called sedition and unrest in India.
This act authorized arrest without trial and trial without appeal for anyone suspected of political crimes. Any Indian found carrying so much as a pamphlet that seemed critical of the Government was liable to a sentence of two years imprisonment.
But the pamphlet wasn't mine I tell you.
THWAK!
THWAK!

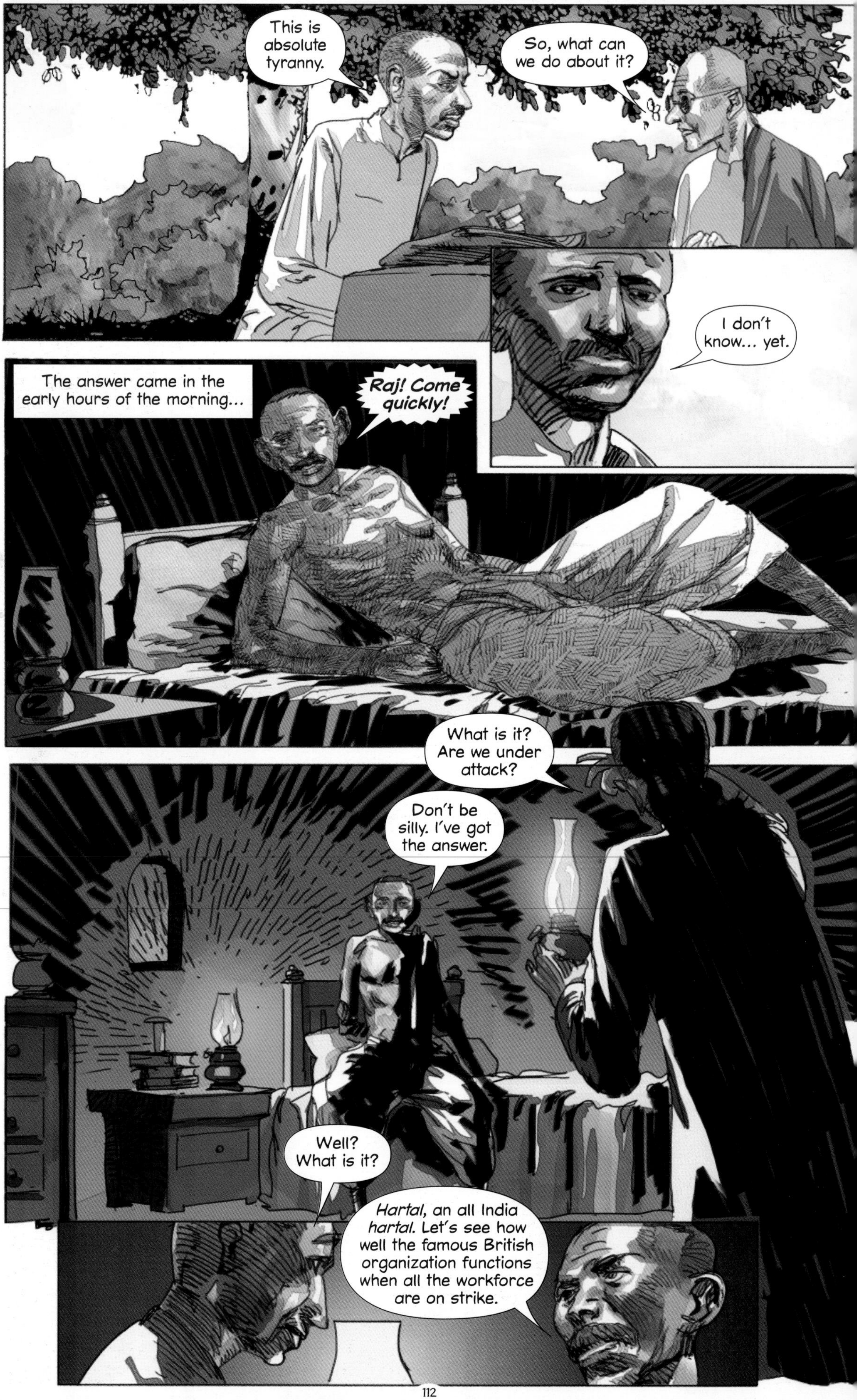
This is absolute tyranny.
So, what can we do about it?
I don't know... yet.
The answer came in the early hours of the morning...
Raj! Come quickly!
What is it? Are we under attack?
Don't be silly. I've got the answer.
Well? What is it?
Hartal, an all India *hartal*. Let's see how well the famous British organization functions when all the workforce are on strike.

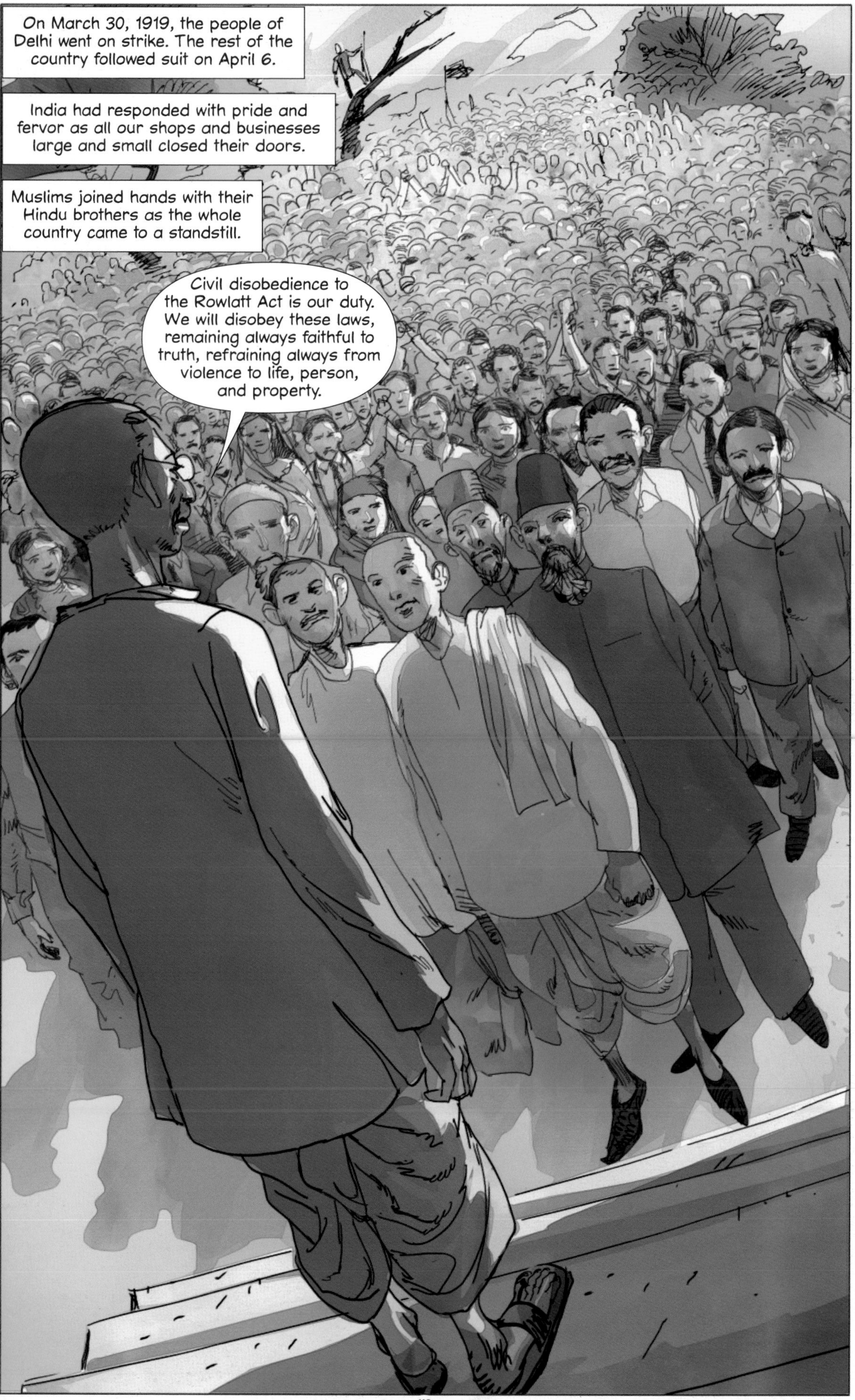
On March 30, 1919, the people of Delhi went on strike. The rest of the country followed suit on April 6.
India had responded with pride and fervor as all our shops and businesses large and small closed their doors.
Muslims joined hands with their Hindu brothers as the whole country came to a standstill.
Civil disobedience to the Rowlatt Act is our duty. We will disobey these laws, remaining always faithful to truth, refraining always from violence to life, person, and property.

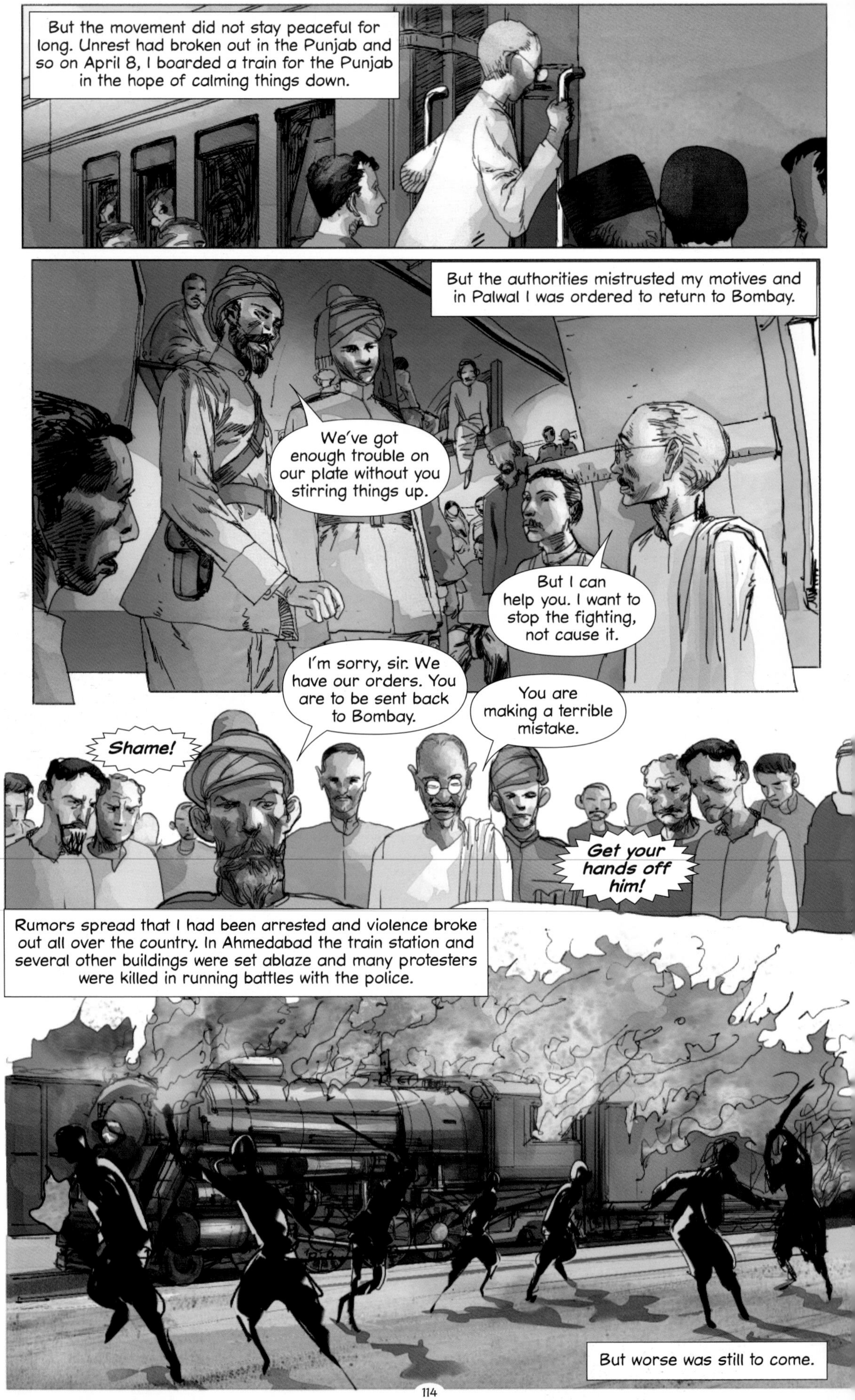

But the movement did not stay peaceful for long. Unrest had broken out in the Punjab and so on April 8, I boarded a train for the Punjab in the hope of calming things down.
But the authorities mistrusted my motives and in Palwal I was ordered to return to Bombay.
We've got enough trouble on our plate without you stirring things up.
But I can help you. I want to stop the fighting, not cause it.
I'm sorry, sir. We have our orders. You are to be sent back to Bombay.
You are making a terrible mistake.
Shame!
Get your hands off him!
Rumors spread that I had been arrested and violence broke out all over the country. In Ahmedabad the train station and several other buildings were set ablaze and many protesters were killed in running battles with the police.
But worse was still to come.

In Amritsar a bank manager tried to defend his bank from an angry mob...

Stay back I say!

CRACK

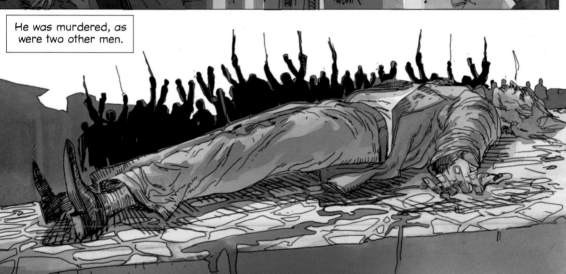

He was murdered, as were two other men.

A young British school teacher was assaulted and left for dead, only to be rescued by a passing Indian.

This woman needs help! Quickly!

I announced the immediate suspension of *Satyagraha*...

Brothers, I am ashamed of the events of the last few days. In the name of *Satyagraha*, we burnt down buildings, killed innocent people, and plundered shops and homes.

We should repent and do penance. I would advise you to fast for twenty four hours. My responsibility is a million times greater. I will therefore fast for seventy two hours.

The people were untrained and unready for *Satyagraha*. It had been a Himalayan miscalculation on my part.

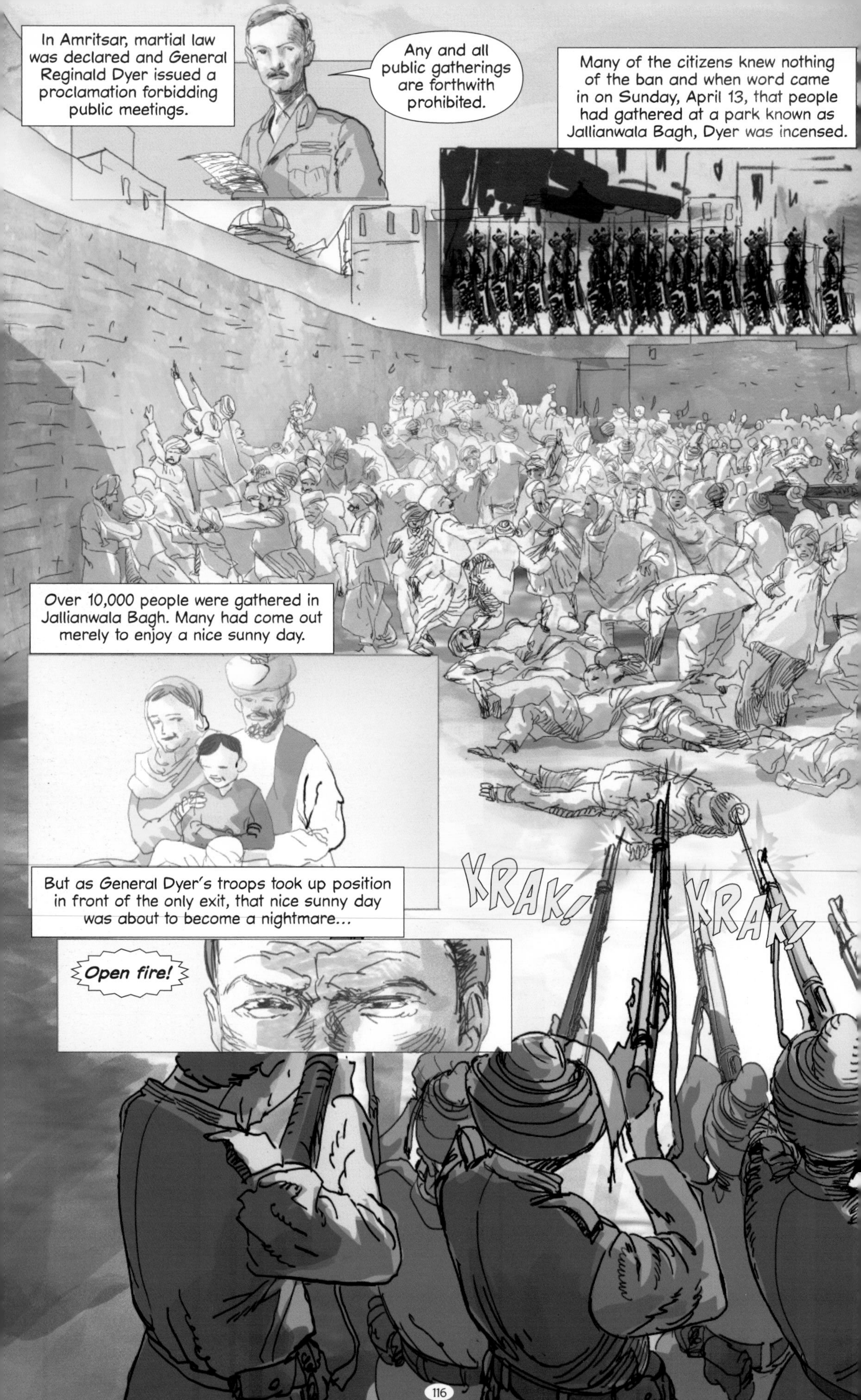

In Amritsar, martial law was declared and General Reginald Dyer issued a proclamation forbidding public meetings.
Any and all public gatherings are forthwith prohibited.
Many of the citizens knew nothing of the ban and when word came in on Sunday, April 13, that people had gathered at a park known as Jallianwala Bagh, Dyer was incensed.
Over 10,000 people were gathered in Jallianwala Bagh. Many had come out merely to enjoy a nice sunny day.
But as General Dyer's troops took up position in front of the only exit, that nice sunny day was about to become a nightmare...
KRAK!
KRAK!
Open fire!

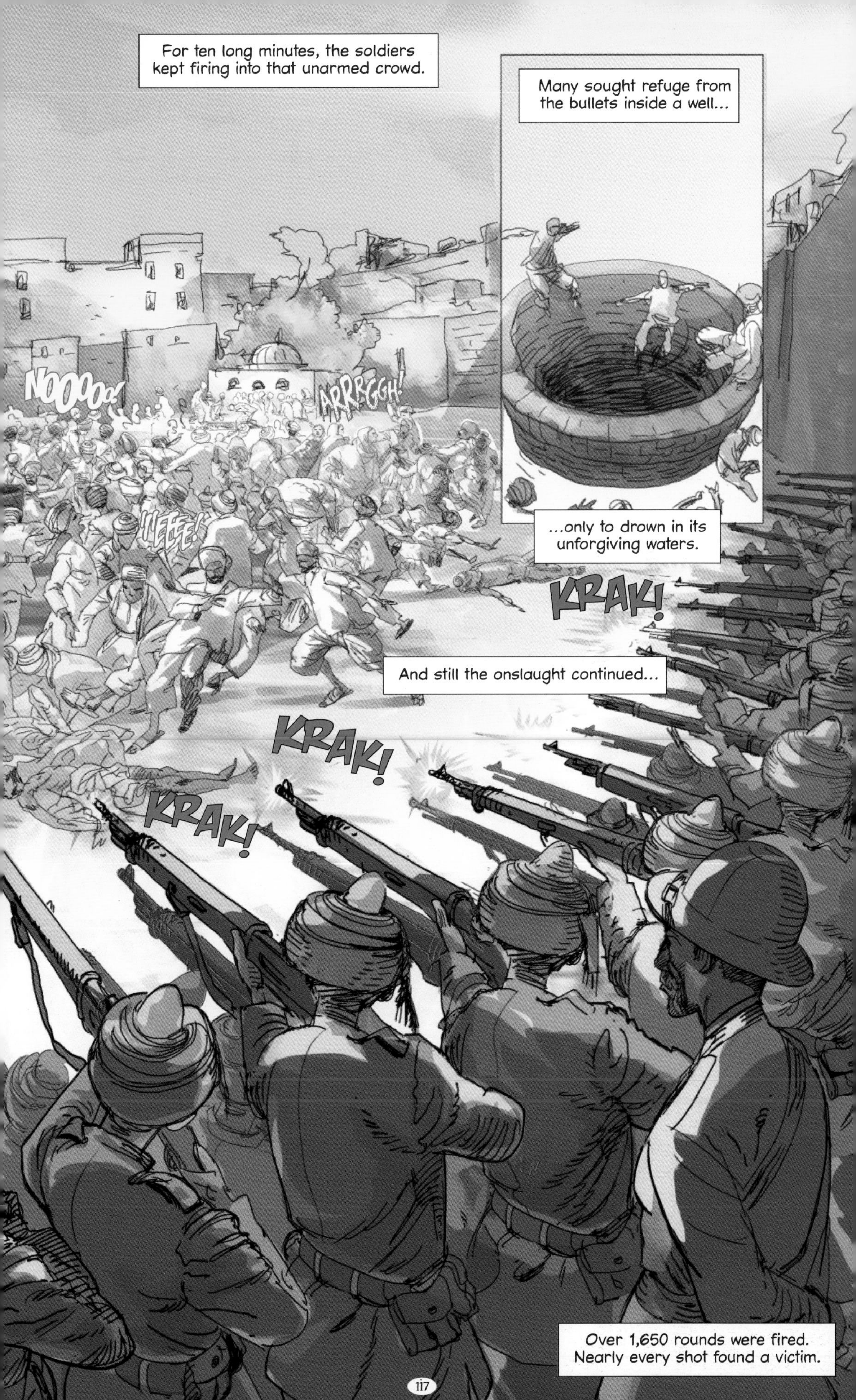
For ten long minutes, the soldiers kept firing into that unarmed crowd.
Many sought refuge from the bullets inside a well...
NOOOOO!
ARRRGGH!
YEEEE!
...only to drown in its unforgiving waters.
KRAK!
And still the onslaught continued...
KRAK!
KRAK!
Over 1,650 rounds were fired. Nearly every shot found a victim.

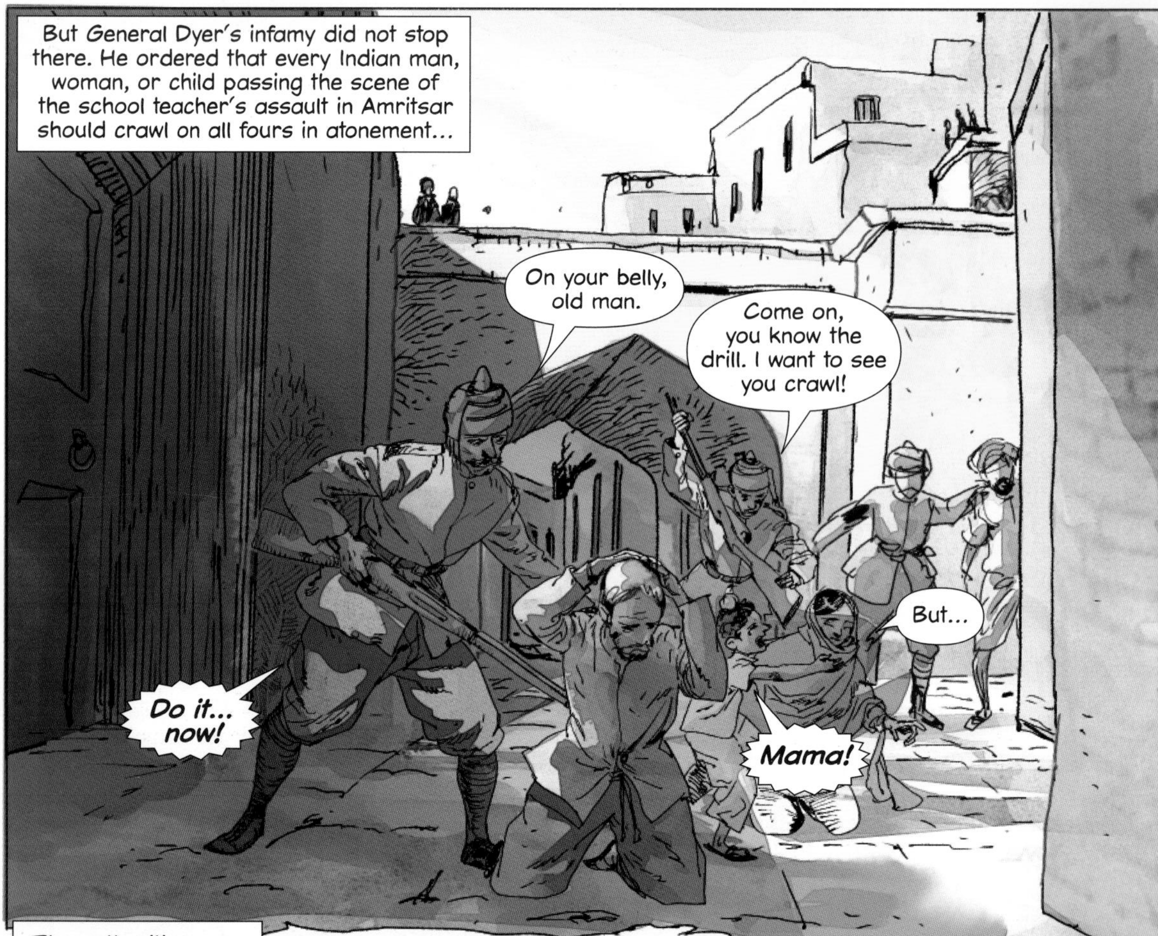
But General Dyer's infamy did not stop there. He ordered that every Indian man, woman, or child passing the scene of the school teacher's assault in Amritsar should crawl on all fours in atonement...
On your belly, old man.
Come on, you know the drill. I want to see you crawl!
But...
Do it... now!
Mama!

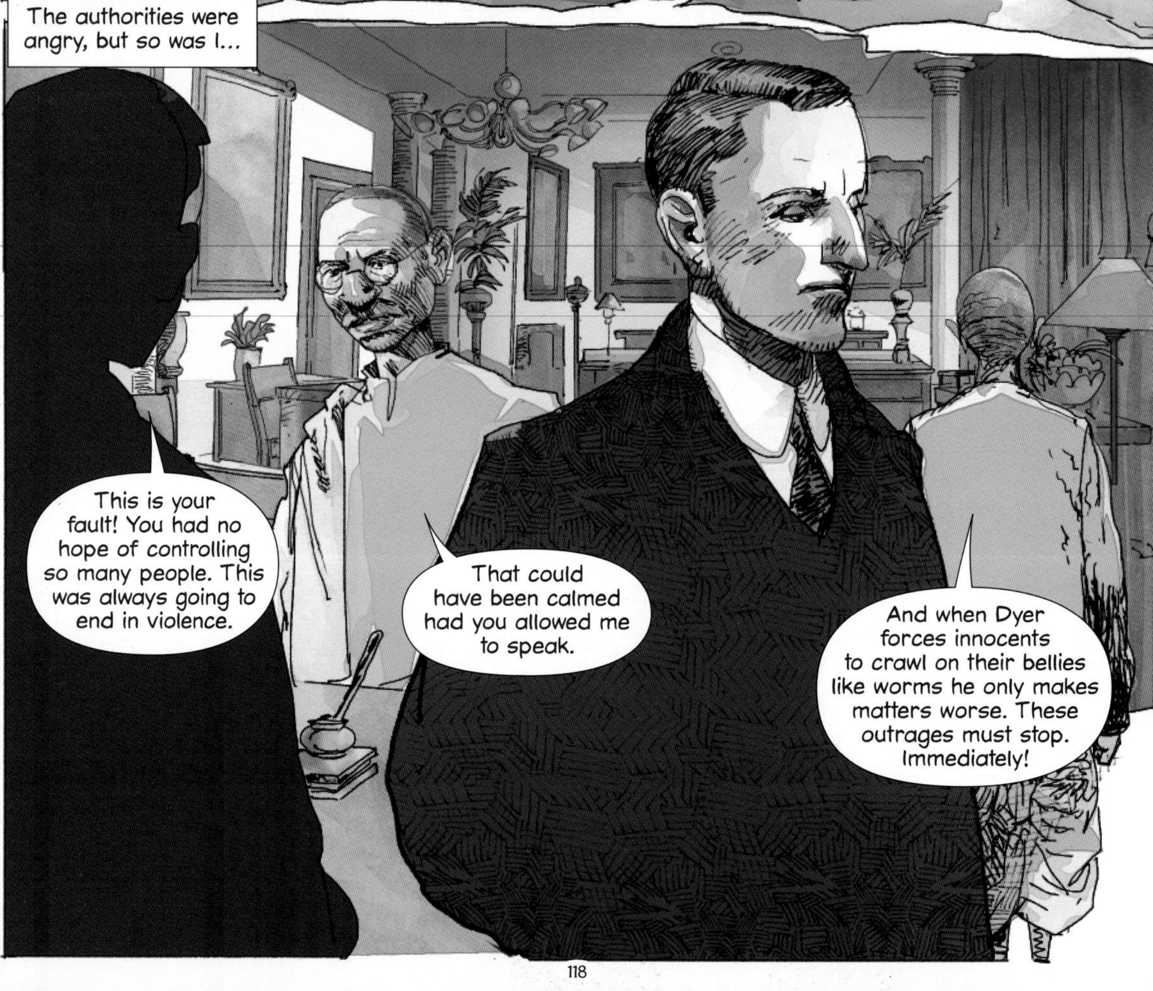
The authorities were angry, but so was I...
This is your fault! You had no hope of controlling so many people. This was always going to end in violence.
That could have been calmed had you allowed me to speak.
And when Dyer forces innocents to crawl on their bellies like worms he only makes matters worse. These outrages must stop. Immediately!

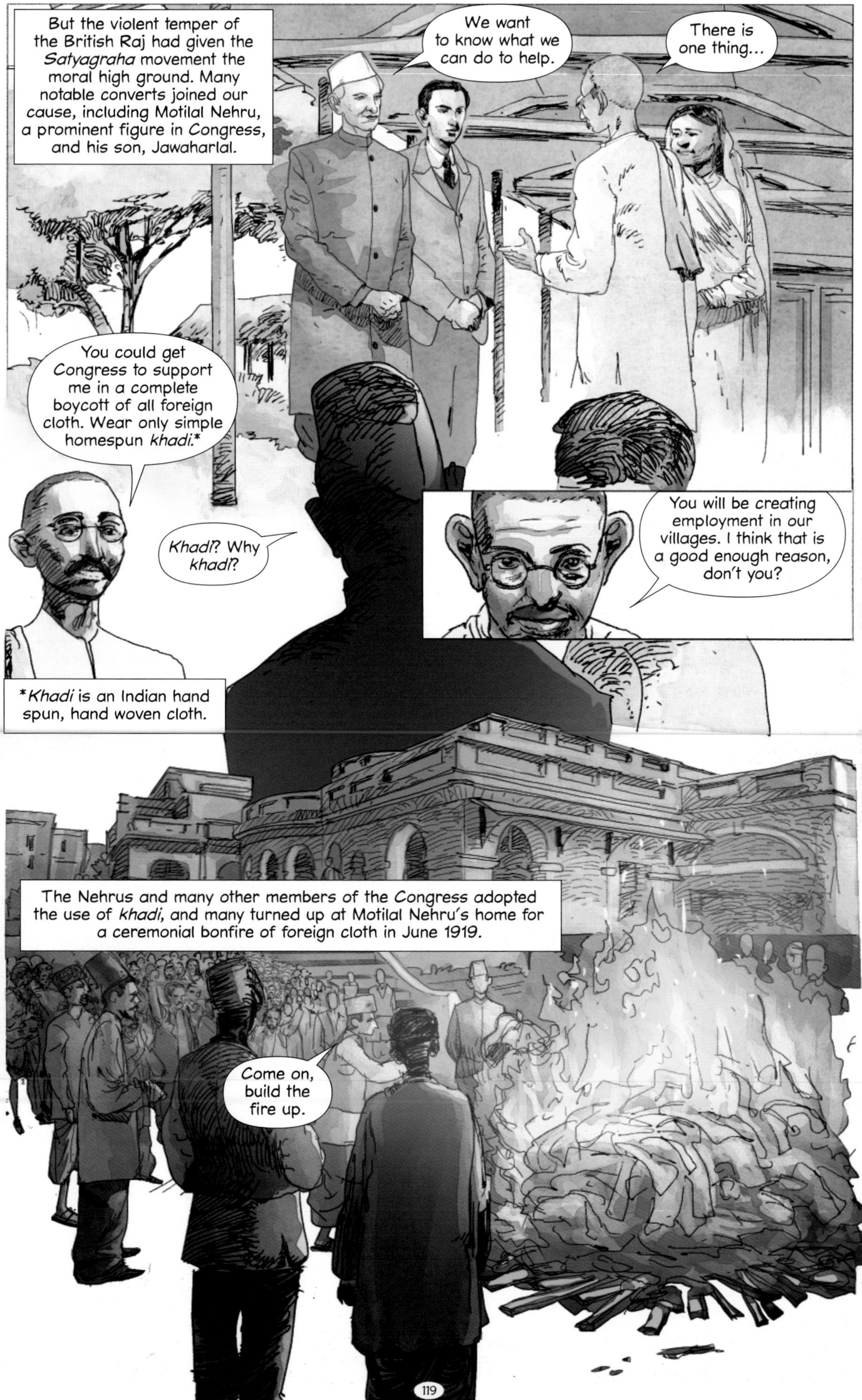
But the violent temper of the British Raj had given the *Satyagraha* movement the moral high ground. Many notable converts joined our cause, including Motilal Nehru, a prominent figure in Congress, and his son, Jawaharlal.
We want to know what we can do to help.
There is one thing...
You could get Congress to support me in a complete boycott of all foreign cloth. Wear only simple homespun *khadi*.*
Khadi? Why *khadi*?
You will be creating employment in our villages. I think that is a good enough reason, don't you?
**Khadi* is an Indian hand spun, hand woven cloth.
The Nehrus and many other members of the Congress adopted the use of *khadi*, and many turned up at Motilal Nehru's home for a ceremonial bonfire of foreign cloth in June 1919.
Come on, build the fire up.

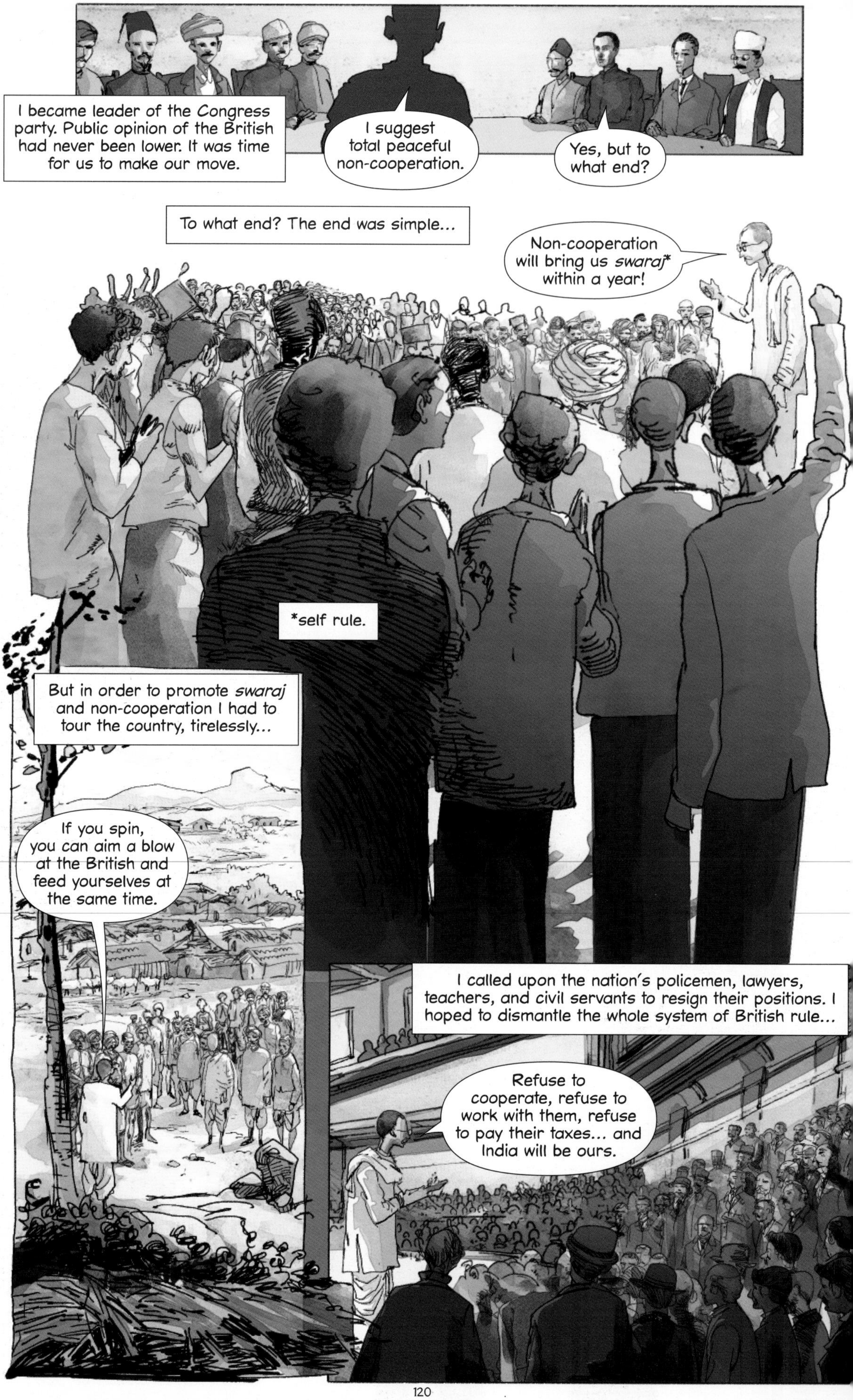
I became leader of the Congress party. Public opinion of the British had never been lower. It was time for us to make our move.
I suggest total peaceful non-cooperation.
Yes, but to what end?
To what end? The end was simple...
Non-cooperation will bring us *swaraj** within a year!
*self rule.
But in order to promote *swaraj* and non-cooperation I had to tour the country, tirelessly...
If you spin, you can aim a blow at the British and feed yourselves at the same time.
I called upon the nation's policemen, lawyers, teachers, and civil servants to resign their positions. I hoped to dismantle the whole system of British rule...
Refuse to cooperate, refuse to work with them, refuse to pay their taxes... and India will be ours.

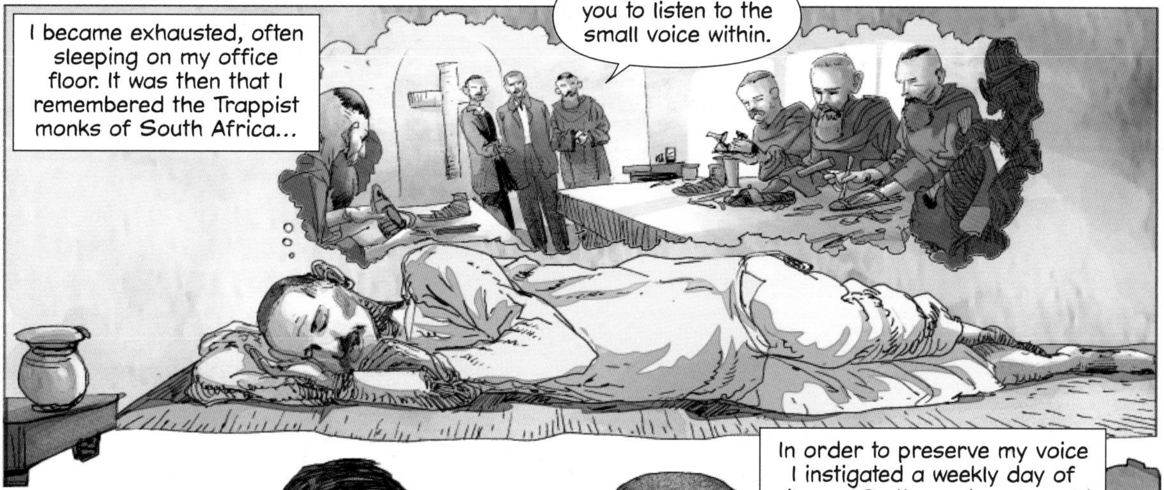
I became exhausted, often sleeping on my office floor. It was then that I remembered the Trappist monks of South Africa...
Silence allows you to listen to the small voice within.

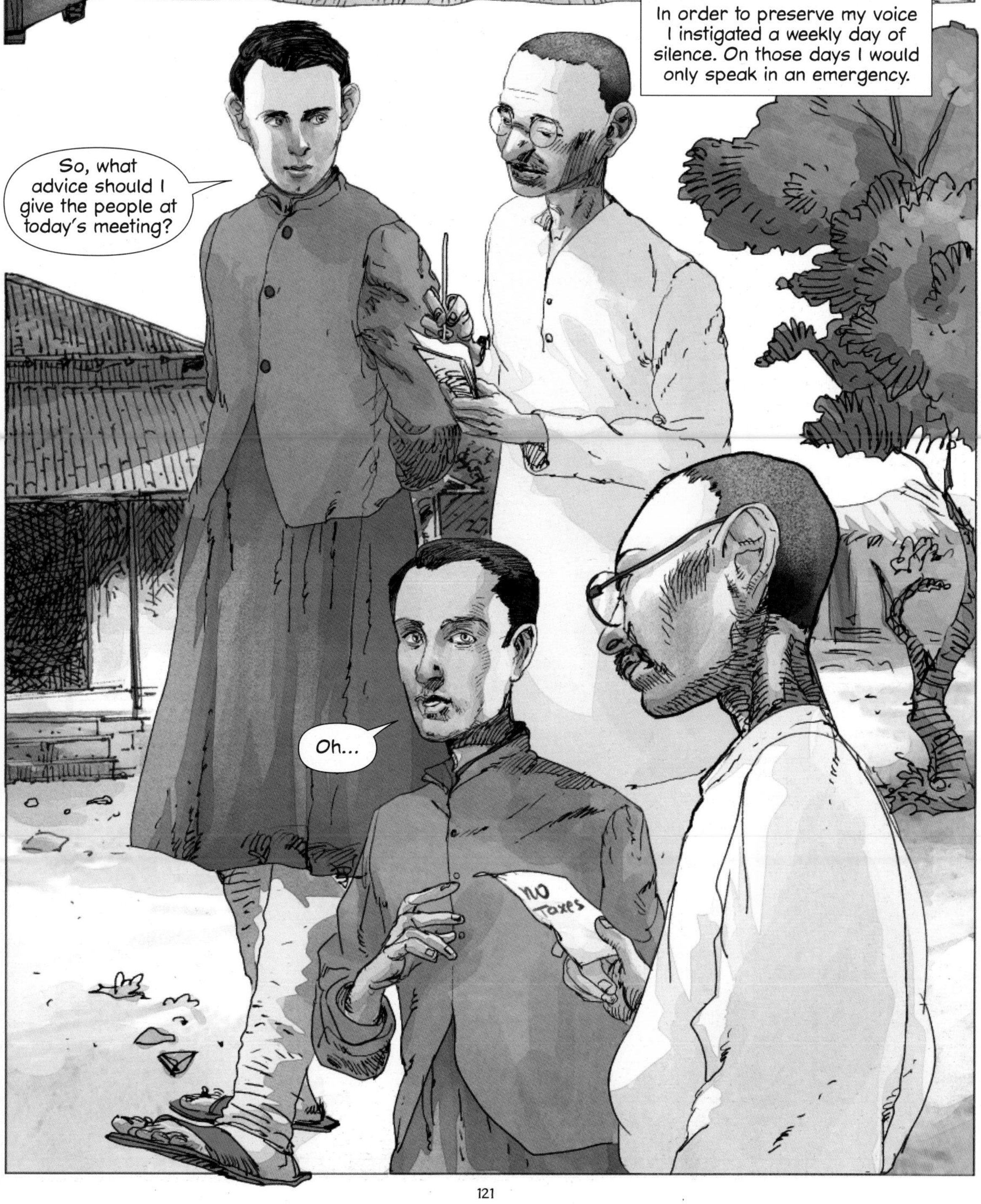
In order to preserve my voice I instigated a weekly day of silence. On those days I would only speak in an emergency.
So, what advice should I give the people at today's meeting?
Oh...
NO Taxes

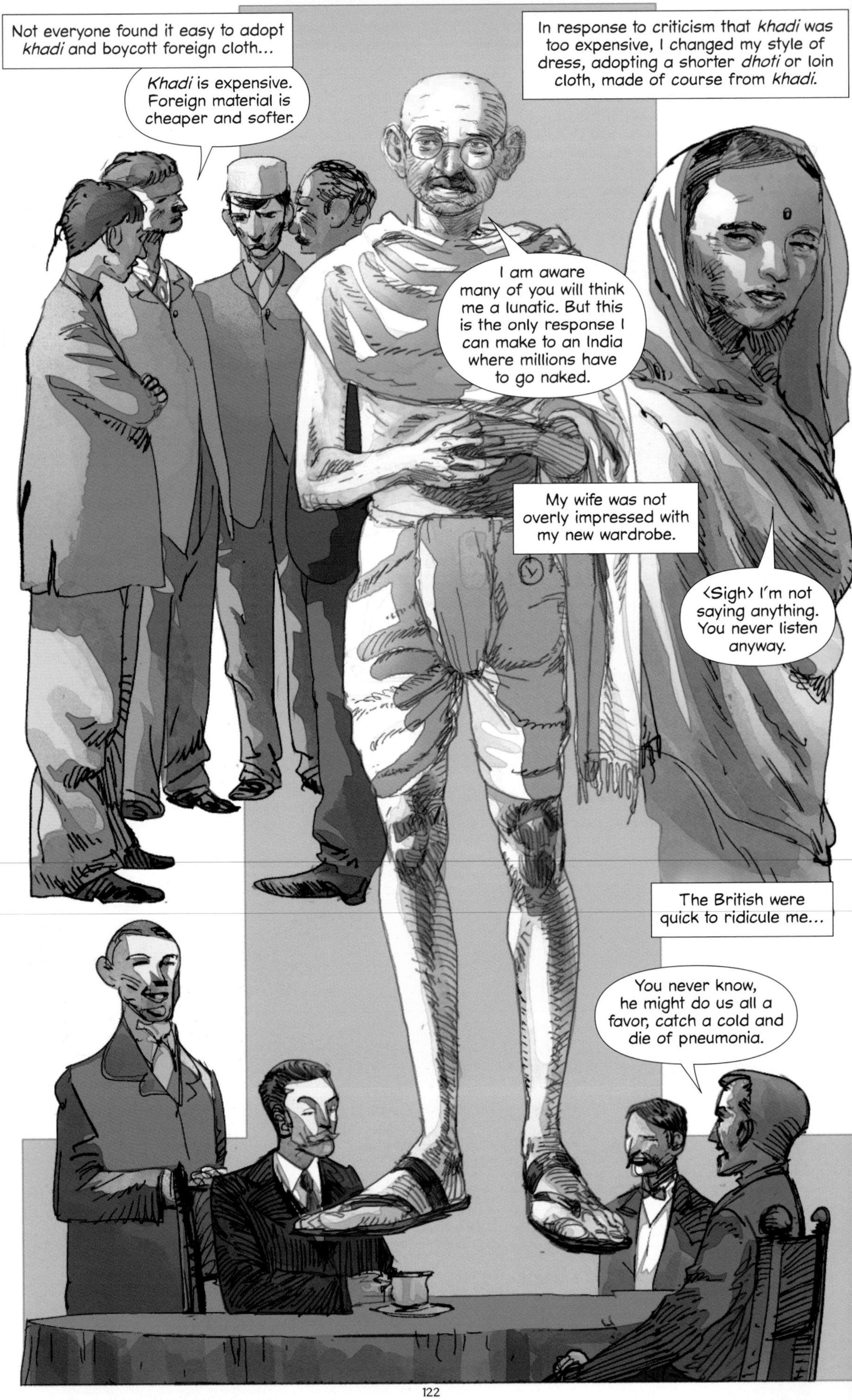

Not everyone found it easy to adopt *khadi* and boycott foreign cloth...
Khadi is expensive. Foreign material is cheaper and softer.
In response to criticism that *khadi* was too expensive, I changed my style of dress, adopting a shorter *dhoti* or loin cloth, made of course from *khadi.*
I am aware many of you will think me a lunatic. But this is the only response I can make to an India where millions have to go naked.
My wife was not overly impressed with my new wardrobe.
<Sigh> I'm not saying anything. You never listen anyway.
The British were quick to ridicule me...
You never know, he might do us all a favor, catch a cold and die of pneumonia.

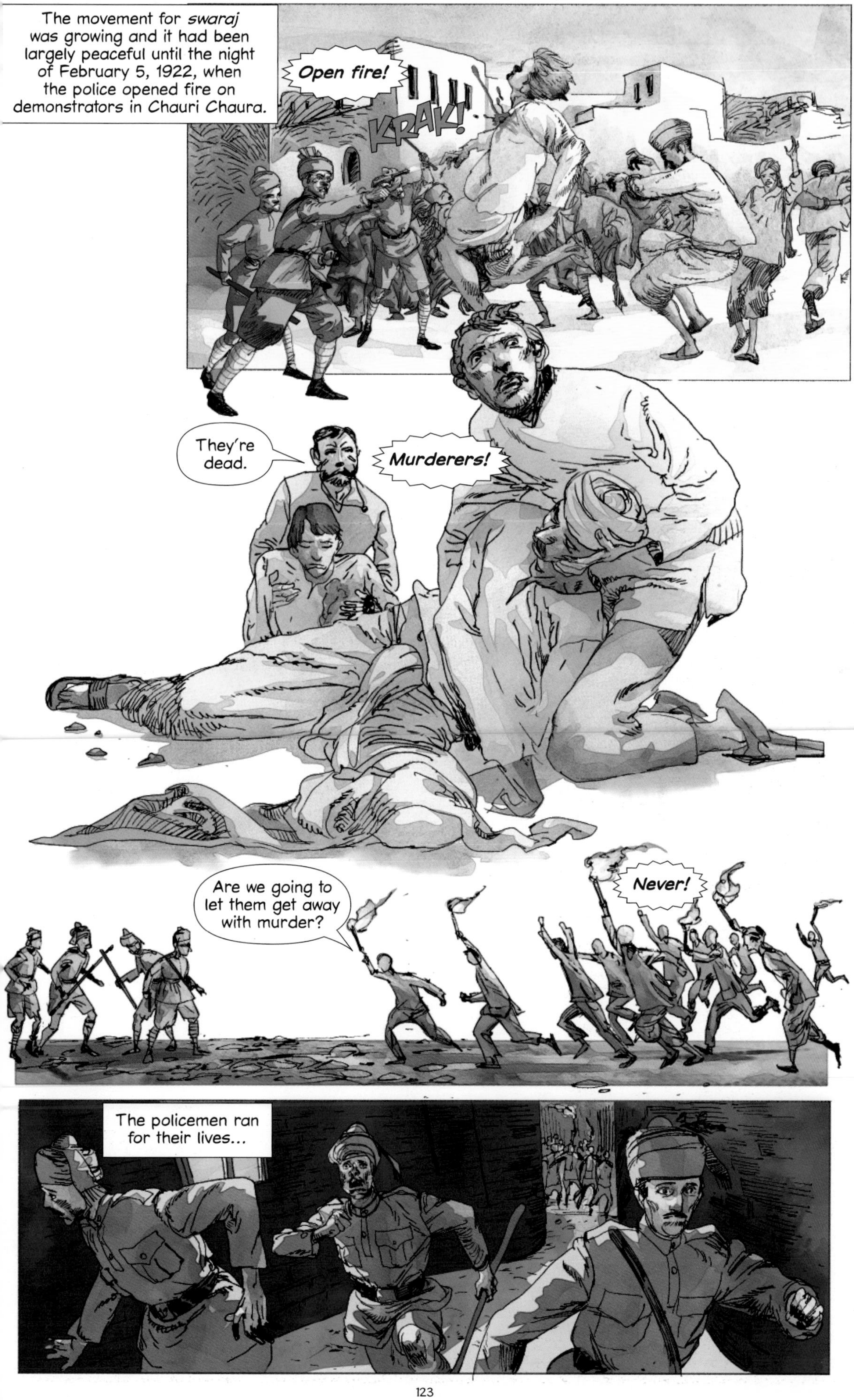
The movement for *swaraj* was growing and it had been largely peaceful until the night of February 5, 1922, when the police opened fire on demonstrators in Chauri Chaura.
Open fire!
KRAK!
They're dead.
Murderers!
Are we going to let them get away with murder?
Never!
The policemen ran for their lives...

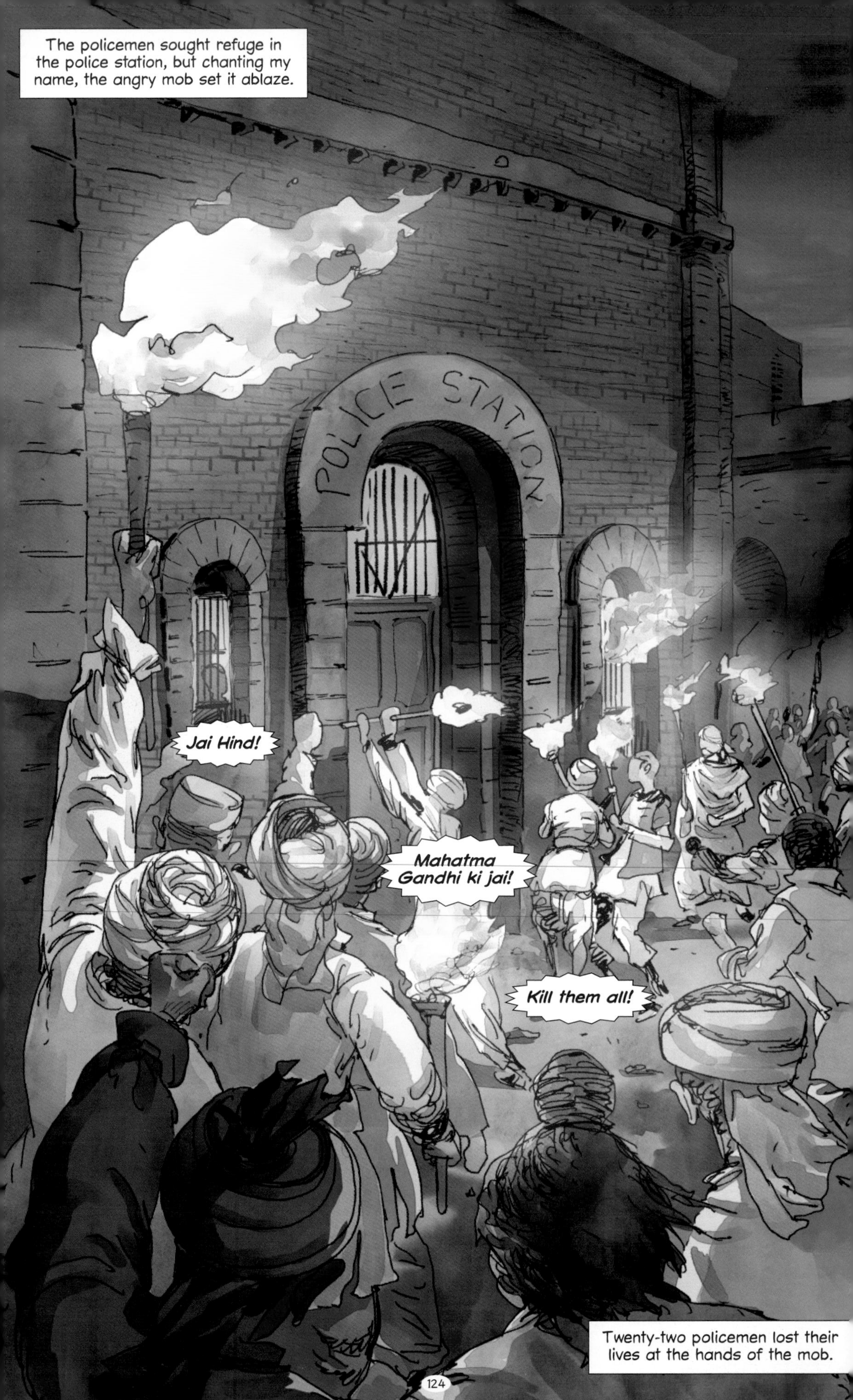
The policemen sought refuge in the police station, but chanting my name, the angry mob set it ablaze.
POLICE STATION
Jai Hind!
Mahatma Gandhi ki jai!
Kill them all!
Twenty-two policemen lost their lives at the hands of the mob.

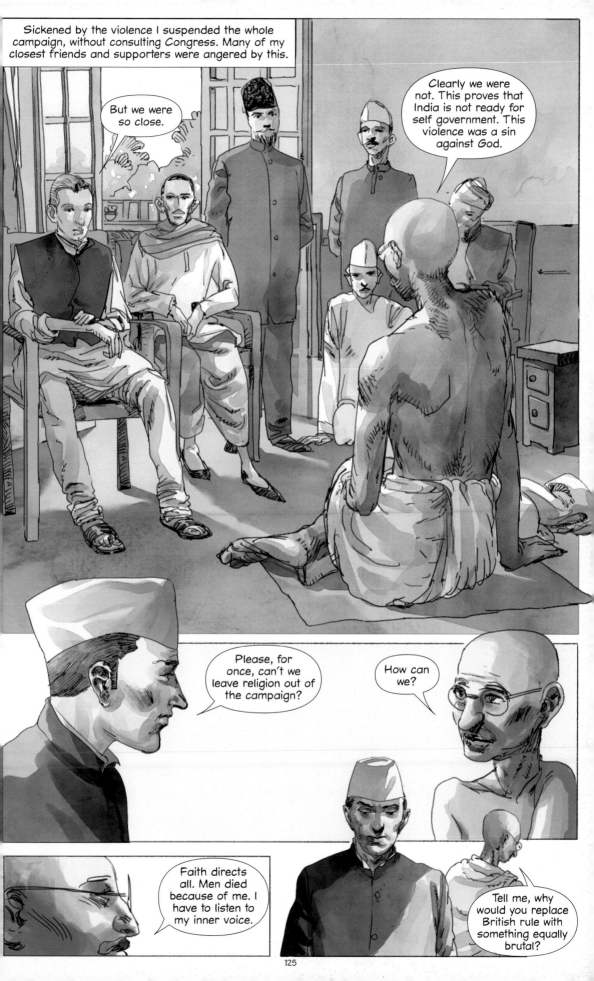

Sickened by the violence I suspended the whole campaign, without consulting Congress. Many of my closest friends and supporters were angered by this.

But we were so close.

Clearly we were not. This proves that India is not ready for self government. This violence was a sin against God.

Please, for once, can't we leave religion out of the campaign?

How can we?

Faith directs all. Men died because of me. I have to listen to my inner voice.

Tell me, why would you replace British rule with something equally brutal?

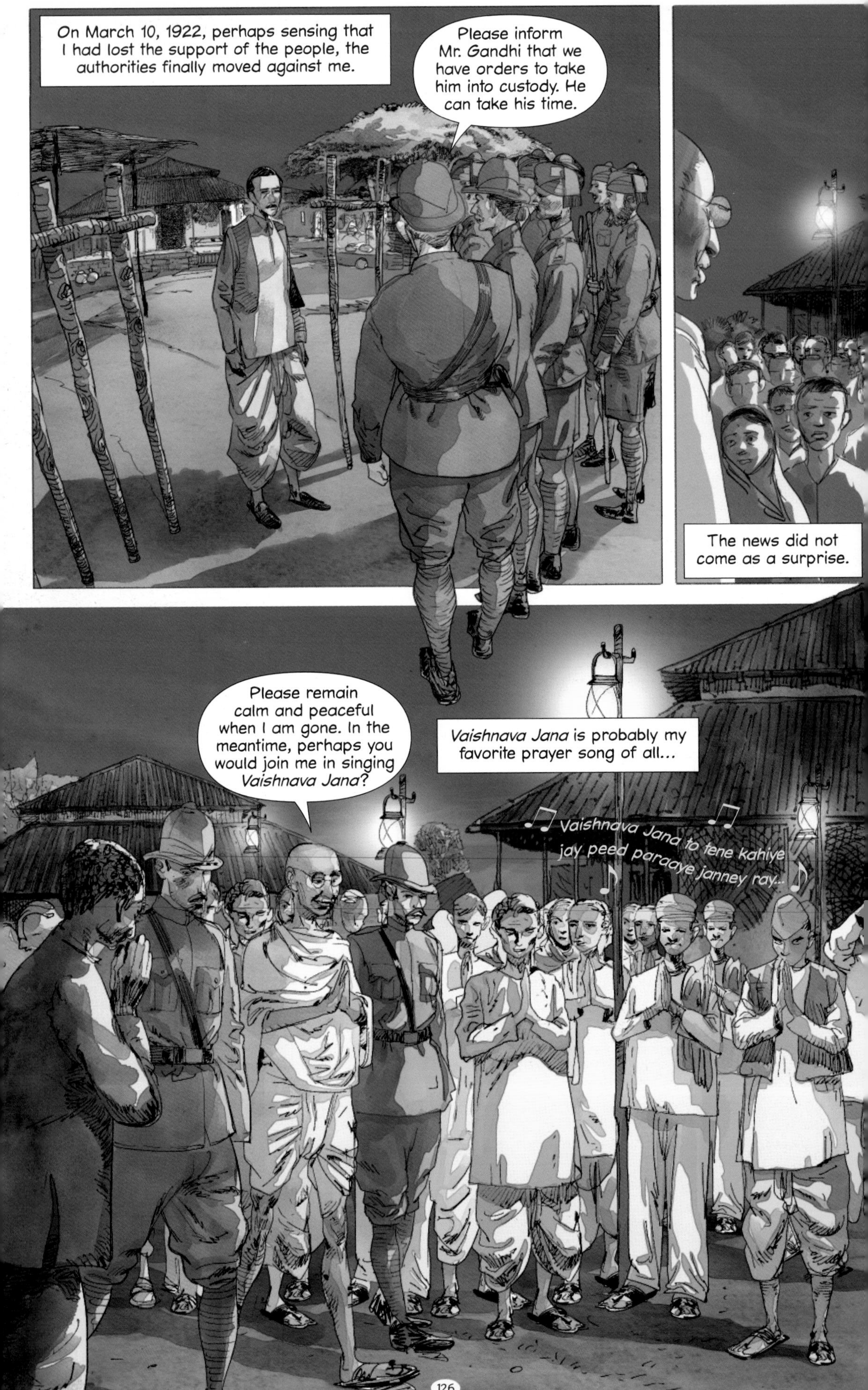
On March 10, 1922, perhaps sensing that I had lost the support of the people, the authorities finally moved against me.
Please inform Mr. Gandhi that we have orders to take him into custody. He can take his time.
The news did not come as a surprise.
Please remain calm and peaceful when I am gone. In the meantime, perhaps you would join me in singing *Vaishnava Jana*?
Vaishnava Jana is probably my favorite prayer song of all...
Vaishnava Jana to tene kahiye jay peed paraaye janney ray...

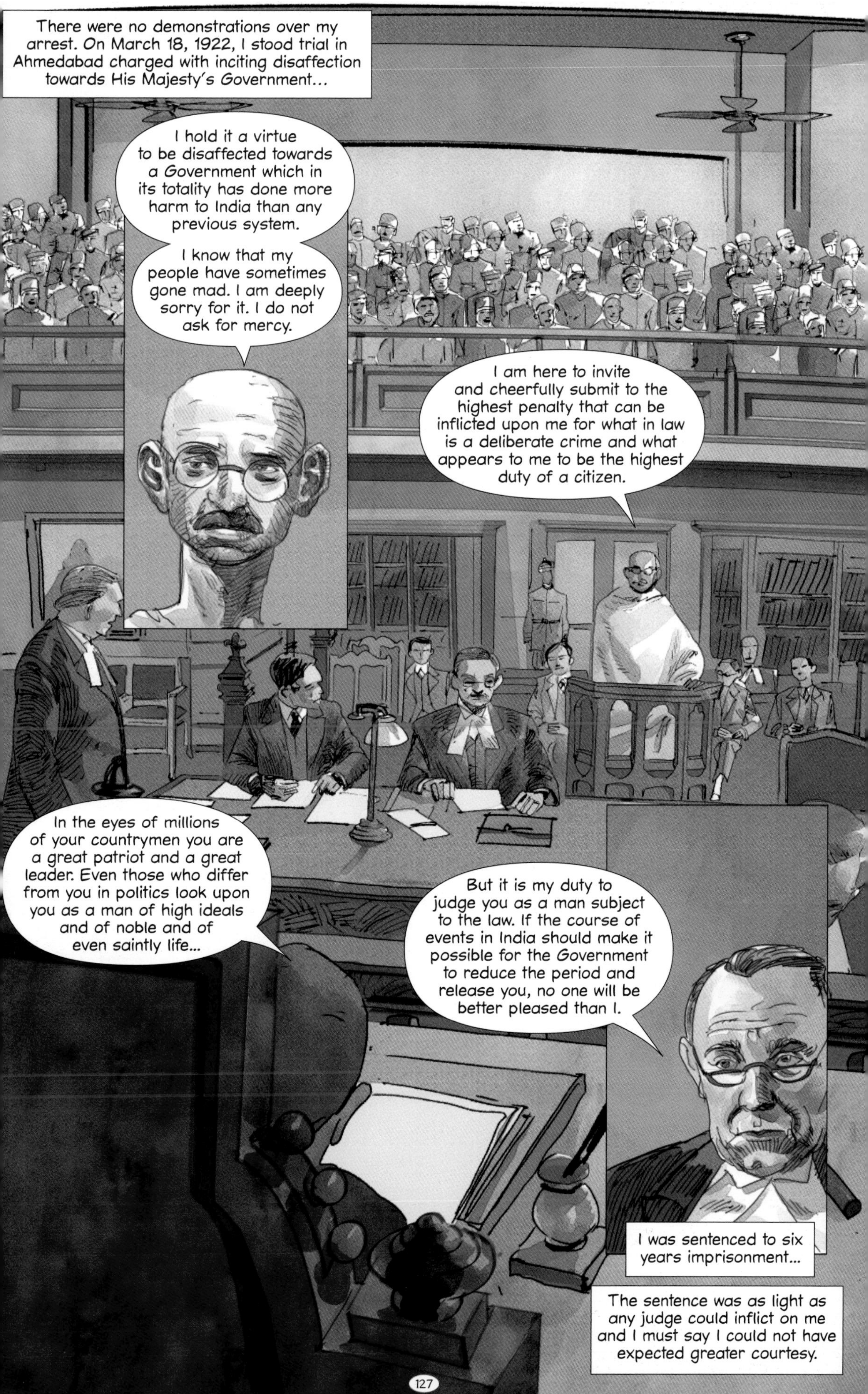
There were no demonstrations over my arrest. On March 18, 1922, I stood trial in Ahmedabad charged with inciting disaffection towards His Majesty's Government...
I hold it a virtue to be disaffected towards a Government which in its totality has done more harm to India than any previous system.
I know that my people have sometimes gone mad. I am deeply sorry for it. I do not ask for mercy.
I am here to invite and cheerfully submit to the highest penalty that can be inflicted upon me for what in law is a deliberate crime and what appears to me to be the highest duty of a citizen.
In the eyes of millions of your countrymen you are a great patriot and a great leader. Even those who differ from you in politics look upon you as a man of high ideals and of noble and of even saintly life...
But it is my duty to judge you as a man subject to the law. If the course of events in India should make it possible for the Government to reduce the period and release you, no one will be better pleased than I.
I was sentenced to six years imprisonment...
The sentence was as light as any judge could inflict on me and I must say I could not have expected greater courtesy.

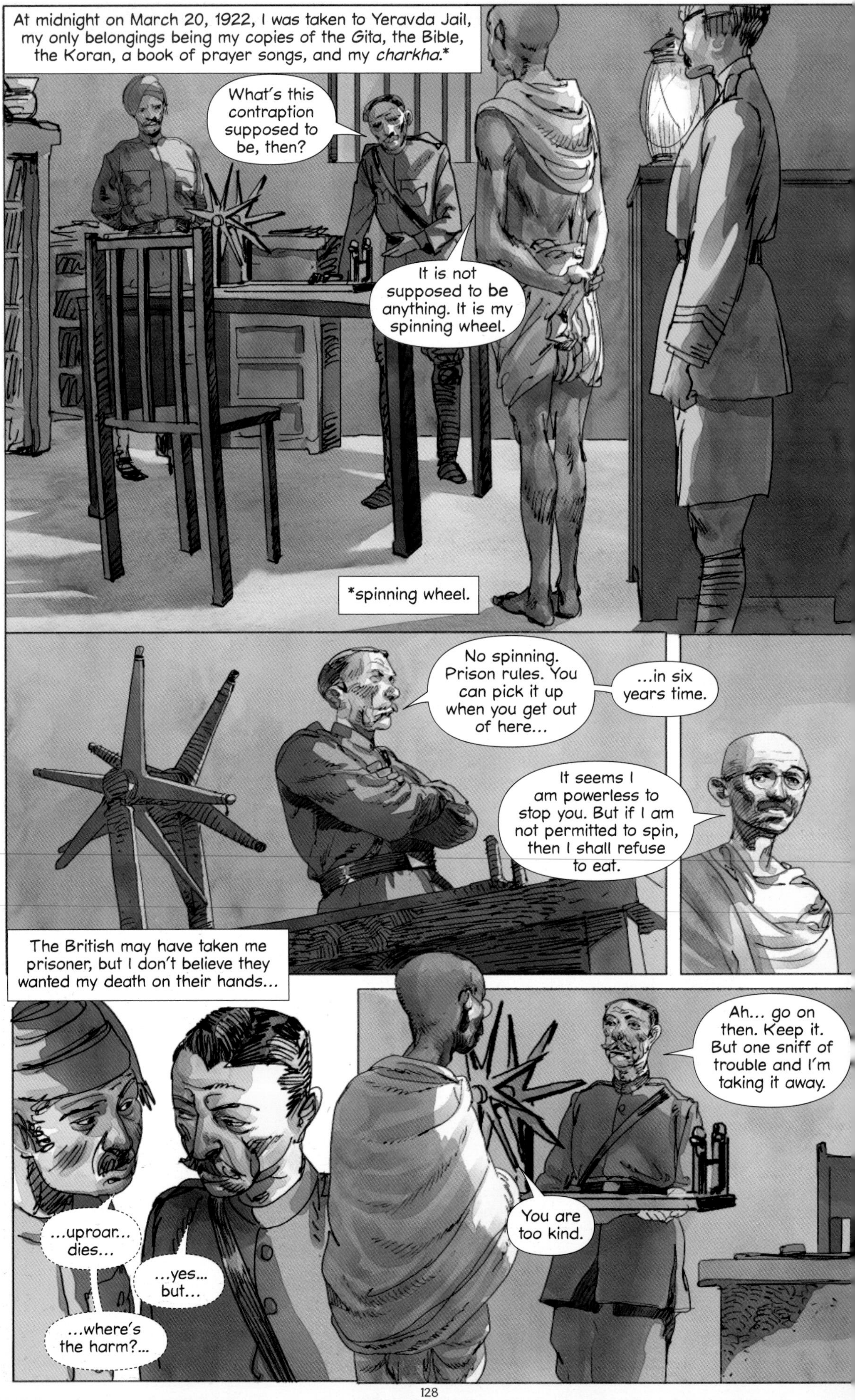

At midnight on March 20, 1922, I was taken to Yeravda Jail, my only belongings being my copies of the *Gita*, the Bible, the Koran, a book of prayer songs, and my *charkha*.*
What's this contraption supposed to be, then?
It is not supposed to be anything. It is my spinning wheel.
*spinning wheel.
No spinning. Prison rules. You can pick it up when you get out of here...
...in six years time.
It seems I am powerless to stop you. But if I am not permitted to spin, then I shall refuse to eat.
The British may have taken me prisoner, but I don't believe they wanted my death on their hands...
...uproar... dies...
...yes... but...
...where's the harm?...
Ah... go on then. Keep it. But one sniff of trouble and I'm taking it away.
You are too kind.

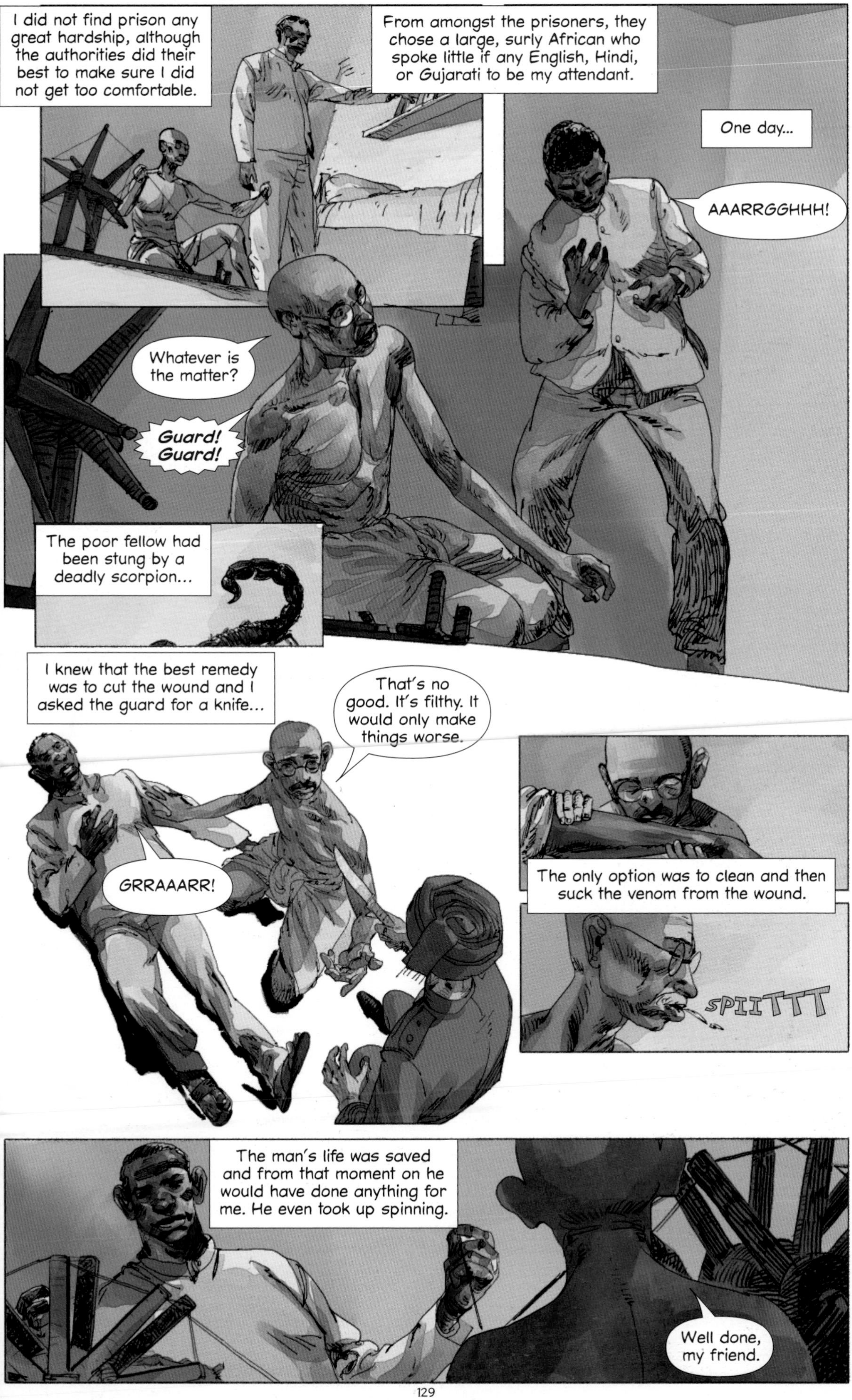
I did not find prison any great hardship, although the authorities did their best to make sure I did not get too comfortable.
From amongst the prisoners, they chose a large, surly African who spoke little if any English, Hindi, or Gujarati to be my attendant.
One day...
AAARRGGHHH!
Whatever is the matter?
Guard! Guard!
The poor fellow had been stung by a deadly scorpion...
I knew that the best remedy was to cut the wound and I asked the guard for a knife...
That's no good. It's filthy. It would only make things worse.
GRRAAARR!
The only option was to clean and then suck the venom from the wound.
SPIITTT
The man's life was saved and from that moment on he would have done anything for me. He even took up spinning.
Well done, my friend.

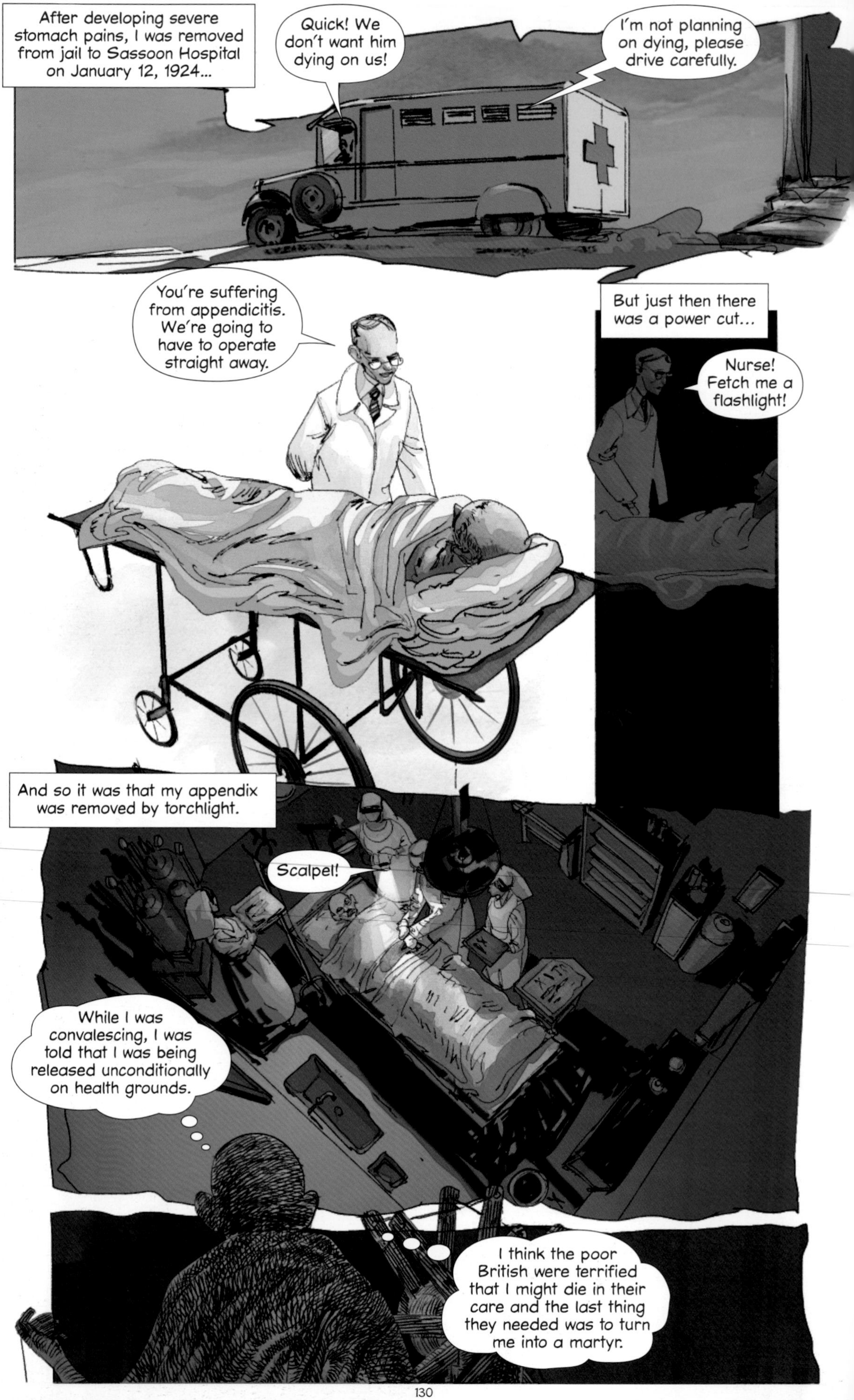
After developing severe stomach pains, I was removed from jail to Sassoon Hospital on January 12, 1924...
Quick! We don't want him dying on us!
I'm not planning on dying, please drive carefully.
You're suffering from appendicitis. We're going to have to operate straight away.
But just then there was a power cut...
Nurse! Fetch me a flashlight!
And so it was that my appendix was removed by torchlight.
Scalpel!
While I was convalescing, I was told that I was being released unconditionally on health grounds.
I think the poor British were terrified that I might die in their care and the last thing they needed was to turn me into a martyr.

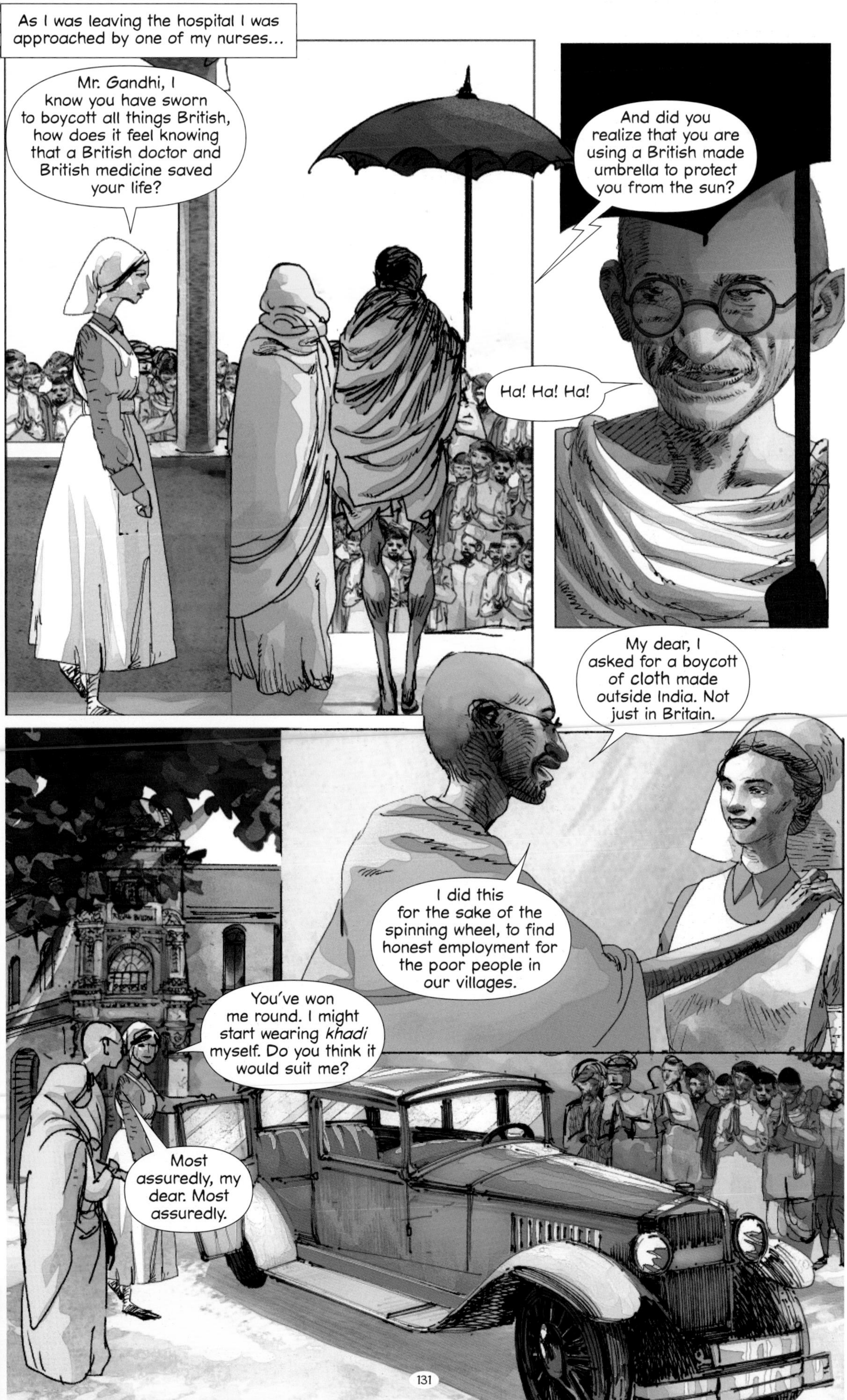

As I was leaving the hospital I was approached by one of my nurses...
Mr. Gandhi, I know you have sworn to boycott all things British, how does it feel knowing that a British doctor and British medicine saved your life?
And did you realize that you are using a British made umbrella to protect you from the sun?
Ha! Ha! Ha!
My dear, I asked for a boycott of cloth made outside India. Not just in Britain.
I did this for the sake of the spinning wheel, to find honest employment for the poor people in our villages.
You've won me round. I might start wearing *khadi* myself. Do you think it would suit me?
Most assuredly, my dear. Most assuredly.

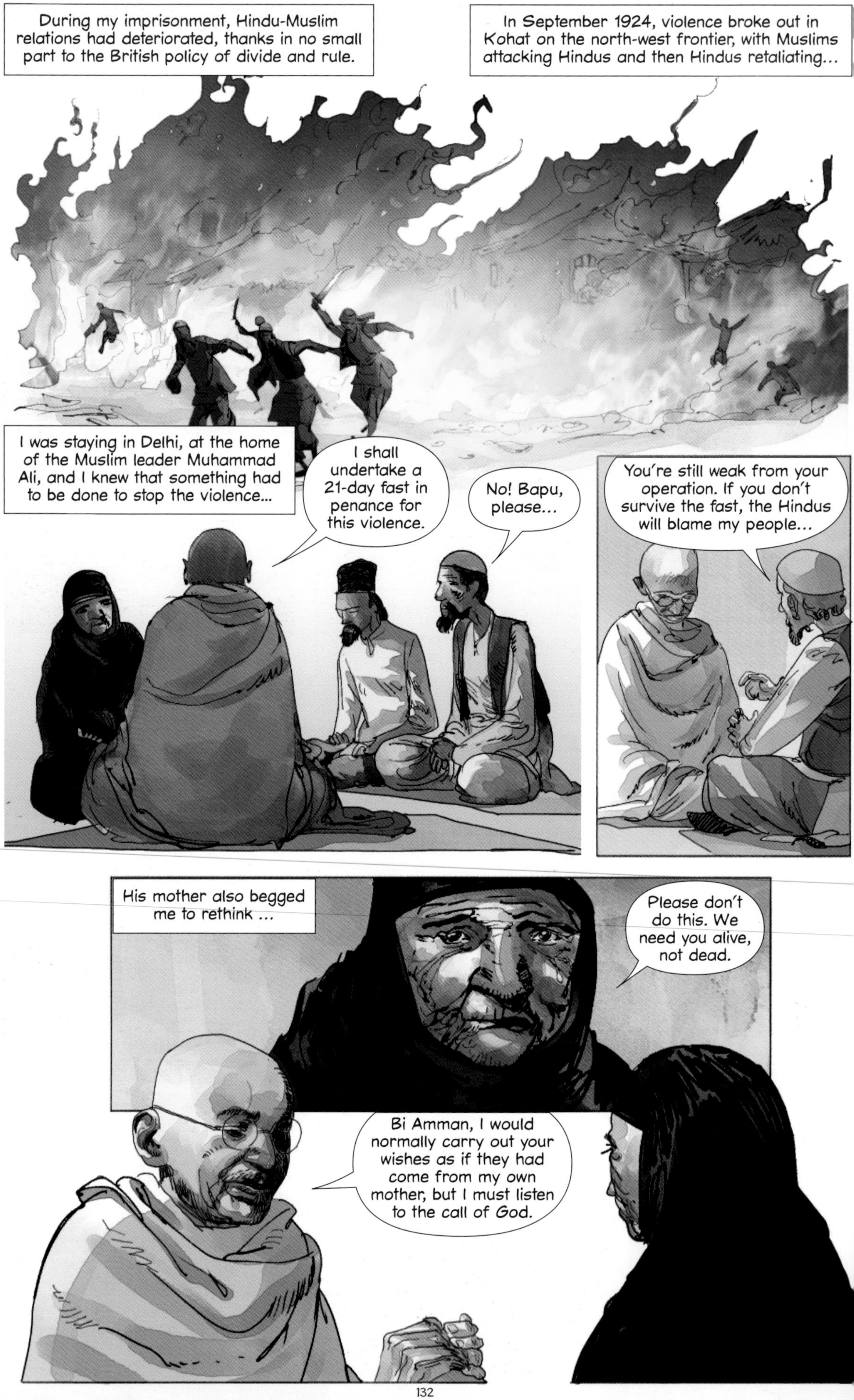
During my imprisonment, Hindu-Muslim relations had deteriorated, thanks in no small part to the British policy of divide and rule.
In September 1924, violence broke out in Kohat on the north-west frontier, with Muslims attacking Hindus and then Hindus retaliating...
I was staying in Delhi, at the home of the Muslim leader Muhammad Ali, and I knew that something had to be done to stop the violence...
I shall undertake a 21-day fast in penance for this violence.
No! Bapu, please...
You're still weak from your operation. If you don't survive the fast, the Hindus will blame my people...
His mother also begged me to rethink ...
Please don't do this. We need you alive, not dead.
Bi Amman, I would normally carry out your wishes as if they had come from my own mother, but I must listen to the call of God.

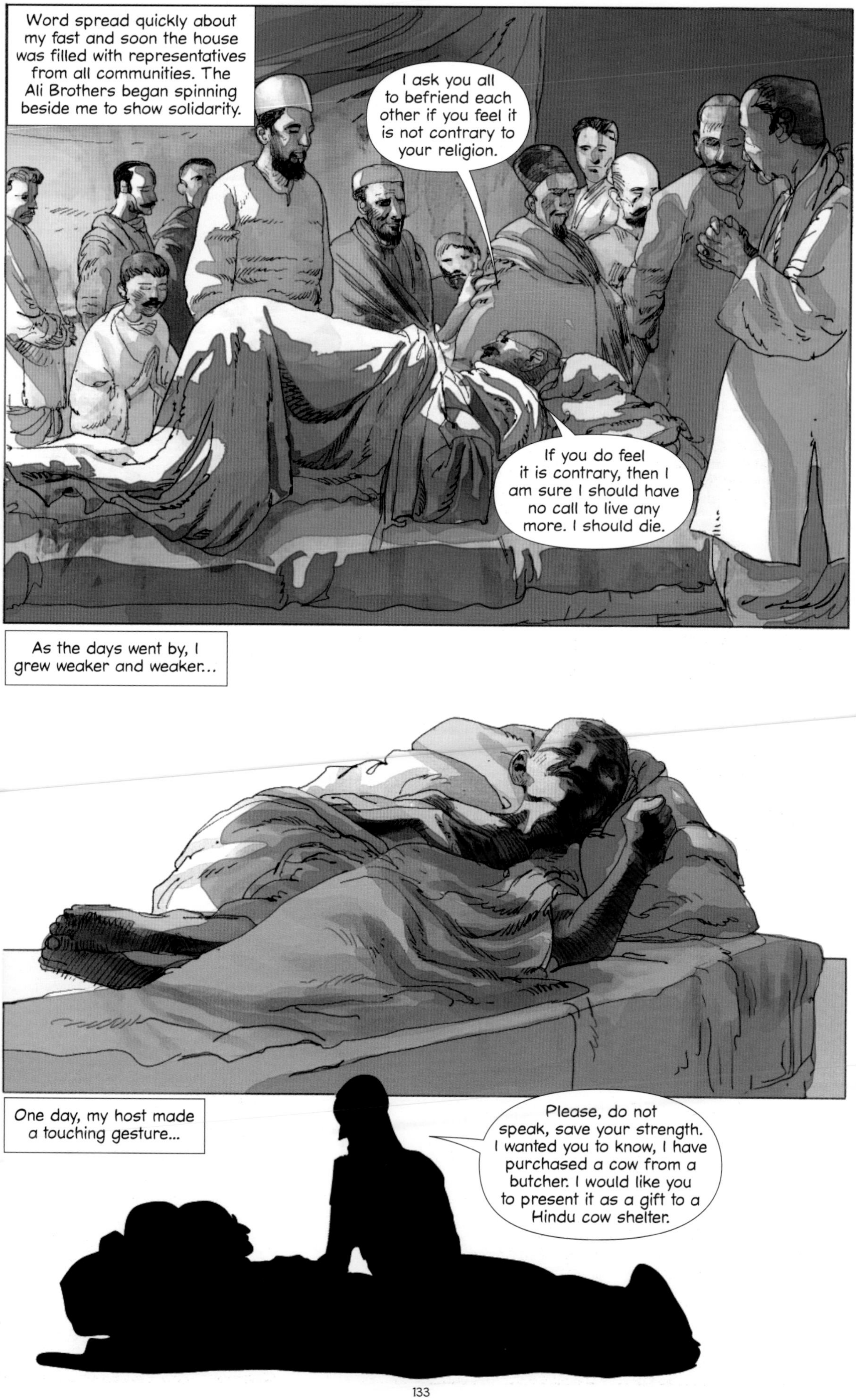
Word spread quickly about my fast and soon the house was filled with representatives from all communities. The Ali Brothers began spinning beside me to show solidarity.
I ask you all to befriend each other if you feel it is not contrary to your religion.
If you do feel it is contrary, then I am sure I should have no call to live any more. I should die.
As the days went by, I grew weaker and weaker...
One day, my host made a touching gesture...
Please, do not speak, save your strength. I wanted you to know, I have purchased a cow from a butcher. I would like you to present it as a gift to a Hindu cow shelter.

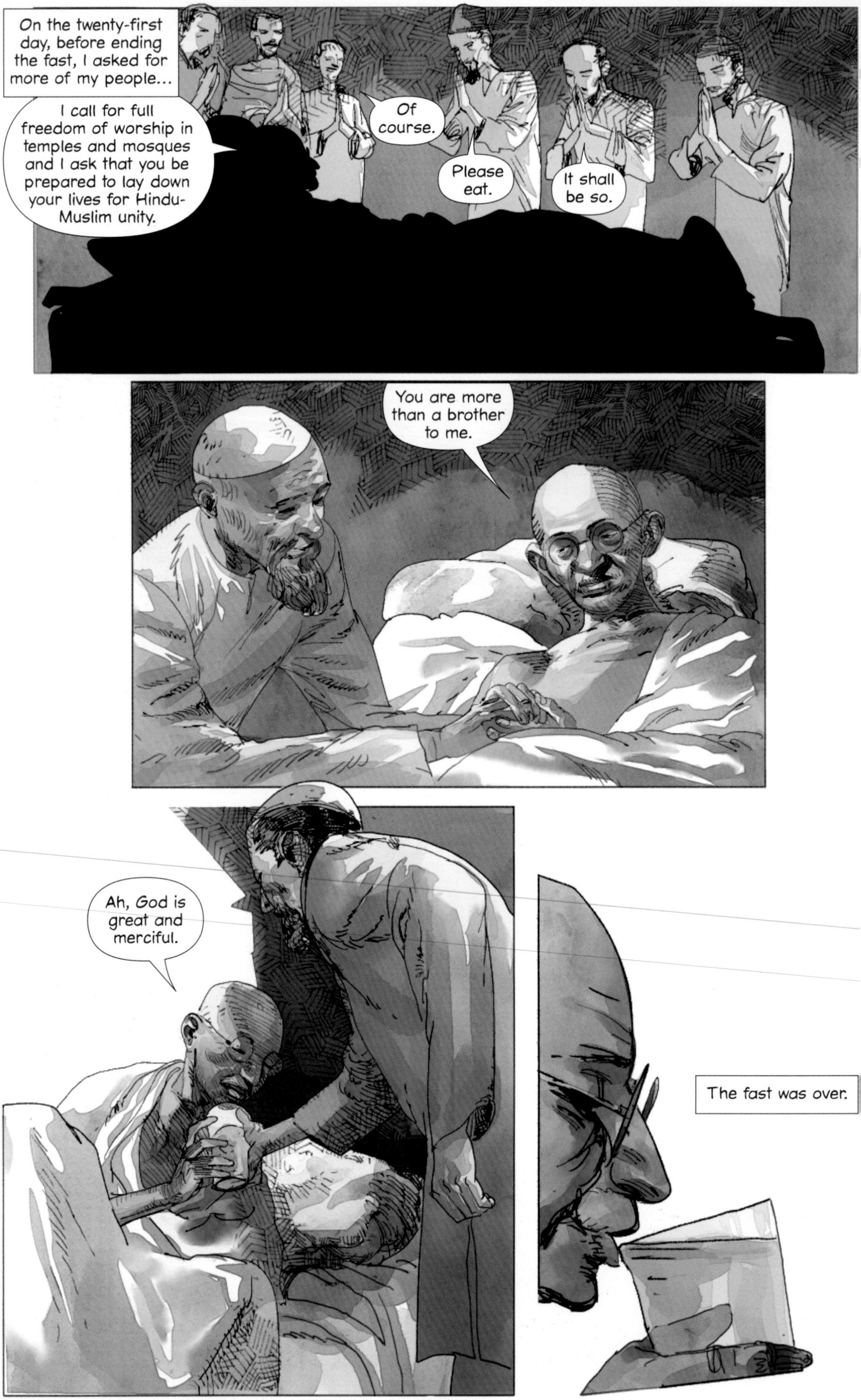

On the twenty-first day, before ending the fast, I asked for more of my people...
I call for full freedom of worship in temples and mosques and I ask that you be prepared to lay down your lives for Hindu-Muslim unity.
Of course.
Please eat.
It shall be so.
You are more than a brother to me.
Ah, God is great and merciful.
The fast was over.

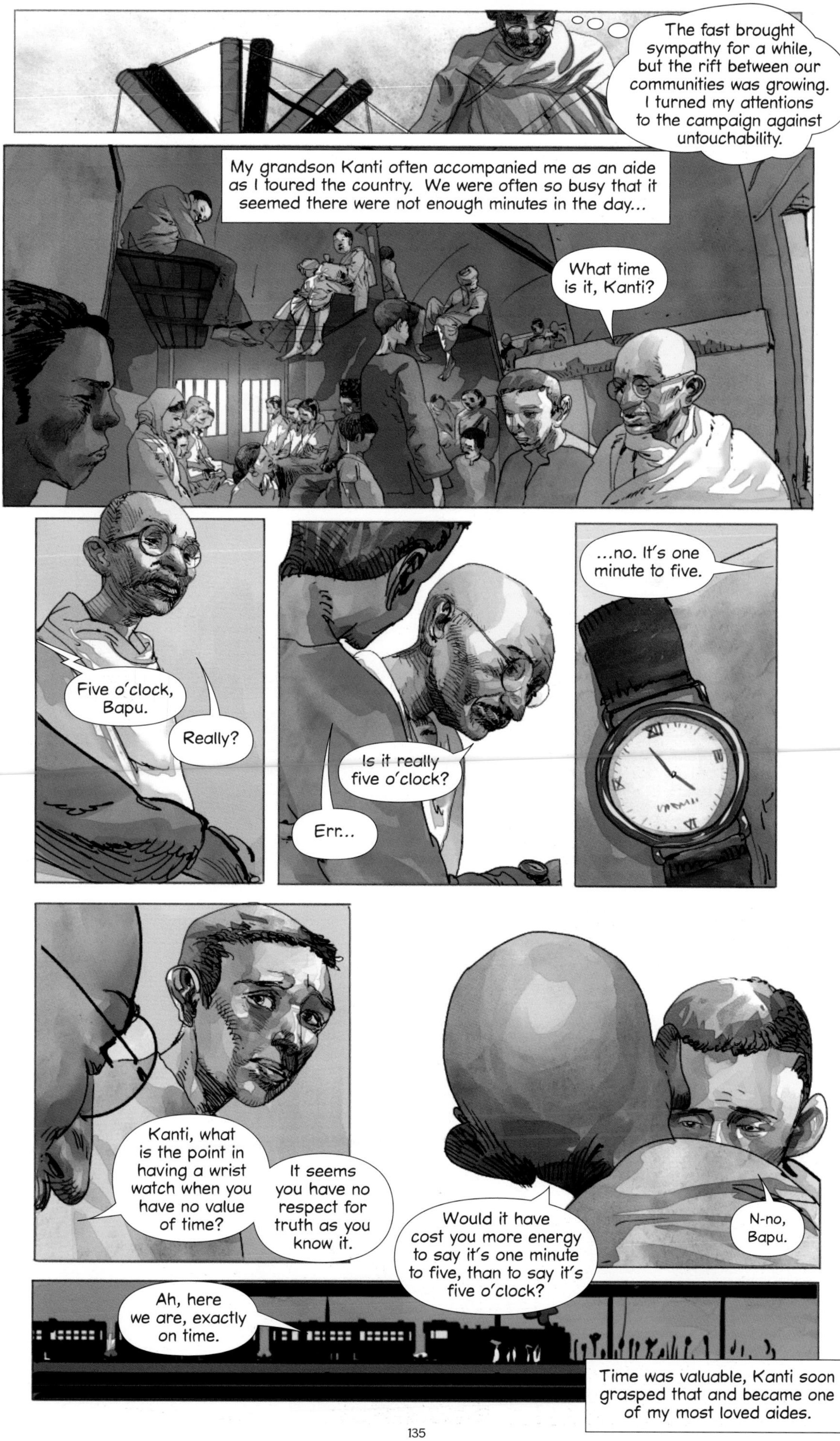

The fast brought sympathy for a while, but the rift between our communities was growing. I turned my attentions to the campaign against untouchability.
My grandson Kanti often accompanied me as an aide as I toured the country. We were often so busy that it seemed there were not enough minutes in the day...
What time is it, Kanti?
Five o'clock, Bapu.
Really?
Is it really five o'clock?
Err...
...no. It's one minute to five.
Kanti, what is the point in having a wrist watch when you have no value of time?
It seems you have no respect for truth as you know it.
Would it have cost you more energy to say it's one minute to five, than to say it's five o'clock?
N-no, Bapu.
Ah, here we are, exactly on time.
Time was valuable, Kanti soon grasped that and became one of my most loved aides.

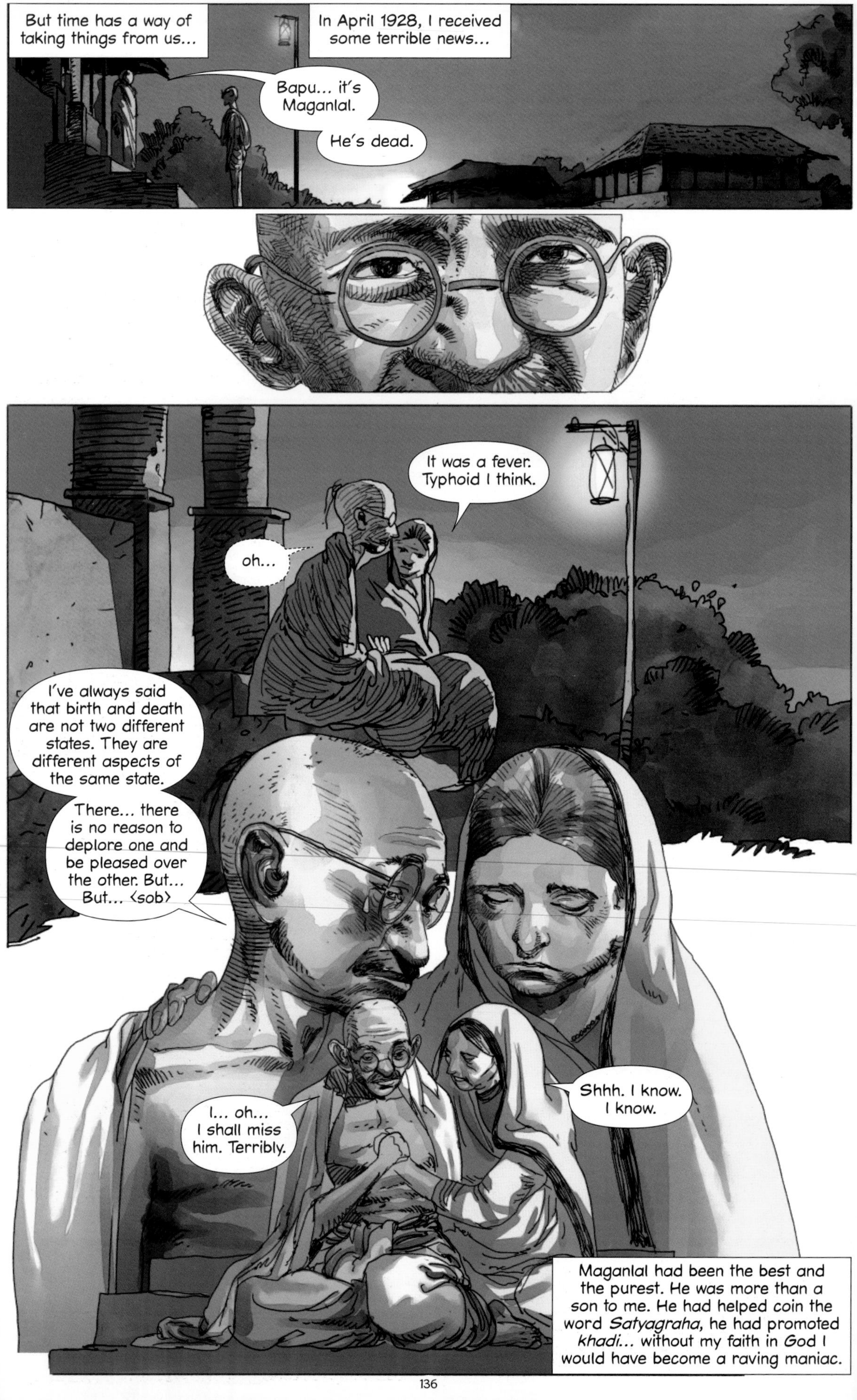

But time has a way of taking things from us...
In April 1928, I received some terrible news...
Bapu... it's Maganlal.
He's dead.
It was a fever. Typhoid I think.
oh...
I've always said that birth and death are not two different states. They are different aspects of the same state.
There... there is no reason to deplore one and be pleased over the other. But... But... <sob>
I... oh... I shall miss him. Terribly.
Shhh. I know. I know.
Maganlal had been the best and the purest. He was more than a son to me. He had helped coin the word *Satyagraha*, he had promoted *khadi*... without my faith in God I would have become a raving maniac.

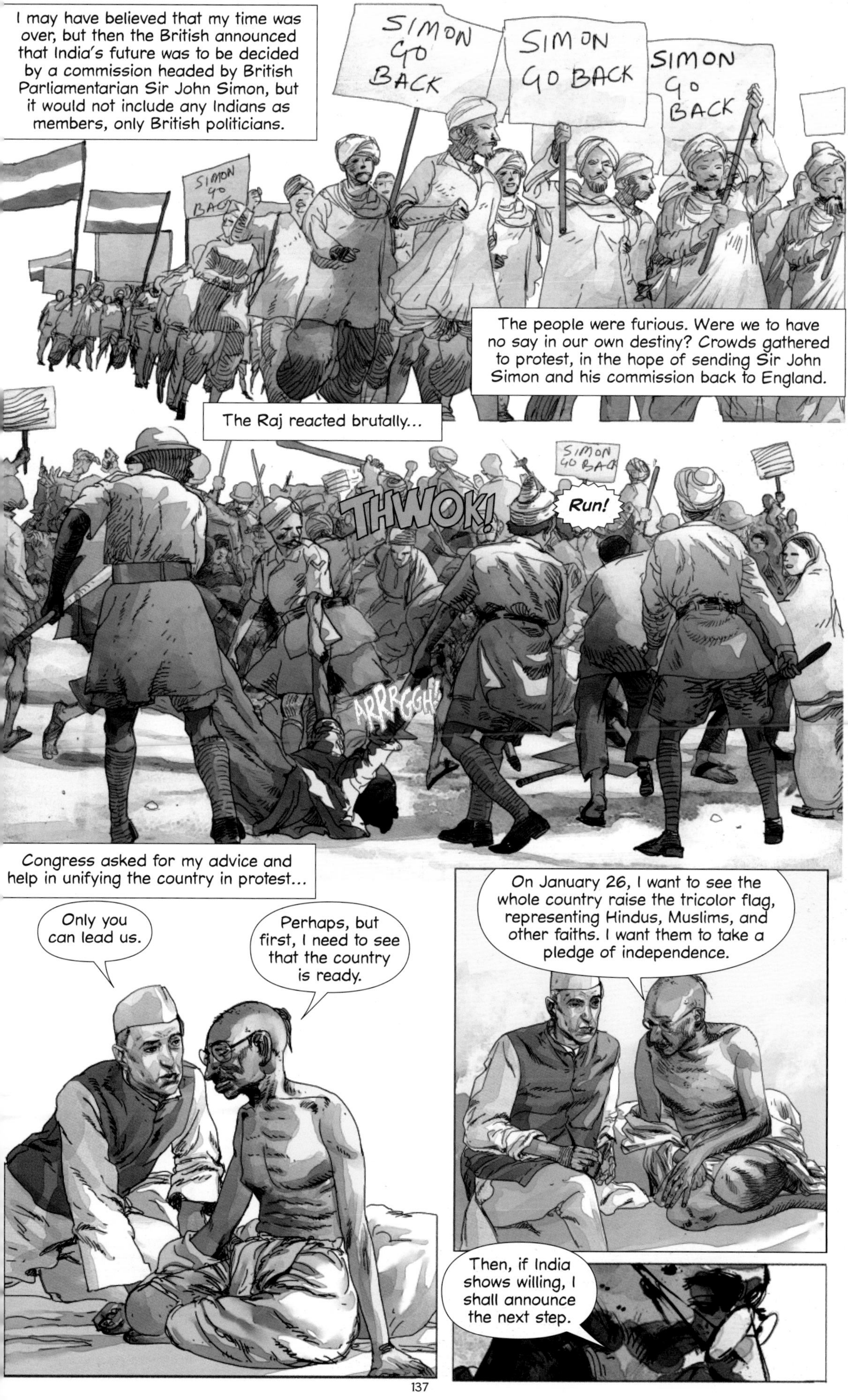
I may have believed that my time was over, but then the British announced that India's future was to be decided by a commission headed by British Parliamentarian Sir John Simon, but it would not include any Indians as members, only British politicians.
SIMON GO BACK
SIMON GO BACK
SIMON GO BACK
SIMON GO BACK
The people were furious. Were we to have no say in our own destiny? Crowds gathered to protest, in the hope of sending Sir John Simon and his commission back to England.
The Raj reacted brutally...
SIMON GO BACK
THWOK!
Run!
ARRRGGH!
Congress asked for my advice and help in unifying the country in protest...
Only you can lead us.
Perhaps, but first, I need to see that the country is ready.
On January 26, I want to see the whole country raise the tricolor flag, representing Hindus, Muslims, and other faiths. I want them to take a pledge of independence.
Then, if India shows willing, I shall announce the next step.

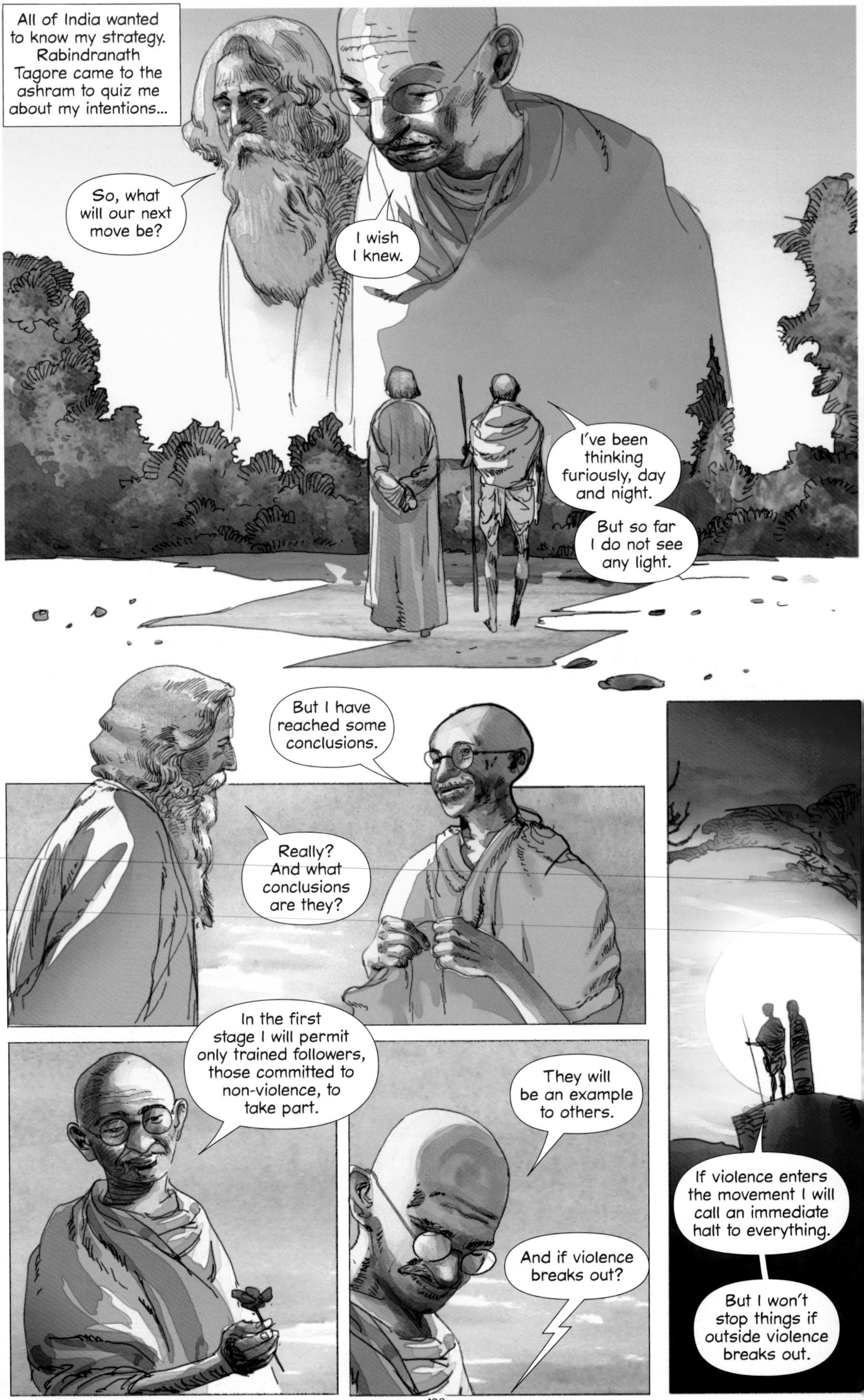

All of India wanted to know my strategy. Rabindranath Tagore came to the ashram to quiz me about my intentions...
So, what will our next move be?
I wish I knew.
I've been thinking furiously, day and night.
But so far I do not see any light.
But I have reached some conclusions.
Really? And what conclusions are they?
In the first stage I will permit only trained followers, those committed to non-violence, to take part.
They will be an example to others.
And if violence breaks out?
If violence enters the movement I will call an immediate halt to everything.
But I won't stop things if outside violence breaks out.

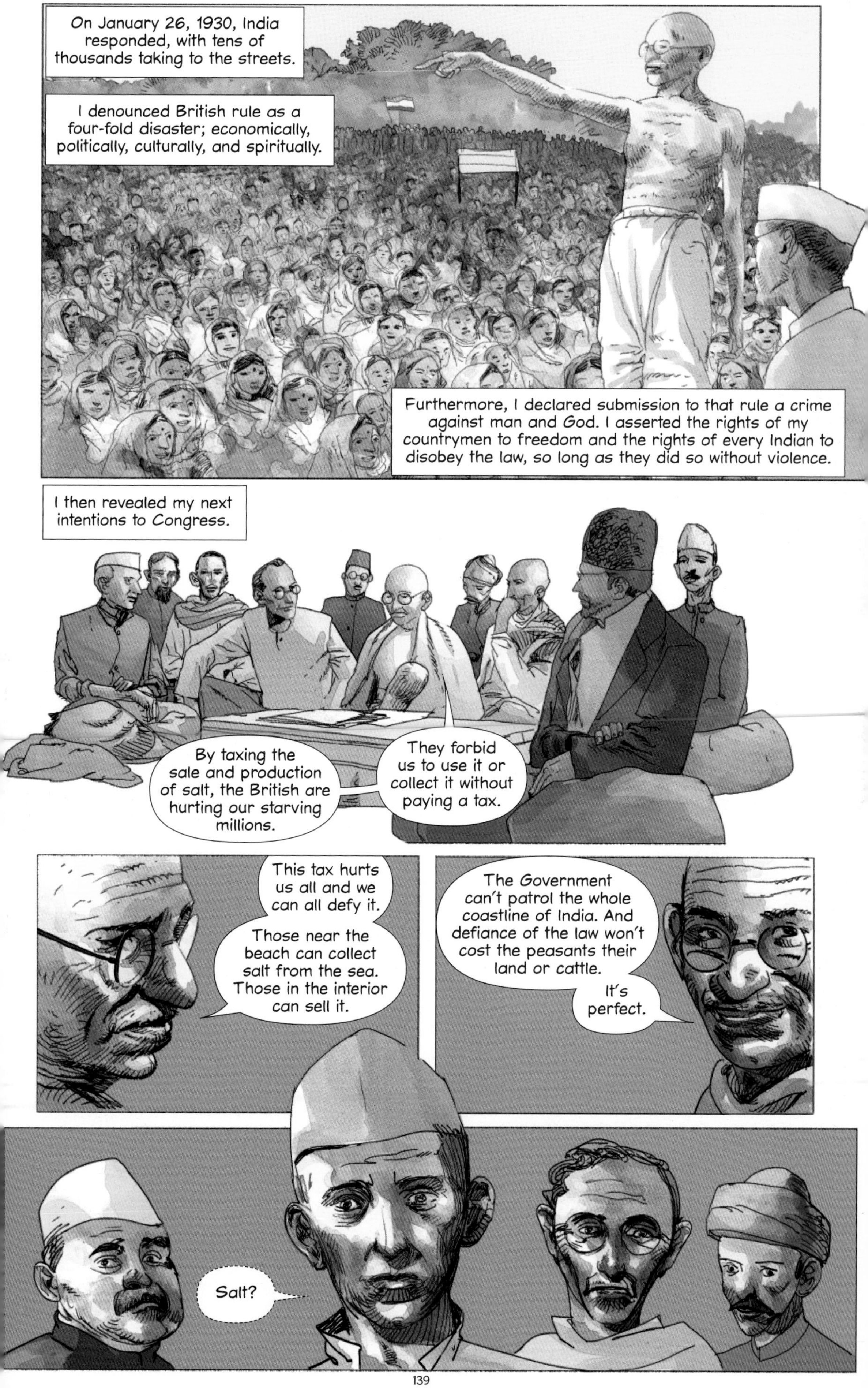
On January 26, 1930, India responded, with tens of thousands taking to the streets.
I denounced British rule as a four-fold disaster; economically, politically, culturally, and spiritually.
Furthermore, I declared submission to that rule a crime against man and God. I asserted the rights of my countrymen to freedom and the rights of every Indian to disobey the law, so long as they did so without violence.
I then revealed my next intentions to Congress.
By taxing the sale and production of salt, the British are hurting our starving millions.
They forbid us to use it or collect it without paying a tax.
This tax hurts us all and we can all defy it.
Those near the beach can collect salt from the sea. Those in the interior can sell it.
The Government can't patrol the whole coastline of India. And defiance of the law won't cost the peasants their land or cattle.
It's perfect.
Salt?

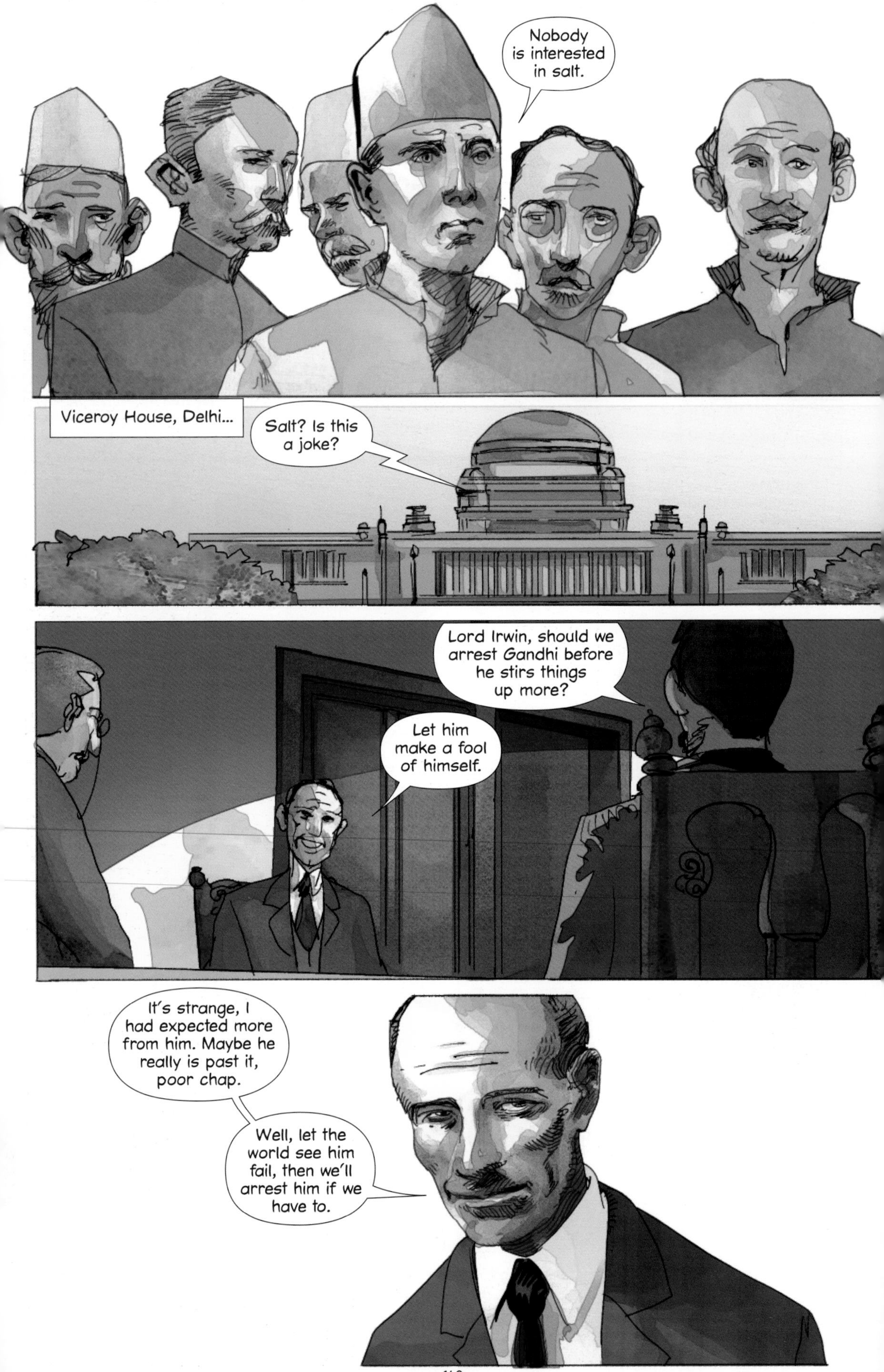
Nobody is interested in salt.
Viceroy House, Delhi...
Salt? Is this a joke?
Lord Irwin, should we arrest Gandhi before he stirs things up more?
Let him make a fool of himself.
It's strange, I had expected more from him. Maybe he really is past it, poor chap.
Well, let the world see him fail, then we'll arrest him if we have to.

I thought it only fair to write to Lord Irwin, the Viceroy, giving him a chance to meet our demands before launching the latest *Satyagraha* campaign...

We demand total prohibition on liquor, the abolition of the salt tax, halving of military expenditure, reduction in official salaries, tariffs on foreign cloths, the release of political prisoners except those convicted for murder or attempted murder...

Vaishnava Jana...

My ambition is to convert the British people through non-violence and thus make them see the wrong they have done to India.

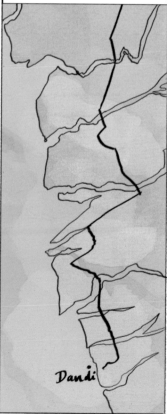

I planned to march, with my most trusted friends 240 miles south from the ashram to the coastal village of Dandi, where we would defy the salt tax by collecting our own salt from the sea.

Dandi

In the early hours of March 12, 1930, we left the ashram...

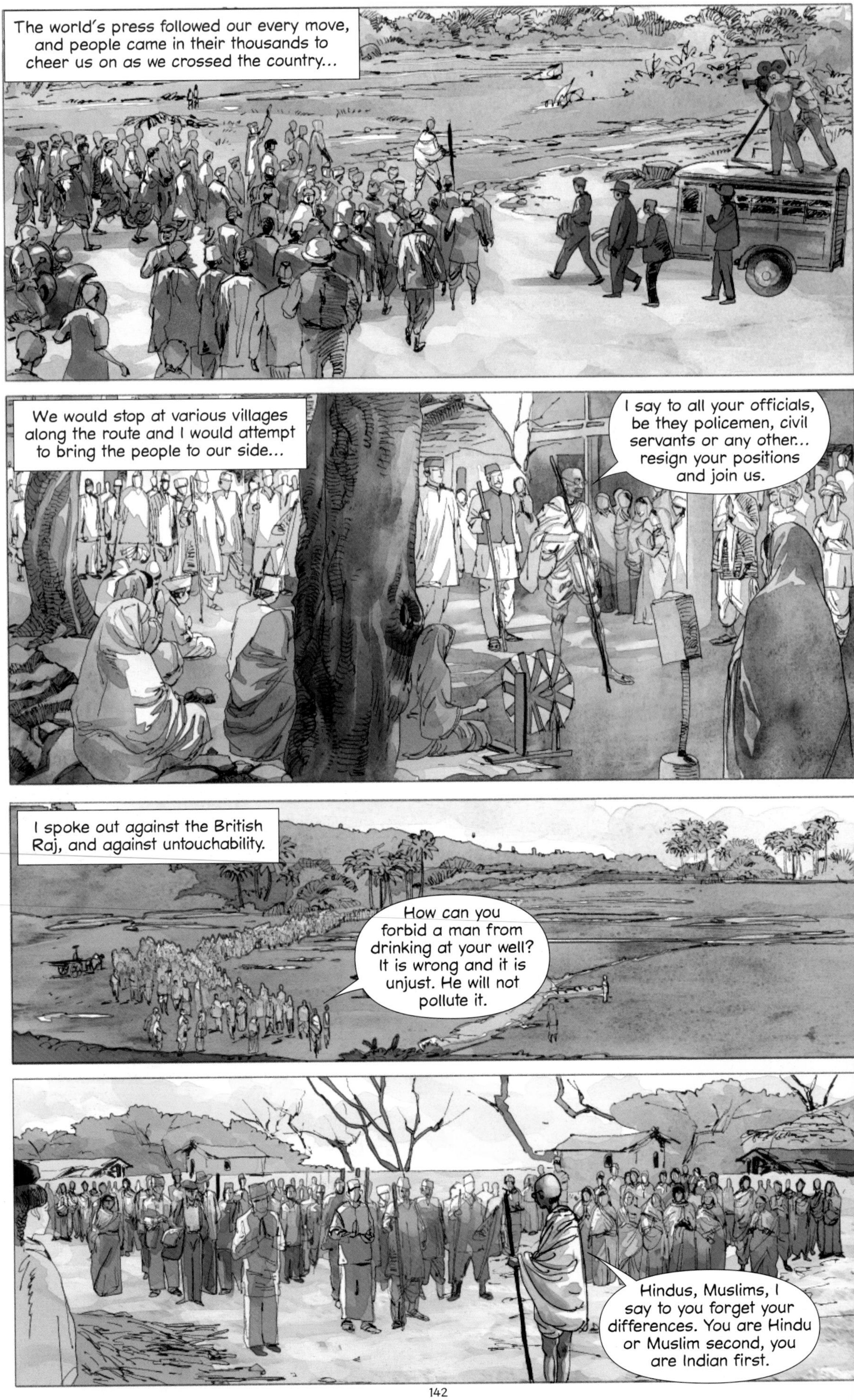
The world's press followed our every move, and people came in their thousands to cheer us on as we crossed the country...
We would stop at various villages along the route and I would attempt to bring the people to our side...
I say to all your officials, be they policemen, civil servants or any other... resign your positions and join us.
I spoke out against the British Raj, and against untouchability.
How can you forbid a man from drinking at your well? It is wrong and it is unjust. He will not pollute it.
Hindus, Muslims, I say to you forget your differences. You are Hindu or Muslim second, you are Indian first.

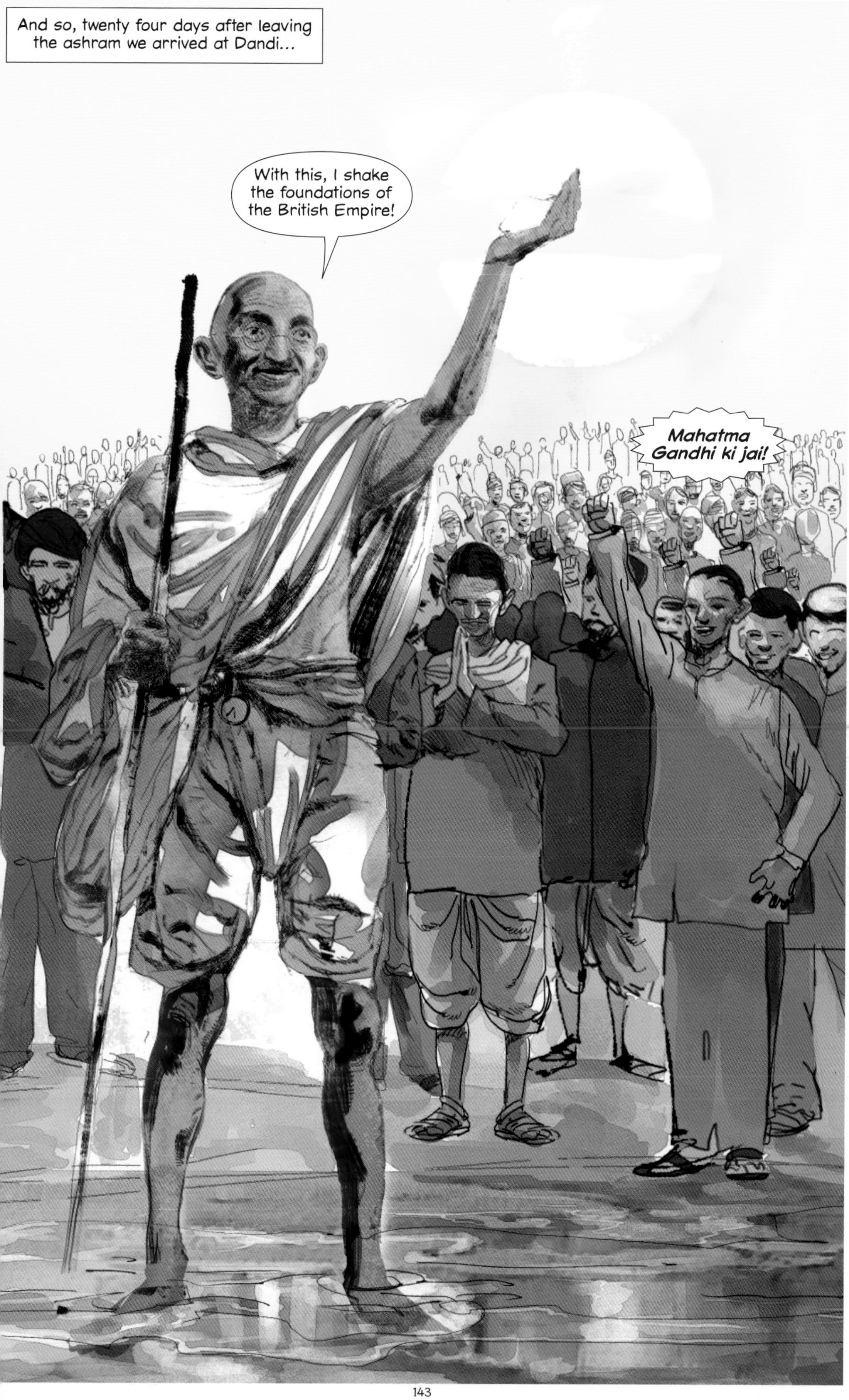
And so, twenty four days after leaving the ashram we arrived at Dandi...
With this, I shake the foundations of the British Empire!
Mahatma Gandhi ki jai!

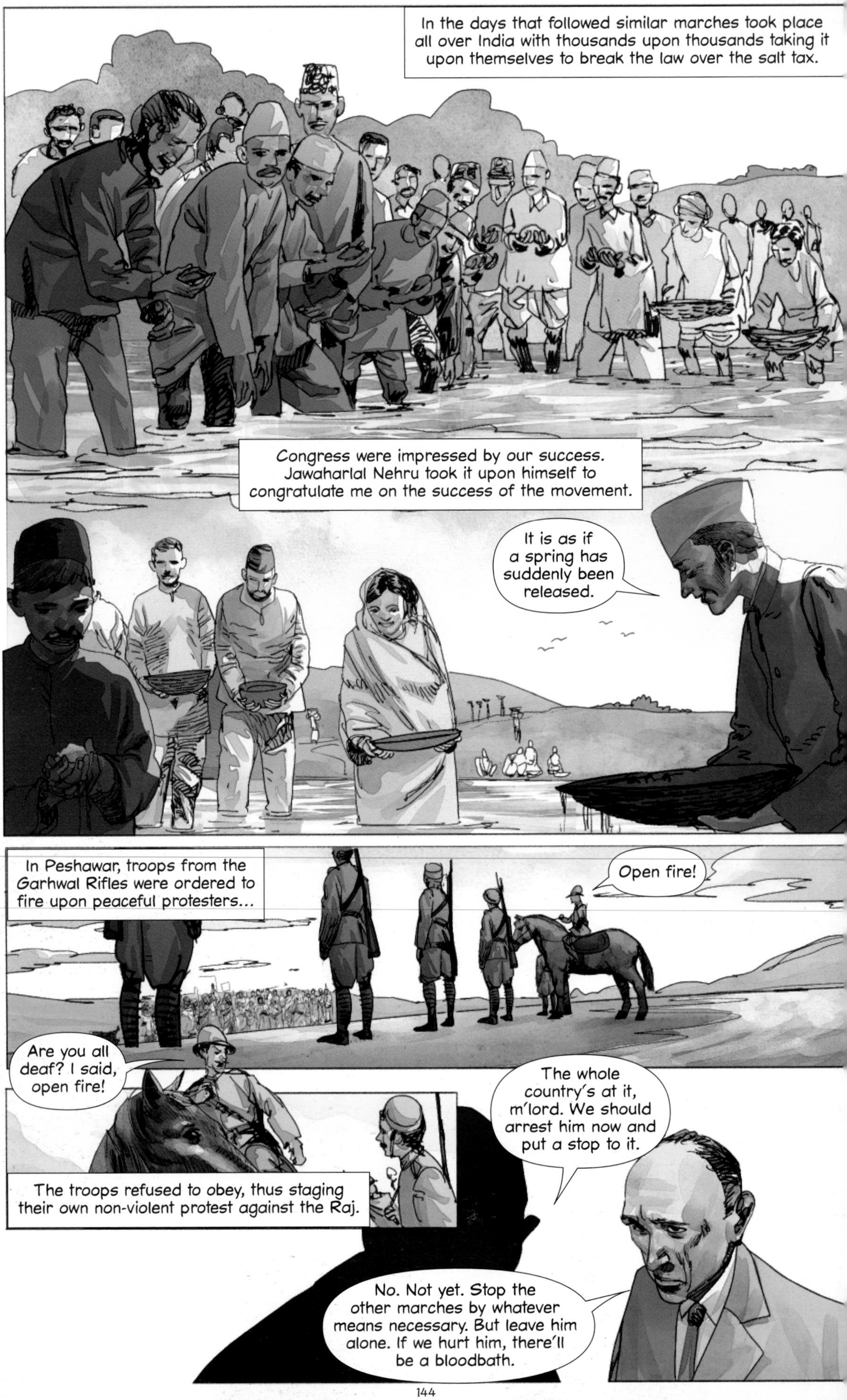

In the days that followed similar marches took place all over India with thousands upon thousands taking it upon themselves to break the law over the salt tax.
Congress were impressed by our success. Jawaharlal Nehru took it upon himself to congratulate me on the success of the movement.
It is as if a spring has suddenly been released.
In Peshawar, troops from the Garhwal Rifles were ordered to fire upon peaceful protesters...
Open fire!
Are you all deaf? I said, open fire!
The troops refused to obey, thus staging their own non-violent protest against the Raj.
The whole country's at it, m'lord. We should arrest him now and put a stop to it.
No. Not yet. Stop the other marches by whatever means necessary. But leave him alone. If we hurt him, there'll be a bloodbath.

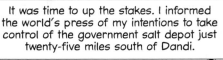
Soon thousands had been arrested all over India, including my son, Devadas and Jawaharlal Nehru, all for breaking the salt tax laws.

It is Indian salt. I shall lead the raid myself.

It was time to up the stakes. I informed the world's press of my intentions to take control of the government salt depot just twenty-five miles south of Dandi.

The authorities were bound to arrest me.

It happened a little after midnight on May 5, 1930...

Shhh!

Huh?

Are you looking for me?

I am arresting you under Regulation 25 of 1827, which authorizes arrest without trial.

For what it's worth, sir, I'm sorry about this. Please take your time. There's no rush.

Thank you. You're very kind.

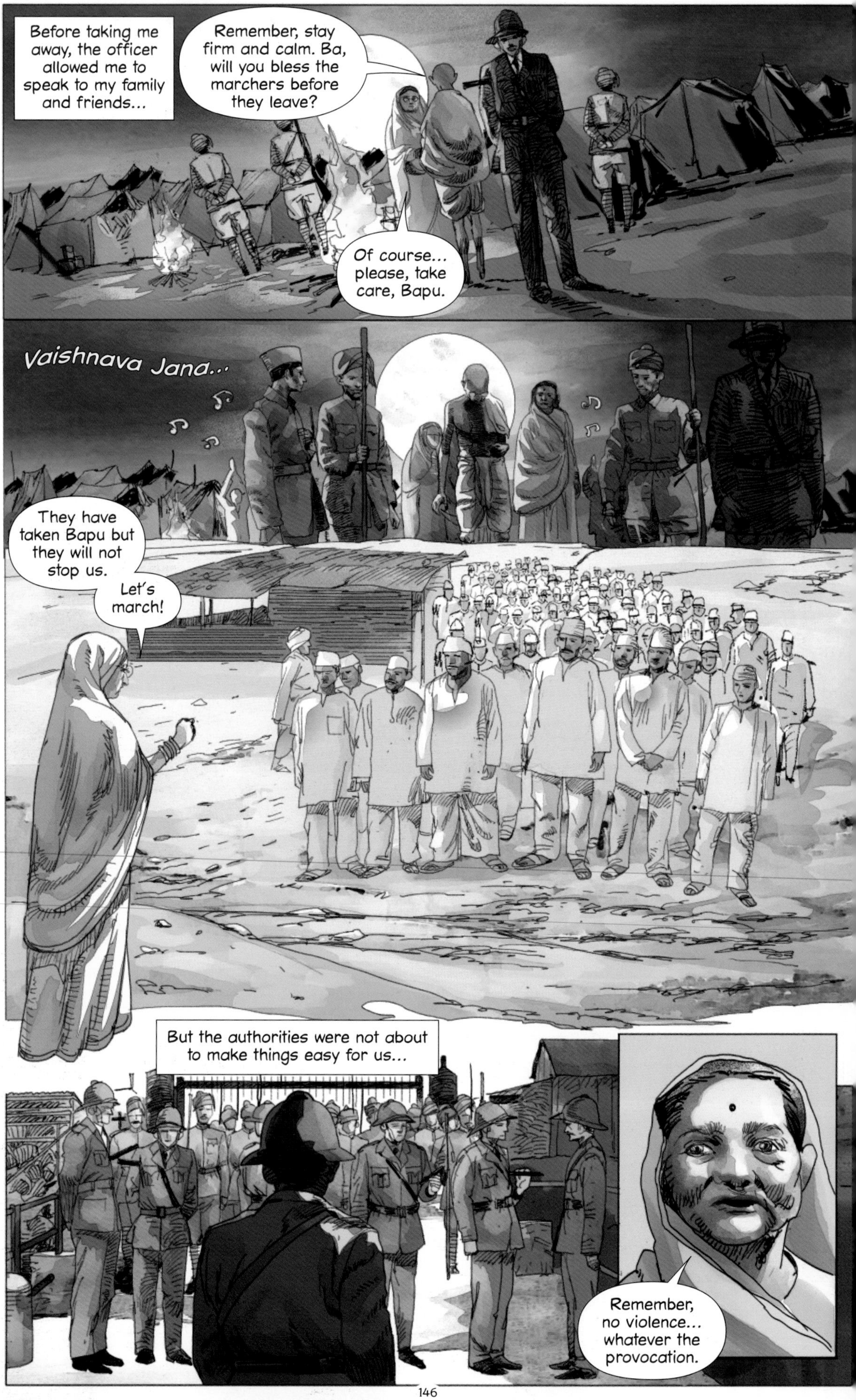
Before taking me away, the officer allowed me to speak to my family and friends...
Remember, stay firm and calm. Ba, will you bless the marchers before they leave?
Of course... please, take care, Bapu.
Vaishnava Jana...
They have taken Bapu but they will not stop us.
Let's march!
But the authorities were not about to make things easy for us...
Remember, no violence... whatever the provocation.

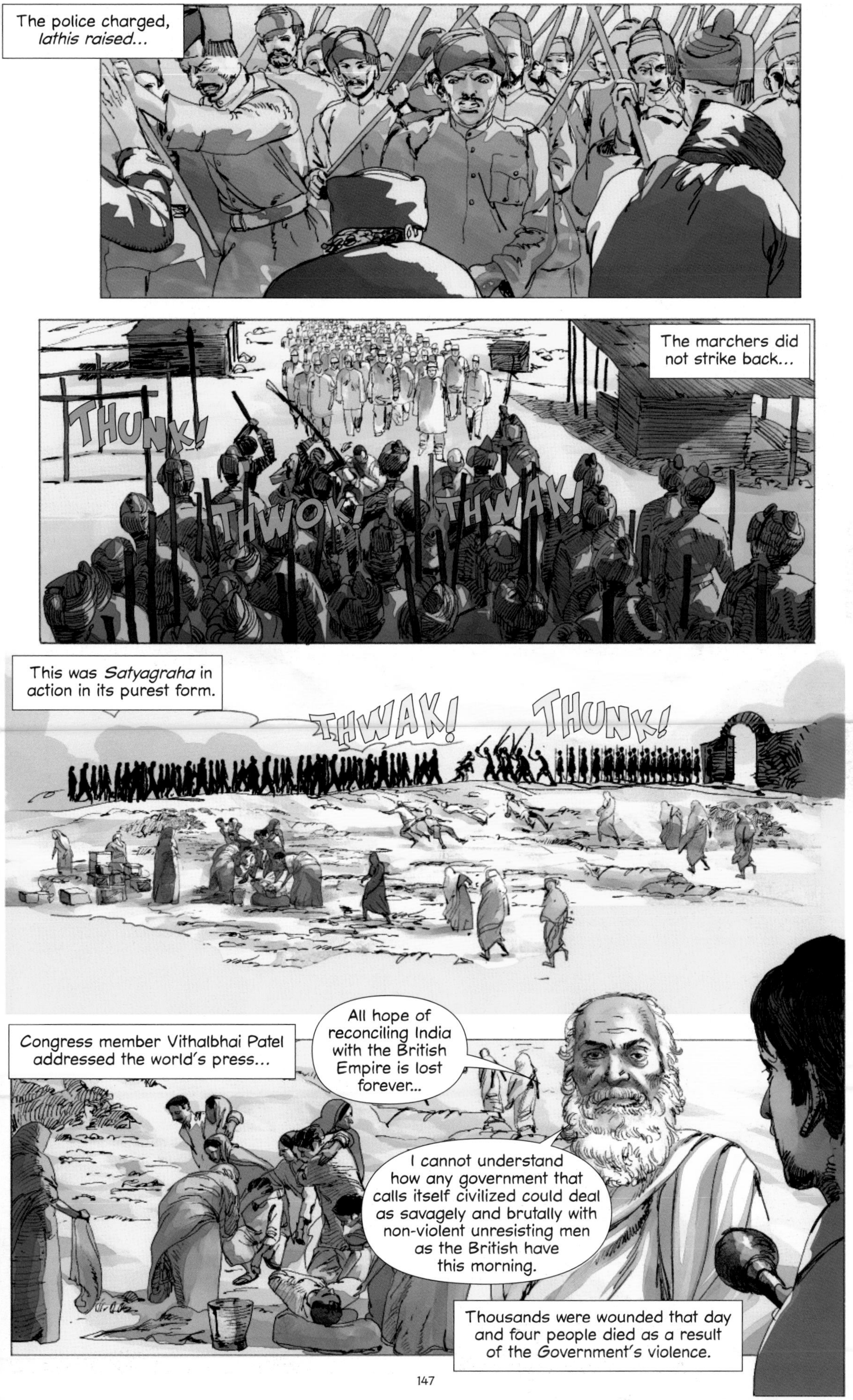
The police charged, *lathis raised...*
The marchers did not strike back...
THUNK!
THWOK!
THWAK!
This was *Satyagraha* in action in its purest form.
THWAK!
THUNK!
Congress member Vithalbhai Patel addressed the world's press...
All hope of reconciling India with the British Empire is lost forever...
I cannot understand how any government that calls itself civilized could deal as savagely and brutally with non-violent unresisting men as the British have this morning.
Thousands were wounded that day and four people died as a result of the Government's violence.

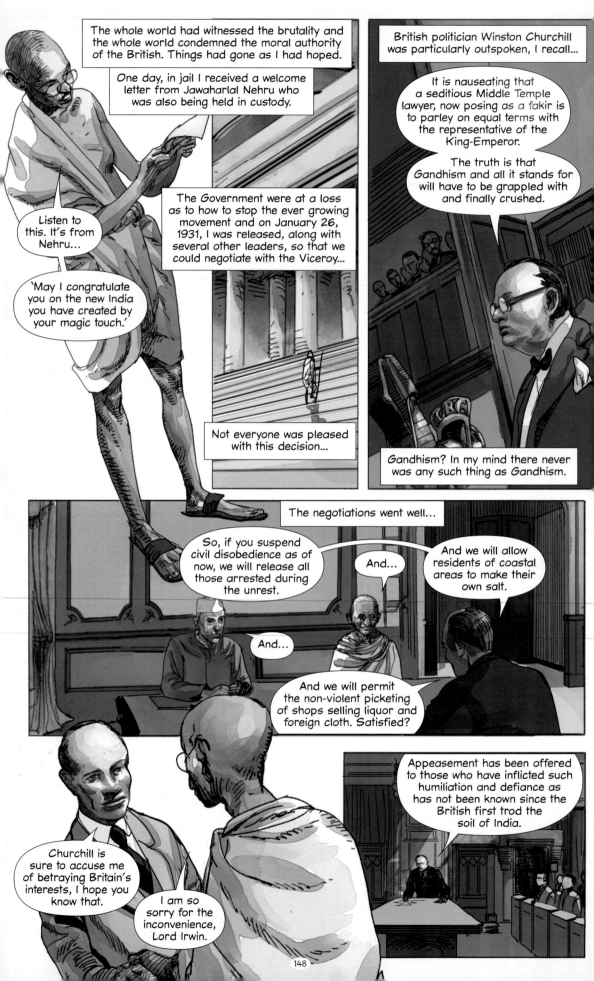

The whole world had witnessed the brutality and the whole world condemned the moral authority of the British. Things had gone as I had hoped.

One day, in jail I received a welcome letter from Jawaharlal Nehru who was also being held in custody.

Listen to this. It's from Nehru...

'May I congratulate you on the new India you have created by your magic touch.'

The Government were at a loss as to how to stop the ever growing movement and on January 26, 1931, I was released, along with several other leaders, so that we could negotiate with the Viceroy...

Not everyone was pleased with this decision...

British politician Winston Churchill was particularly outspoken, I recall...

It is nauseating that a seditious Middle Temple lawyer, now posing as a fakir is to parley on equal terms with the representative of the King-Emperor.

The truth is that Gandhism and all it stands for will have to be grappled with and finally crushed.

Gandhism? In my mind there never was any such thing as Gandhism.

The negotiations went well...

So, if you suspend civil disobedience as of now, we will release all those arrested during the unrest.

And...

And we will allow residents of coastal areas to make their own salt.

And...

And we will permit the non-violent picketing of shops selling liquor and foreign cloth. Satisfied?

Churchill is sure to accuse me of betraying Britain's interests, I hope you know that.

I am so sorry for the inconvenience, Lord Irwin.

Appeasement has been offered to those who have inflicted such humiliation and defiance as has not been known since the British first trod the soil of India.

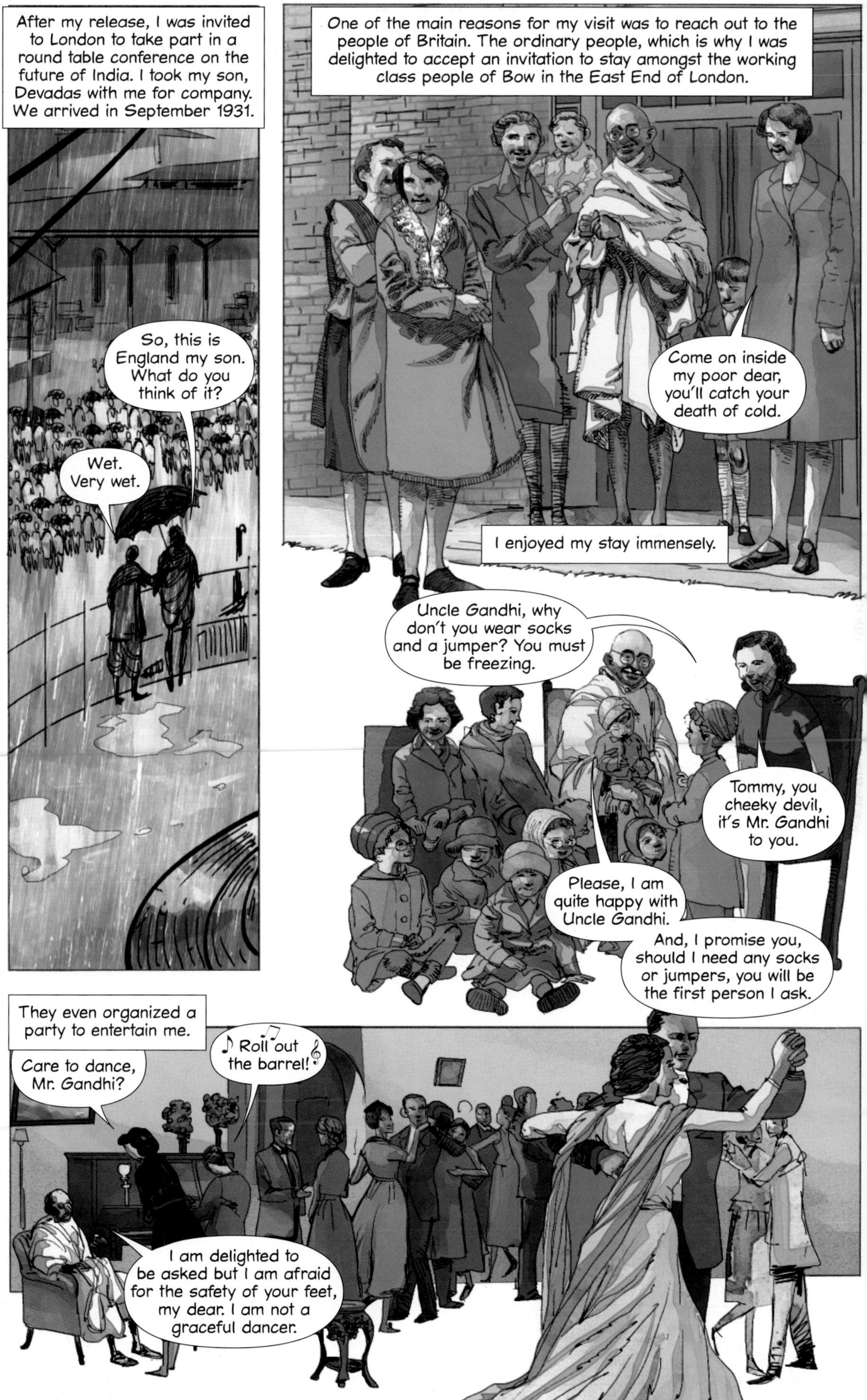

After my release, I was invited to London to take part in a round table conference on the future of India. I took my son, Devadas with me for company. We arrived in September 1931.
So, this is England my son. What do you think of it?
Wet. Very wet.
One of the main reasons for my visit was to reach out to the people of Britain. The ordinary people, which is why I was delighted to accept an invitation to stay amongst the working class people of Bow in the East End of London.
Come on inside my poor dear, you'll catch your death of cold.
I enjoyed my stay immensely.
Uncle Gandhi, why don't you wear socks and a jumper? You must be freezing.
Tommy, you cheeky devil, it's Mr. Gandhi to you.
Please, I am quite happy with Uncle Gandhi.
And, I promise you, should I need any socks or jumpers, you will be the first person I ask.
They even organized a party to entertain me.
Care to dance, Mr. Gandhi?
Roll out the barrel!
I am delighted to be asked but I am afraid for the safety of your feet, my dear. I am not a graceful dancer.

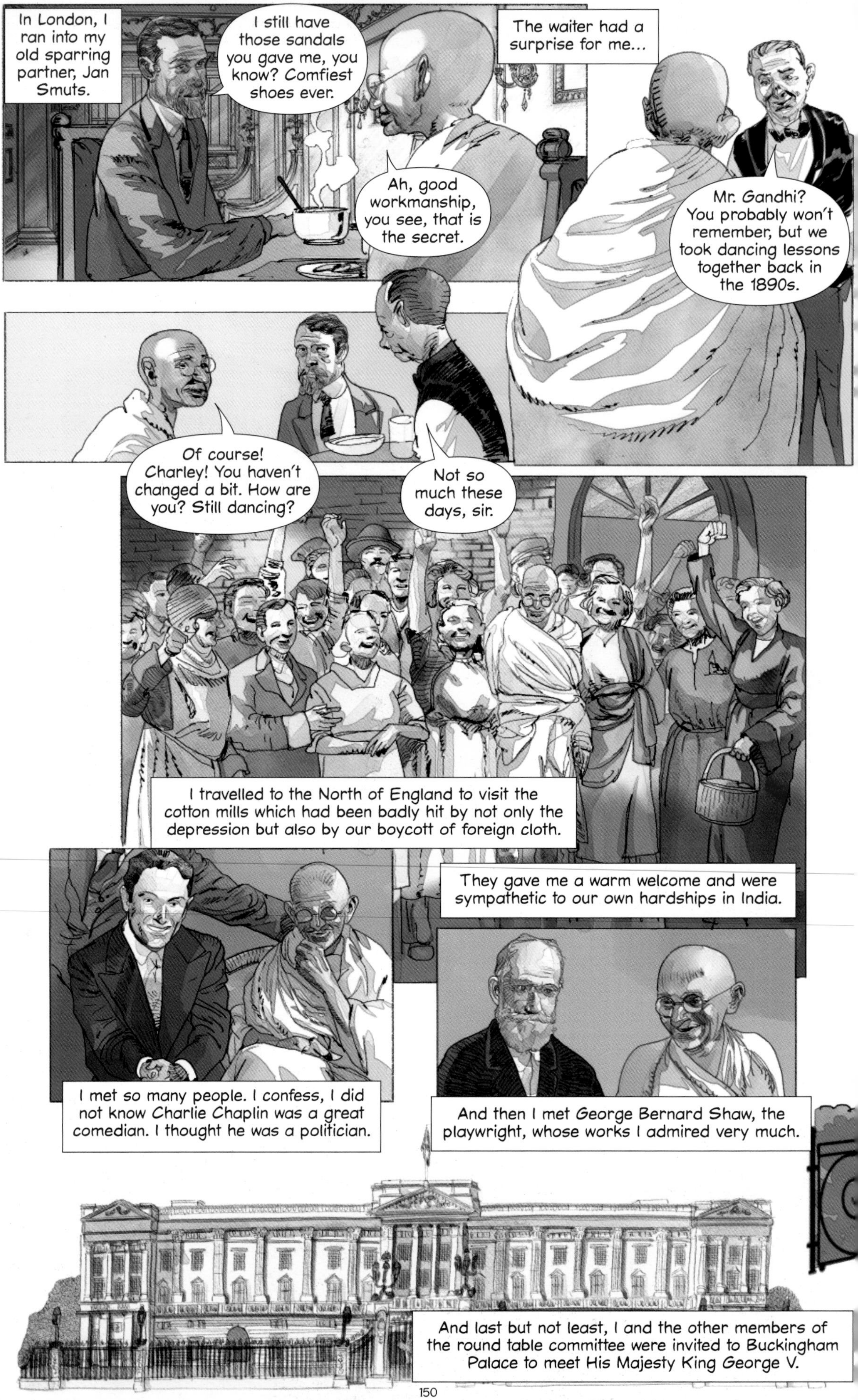
In London, I ran into my old sparring partner, Jan Smuts.
I still have those sandals you gave me, you know? Comfiest shoes ever.
Ah, good workmanship, you see, that is the secret.
The waiter had a surprise for me...
Mr. Gandhi? You probably won't remember, but we took dancing lessons together back in the 1890s.
Of course! Charley! You haven't changed a bit. How are you? Still dancing?
Not so much these days, sir.
I travelled to the North of England to visit the cotton mills which had been badly hit by not only the depression but also by our boycott of foreign cloth.
They gave me a warm welcome and were sympathetic to our own hardships in India.
I met so many people. I confess, I did not know Charlie Chaplin was a great comedian. I thought he was a politician.
And then I met George Bernard Shaw, the playwright, whose works I admired very much.
And last but not least, I and the other members of the round table committee were invited to Buckingham Palace to meet His Majesty King George V.

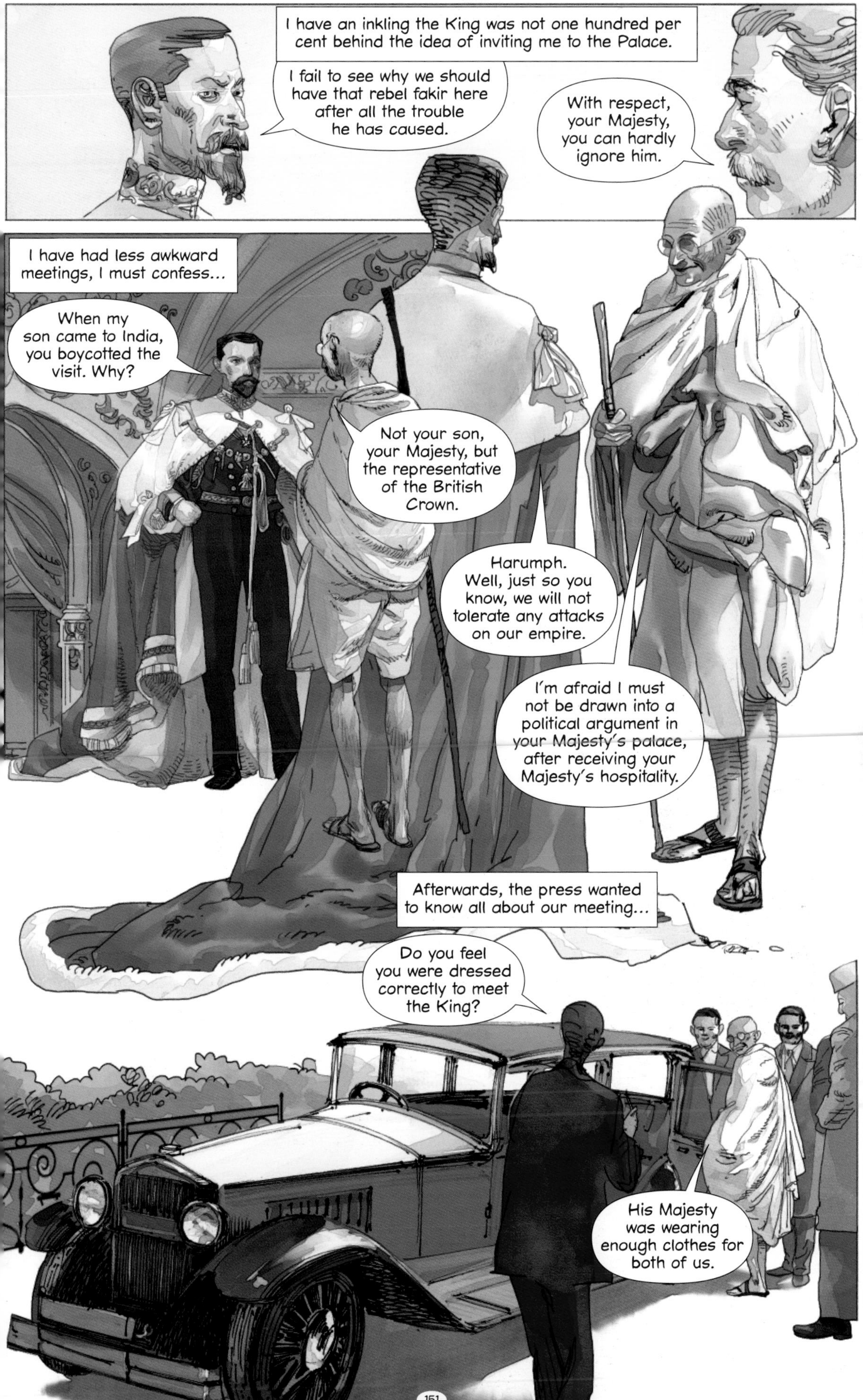

I have an inkling the King was not one hundred per cent behind the idea of inviting me to the Palace.
I fail to see why we should have that rebel fakir here after all the trouble he has caused.
With respect, your Majesty, you can hardly ignore him.
I have had less awkward meetings, I must confess...
When my son came to India, you boycotted the visit. Why?
Not your son, your Majesty, but the representative of the British Crown.
Harumph. Well, just so you know, we will not tolerate any attacks on our empire.
I'm afraid I must not be drawn into a political argument in your Majesty's palace, after receiving your Majesty's hospitality.
Afterwards, the press wanted to know all about our meeting...
Do you feel you were dressed correctly to meet the King?
His Majesty was wearing enough clothes for both of us.

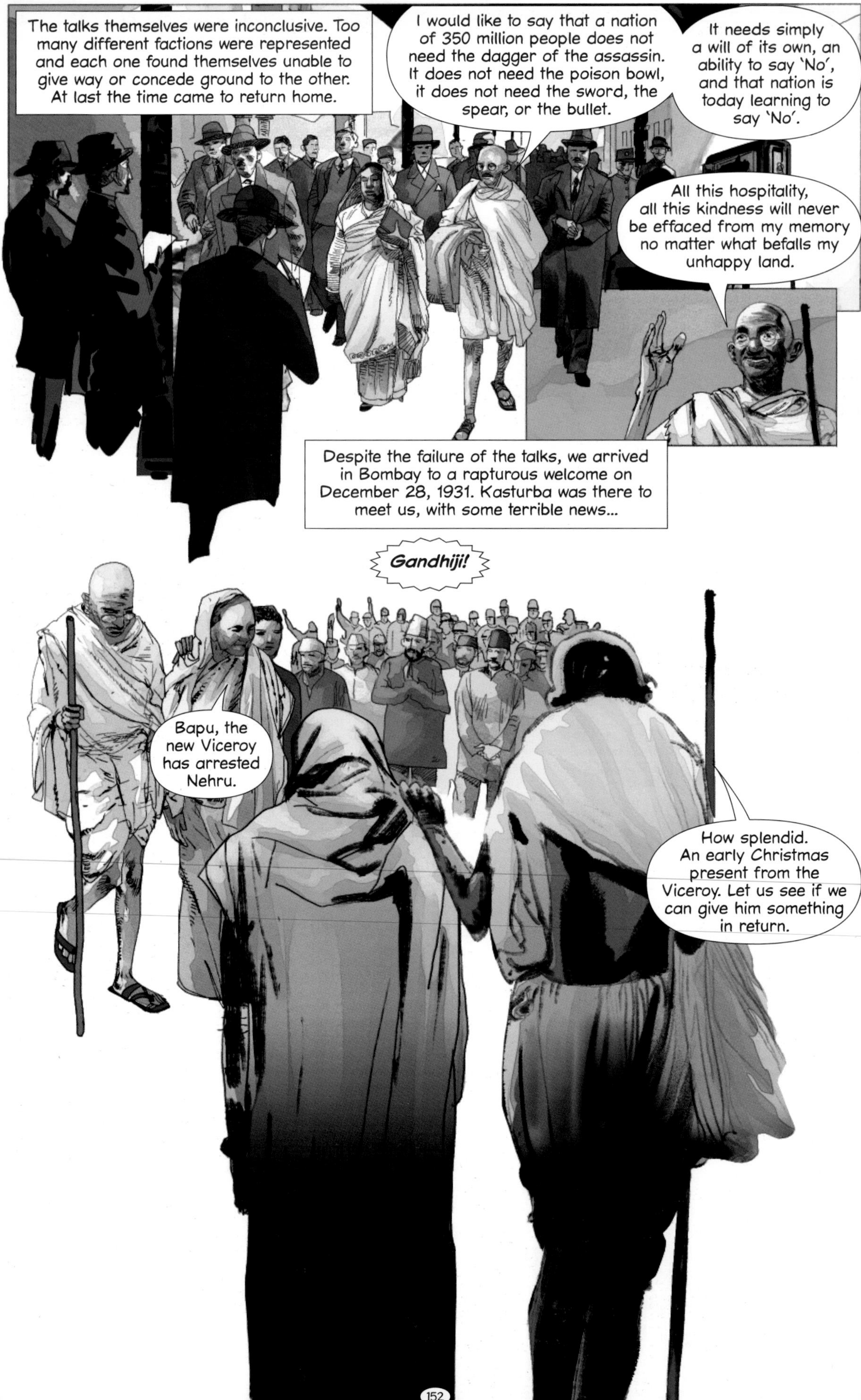

The talks themselves were inconclusive. Too many different factions were represented and each one found themselves unable to give way or concede ground to the other. At last the time came to return home.
I would like to say that a nation of 350 million people does not need the dagger of the assassin. It does not need the poison bowl, it does not need the sword, the spear, or the bullet.
It needs simply a will of its own, an ability to say 'No', and that nation is today learning to say 'No'.
All this hospitality, all this kindness will never be effaced from my memory no matter what befalls my unhappy land.
Despite the failure of the talks, we arrived in Bombay to a rapturous welcome on December 28, 1931. Kasturba was there to meet us, with some terrible news...
Gandhiji!
Bapu, the new Viceroy has arrested Nehru.
How splendid. An early Christmas present from the Viceroy. Let us see if we can give him something in return.

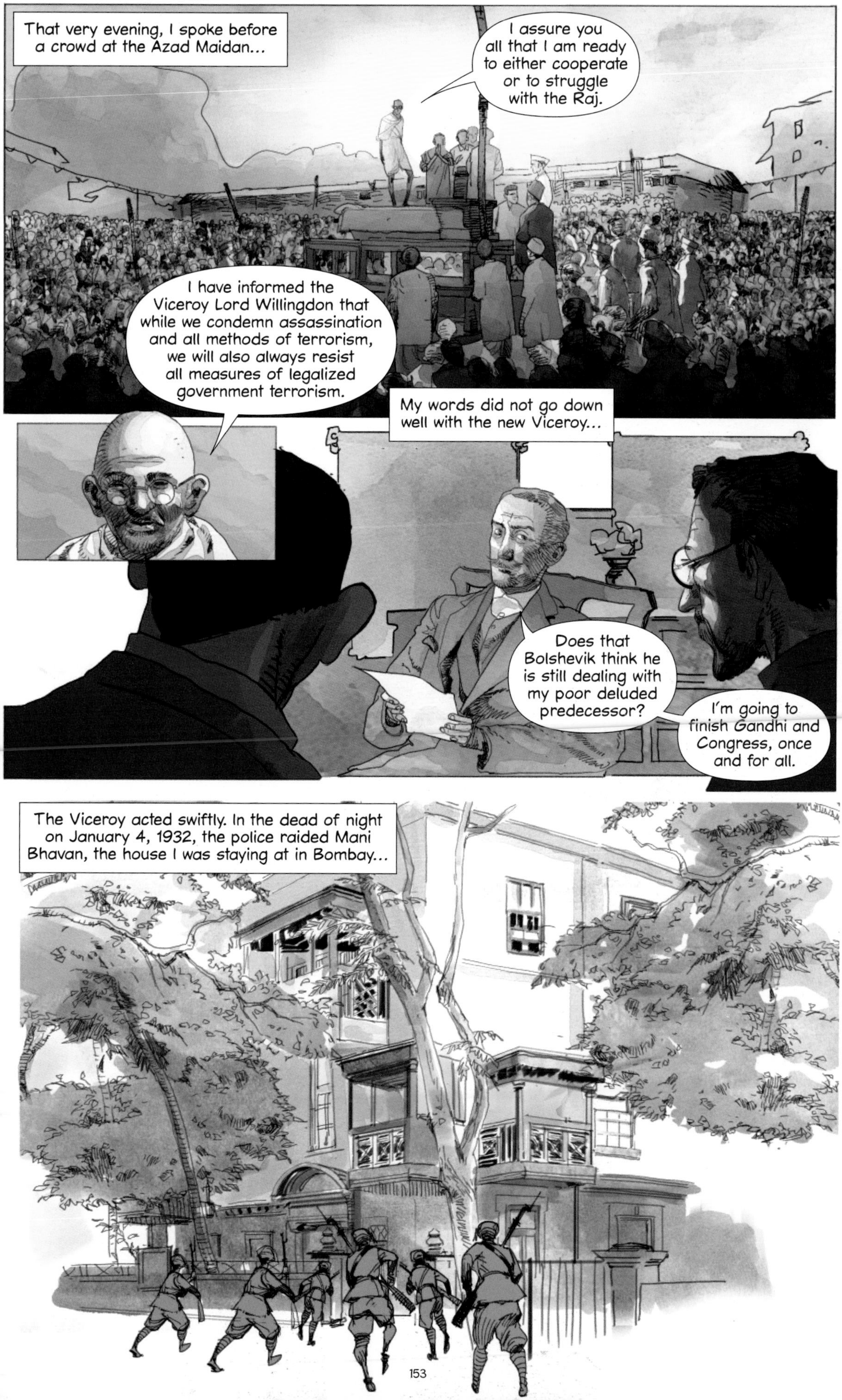
That very evening, I spoke before a crowd at the Azad Maidan...
I assure you all that I am ready to either cooperate or to struggle with the Raj.
I have informed the Viceroy Lord Willingdon that while we condemn assassination and all methods of terrorism, we will also always resist all measures of legalized government terrorism.
My words did not go down well with the new Viceroy...
Does that Bolshevik think he is still dealing with my poor deluded predecessor?
I'm going to finish Gandhi and Congress, once and for all.
The Viceroy acted swiftly. In the dead of night on January 4, 1932, the police raided Mani Bhavan, the house I was staying at in Bombay...

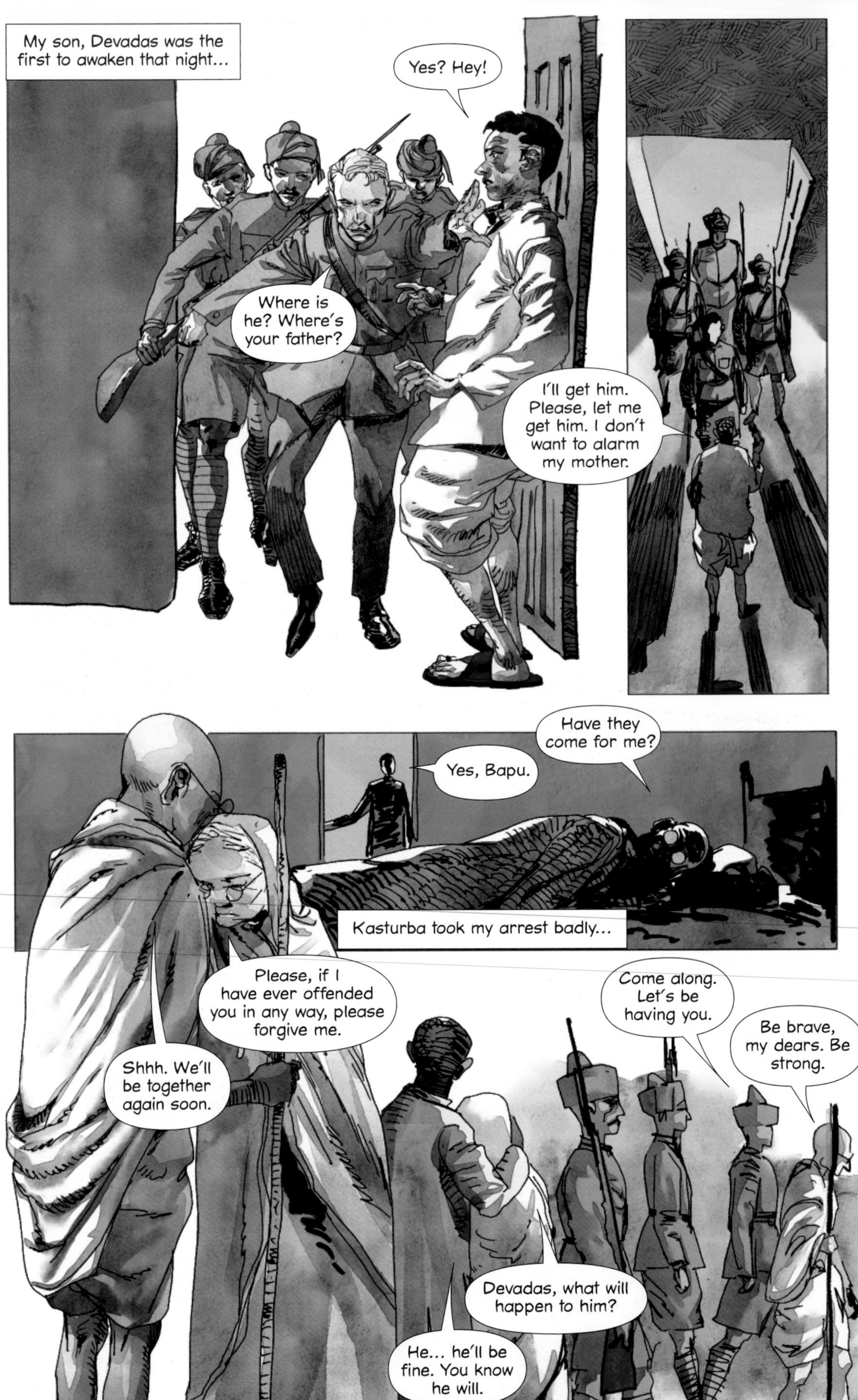
My son, Devadas was the first to awaken that night...
Yes? Hey!
Where is he? Where's your father?
I'll get him. Please, let me get him. I don't want to alarm my mother.
Have they come for me?
Yes, Bapu.
Kasturba took my arrest badly...
Please, if I have ever offended you in any way, please forgive me.
Shhh. We'll be together again soon.
Come along. Let's be having you.
Be brave, my dears. Be strong.
Devadas, what will happen to him?
He... he'll be fine. You know he will.

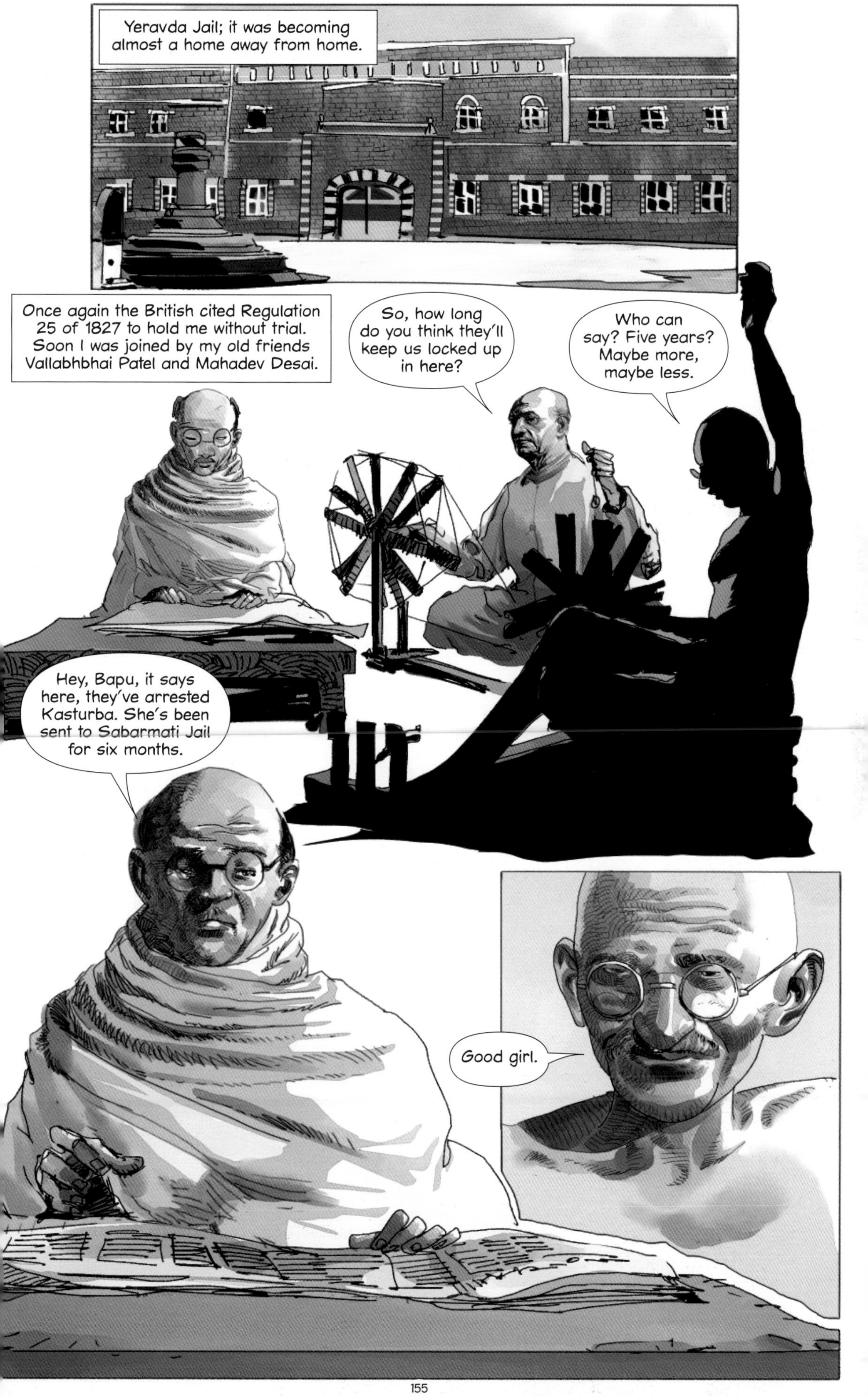
Yeravda Jail; it was becoming almost a home away from home.
Once again the British cited Regulation 25 of 1827 to hold me without trial. Soon I was joined by my old friends Vallabhbhai Patel and Mahadev Desai.
So, how long do you think they'll keep us locked up in here?
Who can say? Five years? Maybe more, maybe less.
Hey, Bapu, it says here, they've arrested Kasturba. She's been sent to Sabarmati Jail for six months.
Good girl.

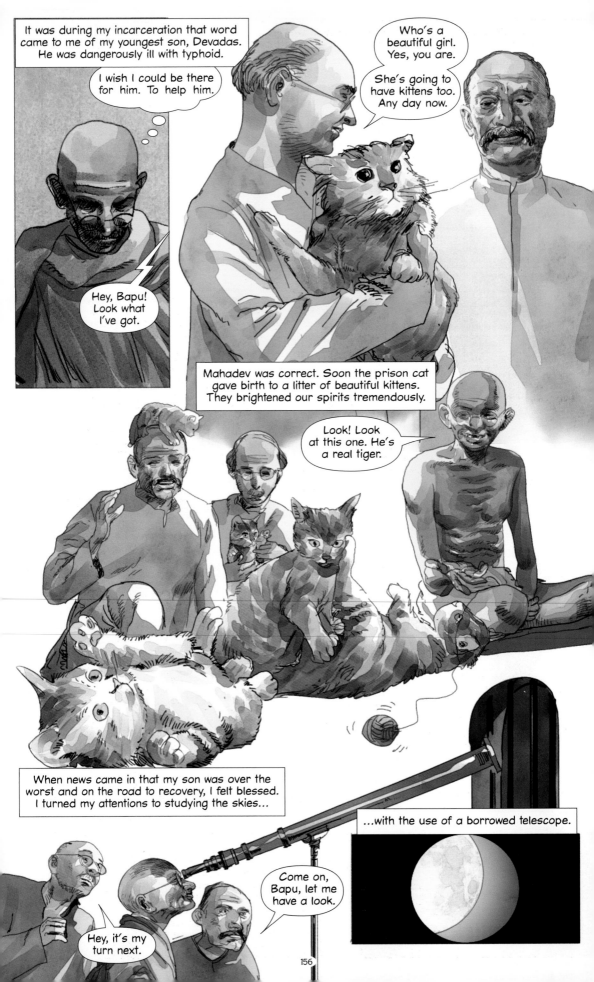

It was during my incarceration that word came to me of my youngest son, Devadas. He was dangerously ill with typhoid.

I wish I could be there for him. To help him.

Who's a beautiful girl. Yes, you are.

She's going to have kittens too. Any day now.

Hey, Bapu! Look what I've got.

Mahadev was correct. Soon the prison cat gave birth to a litter of beautiful kittens. They brightened our spirits tremendously.

Look! Look at this one. He's a real tiger.

When news came in that my son was over the worst and on the road to recovery, I felt blessed. I turned my attentions to studying the skies...

...with the use of a borrowed telescope.

Come on, Bapu, let me have a look.

Hey, it's my turn next.

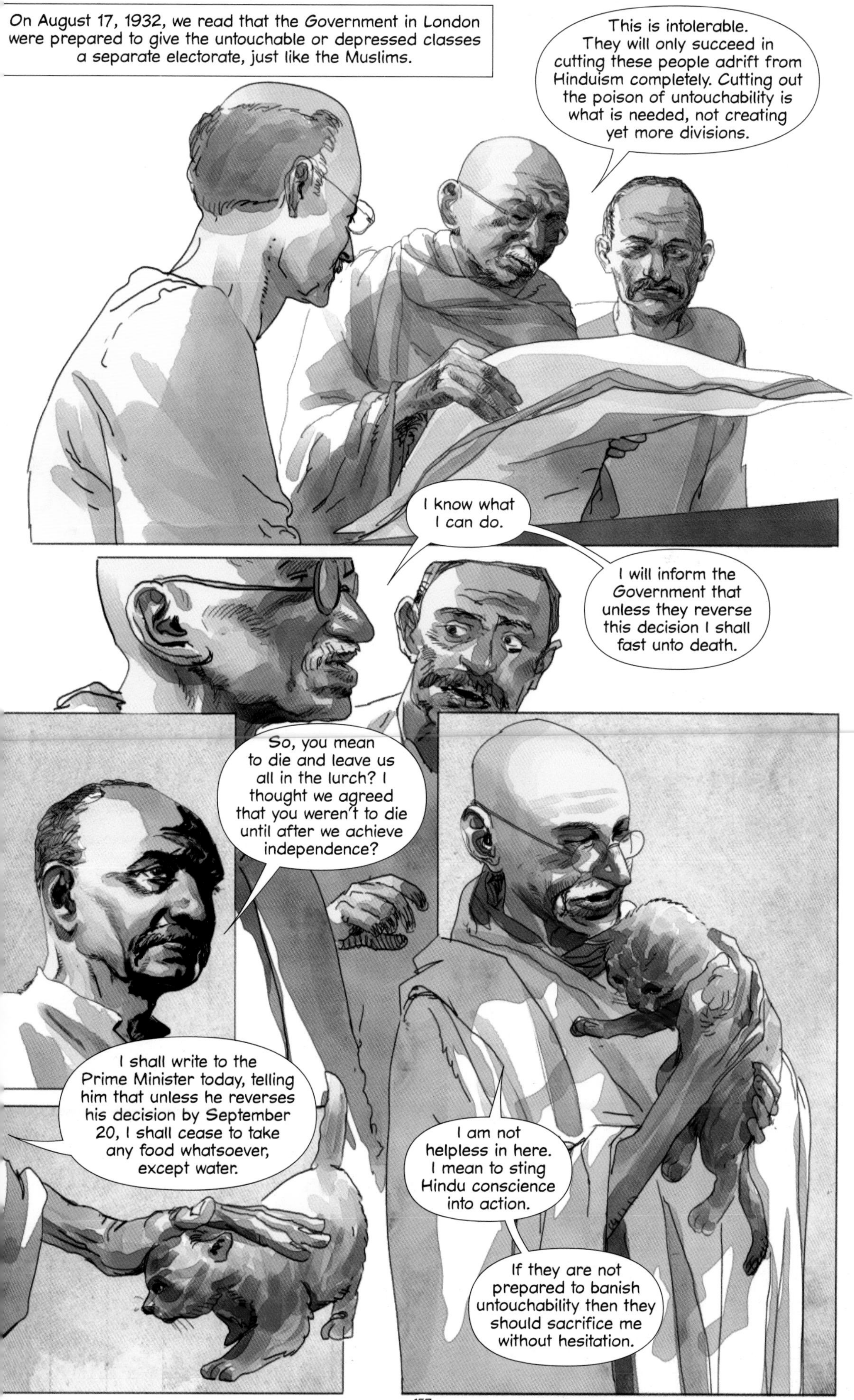
On August 17, 1932, we read that the *Government* in London were prepared to give the untouchable or depressed classes a separate electorate, just like the Muslims.
This is intolerable. They will only succeed in cutting these people adrift from Hinduism completely. Cutting out the poison of untouchability is what is needed, not creating yet more divisions.
I know what I can do.
I will inform the Government that unless they reverse this decision I shall fast unto death.
So, you mean to die and leave us all in the lurch? I thought we agreed that you weren't to die until after we achieve independence?
I shall write to the Prime Minister today, telling him that unless he reverses his decision by September 20, I shall cease to take any food whatsoever, except water.
I am not helpless in here. I mean to sting Hindu conscience into action.
If they are not prepared to banish untouchability then they should sacrifice me without hesitation.

Gandhiji says he will fast to the death unless the British reverse their decision.

Of course, I needed to win support from the untouchable classes themselves and I contacted Bhimrao Ramji Ambedkar, a leading spokesman and figurehead.

To win our support, he has promised us twice as many seats as the British do, on condition that our legislators be elected by general and not separate vote.

I don't see how we can refuse.

As news spread regarding the impending fast, it seemed that many Hindus were in fact being stung into action.

In Bombay, a meeting of caste Hindus declared that upon gaining self rule, they would ensure that untouchables had equal use of public wells, roads, schools, and other institutions.

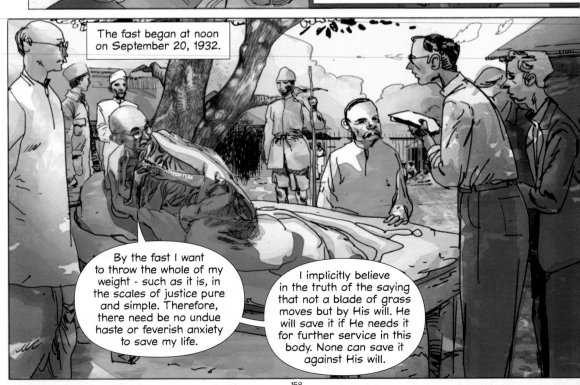

The fast began at noon on September 20, 1932.

By the fast I want to throw the whole of my weight - such as it is, in the scales of justice pure and simple. Therefore, there need be no undue haste or feverish anxiety to save my life.

I implicitly believe in the truth of the saying that not a blade of grass moves but by His will. He will save it if He needs it for further service in this body. None can save it against His will.

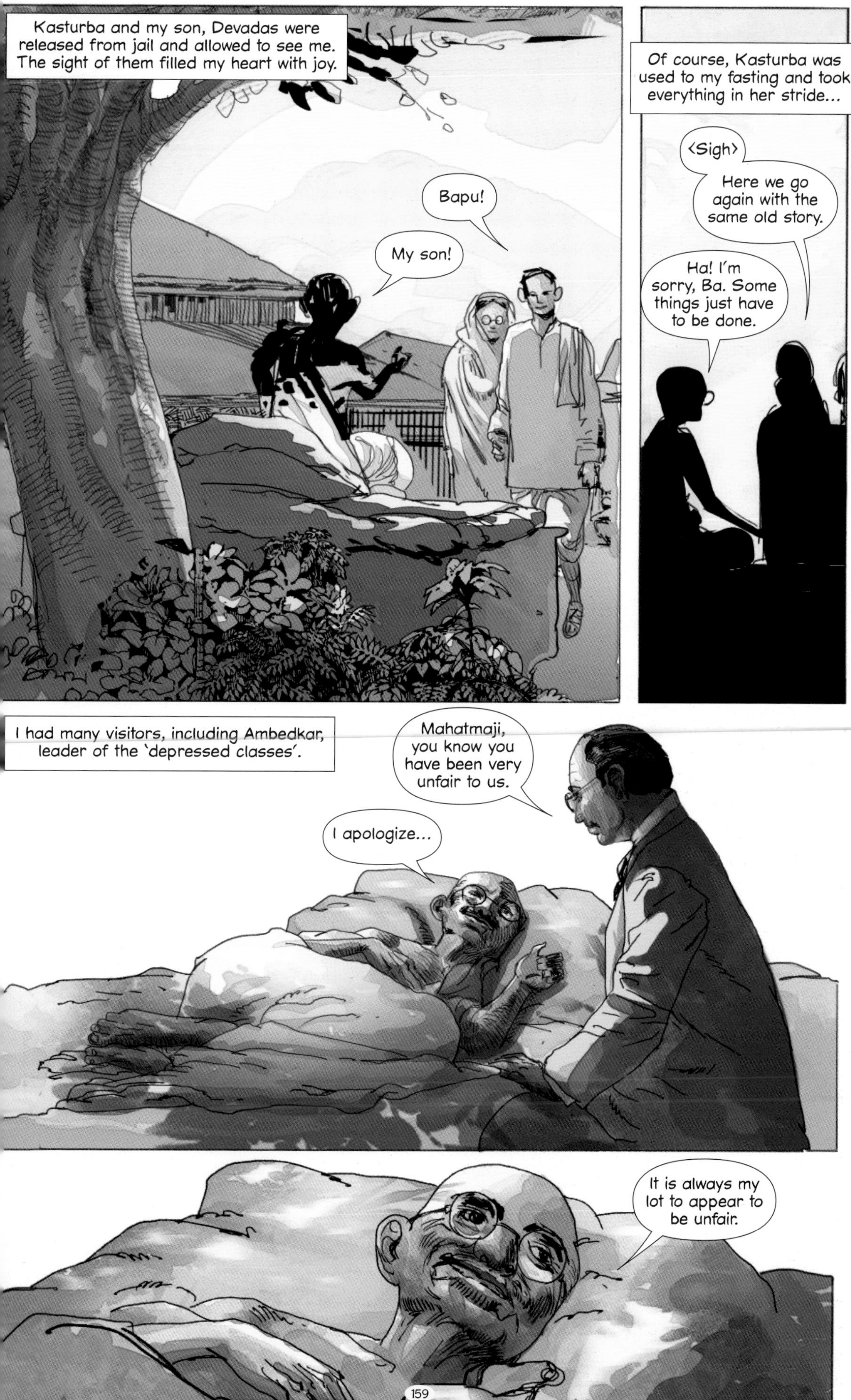
Kasturba and my son, Devadas were released from jail and allowed to see me. The sight of them filled my heart with joy.
Bapu!
My son!
Of course, Kasturba was used to my fasting and took everything in her stride...
<Sigh>
Here we go again with the same old story.
Ha! I'm sorry, Ba. Some things just have to be done.
I had many visitors, including Ambedkar, leader of the 'depressed classes'.
Mahatmaji, you know you have been very unfair to us.
I apologize...
It is always my lot to appear to be unfair.

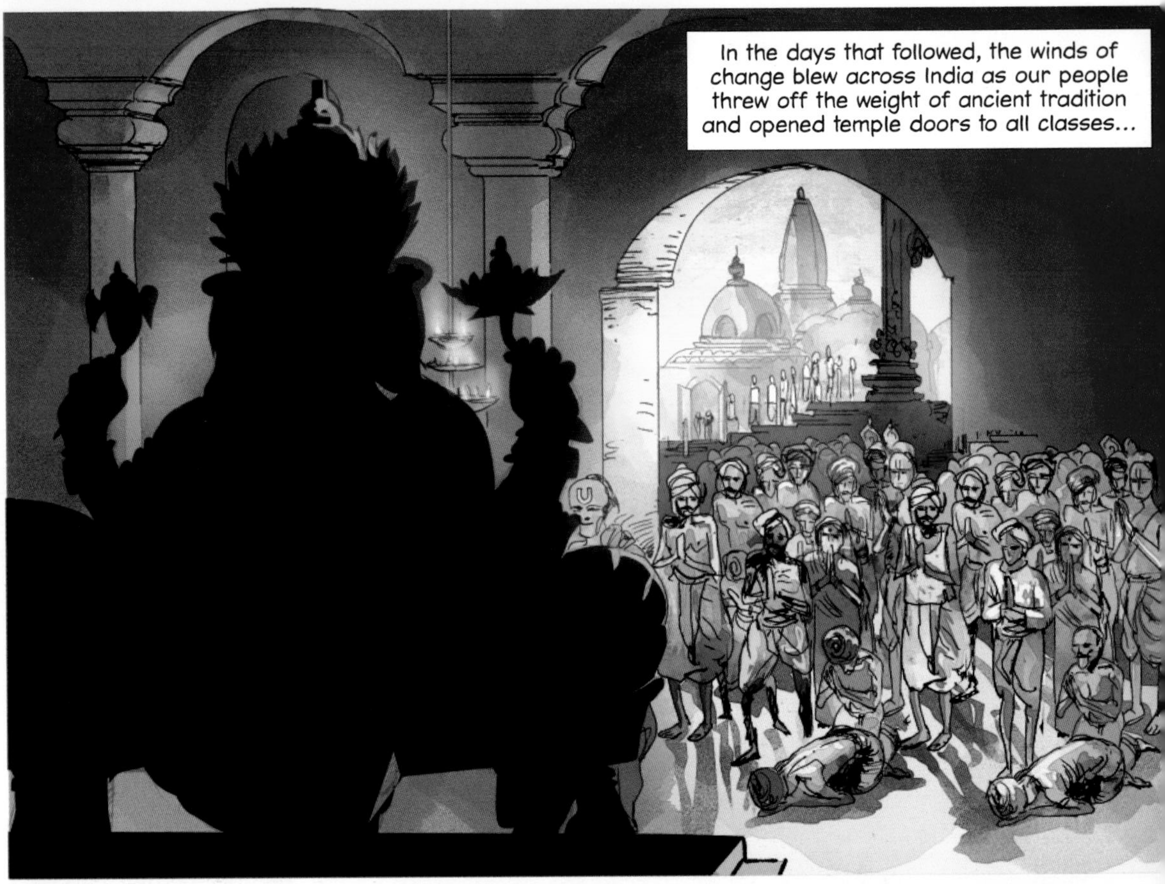
In the days that followed, the winds of change blew across India as our people threw off the weight of ancient tradition and opened temple doors to all classes...

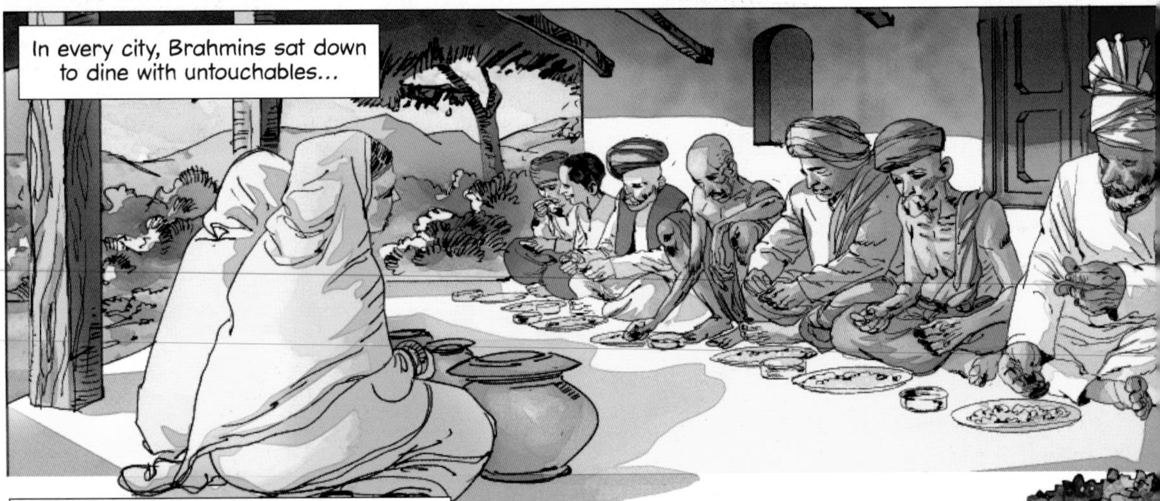
In every city, Brahmins sat down to dine with untouchables...

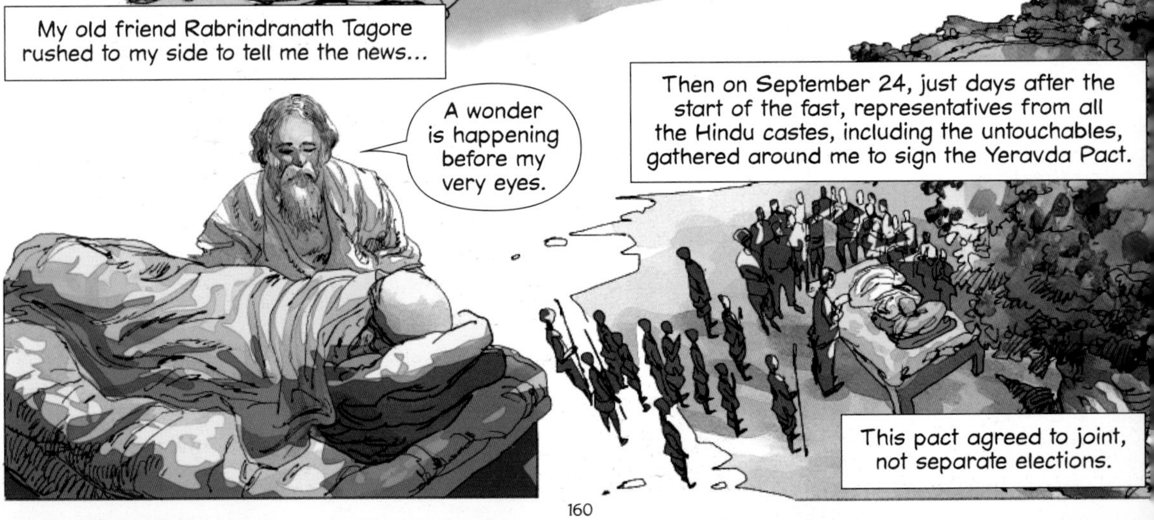
My old friend Rabrindranath Tagore rushed to my side to tell me the news...
A wonder is happening before my very eyes.
Then on September 24, just days after the start of the fast, representatives from all the Hindu castes, including the untouchables, gathered around me to sign the Yeravda Pact.
This pact agreed to joint, not separate elections.

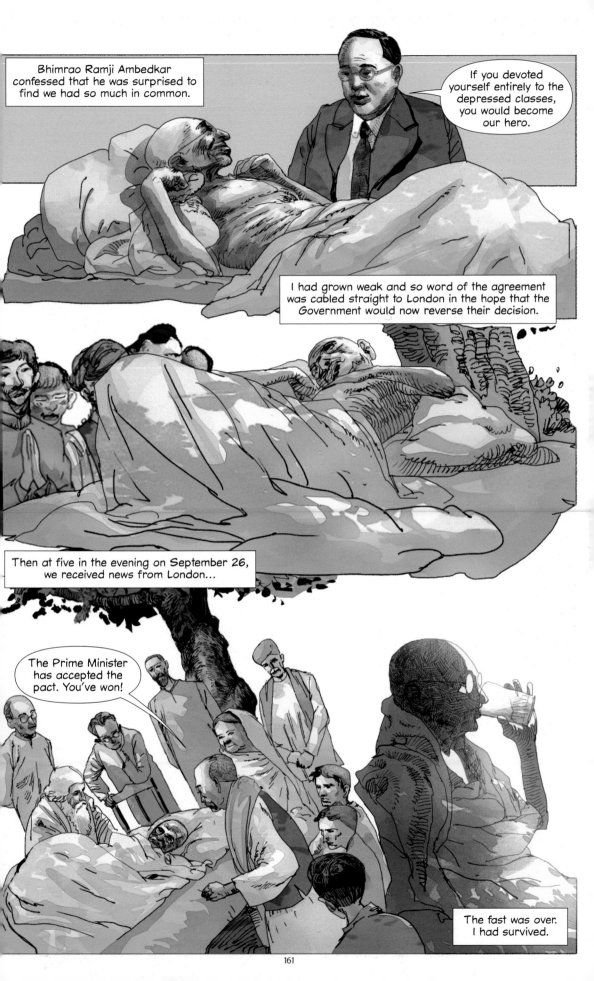

Bhimrao Ramji Ambedkar confessed that he was surprised to find we had so much in common.

If you devoted yourself entirely to the depressed classes, you would become our hero.

I had grown weak and so word of the agreement was cabled straight to London in the hope that the Government would now reverse their decision.

Then at five in the evening on September 26, we received news from London...

The Prime Minister has accepted the pact. You've won!

The fast was over. I had survived.

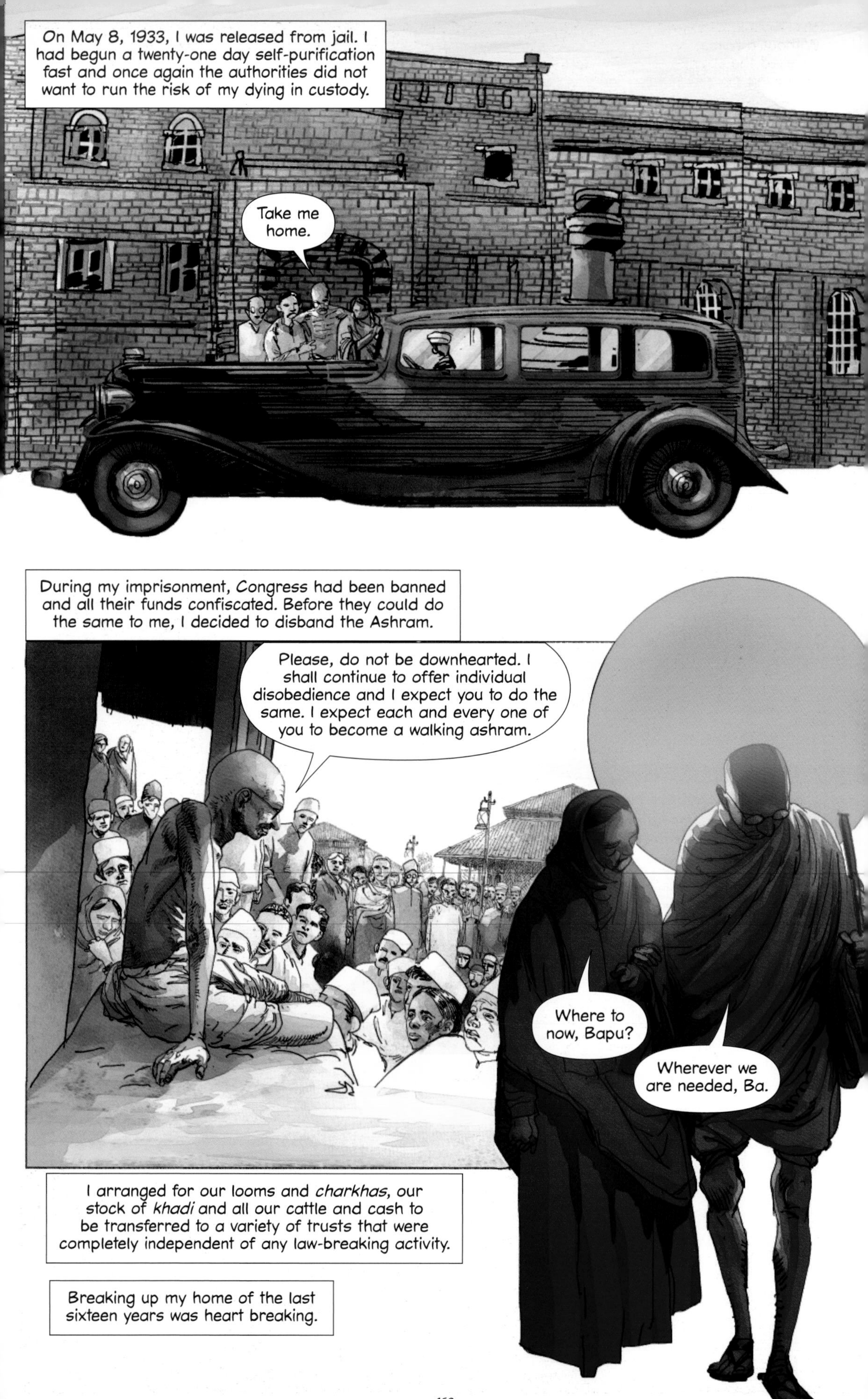

On May 8, 1933, I was released from jail. I had begun a twenty-one day self-purification fast and once again the authorities did not want to run the risk of my dying in custody.
Take me home.
During my imprisonment, Congress had been banned and all their funds confiscated. Before they could do the same to me, I decided to disband the Ashram.
Please, do not be downhearted. I shall continue to offer individual disobedience and I expect you to do the same. I expect each and every one of you to become a walking ashram.
Where to now, Bapu?
Wherever we are needed, Ba.
I arranged for our looms and *charkhas*, our stock of *khadi* and all our cattle and cash to be transferred to a variety of trusts that were completely independent of any law-breaking activity.
Breaking up my home of the last sixteen years was heart breaking.

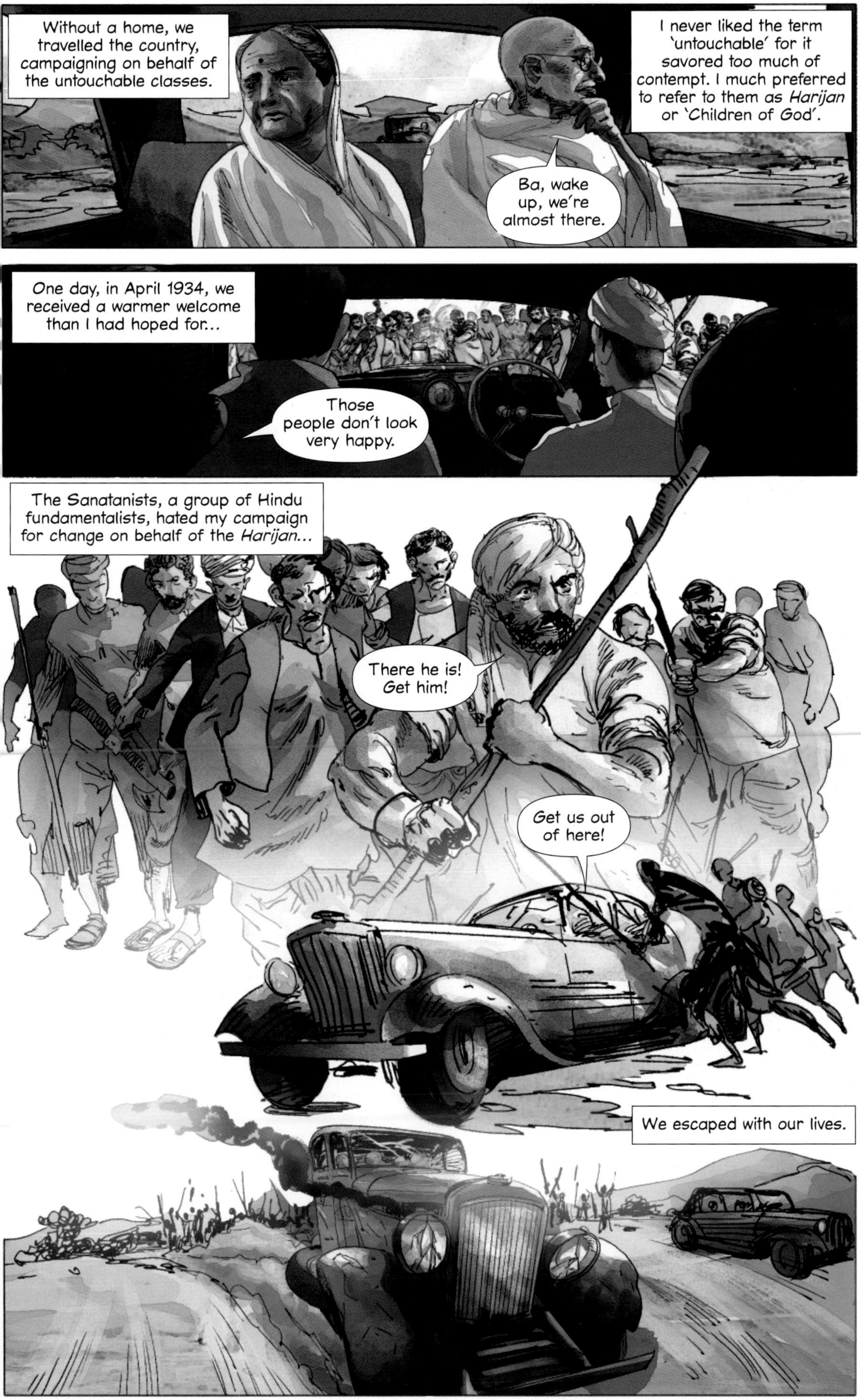
Without a home, we travelled the country, campaigning on behalf of the untouchable classes.
I never liked the term 'untouchable' for it savored too much of contempt. I much preferred to refer to them as *Harijan* or 'Children of God'.
Ba, wake up, we're almost there.
One day, in April 1934, we received a warmer welcome than I had hoped for...
Those people don't look very happy.
The Sanatanists, a group of Hindu fundamentalists, hated my campaign for change on behalf of the *Harijan*...
There he is! Get him!
Get us out of here!
We escaped with our lives.

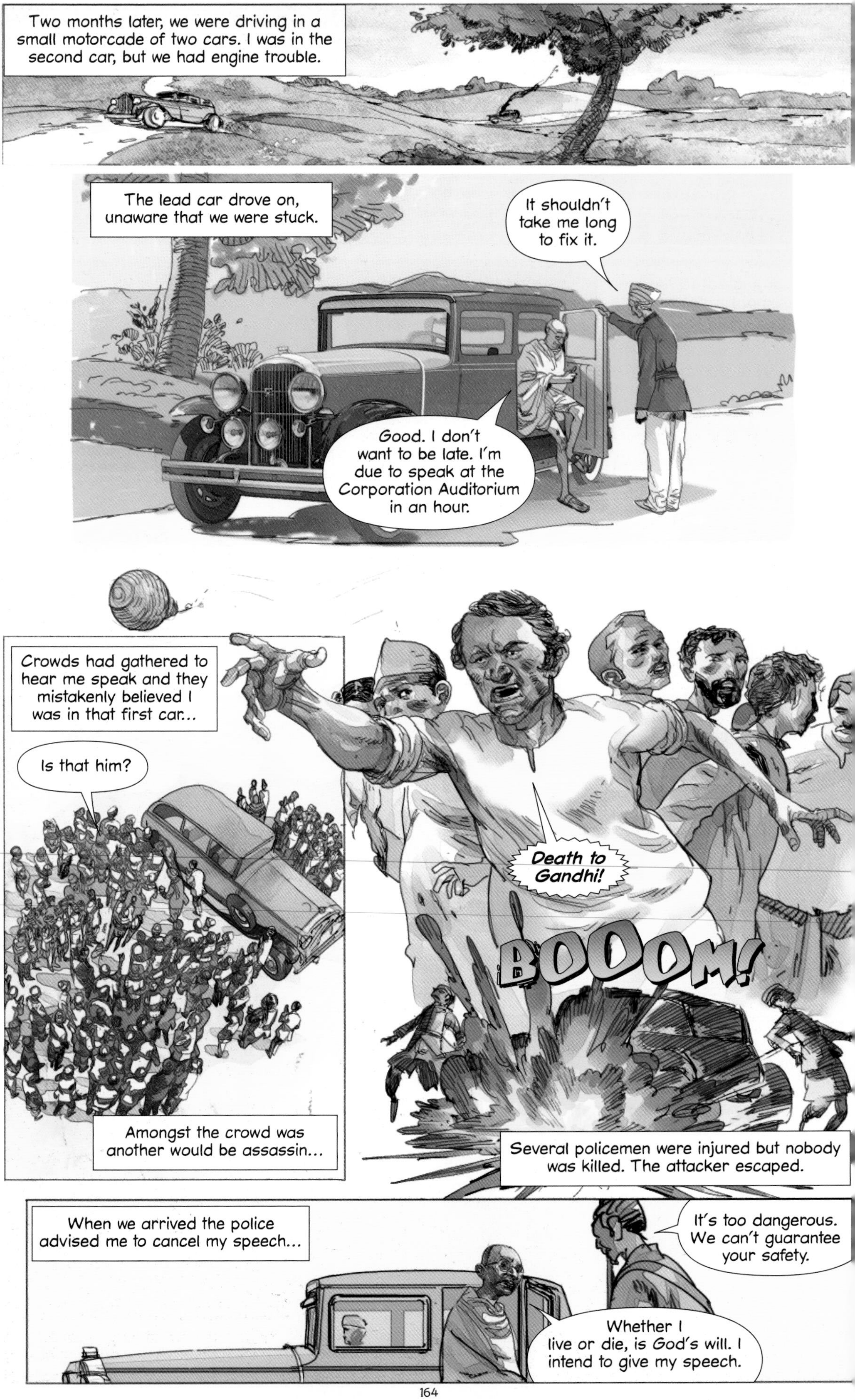
Two months later, we were driving in a small motorcade of two cars. I was in the second car, but we had engine trouble.
The lead car drove on, unaware that we were stuck.
It shouldn't take me long to fix it.
Good. I don't want to be late. I'm due to speak at the Corporation Auditorium in an hour.
Crowds had gathered to hear me speak and they mistakenly believed I was in that first car...
Is that him?
Amongst the crowd was another would be assassin...
Death to Gandhi!
BOOOM!
Several policemen were injured but nobody was killed. The attacker escaped.
When we arrived the police advised me to cancel my speech...
It's too dangerous. We can't guarantee your safety.
Whether I live or die, is God's will. I intend to give my speech.

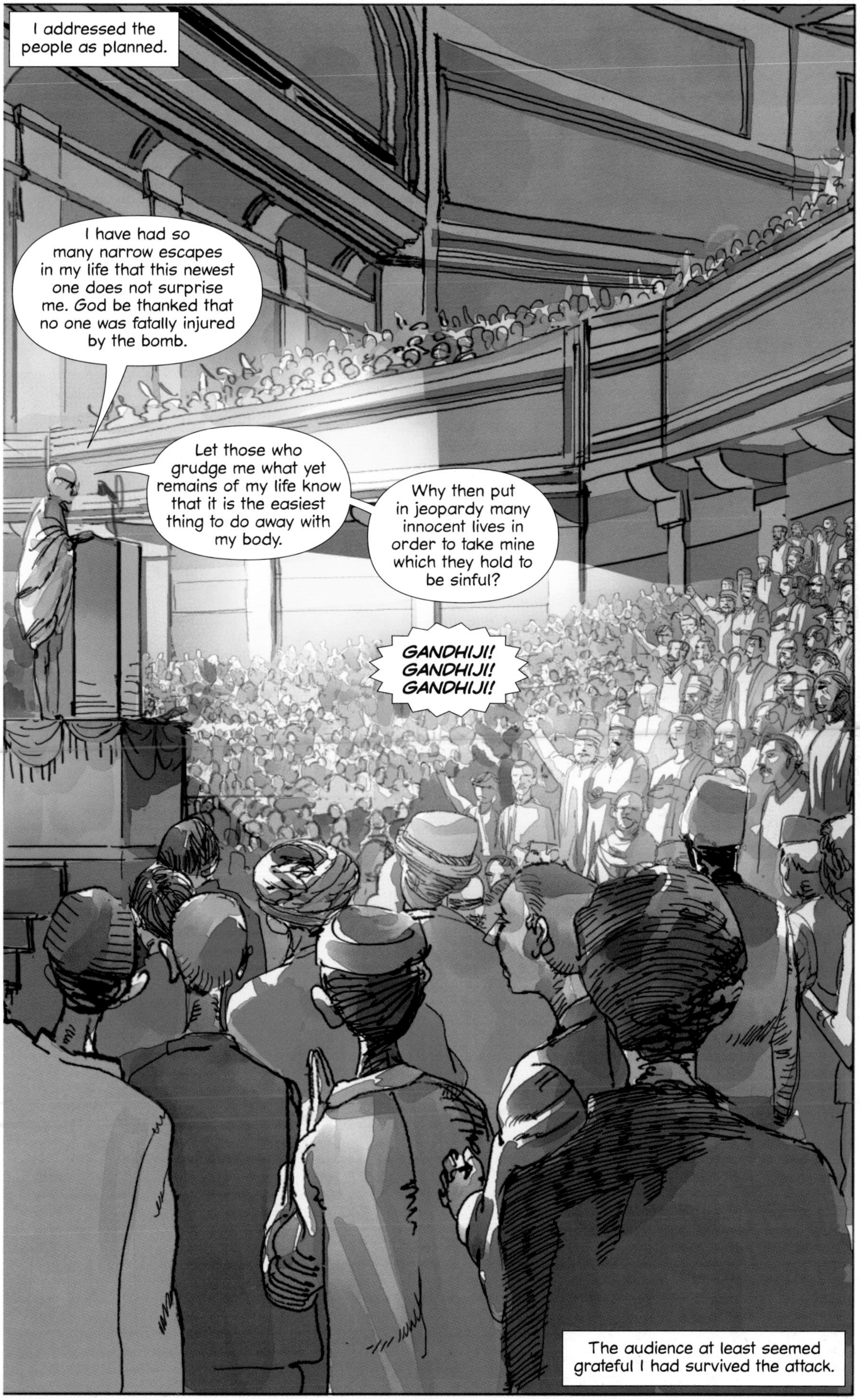
I addressed the people as planned.
I have had so many narrow escapes in my life that this newest one does not surprise me. God be thanked that no one was fatally injured by the bomb.
Let those who grudge me what yet remains of my life know that it is the easiest thing to do away with my body.
Why then put in jeopardy many innocent lives in order to take mine which they hold to be sinful?
GANDHIJI! GANDHIJI! GANDHIJI!
The audience at least seemed grateful I had survived the attack.

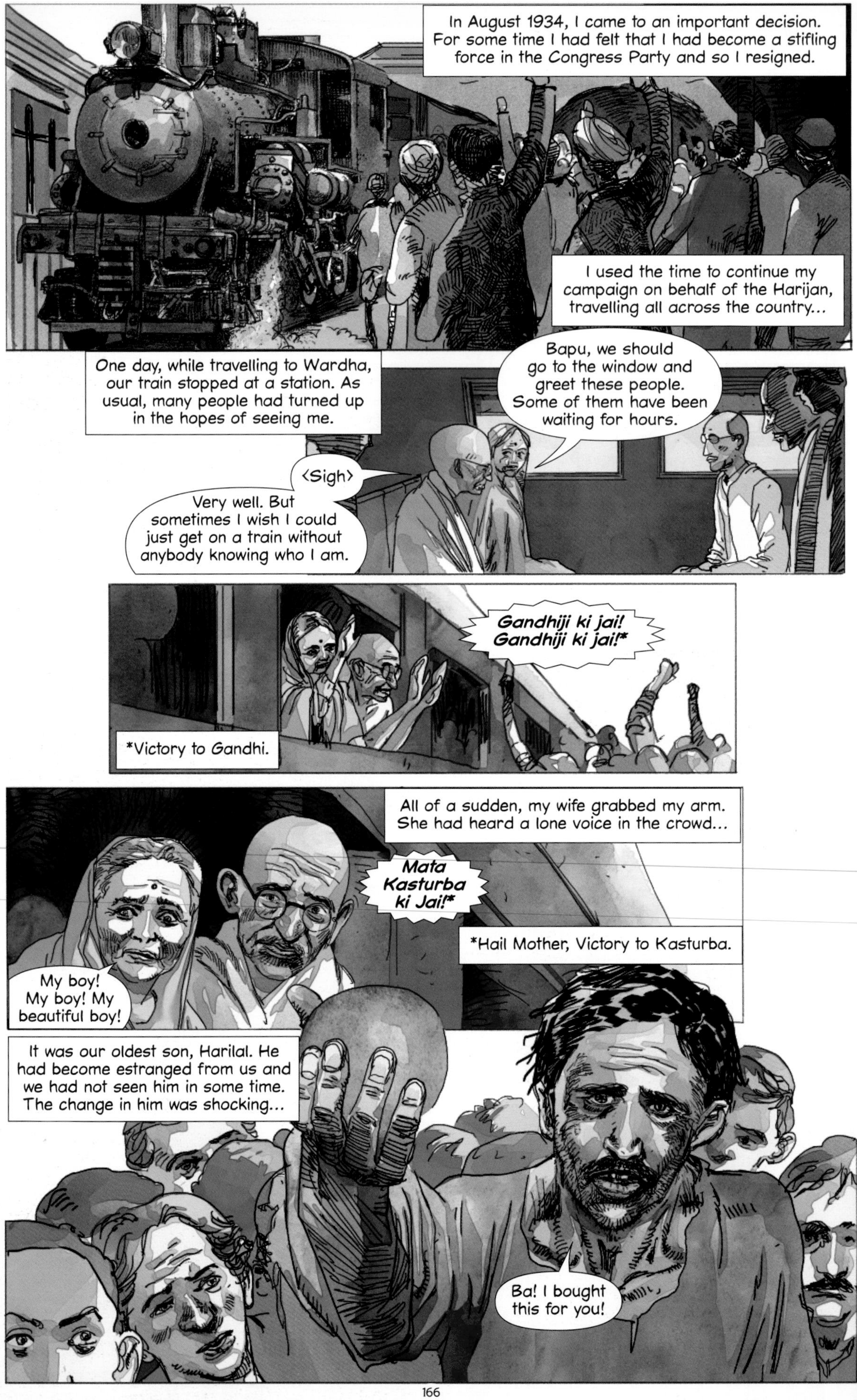

In August 1934, I came to an important decision. For some time I had felt that I had become a stifling force in the Congress Party and so I resigned.
I used the time to continue my campaign on behalf of the Harijan, travelling all across the country...
One day, while travelling to Wardha, our train stopped at a station. As usual, many people had turned up in the hopes of seeing me.
Bapu, we should go to the window and greet these people. Some of them have been waiting for hours.
<Sigh>
Very well. But sometimes I wish I could just get on a train without anybody knowing who I am.
Gandhiji ki jai! Gandhiji ki jai!*
*Victory to Gandhi.
All of a sudden, my wife grabbed my arm. She had heard a lone voice in the crowd...
Mata Kasturba ki Jai!*
*Hail Mother, Victory to Kasturba.
My boy! My boy! My beautiful boy!
It was our oldest son, Harilal. He had become estranged from us and we had not seen him in some time. The change in him was shocking...
Ba! I bought this for you!

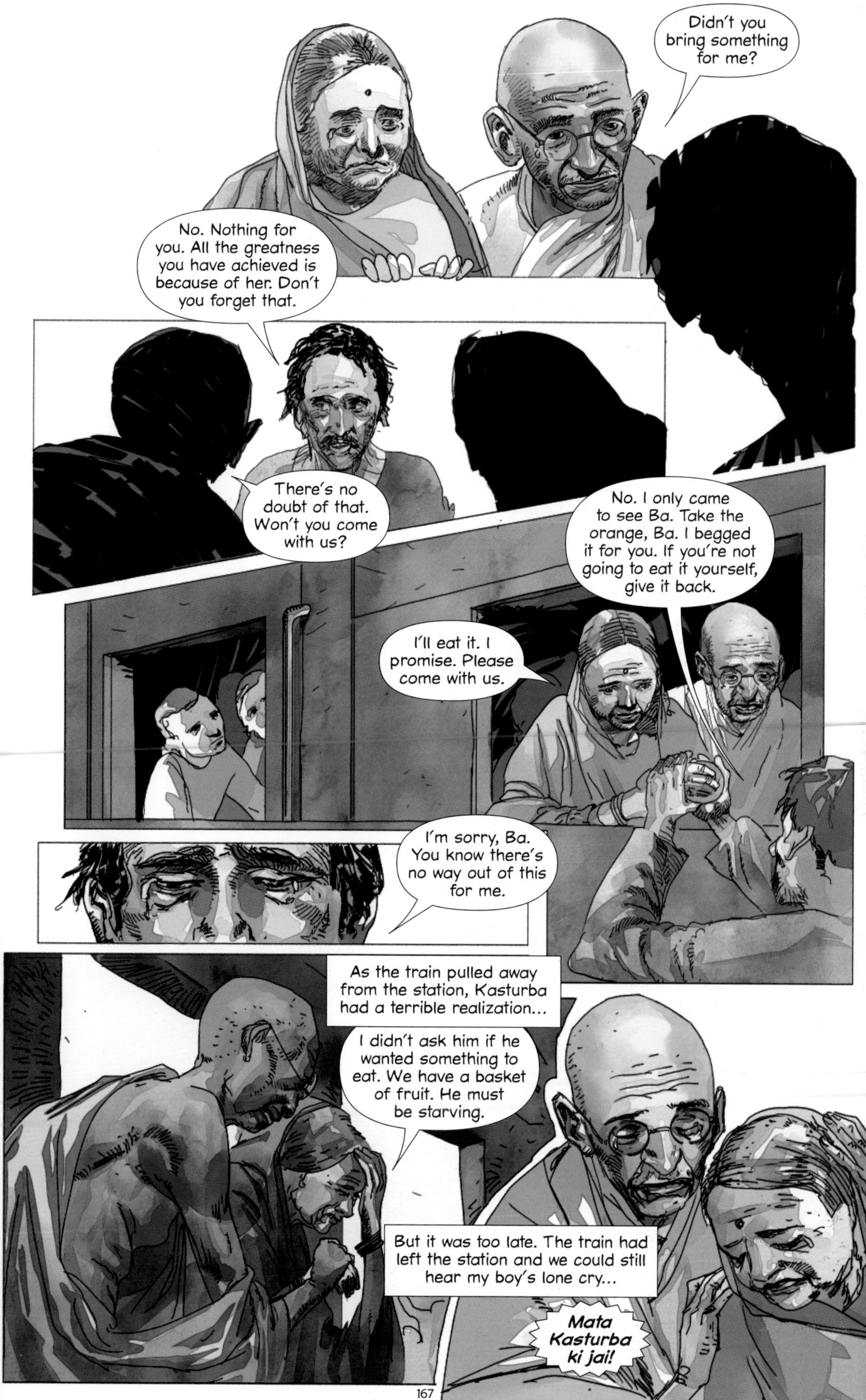
Didn't you bring something for me?
No. Nothing for you. All the greatness you have achieved is because of her. Don't you forget that.
There's no doubt of that. Won't you come with us?
No. I only came to see Ba. Take the orange, Ba. I begged it for you. If you're not going to eat it yourself, give it back.
I'll eat it. I promise. Please come with us.
I'm sorry, Ba. You know there's no way out of this for me.
As the train pulled away from the station, Kasturba had a terrible realization...
I didn't ask him if he wanted something to eat. We have a basket of fruit. He must be starving.
But it was too late. The train had left the station and we could still hear my boy's lone cry...
Mata Kasturba ki jai!

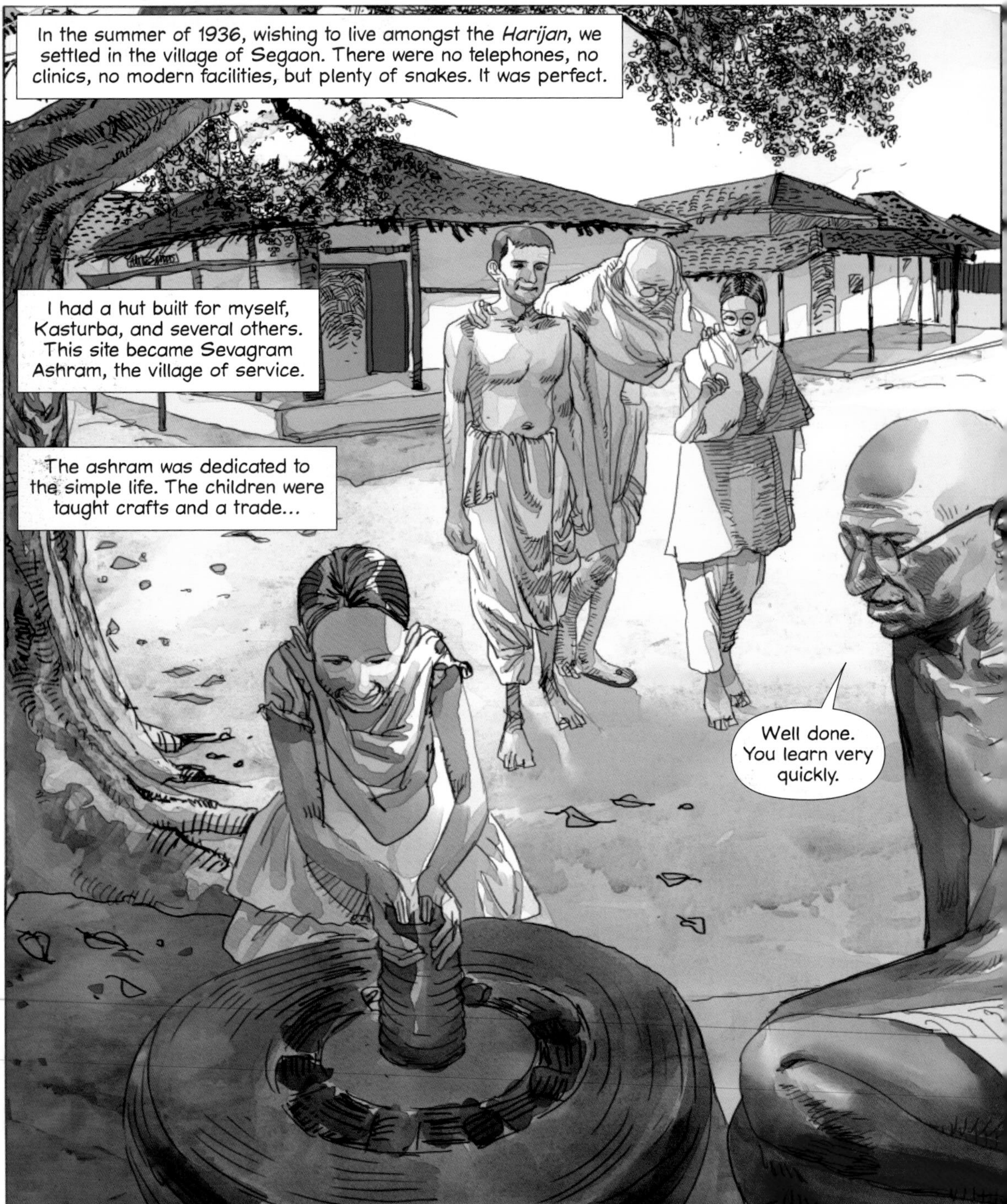
In the summer of 1936, wishing to live amongst the *Harijan*, we settled in the village of Segaon. There were no telephones, no clinics, no modern facilities, but plenty of snakes. It was perfect.
I had a hut built for myself, Kasturba, and several others. This site became Sevagram Ashram, the village of service.
The ashram was dedicated to the simple life. The children were taught crafts and a trade...
Well done. You learn very quickly.

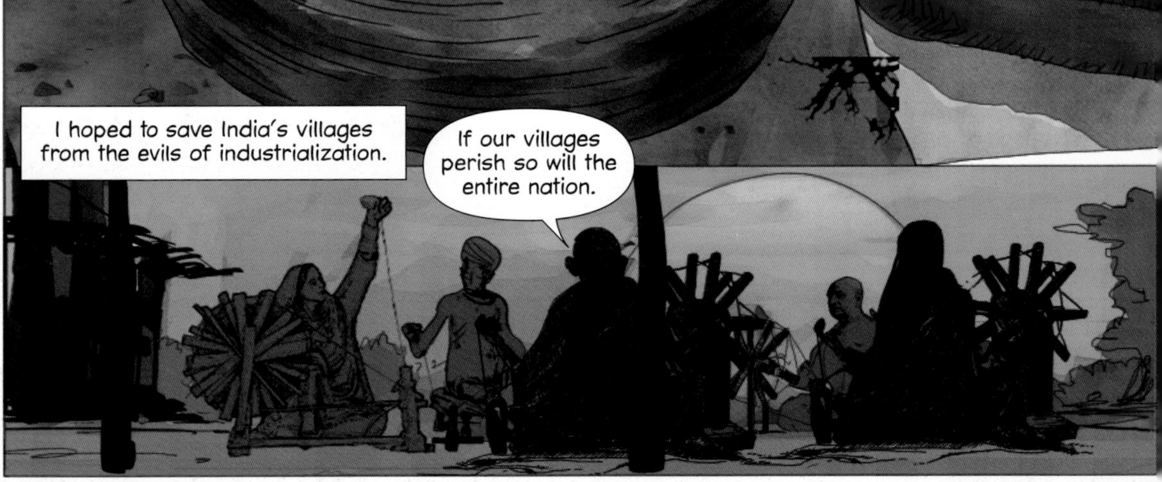
I hoped to save India's villages from the evils of industrialization.
If our villages perish so will the entire nation.

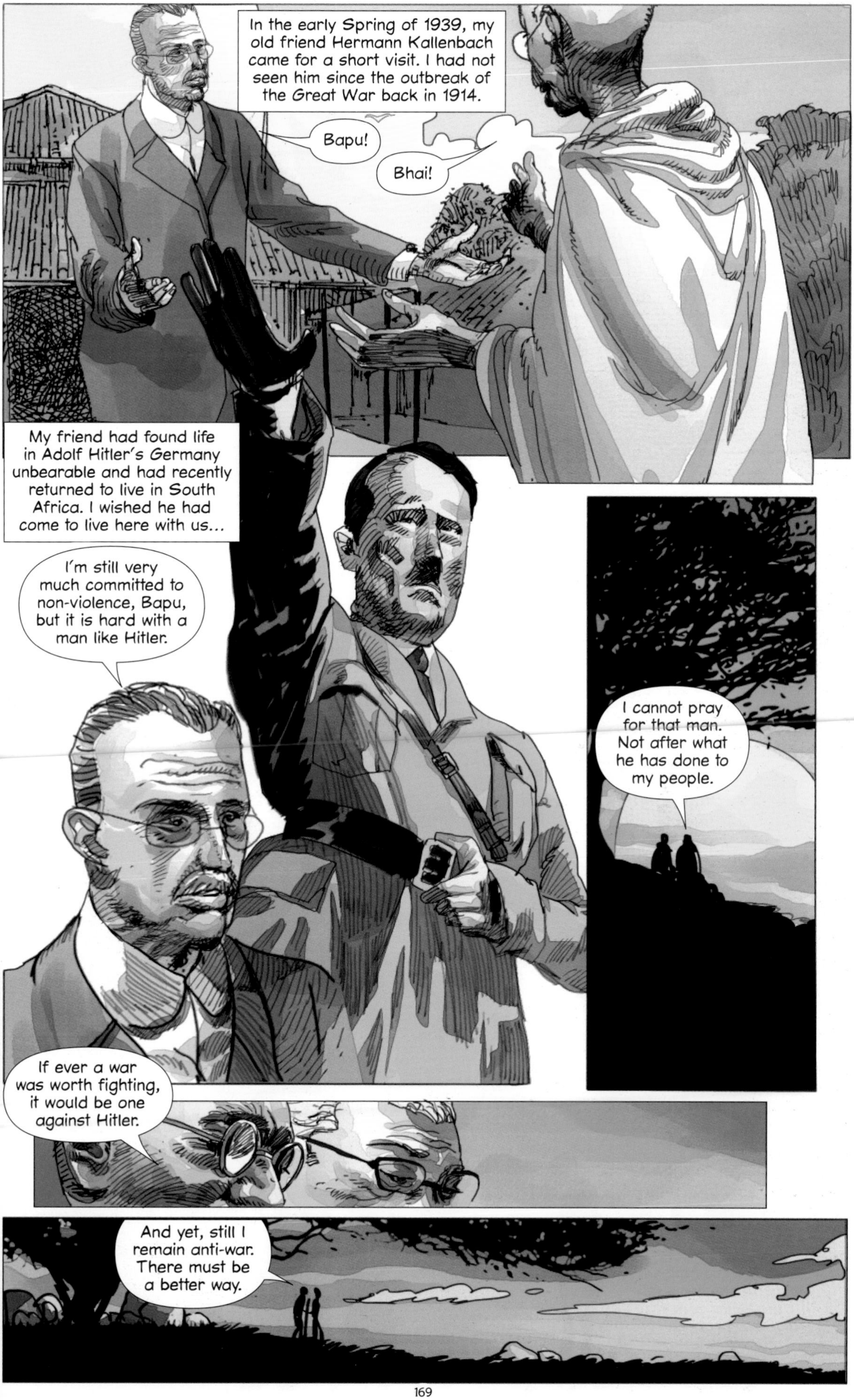
In the early Spring of 1939, my old friend Hermann Kallenbach came for a short visit. I had not seen him since the outbreak of the Great War back in 1914.
Bapu!
Bhai!
My friend had found life in Adolf Hitler's Germany unbearable and had recently returned to live in South Africa. I wished he had come to live here with us...
I'm still very much committed to non-violence, Bapu, but it is hard with a man like Hitler.
I cannot pray for that man. Not after what he has done to my people.
If ever a war was worth fighting, it would be one against Hitler.
And yet, still I remain anti-war. There must be a better way.

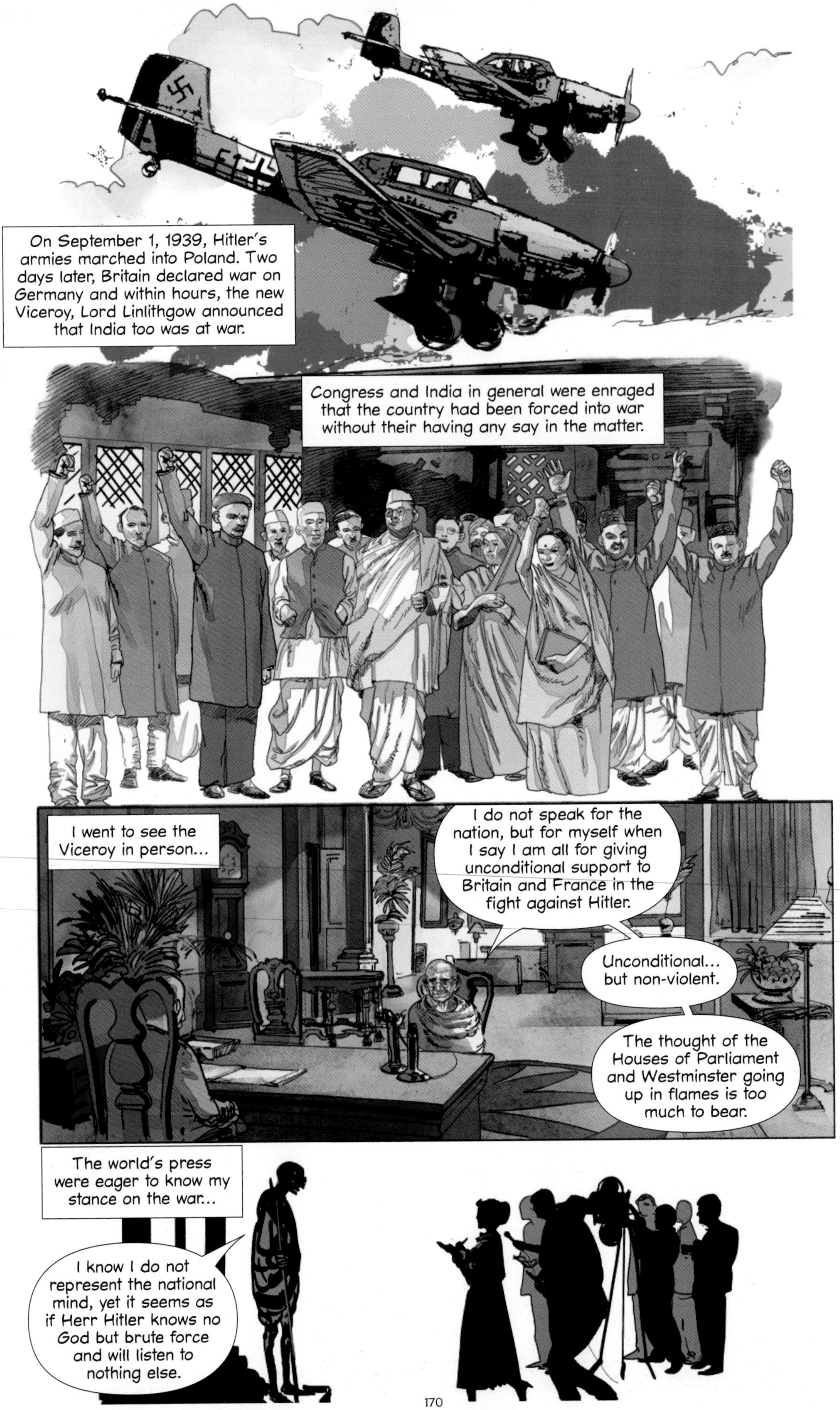
On September 1, 1939, Hitler's armies marched into Poland. Two days later, Britain declared war on Germany and within hours, the new Viceroy, Lord Linlithgow announced that India too was at war.
Congress and India in general were enraged that the country had been forced into war without their having any say in the matter.
I went to see the Viceroy in person...
I do not speak for the nation, but for myself when I say I am all for giving unconditional support to Britain and France in the fight against Hitler.
Unconditional... but non-violent.
The thought of the Houses of Parliament and Westminster going up in flames is too much to bear.
The world's press were eager to know my stance on the war...
I know I do not represent the national mind, yet it seems as if Herr Hitler knows no God but brute force and will listen to nothing else.

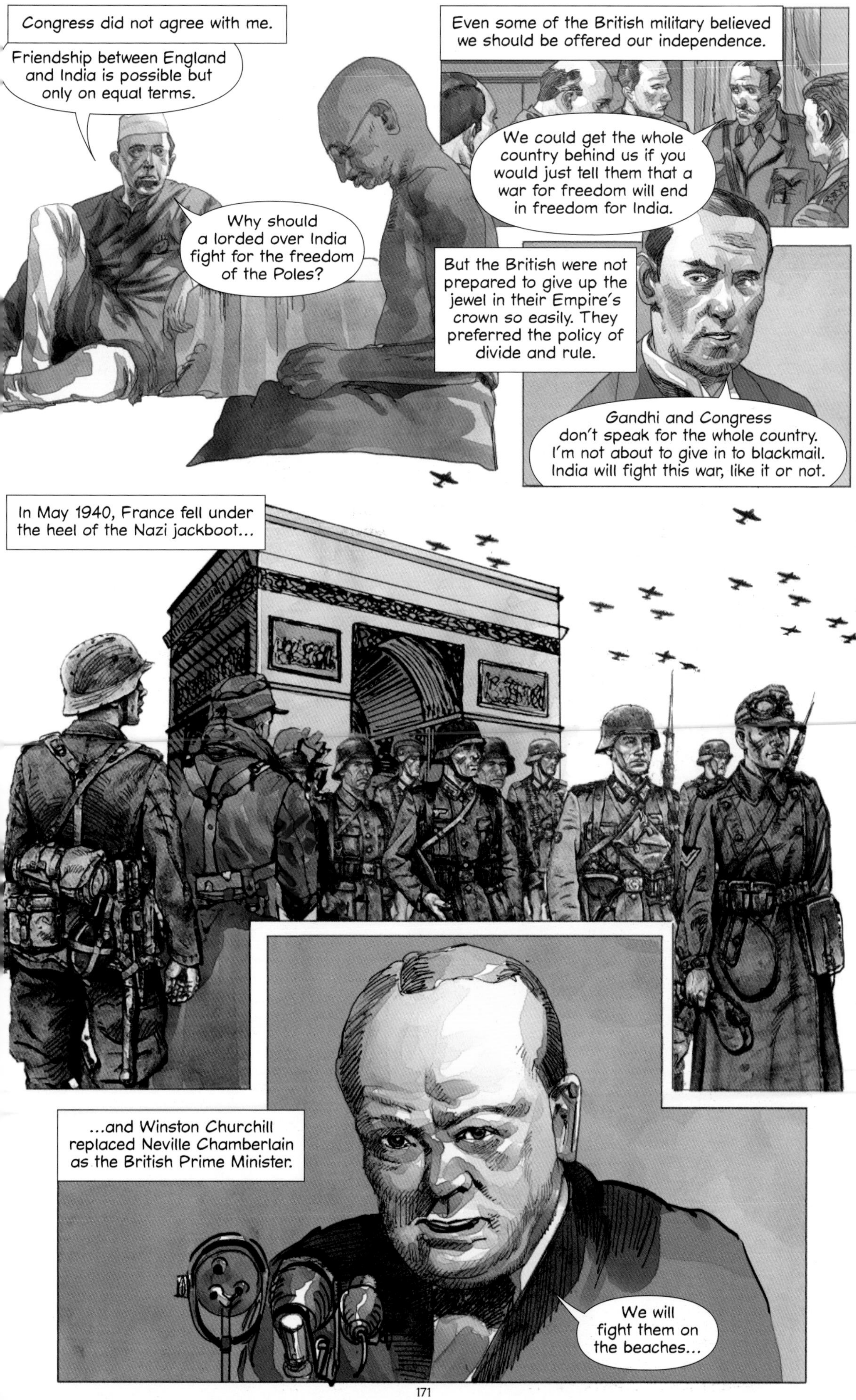
Congress did not agree with me.
Friendship between England and India is possible but only on equal terms.
Why should a lorded over India fight for the freedom of the Poles?
Even some of the British military believed we should be offered our independence.
We could get the whole country behind us if you would just tell them that a war for freedom will end in freedom for India.
But the British were not prepared to give up the jewel in their Empire's crown so easily. They preferred the policy of divide and rule.
Gandhi and Congress don't speak for the whole country. I'm not about to give in to blackmail. India will fight this war, like it or not.
In May 1940, France fell under the heel of the Nazi jackboot...
...and Winston Churchill replaced Neville Chamberlain as the British Prime Minister.
We will fight them on the beaches...

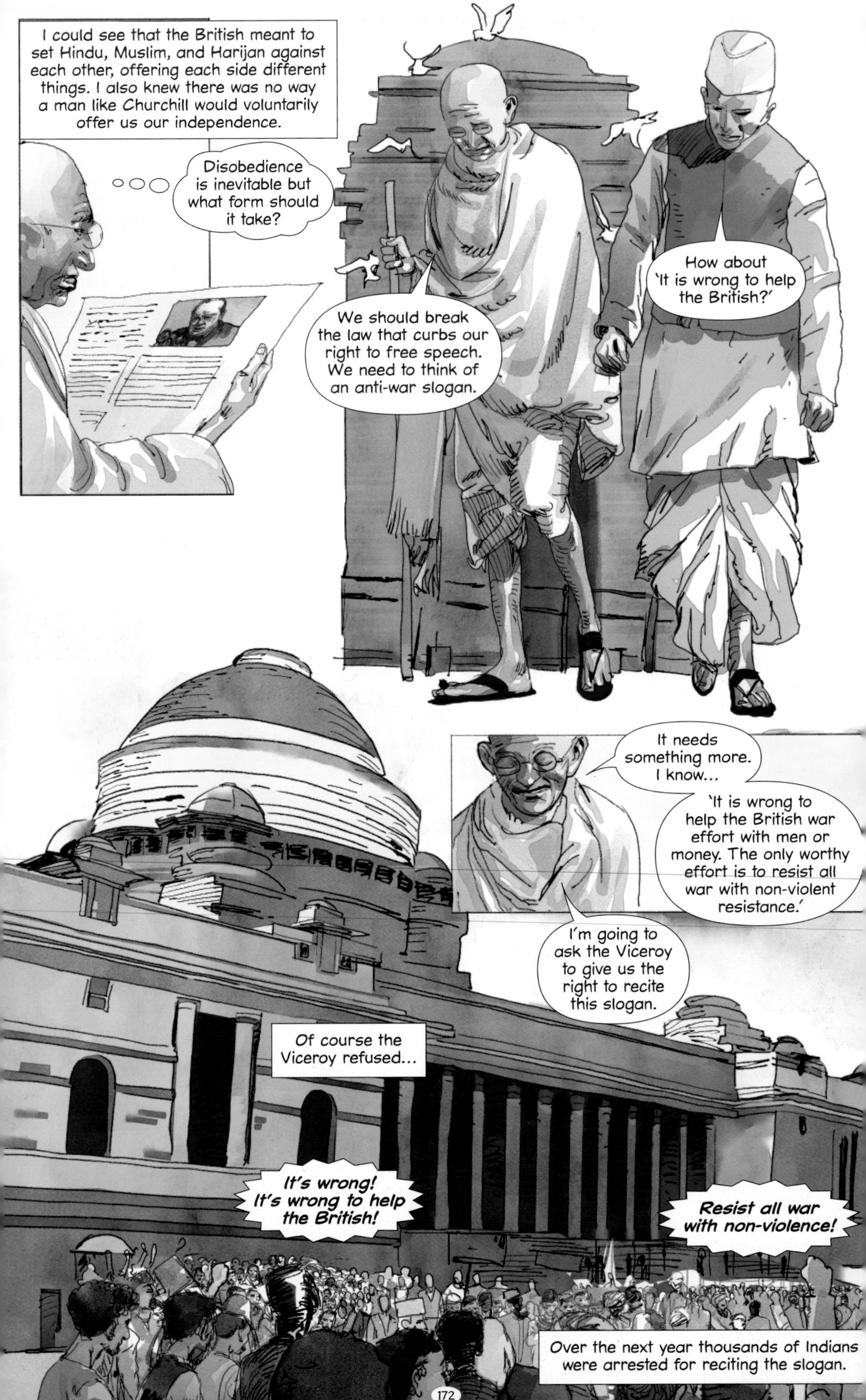
I could see that the British meant to set Hindu, Muslim, and Harijan against each other, offering each side different things. I also knew there was no way a man like Churchill would voluntarily offer us our independence.
Disobedience is inevitable but what form should it take?
We should break the law that curbs our right to free speech. We need to think of an anti-war slogan.
How about 'It is wrong to help the British?'
It needs something more. I know...
'It is wrong to help the British war effort with men or money. The only worthy effort is to resist all war with non-violent resistance.'
I'm going to ask the Viceroy to give us the right to recite this slogan.
Of course the Viceroy refused...
It's wrong! It's wrong to help the British!
Resist all war with non-violence!
Over the next year thousands of Indians were arrested for reciting the slogan.

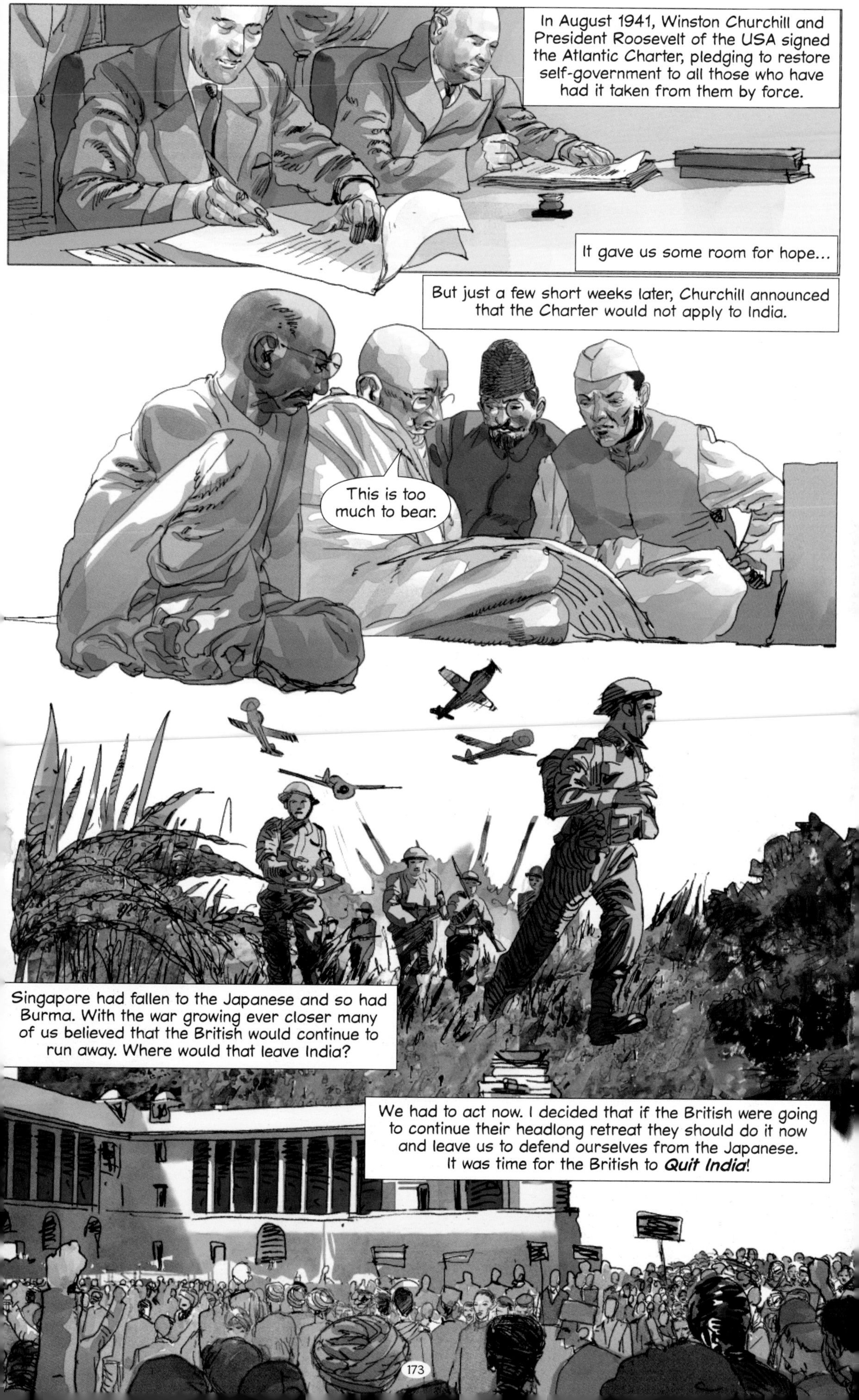
In August 1941, Winston Churchill and President Roosevelt of the USA signed the Atlantic Charter, pledging to restore self-government to all those who have had it taken from them by force.
It gave us some room for hope...
But just a few short weeks later, Churchill announced that the Charter would not apply to India.
This is too much to bear.
Singapore had fallen to the Japanese and so had Burma. With the war growing ever closer many of us believed that the British would continue to run away. Where would that leave India?
We had to act now. I decided that if the British were going to continue their headlong retreat they should do it now and leave us to defend ourselves from the Japanese. It was time for the British to ***Quit India***!

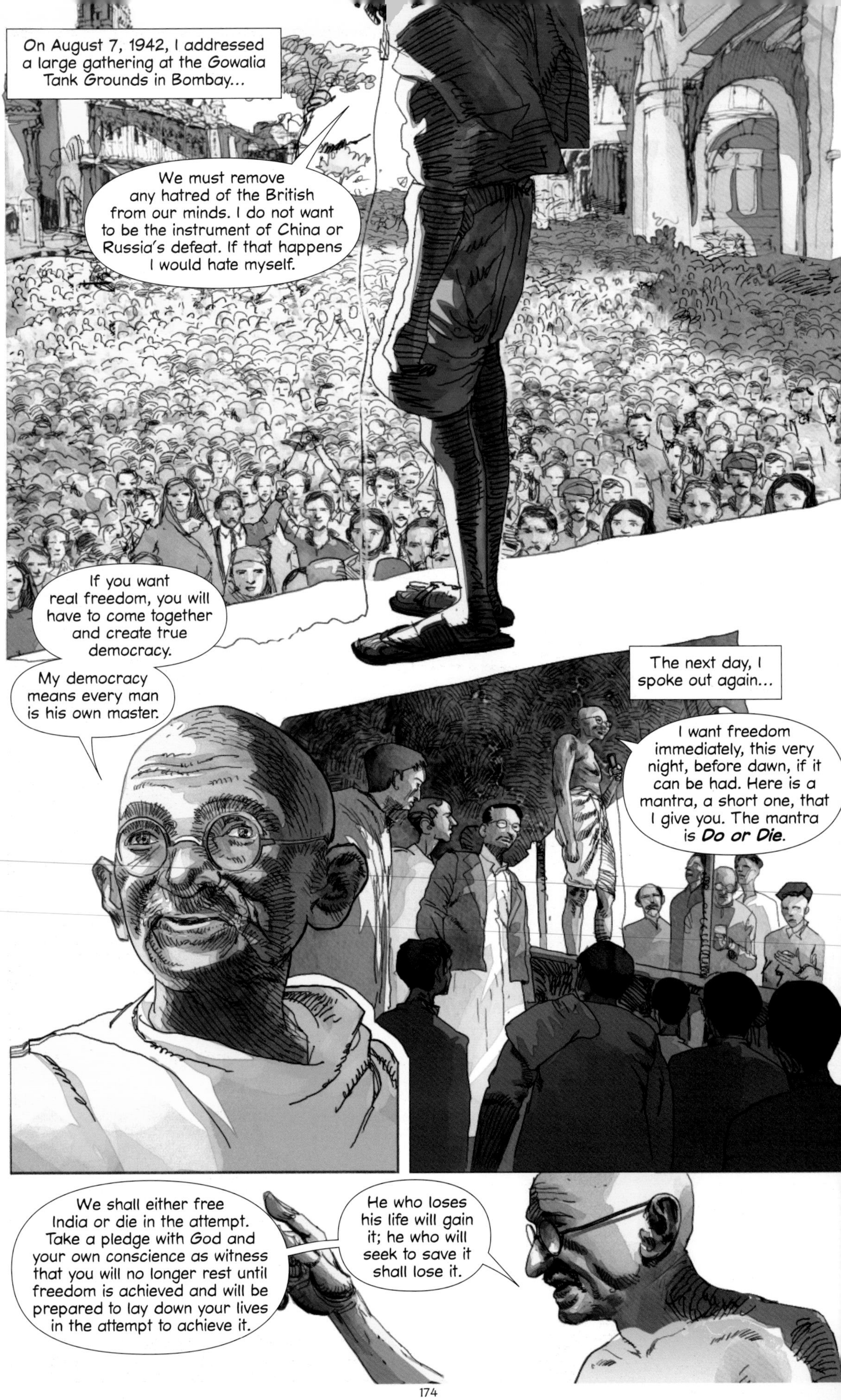

On August 7, 1942, I addressed a large gathering at the Gowalia Tank Grounds in Bombay...
We must remove any hatred of the British from our minds. I do not want to be the instrument of China or Russia's defeat. If that happens I would hate myself.
If you want real freedom, you will have to come together and create true democracy.
My democracy means every man is his own master.
The next day, I spoke out again...
I want freedom immediately, this very night, before dawn, if it can be had. Here is a mantra, a short one, that I give you. The mantra is ***Do or Die***.
We shall either free India or die in the attempt. Take a pledge with God and your own conscience as witness that you will no longer rest until freedom is achieved and will be prepared to lay down your lives in the attempt to achieve it.
He who loses his life will gain it; he who will seek to save it shall lose it.

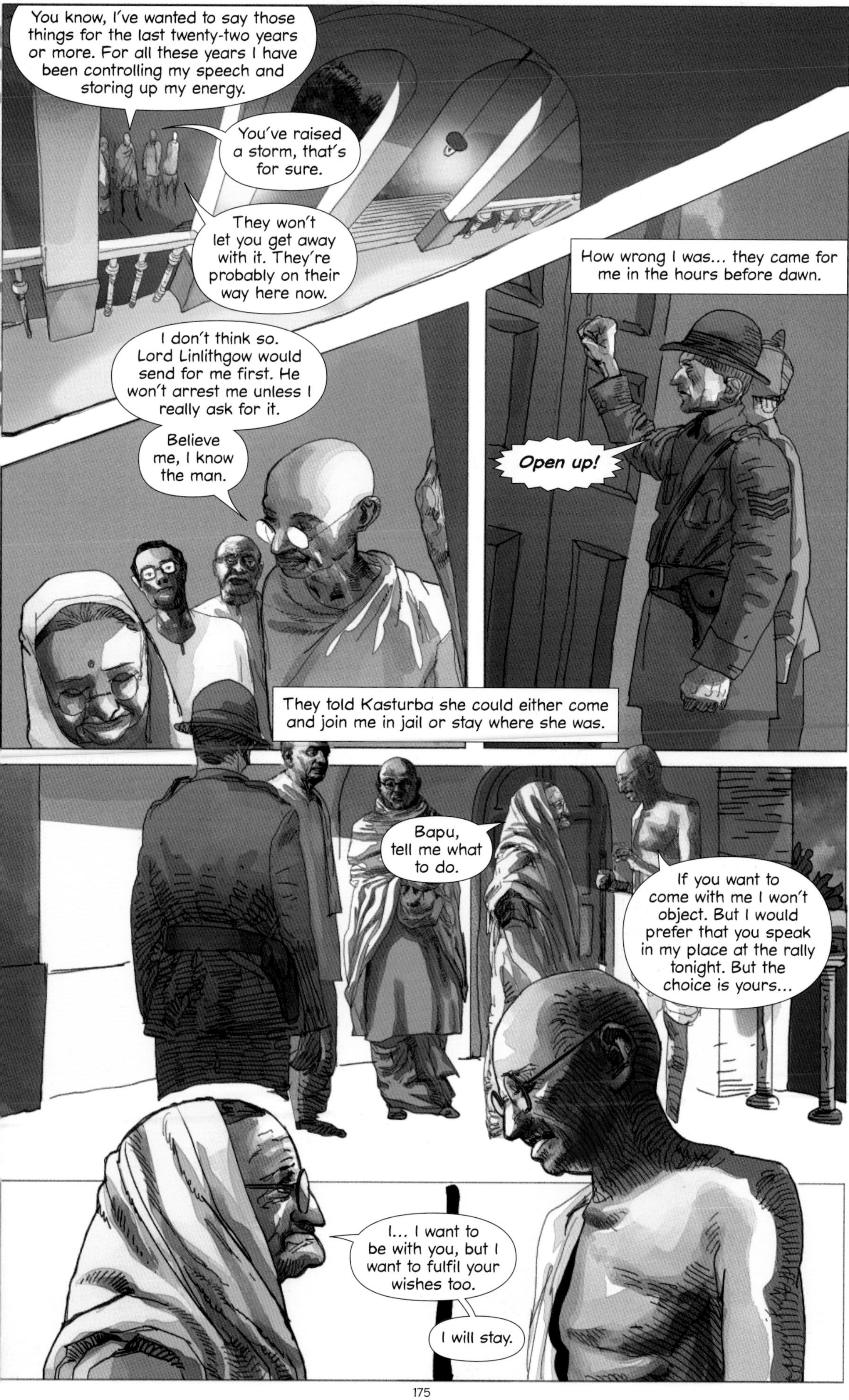
You know, I've wanted to say those things for the last twenty-two years or more. For all these years I have been controlling my speech and storing up my energy.
You've raised a storm, that's for sure.
They won't let you get away with it. They're probably on their way here now.
I don't think so. Lord Linlithgow would send for me first. He won't arrest me unless I really ask for it.
Believe me, I know the man.
How wrong I was... they came for me in the hours before dawn.
Open up!
They told Kasturba she could either come and join me in jail or stay where she was.
Bapu, tell me what to do.
If you want to come with me I won't object. But I would prefer that you speak in my place at the rally tonight. But the choice is yours...
I... I want to be with you, but I want to fulfil your wishes too.
I will stay.

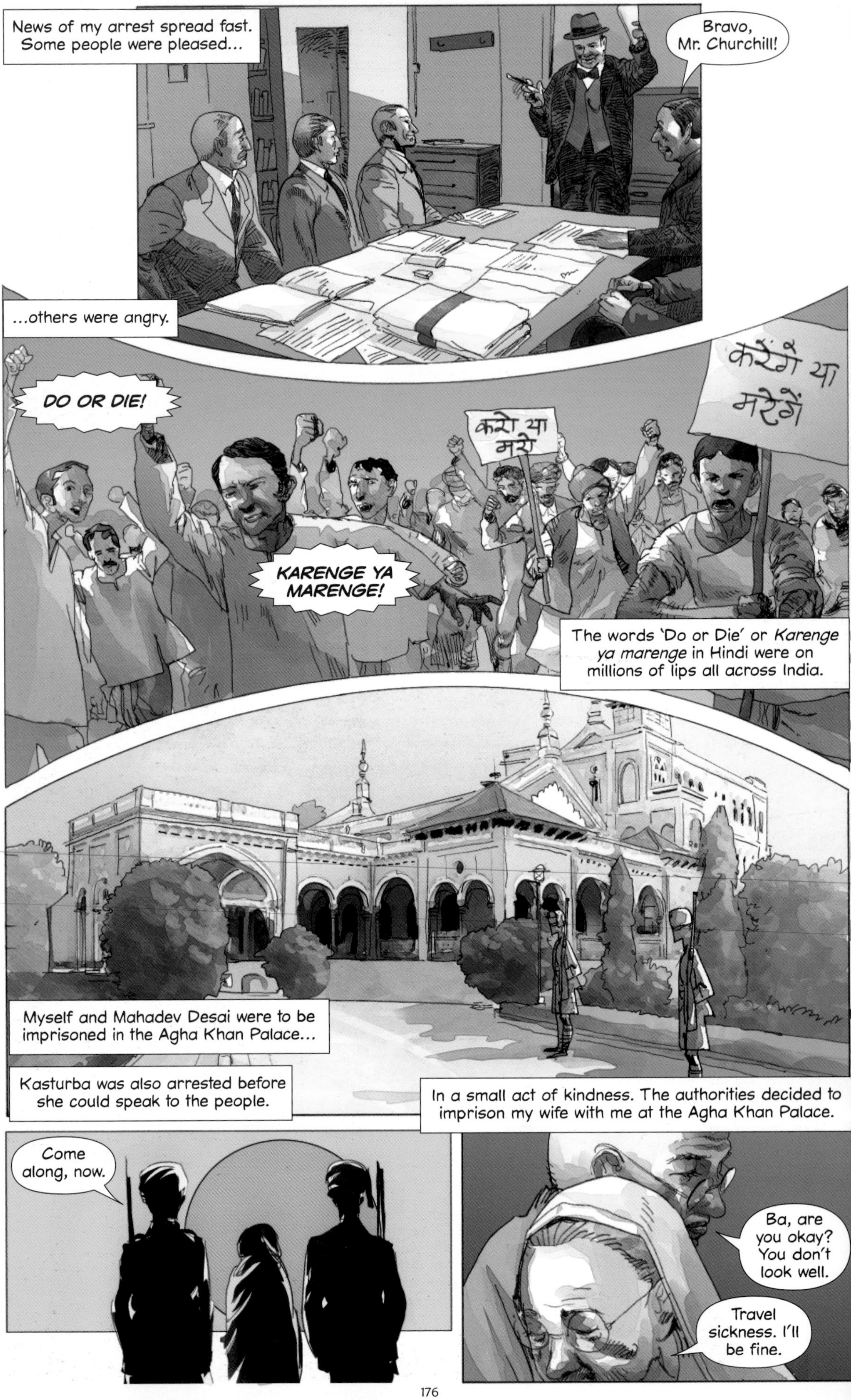
News of my arrest spread fast. Some people were pleased...
Bravo, Mr. Churchill!
...others were angry.
DO OR DIE!
करो या मरो
करेंगे या मरेंगे
KARENGE YA MARENGE!
The words 'Do or Die' or *Karenge ya marenge* in Hindi were on millions of lips all across India.
Myself and Mahadev Desai were to be imprisoned in the Agha Khan Palace...
Kasturba was also arrested before she could speak to the people.
In a small act of kindness. The authorities decided to imprison my wife with me at the Agha Khan Palace.
Come along, now.
Ba, are you okay? You don't look well.
Travel sickness. I'll be fine.

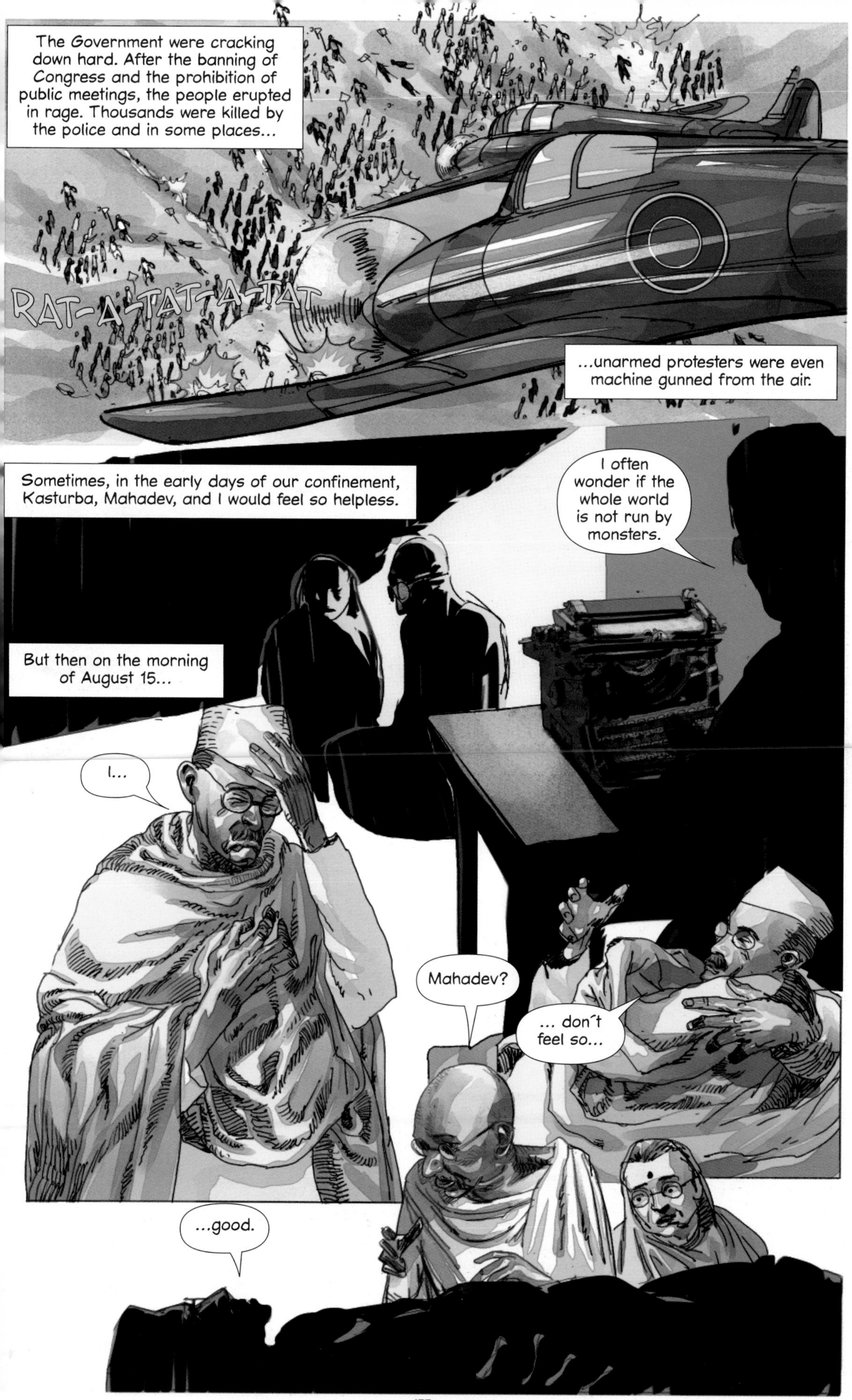
The Government were cracking down hard. After the banning of Congress and the prohibition of public meetings, the people erupted in rage. Thousands were killed by the police and in some places...
RAT-A-TAT-A-TAT
...unarmed protesters were even machine gunned from the air.
Sometimes, in the early days of our confinement, Kasturba, Mahadev, and I would feel so helpless.
I often wonder if the whole world is not run by monsters.
But then on the morning of August 15...
I...
Mahadev?
... don´t feel so...
...good.

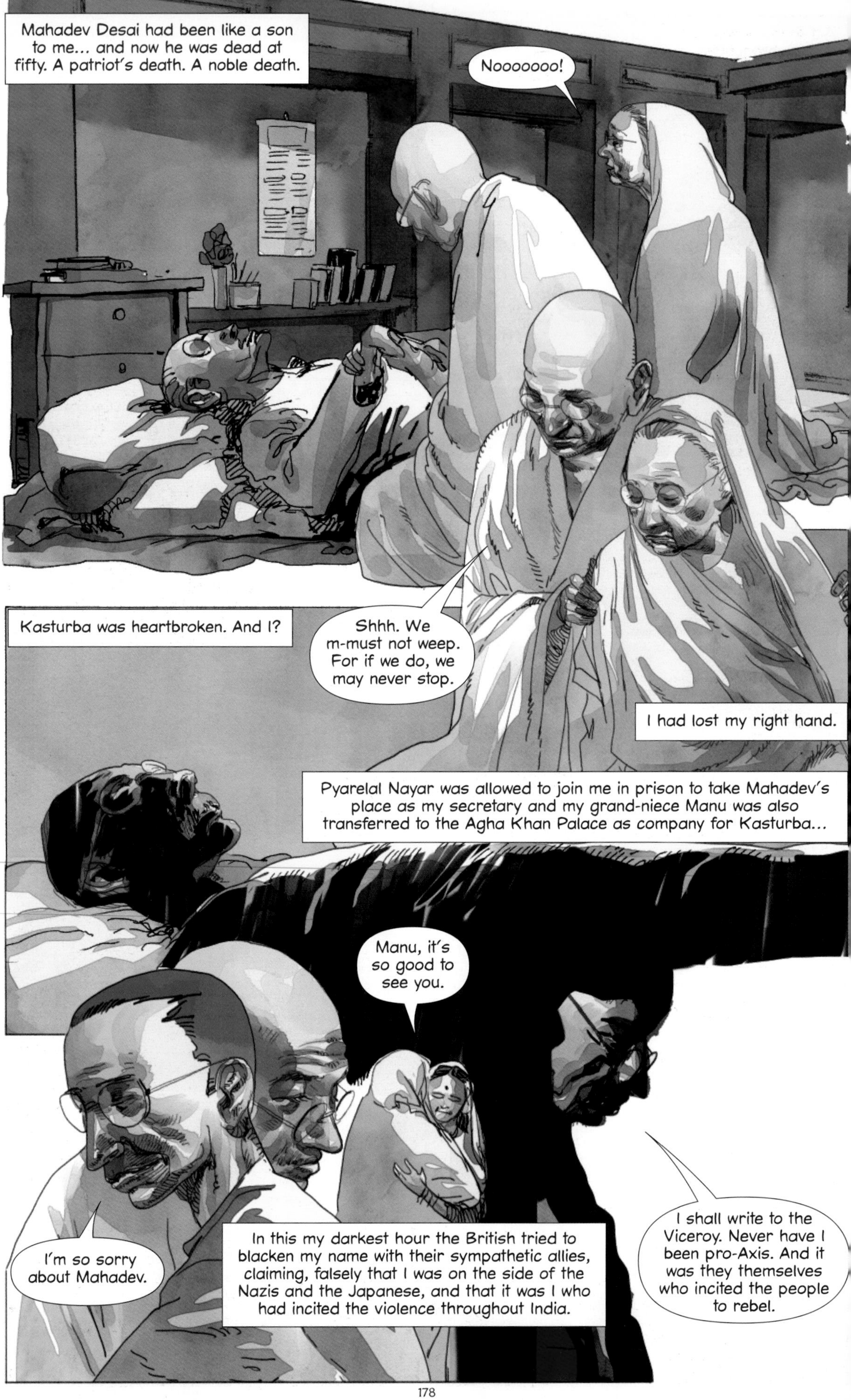
Mahadev Desai had been like a son to me... and now he was dead at fifty. A patriot's death. A noble death.
Noooooooo!
Kasturba was heartbroken. And I?
Shhh. We m-must not weep. For if we do, we may never stop.
I had lost my right hand.
Pyarelal Nayar was allowed to join me in prison to take Mahadev's place as my secretary and my grand-niece Manu was also transferred to the Agha Khan Palace as company for Kasturba...
Manu, it's so good to see you.
I'm so sorry about Mahadev.
In this my darkest hour the British tried to blacken my name with their sympathetic allies, claiming, falsely that I was on the side of the Nazis and the Japanese, and that it was I who had incited the violence throughout India.
I shall write to the Viceroy. Never have I been pro-Axis. And it was they themselves who incited the people to rebel.

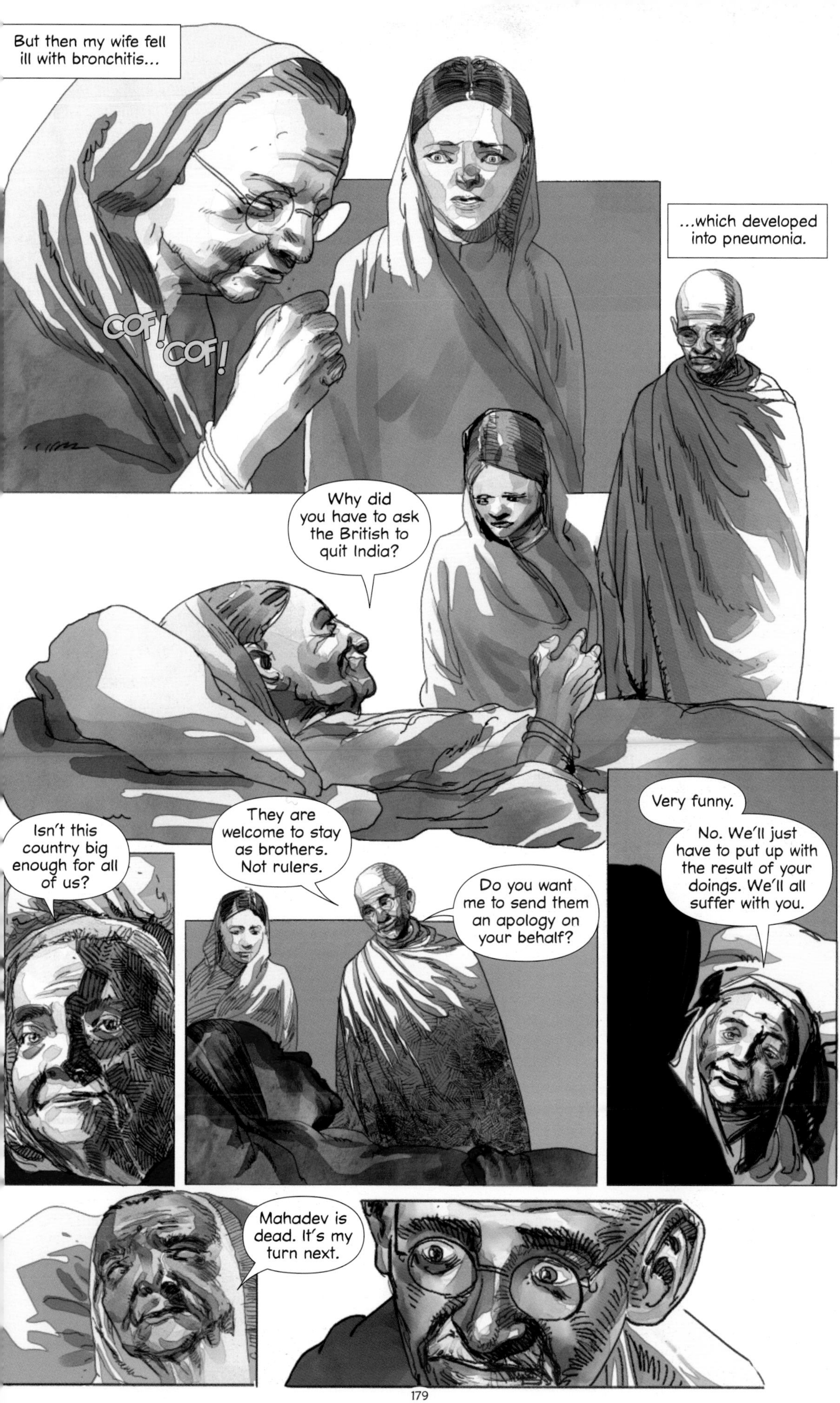

But then my wife fell ill with bronchitis...
COF! COF!
...which developed into pneumonia.
Why did you have to ask the British to quit India?
Isn't this country big enough for all of us?
They are welcome to stay as brothers. Not rulers.
Do you want me to send them an apology on your behalf?
Very funny.
No. We'll just have to put up with the result of your doings. We'll all suffer with you.
Mahadev is dead. It's my turn next.

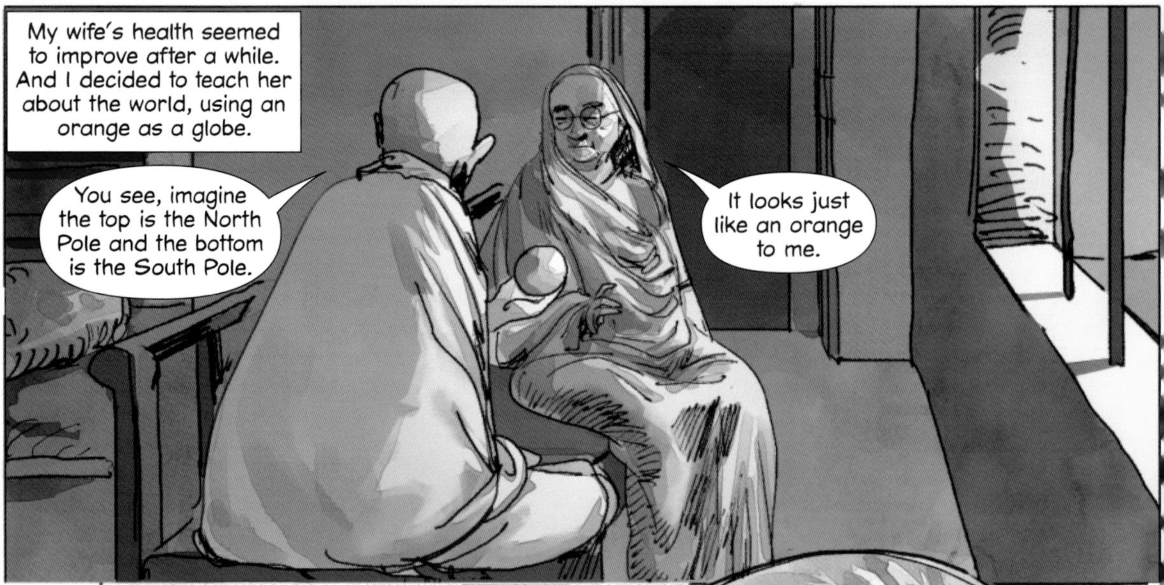
My wife's health seemed to improve after a while. And I decided to teach her about the world, using an orange as a globe.
You see, imagine the top is the North Pole and the bottom is the South Pole.
It looks just like an orange to me.

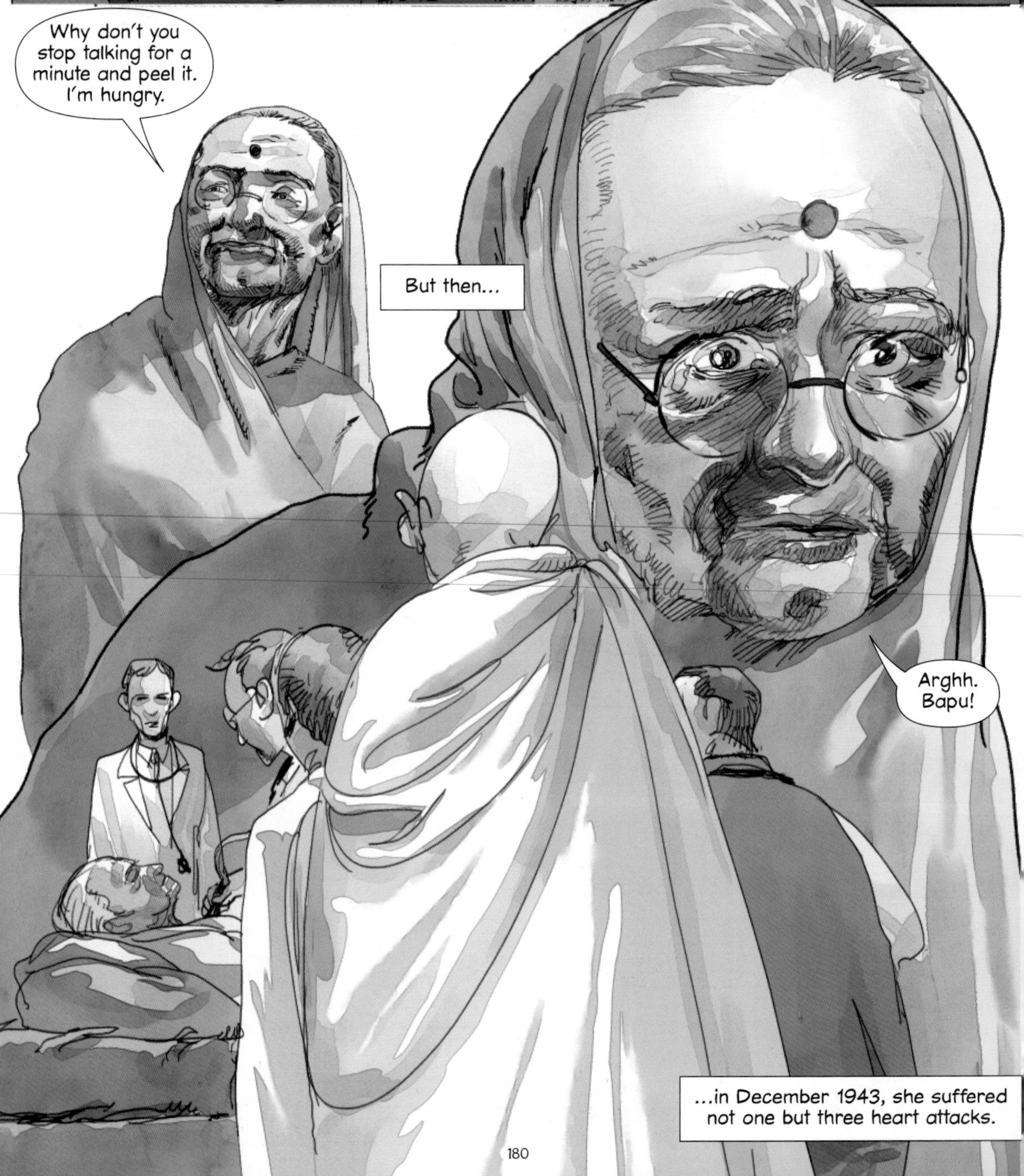
Why don't you stop talking for a minute and peel it. I'm hungry.
But then...
Arghh. Bapu!
...in December 1943, she suffered not one but three heart attacks.

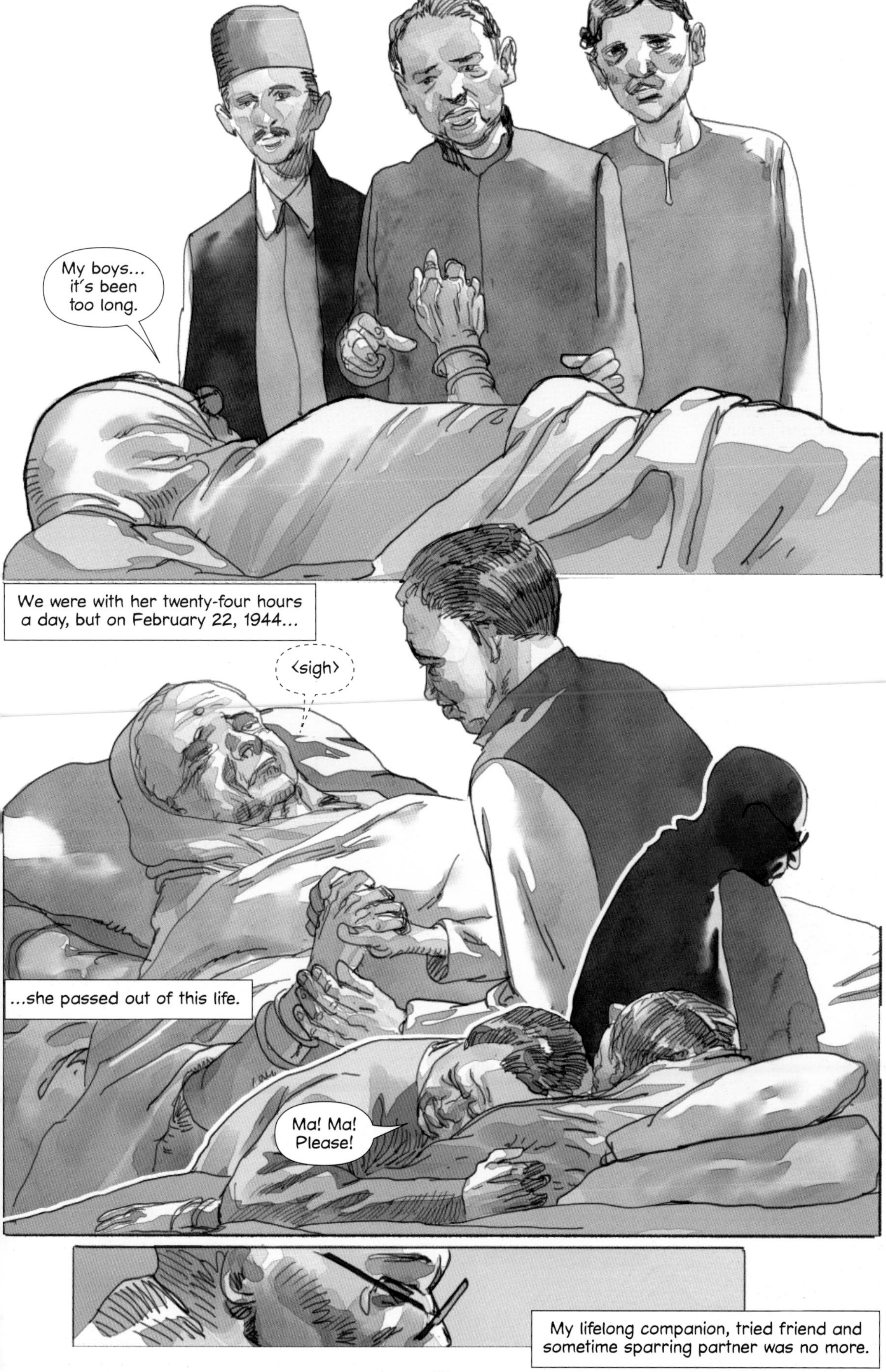
My boys... it's been too long.
We were with her twenty-four hours a day, but on February 22, 1944...
<sigh>
...she passed out of this life.
Ma! Ma! Please!
My lifelong companion, tried friend and sometime sparring partner was no more.

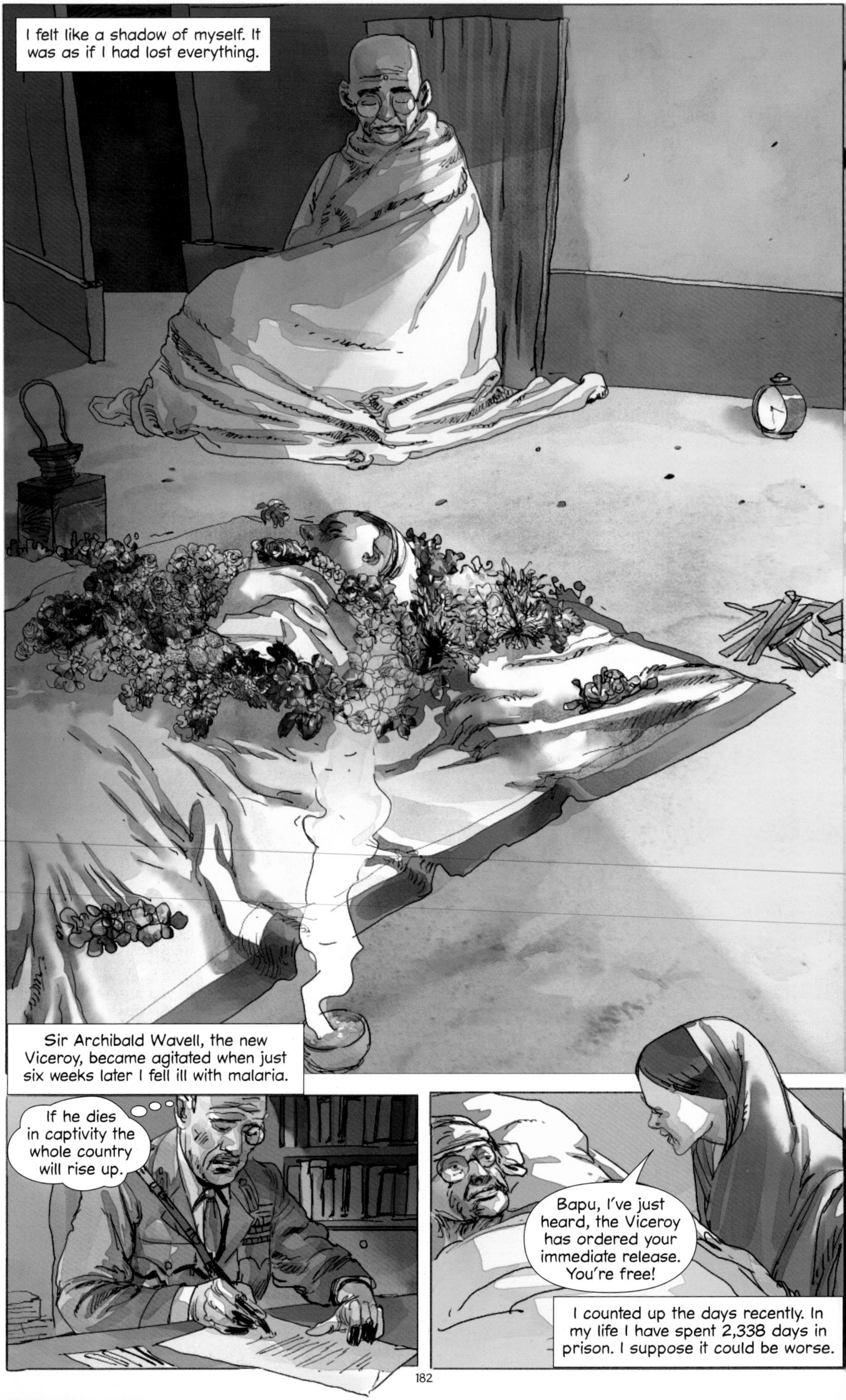

I felt like a shadow of myself. It was as if I had lost everything.
Sir Archibald Wavell, the new Viceroy, became agitated when just six weeks later I fell ill with malaria.
If he dies in captivity the whole country will rise up.
Bapu, I've just heard, the Viceroy has ordered your immediate release. You're free!
I counted up the days recently. In my life I have spent 2,338 days in prison. I suppose it could be worse.

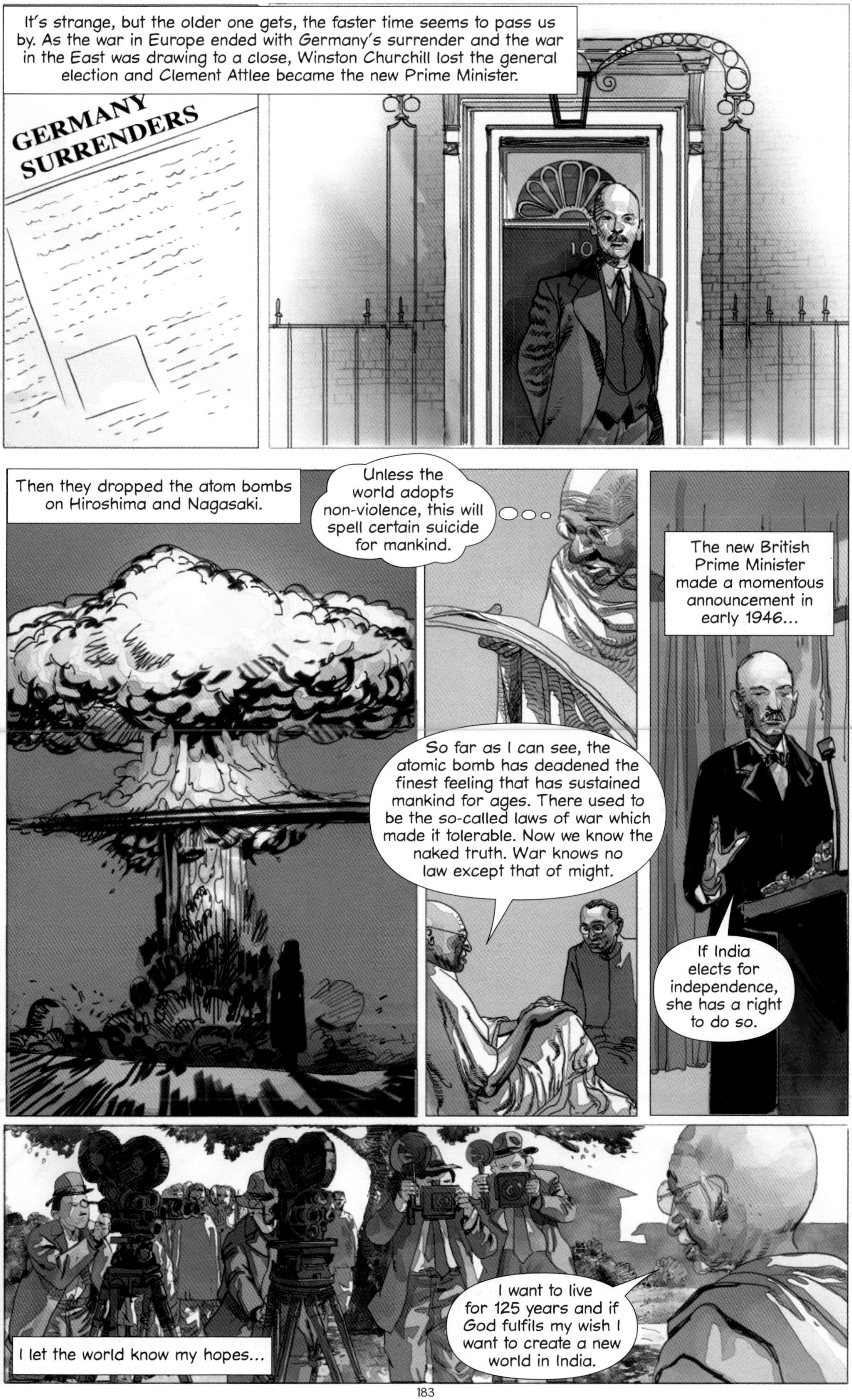
It's strange, but the older one gets, the faster time seems to pass us by. As the war in Europe ended with Germany's surrender and the war in the East was drawing to a close, Winston Churchill lost the general election and Clement Attlee became the new Prime Minister.
GERMANY SURRENDERS
10
Then they dropped the atom bombs on Hiroshima and Nagasaki.
Unless the world adopts non-violence, this will spell certain suicide for mankind.
So far as I can see, the atomic bomb has deadened the finest feeling that has sustained mankind for ages. There used to be the so-called laws of war which made it tolerable. Now we know the naked truth. War knows no law except that of might.
The new British Prime Minister made a momentous announcement in early 1946...
If India elects for independence, she has a right to do so.
I let the world know my hopes...
I want to live for 125 years and if God fulfils my wish I want to create a new world in India.

The moment we had been fighting for all our lives was almost upon us. But I did not feel like rejoicing. Muhammad Ali Jinnah and the Muslim League were calling for a separate nation of Pakistan for India's Muslim community.
I could not bring myself to accept the idea of a separate state for Muslims.
It is time for Direct Action. Today we bid goodbye to constitutional methods. We have forged a pistol and are in a position to use it.
This is vivisection. It will lead to nothing but heartbreak and strife. We are all Indian.
Unrest broke out all across the country, with Muslims attacking Hindus and Hindus attacking Muslims. I decided to travel to Noakhali, where some of the worst atrocities were taking place.
In this largely Muslim region, the violence had begun with reports of Hindus attacking Muslims. The local Muslim population had reacted with fury, turning on their Hindu neighbors.
We are all Indians be we Muslims, Hindus or any other faith.
With *swaraj* within touching distance, it was vital we began building bridges with our neighbors.
It was only a few of us who took part in the attacks.
A fence-sitting majority is as guilty as the actual attackers.
Try to forgive and forget what has happened here.
Recalling the unpleasant past can serve no purpose.

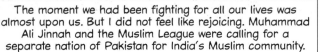

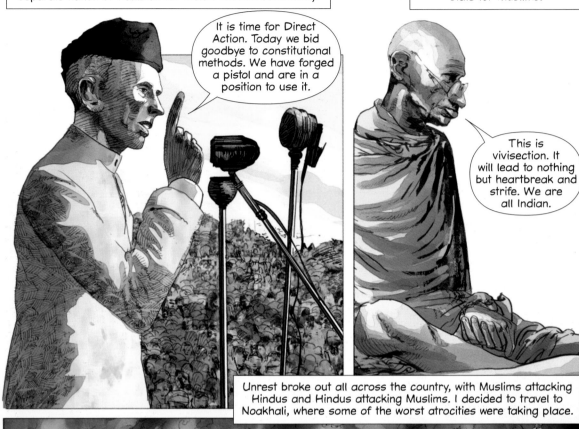

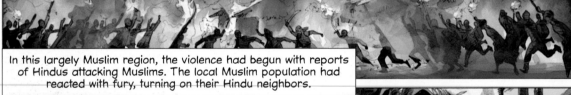

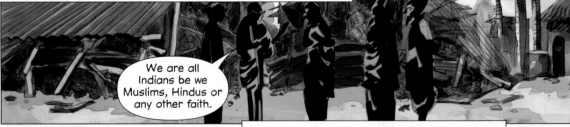

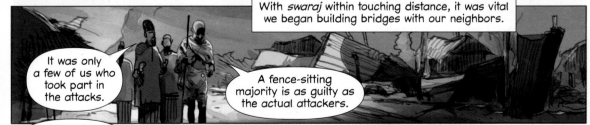

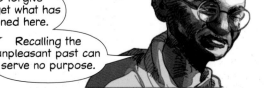

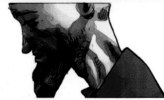

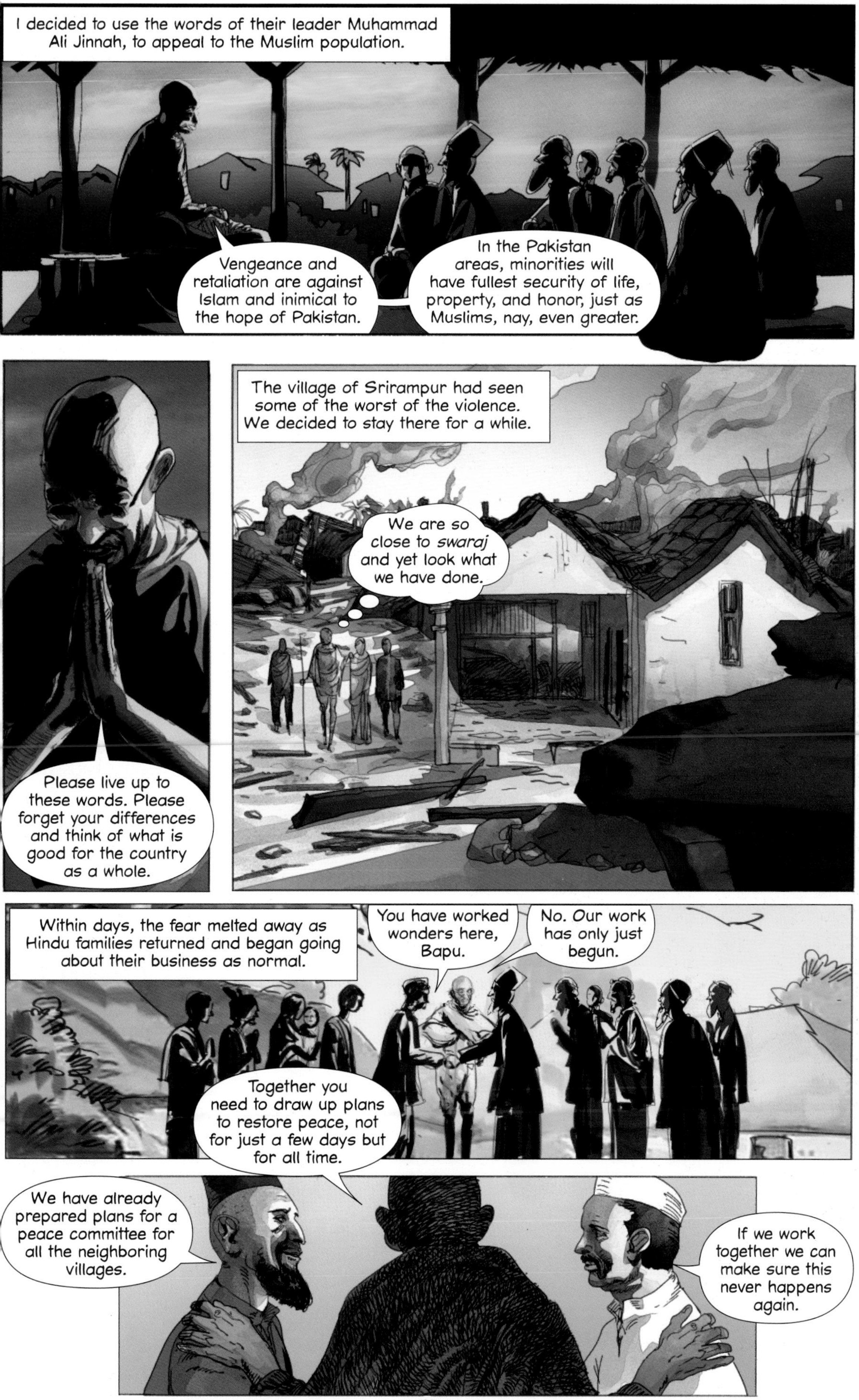
I decided to use the words of their leader Muhammad Ali Jinnah, to appeal to the Muslim population.
Vengeance and retaliation are against Islam and inimical to the hope of Pakistan.
In the Pakistan areas, minorities will have fullest security of life, property, and honor, just as Muslims, nay, even greater.
Please live up to these words. Please forget your differences and think of what is good for the country as a whole.
The village of Srirampur had seen some of the worst of the violence. We decided to stay there for a while.
We are so close to *swaraj* and yet look what we have done.
Within days, the fear melted away as Hindu families returned and began going about their business as normal.
You have worked wonders here, Bapu.
No. Our work has only just begun.
Together you need to draw up plans to restore peace, not for just a few days but for all time.
We have already prepared plans for a peace committee for all the neighboring villages.
If we work together we can make sure this never happens again.

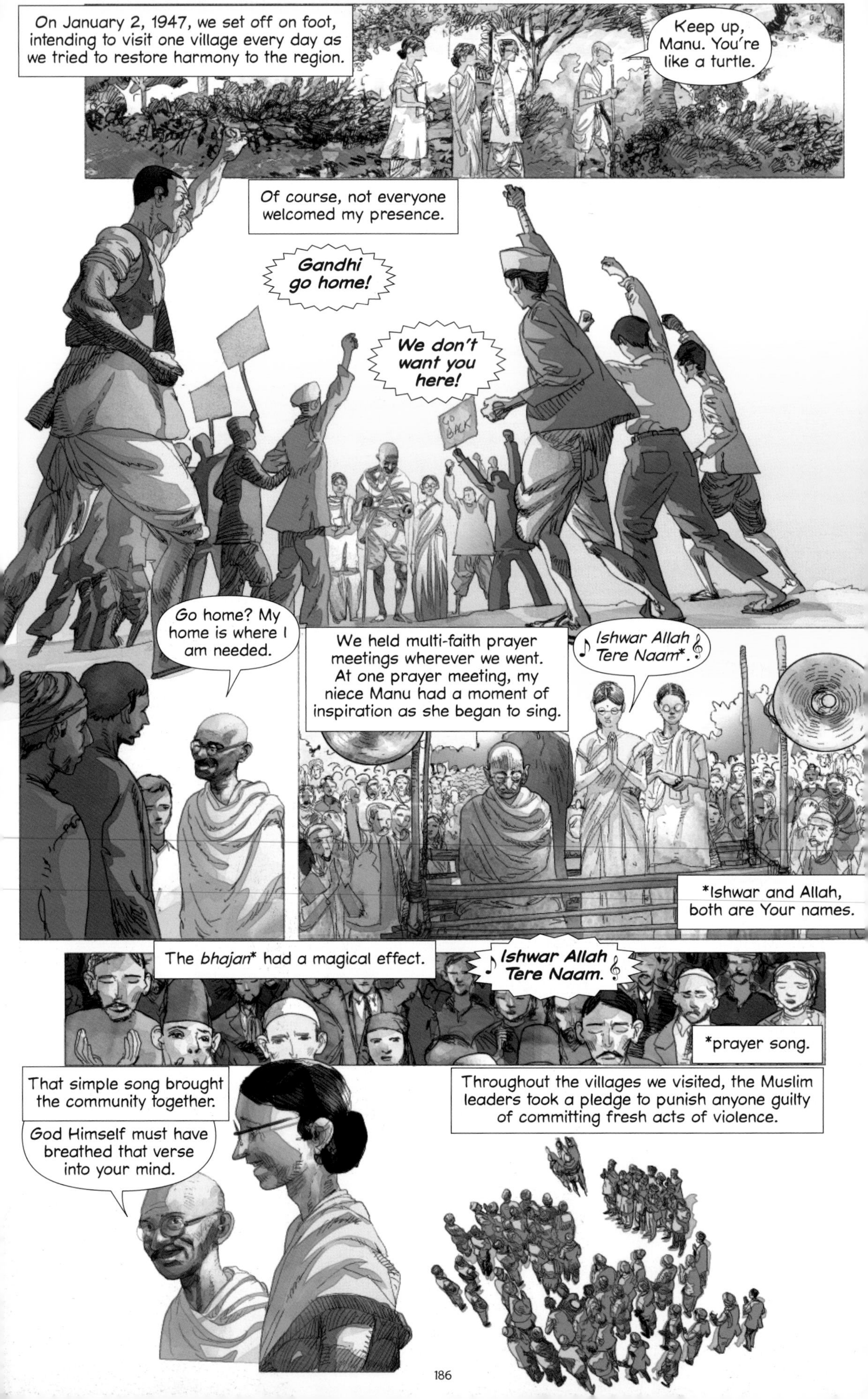
On January 2, 1947, we set off on foot, intending to visit one village every day as we tried to restore harmony to the region.
Keep up, Manu. You're like a turtle.
Of course, not everyone welcomed my presence.
Gandhi go home!
We don't want you here!
GO BACK
Go home? My home is where I am needed.
We held multi-faith prayer meetings wherever we went. At one prayer meeting, my niece Manu had a moment of inspiration as she began to sing.
Ishwar Allah Tere Naam*.
*Ishwar and Allah, both are Your names.
The bhajan* had a magical effect.
Ishwar Allah Tere Naam.
*prayer song.
That simple song brought the community together.
God Himself must have breathed that verse into your mind.
Throughout the villages we visited, the Muslim leaders took a pledge to punish anyone guilty of committing fresh acts of violence.

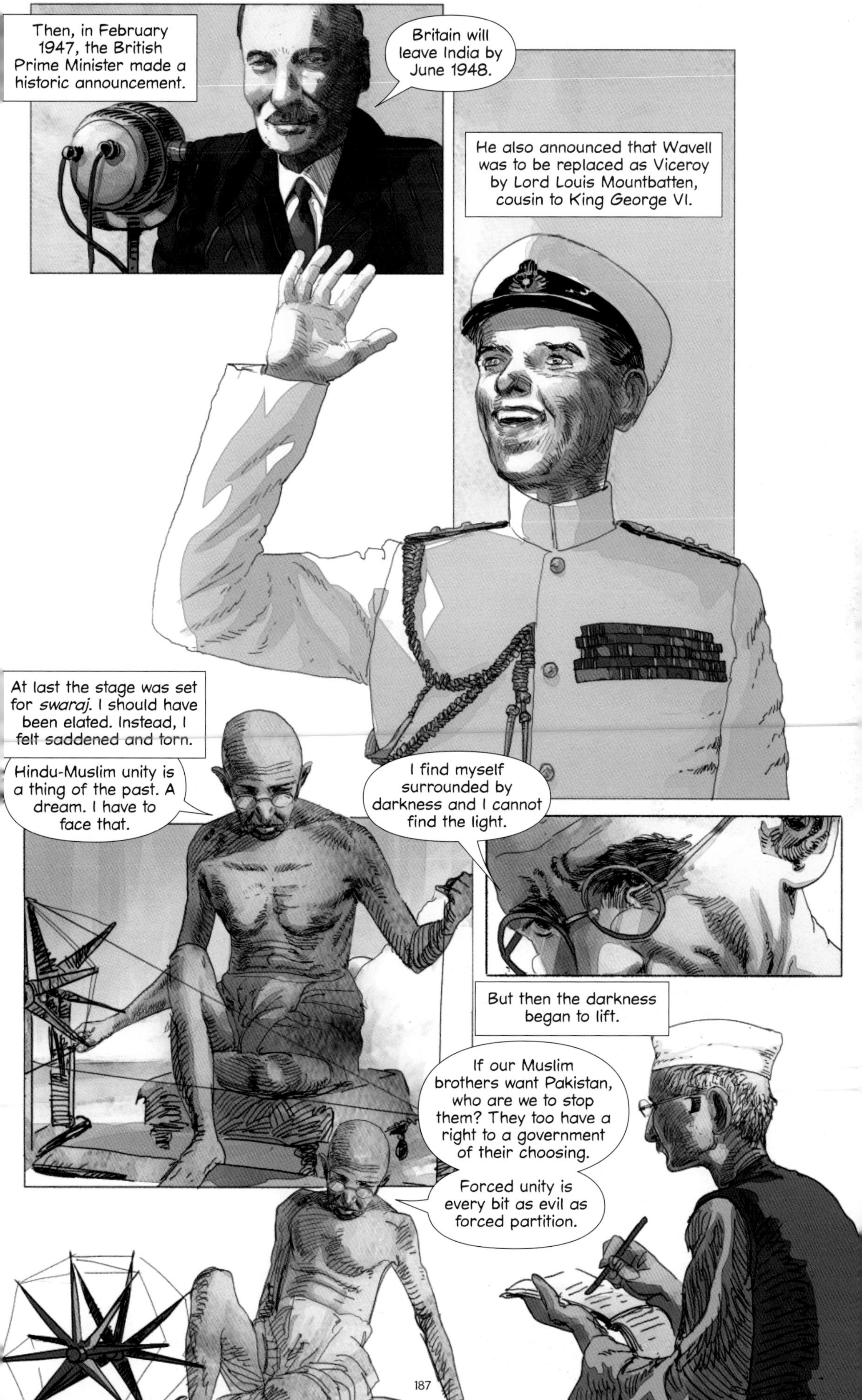

Then, in February 1947, the British Prime Minister made a historic announcement.
Britain will leave India by June 1948.
He also announced that Wavell was to be replaced as Viceroy by Lord Louis Mountbatten, cousin to King George VI.
At last the stage was set for *swaraj*. I should have been elated. Instead, I felt saddened and torn.
Hindu-Muslim unity is a thing of the past. A dream. I have to face that.
I find myself surrounded by darkness and I cannot find the light.
But then the darkness began to lift.
If our Muslim brothers want Pakistan, who are we to stop them? They too have a right to a government of their choosing.
Forced unity is every bit as evil as forced partition.

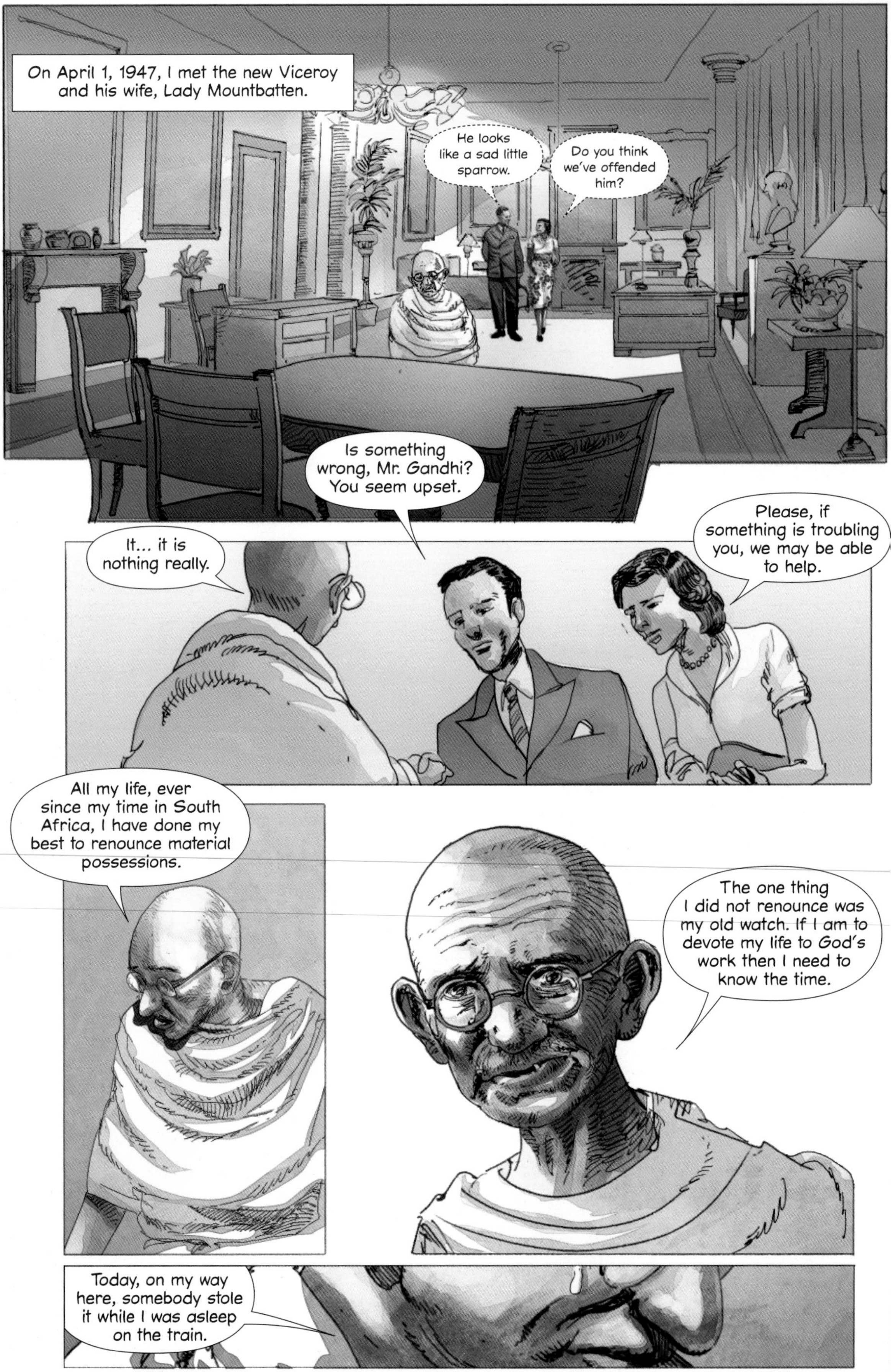

On April 1, 1947, I met the new Viceroy and his wife, Lady Mountbatten.
He looks like a sad little sparrow.
Do you think we've offended him?
Is something wrong, Mr. Gandhi? You seem upset.
It... it is nothing really.
Please, if something is troubling you, we may be able to help.
All my life, ever since my time in South Africa, I have done my best to renounce material possessions.
The one thing I did not renounce was my old watch. If I am to devote my life to *God's* work then I need to know the time.
Today, on my way here, somebody stole it while I was asleep on the train.

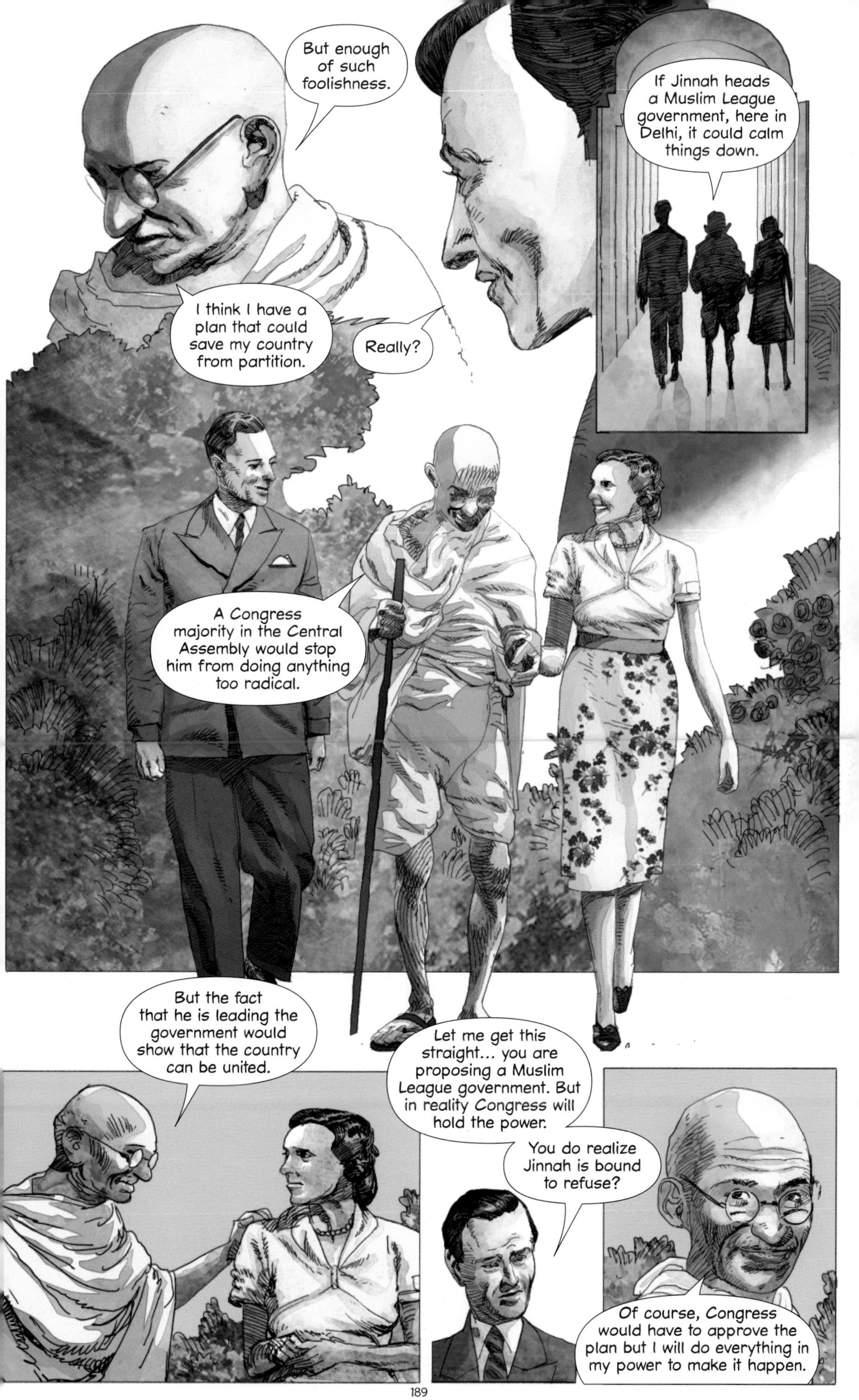
But enough of such foolishness.
I think I have a plan that could save my country from partition.
Really?
If Jinnah heads a Muslim League government, here in Delhi, it could calm things down.
A Congress majority in the Central Assembly would stop him from doing anything too radical.
But the fact that he is leading the government would show that the country can be united.
Let me get this straight... you are proposing a Muslim League government. But in reality Congress will hold the power.
You do realize Jinnah is bound to refuse?
Of course, Congress would have to approve the plan but I will do everything in my power to make it happen.

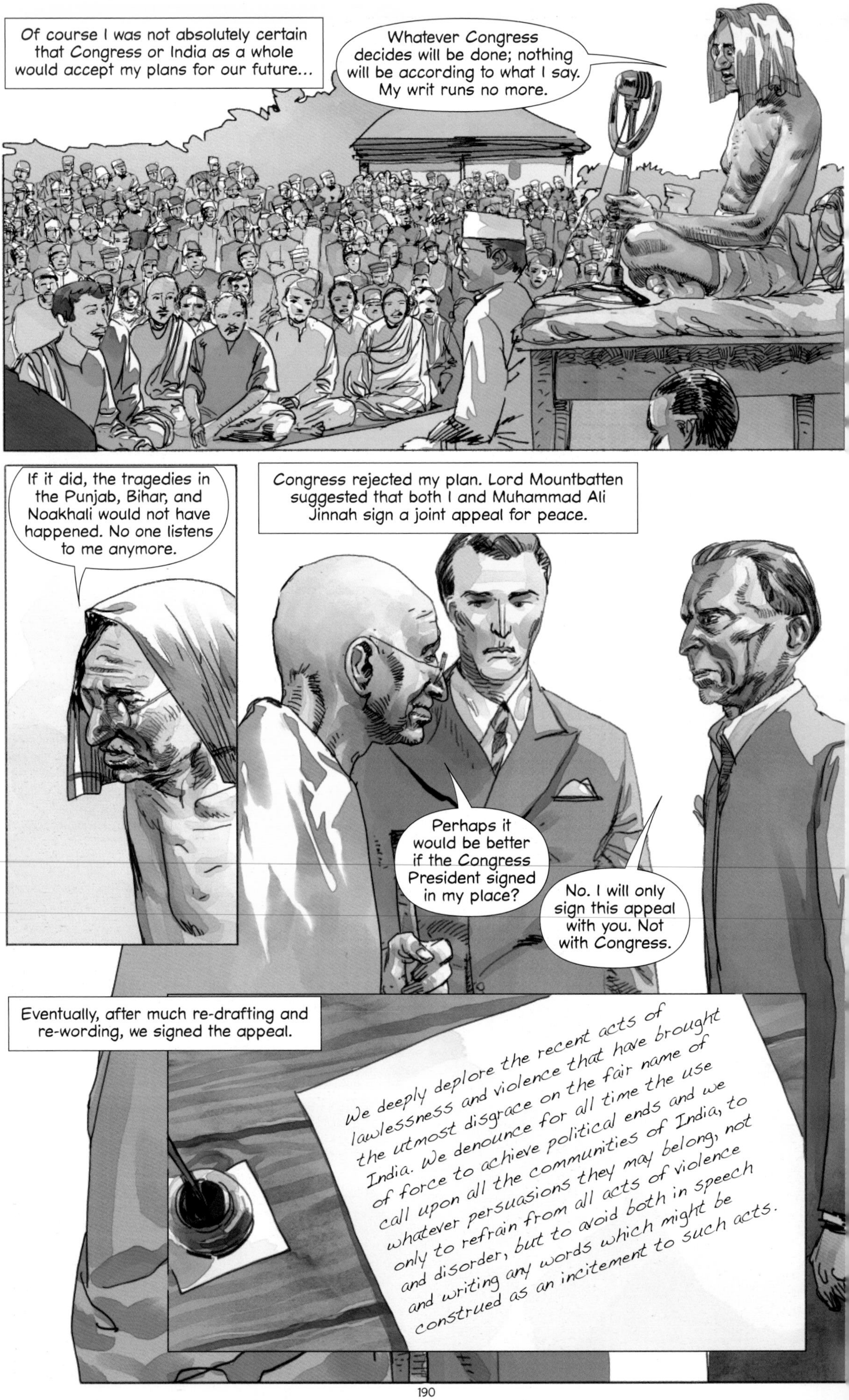
Of course I was not absolutely certain that Congress or India as a whole would accept my plans for our future...
Whatever Congress decides will be done; nothing will be according to what I say. My writ runs no more.
If it did, the tragedies in the Punjab, Bihar, and Noakhali would not have happened. No one listens to me anymore.
Congress rejected my plan. Lord Mountbatten suggested that both I and Muhammad Ali Jinnah sign a joint appeal for peace.
Perhaps it would be better if the Congress President signed in my place?
No. I will only sign this appeal with you. Not with Congress.
Eventually, after much re-drafting and re-wording, we signed the appeal.
We deeply deplore the recent acts of lawlessness and violence that have brought the utmost disgrace on the fair name of India. We denounce for all time the use of force to achieve political ends and we call upon all the communities of India, to whatever persuasions they may belong, not only to refrain from all acts of violence and disorder, but to avoid both in speech and writing any words which might be construed as an incitement to such acts.

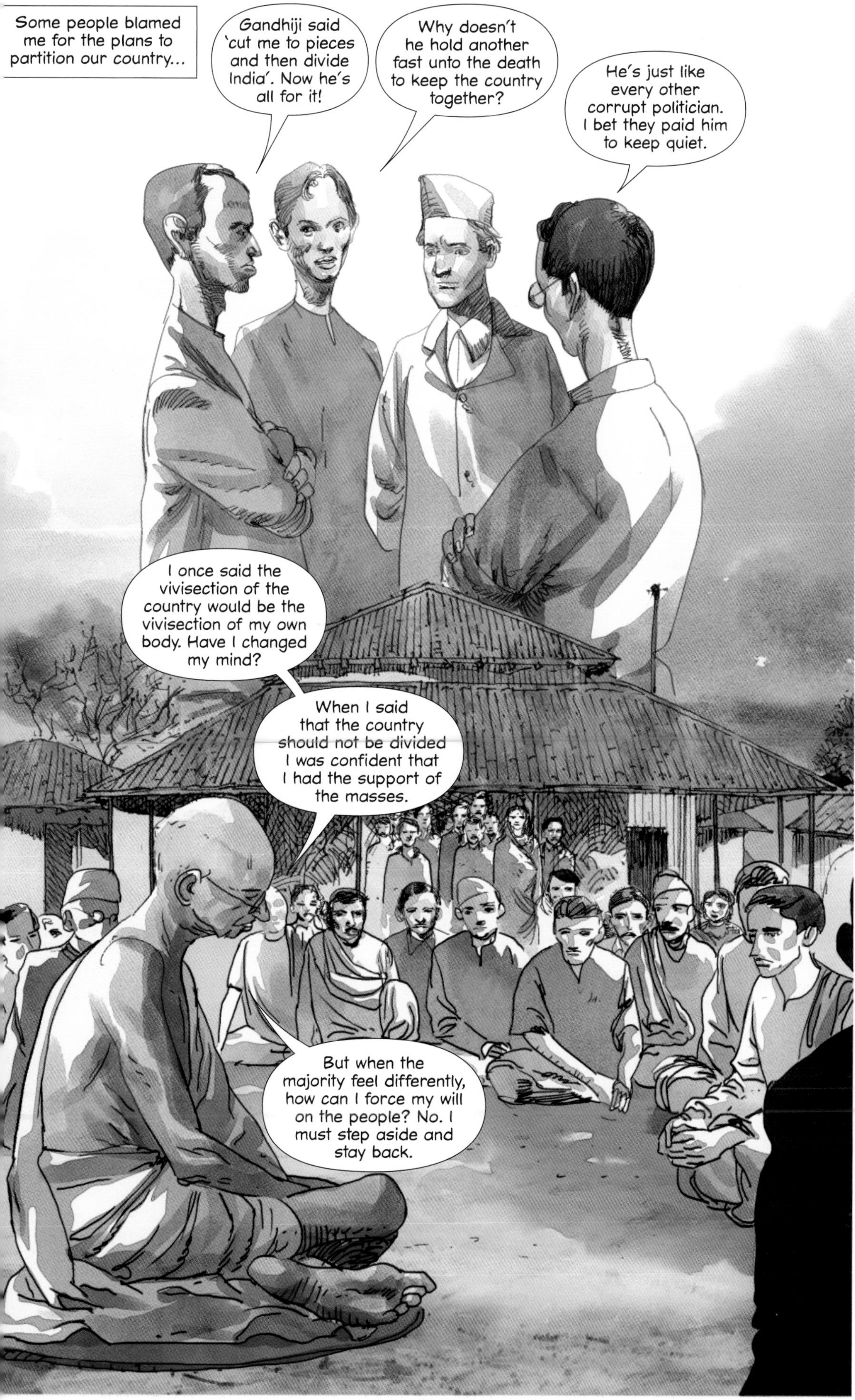
Some people blamed me for the plans to partition our country...
Gandhiji said 'cut me to pieces and then divide India'. Now he's all for it!
Why doesn't he hold another fast unto the death to keep the country together?
He's just like every other corrupt politician. I bet they paid him to keep quiet.
I once said the vivisection of the country would be the vivisection of my own body. Have I changed my mind?
When I said that the country should not be divided I was confident that I had the support of the masses.
But when the majority feel differently, how can I force my will on the people? No. I must step aside and stay back.

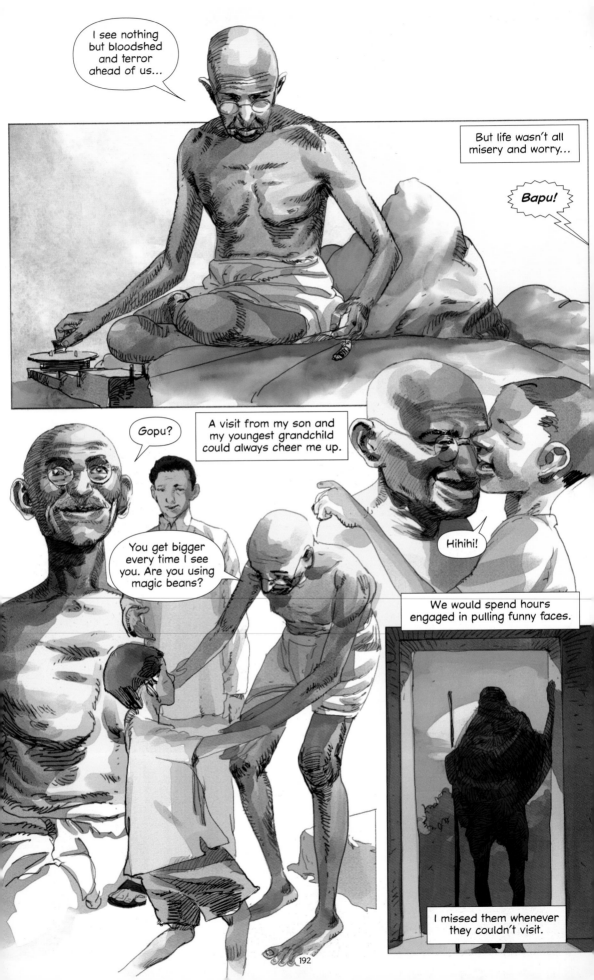

I see nothing but bloodshed and terror ahead of us...

But life wasn't all misery and worry...

Bapu!

Gopu?

A visit from my son and my youngest grandchild could always cheer me up.

You get bigger every time I see you. Are you using magic beans?

Hihihi!

We would spend hours engaged in pulling funny faces.

I missed them whenever they couldn't visit.

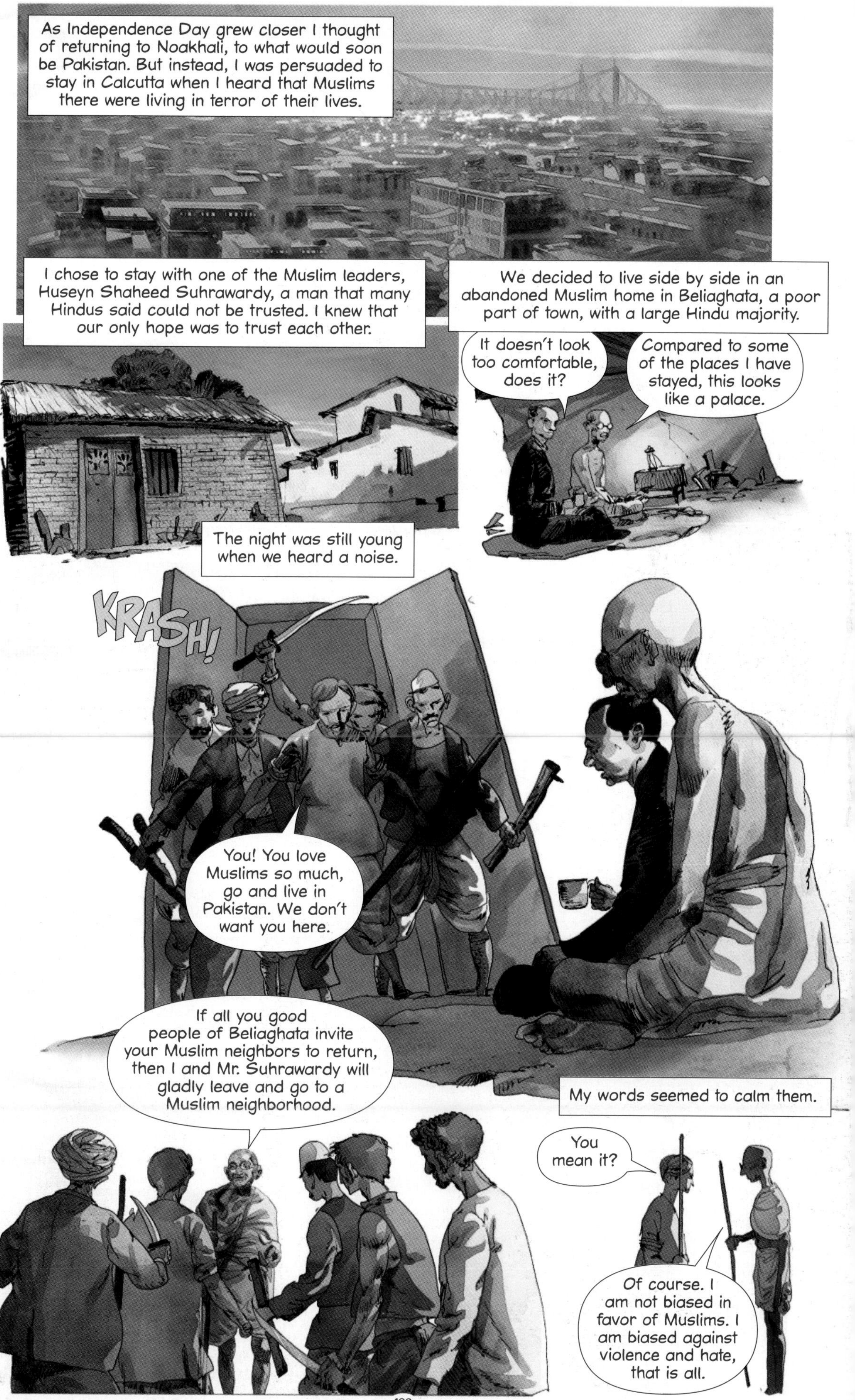
As Independence Day grew closer I thought of returning to Noakhali, to what would soon be Pakistan. But instead, I was persuaded to stay in Calcutta when I heard that Muslims there were living in terror of their lives.
I chose to stay with one of the Muslim leaders, Huseyn Shaheed Suhrawardy, a man that many Hindus said could not be trusted. I knew that our only hope was to trust each other.
We decided to live side by side in an abandoned Muslim home in Beliaghata, a poor part of town, with a large Hindu majority.
It doesn't look too comfortable, does it?
Compared to some of the places I have stayed, this looks like a palace.
The night was still young when we heard a noise.
KRASH!
You! You love Muslims so much, go and live in Pakistan. We don't want you here.
If all you good people of Beliaghata invite your Muslim neighbors to return, then I and Mr. Suhrawardy will gladly leave and go to a Muslim neighborhood.
My words seemed to calm them.
You mean it?
Of course. I am not biased in favor of Muslims. I am biased against violence and hate, that is all.

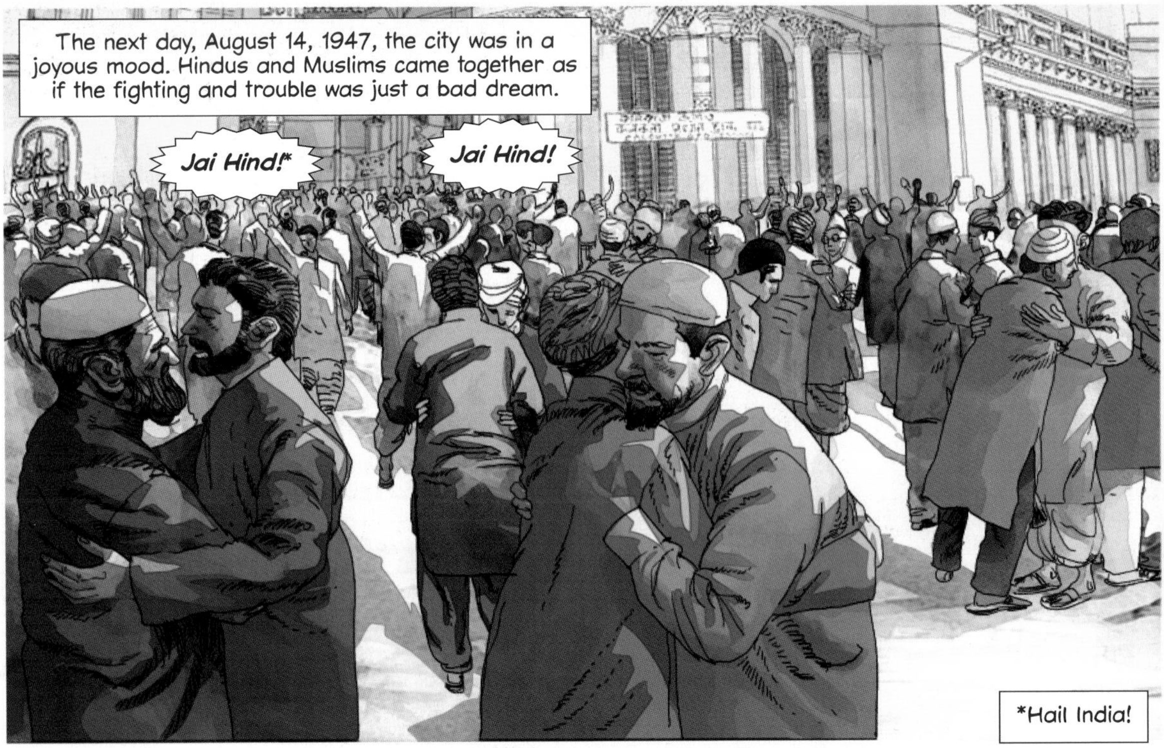
The next day, August 14, 1947, the city was in a joyous mood. Hindus and Muslims came together as if the fighting and trouble was just a bad dream.
Jai Hind!*
Jai Hind!
*Hail India!

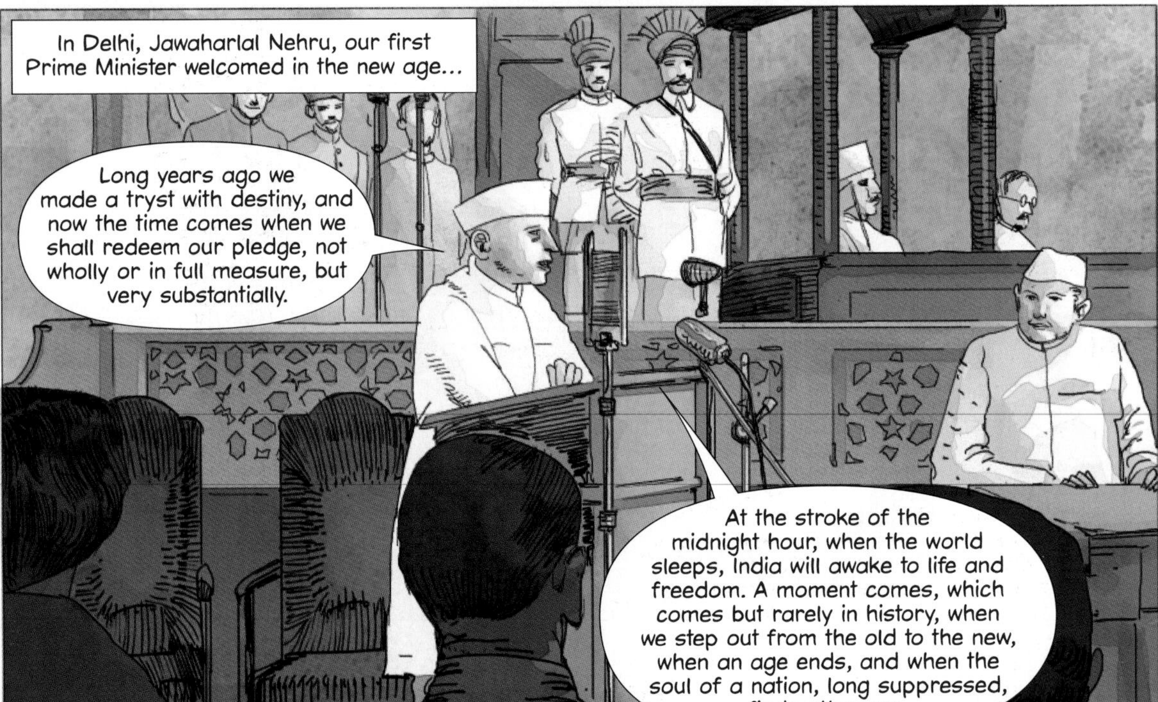
In Delhi, Jawaharlal Nehru, our first Prime Minister welcomed in the new age...
Long years ago we made a tryst with destiny, and now the time comes when we shall redeem our pledge, not wholly or in full measure, but very substantially.
At the stroke of the midnight hour, when the world sleeps, India will awake to life and freedom. A moment comes, which comes but rarely in history, when we step out from the old to the new, when an age ends, and when the soul of a nation, long suppressed, finds utterance.

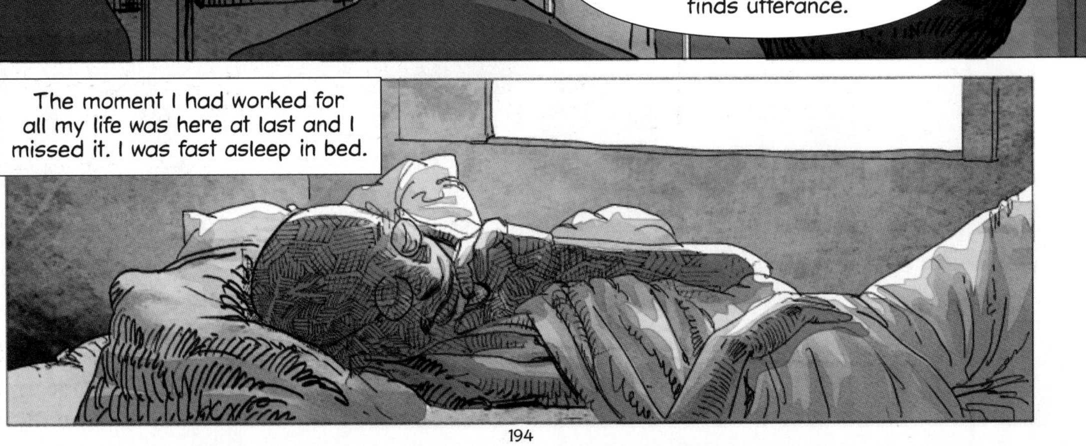
The moment I had worked for all my life was here at last and I missed it. I was fast asleep in bed.

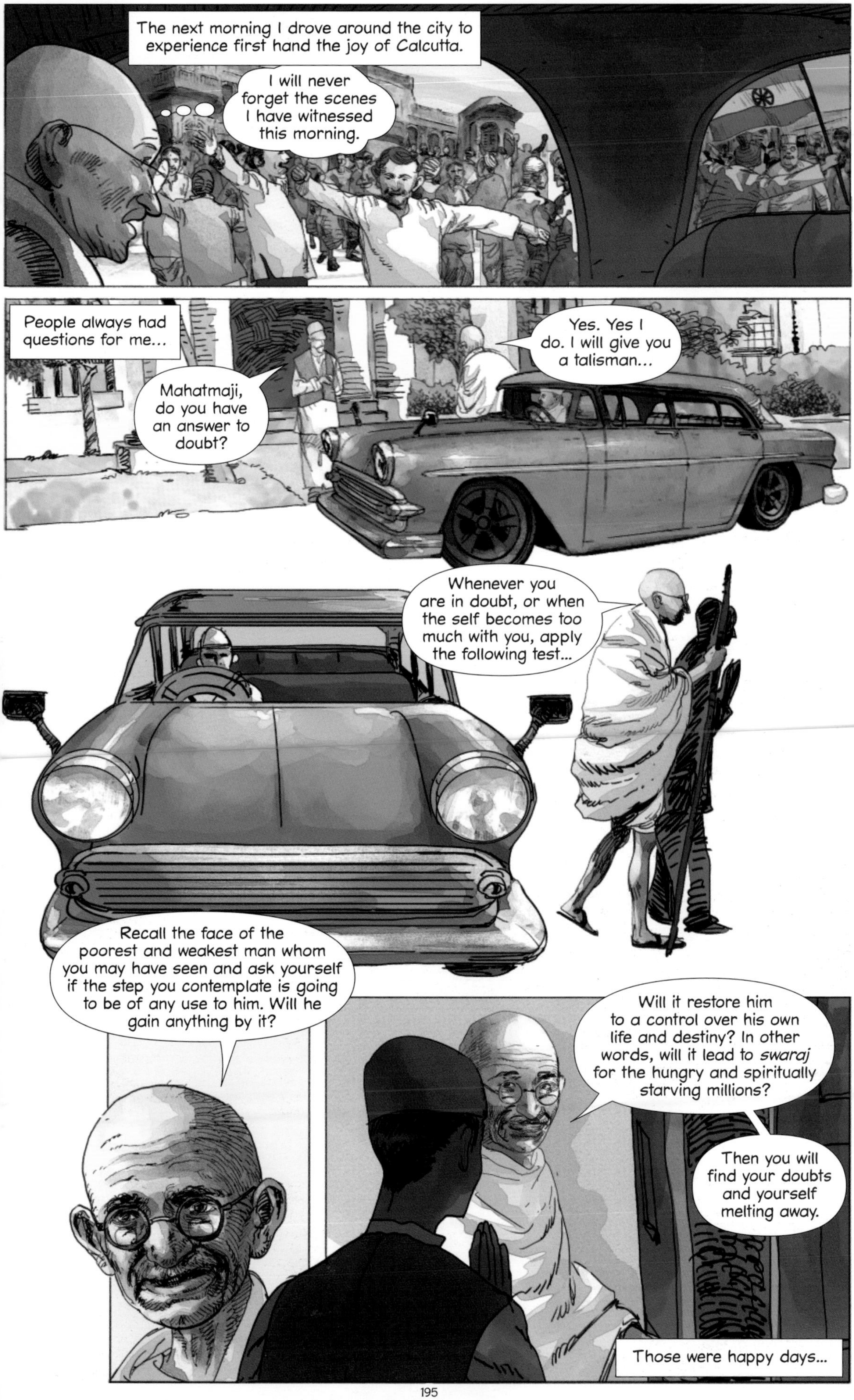
The next morning I drove around the city to experience first hand the joy of Calcutta.
I will never forget the scenes I have witnessed this morning.
People always had questions for me...
Mahatmaji, do you have an answer to doubt?
Yes. Yes I do. I will give you a talisman...
Whenever you are in doubt, or when the self becomes too much with you, apply the following test...
Recall the face of the poorest and weakest man whom you may have seen and ask yourself if the step you contemplate is going to be of any use to him. Will he gain anything by it?
Will it restore him to a control over his own life and destiny? In other words, will it lead to *swaraj* for the hungry and spiritually starving millions?
Then you will find your doubts and yourself melting away.
Those were happy days...

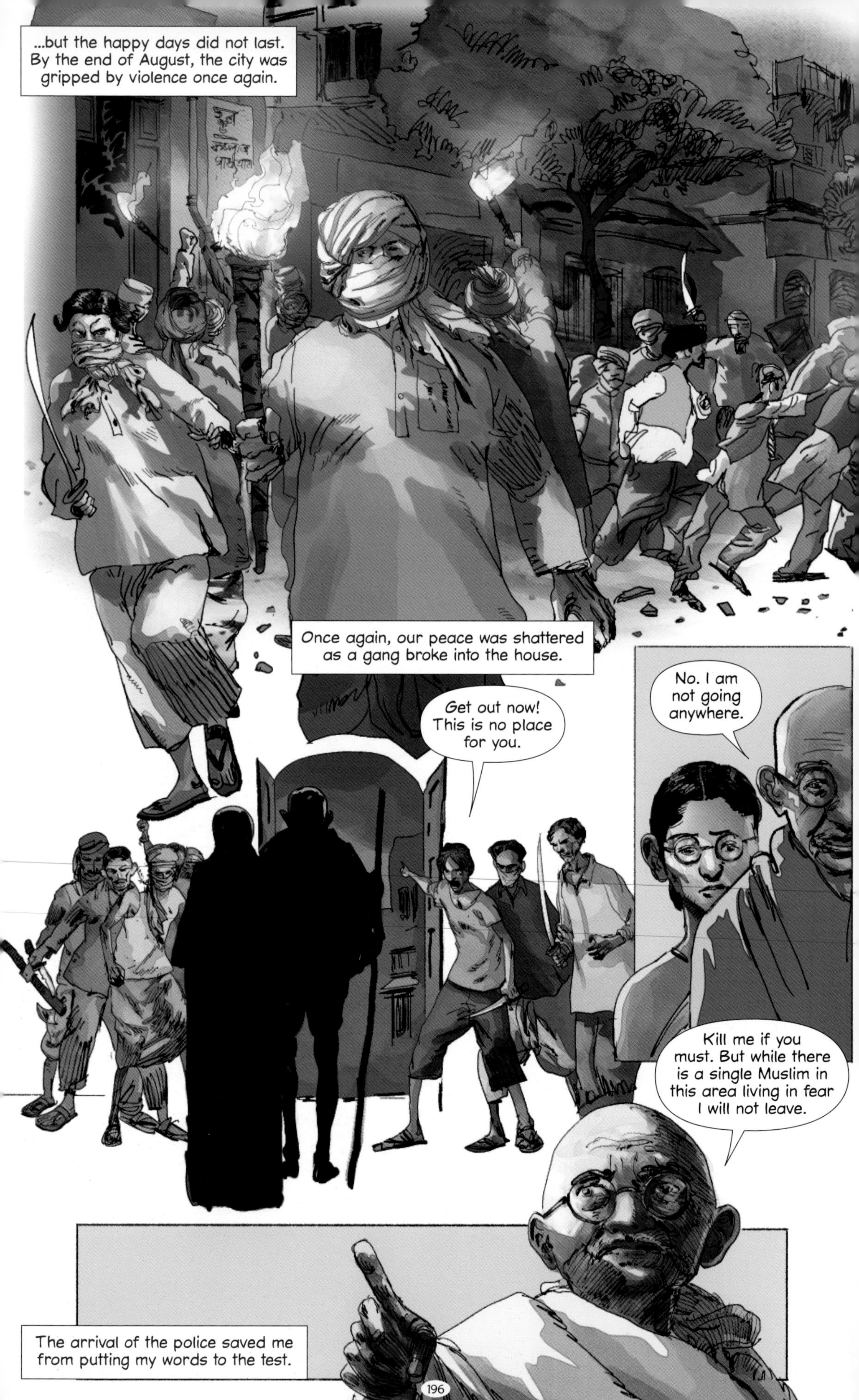
...but the happy days did not last. By the end of August, the city was gripped by violence once again.
Once again, our peace was shattered as a gang broke into the house.
Get out now! This is no place for you.
No. I am not going anywhere.
Kill me if you must. But while there is a single Muslim in this area living in fear I will not leave.
The arrival of the police saved me from putting my words to the test.

Everyone was at a loss as to what to do, but then the Governor, Rajagopalachari asked me a question...

Could you not fast against these *goondas*?*

Against the goondas, no. But maybe I can win the hearts of their supporters.

*Thugs.

The fast was announced on September 1. The violence died down immediately.

Many Hindus admitted their violent acts and handed in their weapons in an act of contrition.

Hindus and Muslims marched together for peace.

Is that really a sten gun? How fascinating. I've never seen one before.

I ended the fast after seventy-three hours. I met with the newly formed Shanti Sena (Peace Brigade), a group of young people prepared to take non-violent action to stop further disturbances. I enjoyed meeting their secretary...

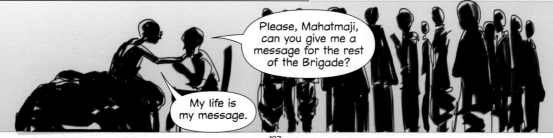

Please, Mahatmaji, can you give me a message for the rest of the Brigade?

My life is my message.

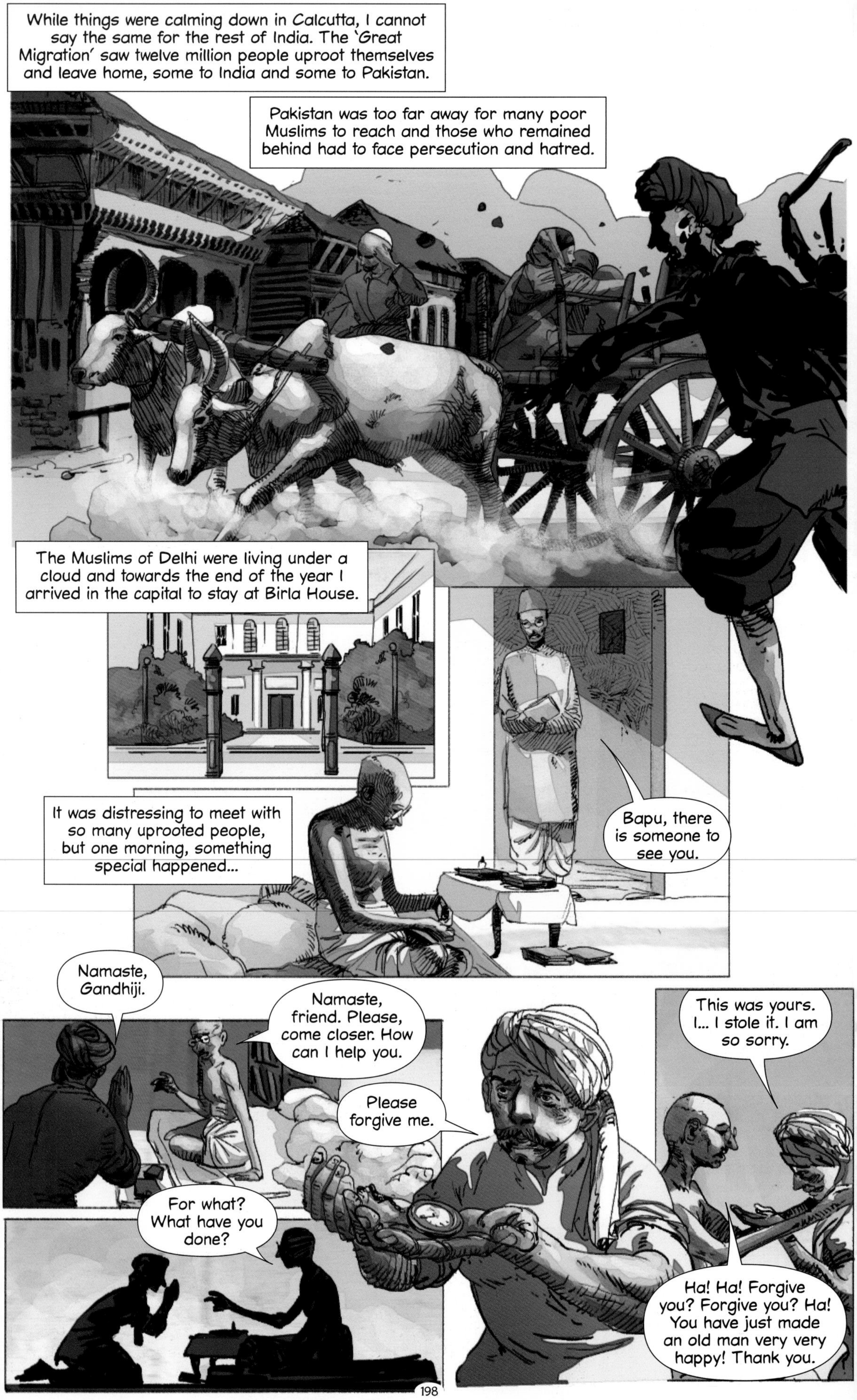
While things were calming down in Calcutta, I cannot say the same for the rest of India. The 'Great Migration' saw twelve million people uproot themselves and leave home, some to India and some to Pakistan.
Pakistan was too far away for many poor Muslims to reach and those who remained behind had to face persecution and hatred.
The Muslims of Delhi were living under a cloud and towards the end of the year I arrived in the capital to stay at Birla House.
It was distressing to meet with so many uprooted people, but one morning, something special happened...
Bapu, there is someone to see you.
Namaste, Gandhiji.
Namaste, friend. Please, come closer. How can I help you.
Please forgive me.
For what? What have you done?
This was yours. I... I stole it. I am so sorry.
Ha! Ha! Forgive you? Forgive you? Ha! You have just made an old man very very happy! Thank you.

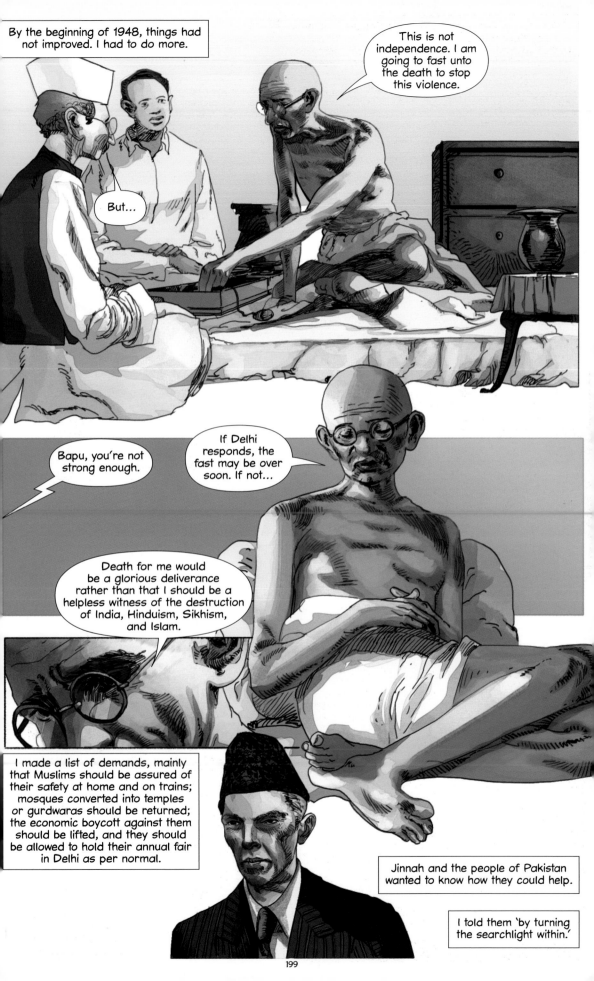

By the beginning of 1948, things had not improved. I had to do more.

This is not independence. I am going to fast unto the death to stop this violence.

But...

Bapu, you're not strong enough.

If Delhi responds, the fast may be over soon. If not...

Death for me would be a glorious deliverance rather than that I should be a helpless witness of the destruction of India, Hinduism, Sikhism, and Islam.

I made a list of demands, mainly that Muslims should be assured of their safety at home and on trains; mosques converted into temples or gurdwaras should be returned; the economic boycott against them should be lifted, and they should be allowed to hold their annual fair in Delhi as per normal.

Jinnah and the people of Pakistan wanted to know how they could help.

I told them 'by turning the searchlight within.'

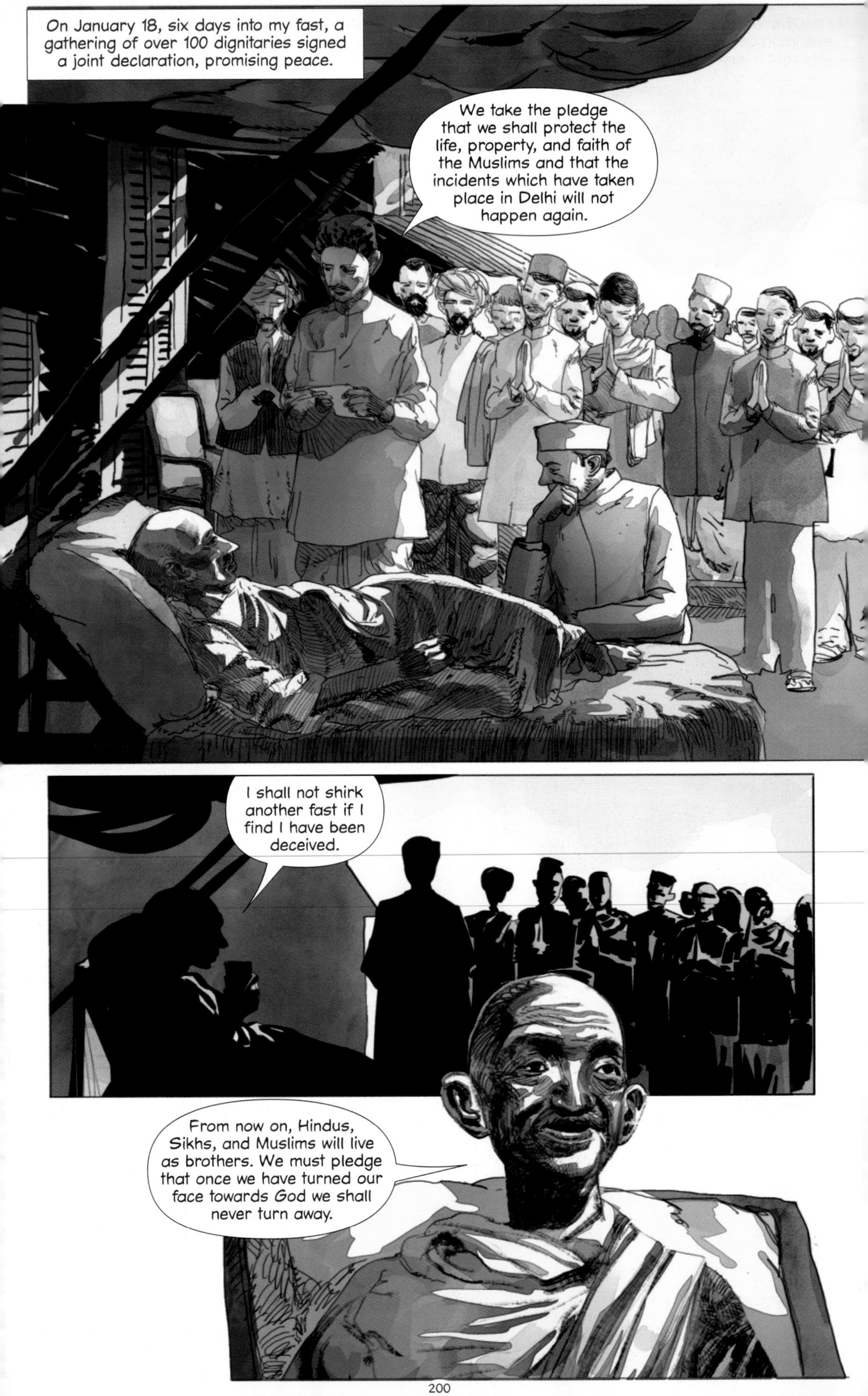
On January 18, six days into my fast, a gathering of over 100 dignitaries signed a joint declaration, promising peace.
We take the pledge that we shall protect the life, property, and faith of the Muslims and that the incidents which have taken place in Delhi will not happen again.
I shall not shirk another fast if I find I have been deceived.
From now on, Hindus, Sikhs, and Muslims will live as brothers. We must pledge that once we have turned our face towards God we shall never turn away.

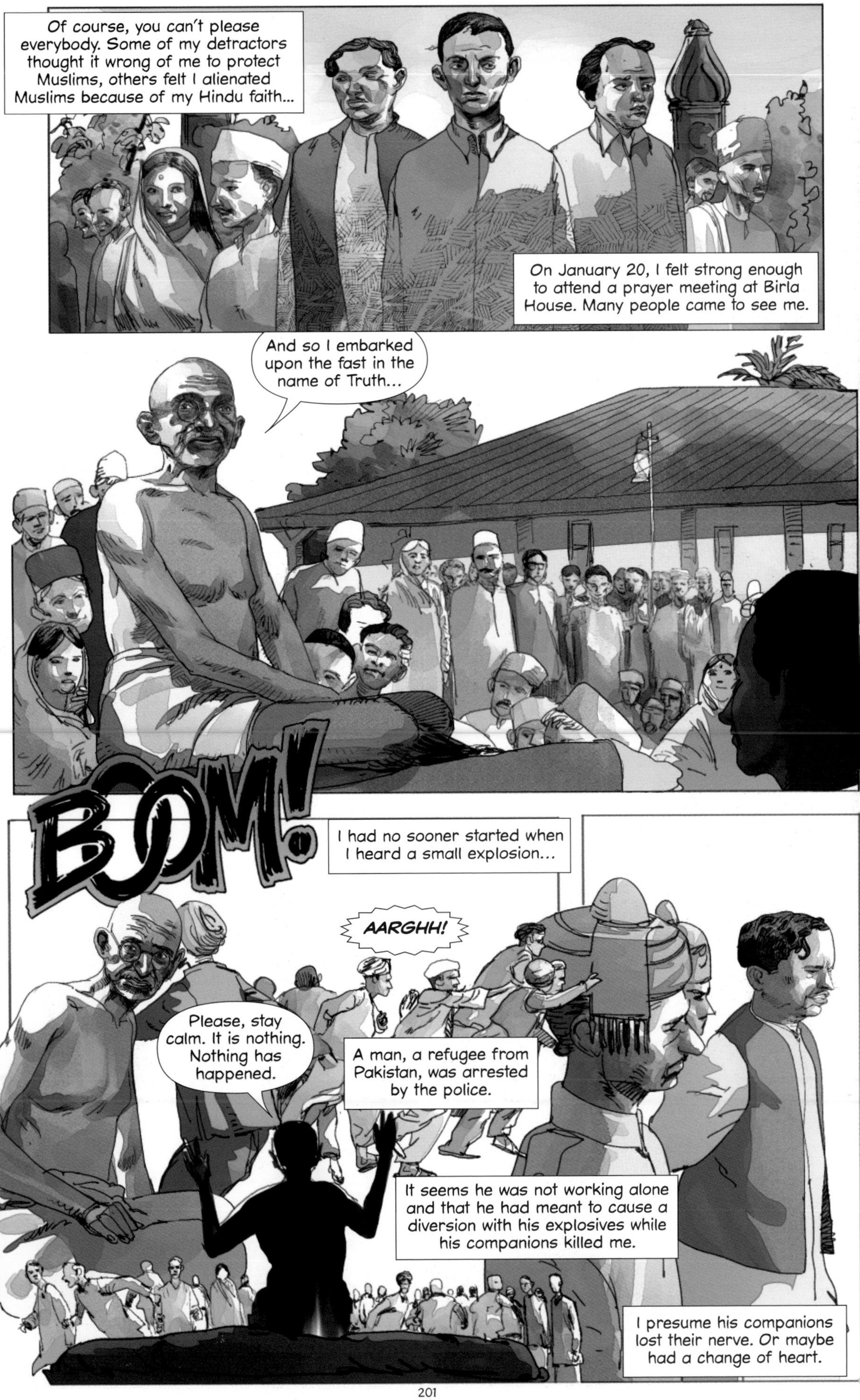

Of course, you can't please everybody. Some of my detractors thought it wrong of me to protect Muslims, others felt I alienated Muslims because of my Hindu faith...
On January 20, I felt strong enough to attend a prayer meeting at Birla House. Many people came to see me.
And so I embarked upon the fast in the name of Truth...
BOOM!
I had no sooner started when I heard a small explosion...
AARGHH!
Please, stay calm. It is nothing. Nothing has happened.
A man, a refugee from Pakistan, was arrested by the police.
It seems he was not working alone and that he had meant to cause a diversion with his explosives while his companions killed me.
I presume his companions lost their nerve. Or maybe had a change of heart.

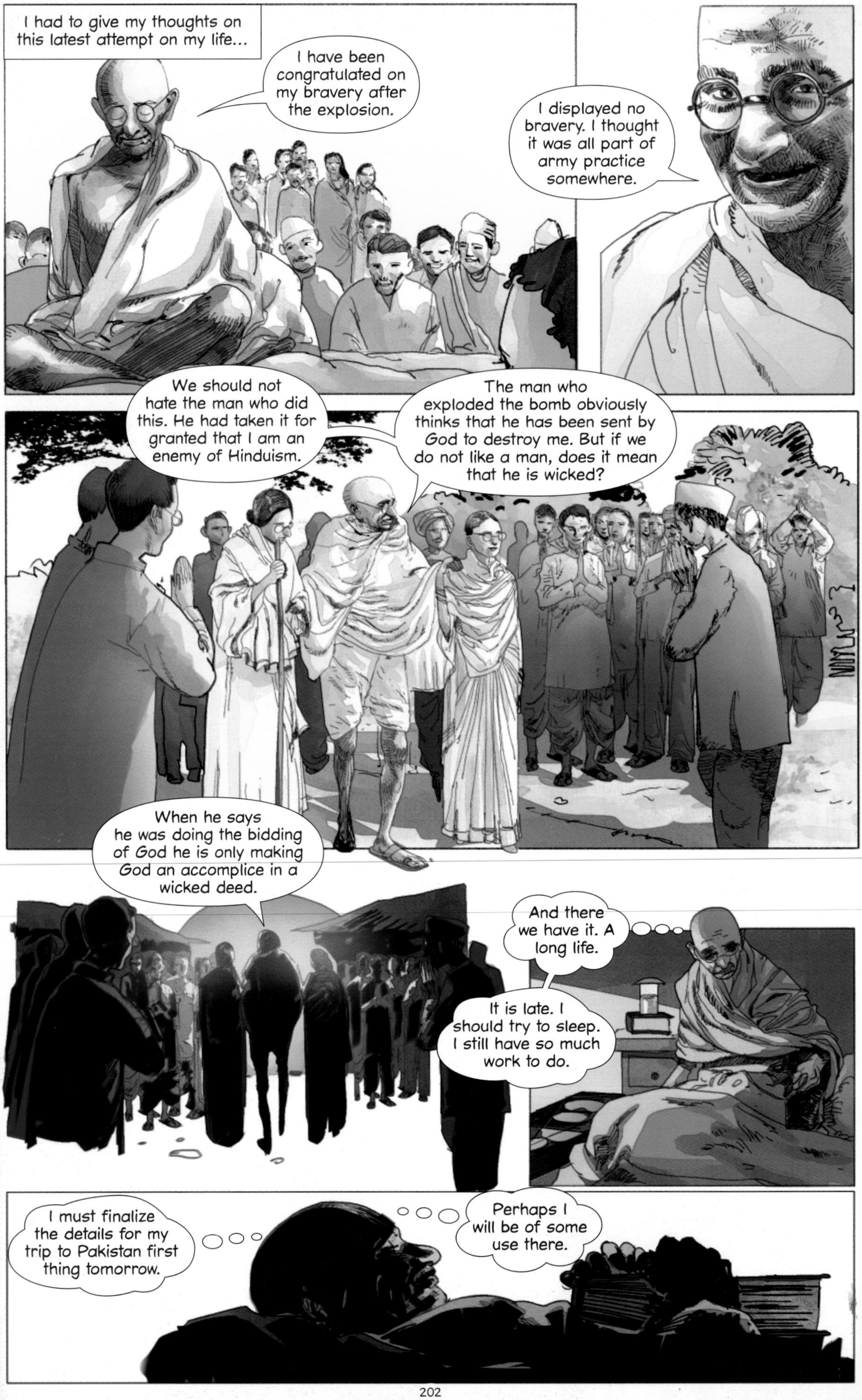

I had to give my thoughts on this latest attempt on my life...
I have been congratulated on my bravery after the explosion.
I displayed no bravery. I thought it was all part of army practice somewhere.
We should not hate the man who did this. He had taken it for granted that I am an enemy of Hinduism.
The man who exploded the bomb obviously thinks that he has been sent by God to destroy me. But if we do not like a man, does it mean that he is wicked?
When he says he was doing the bidding of God he is only making God an accomplice in a wicked deed.
And there we have it. A long life.
It is late. I should try to sleep. I still have so much work to do.
I must finalize the details for my trip to Pakistan first thing tomorrow.
Perhaps I will be of some use there.

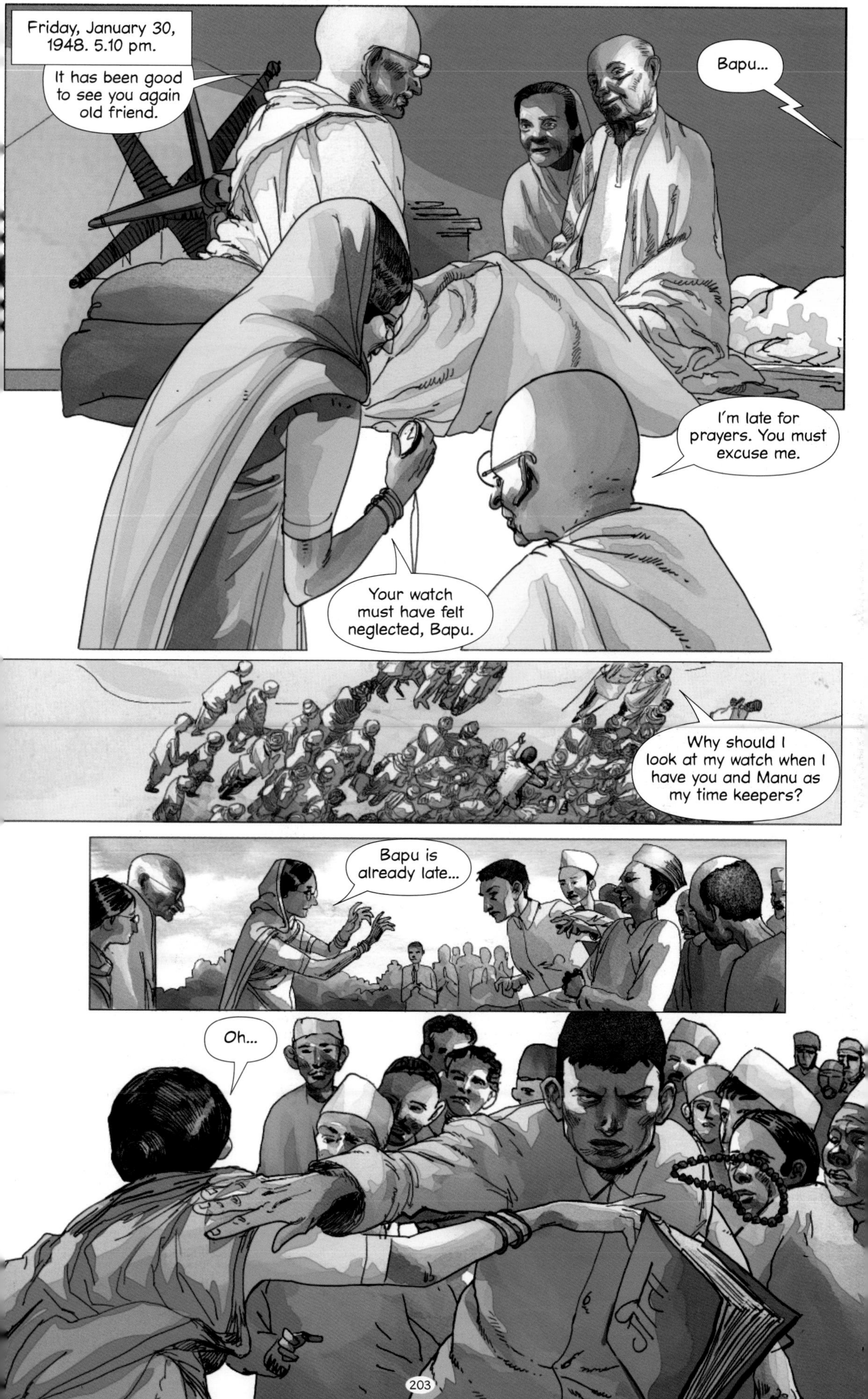
Friday, January 30, 1948. 5.10 pm.
It has been good to see you again old friend.
Bapu...
I'm late for prayers. You must excuse me.
Your watch must have felt neglected, Bapu.
Why should I look at my watch when I have you and Manu as my time keepers?
Bapu is already late...
Oh...

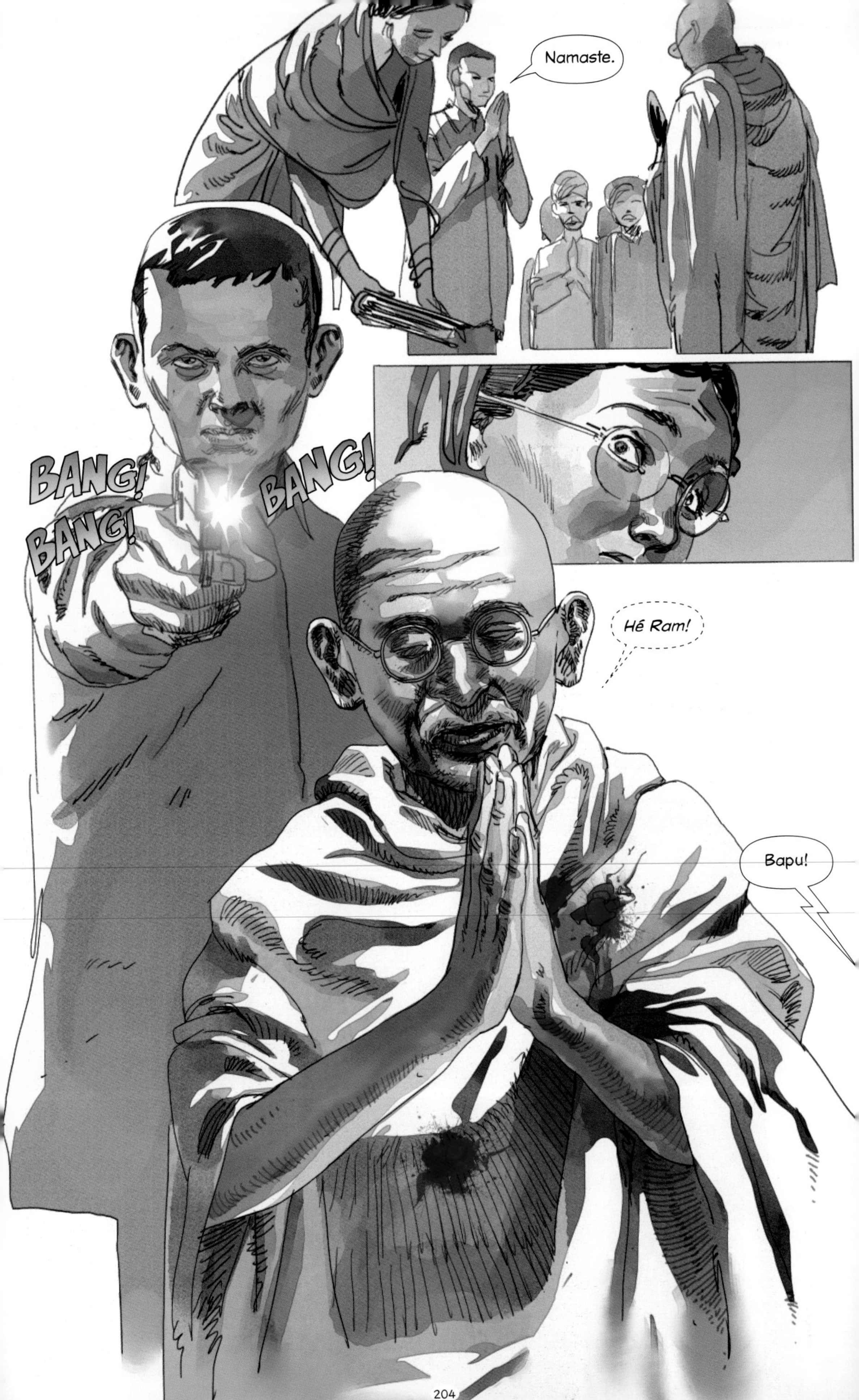
Namaste.
BANG!
BANG!
BANG!
Hé Ram!
Bapu!

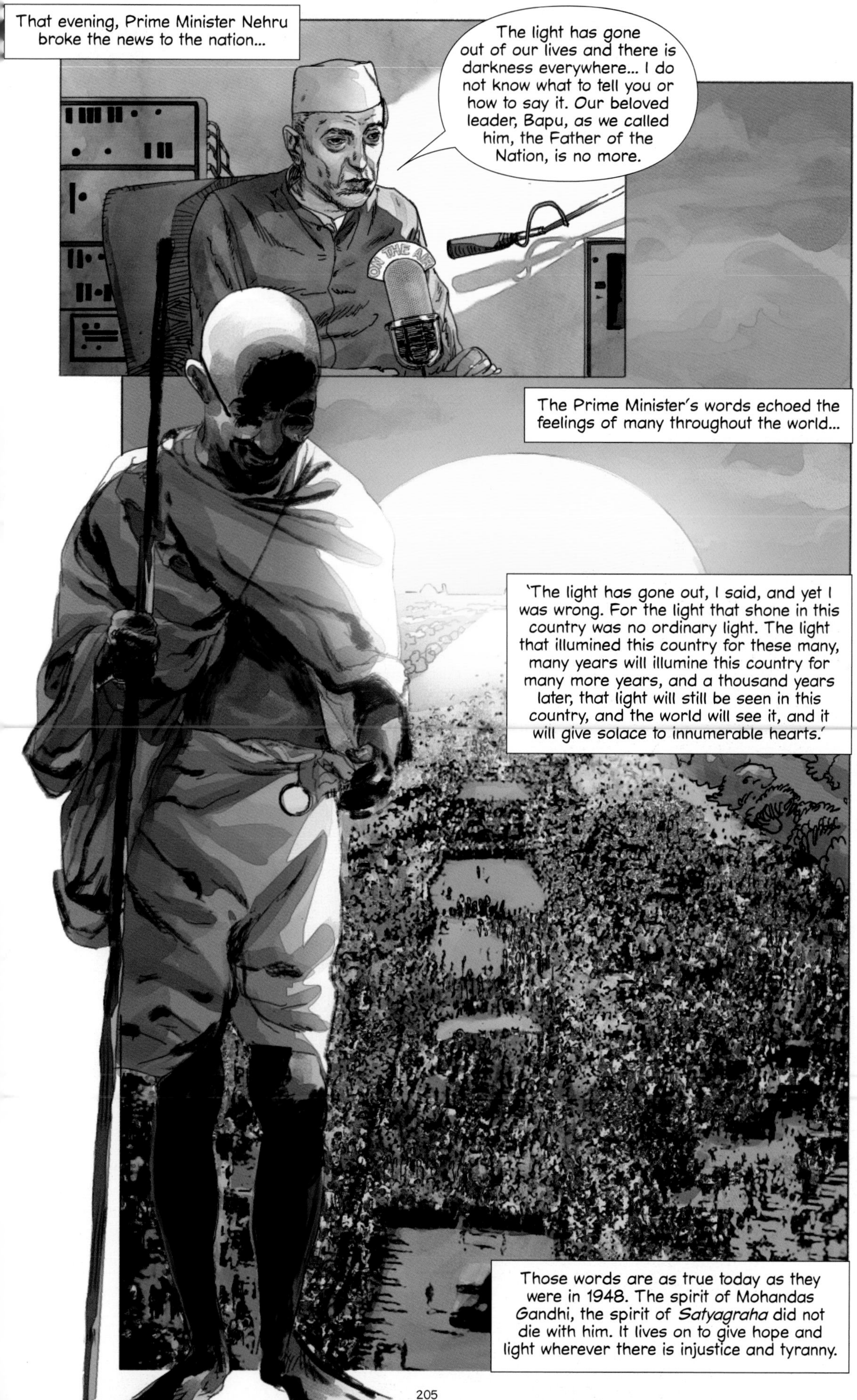
That evening, Prime Minister Nehru broke the news to the nation...
The light has gone out of our lives and there is darkness everywhere... I do not know what to tell you or how to say it. Our beloved leader, Bapu, as we called him, the Father of the Nation, is no more.
ON THE AIR
The Prime Minister's words echoed the feelings of many throughout the world...
'The light has gone out, I said, and yet I was wrong. For the light that shone in this country was no ordinary light. The light that illumined this country for these many, many years will illumine this country for many more years, and a thousand years later, that light will still be seen in this country, and the world will see it, and it will give solace to innumerable hearts.'
Those words are as true today as they were in 1948. The spirit of Mohandas Gandhi, the spirit of *Satyagraha* did not die with him. It lives on to give hope and light wherever there is injustice and tyranny.

Memorable Quotes
of the Mahatma

Gandhi's shyness made him think carefully about everything he ever said, so as he himself claimed, a thoughtless word hardly ever escaped his tongue or pen. Here are just a few of his most insightful thoughts and sayings.

on Ahimsa (non-violence)

"Ahimsa is not the way of the timid or cowardly. It is the way of the brave ready to face death. He who perishes sword in hand is no doubt brave; but he who faces death without raising his little finger and without flinching is braver."

on Conflict

"Having flung aside the sword, there is nothing except the cup of love which I can offer to those who oppose me."

on Satyagraha (soul force)

"Satyagraha is the weapon of the strong, it admits of no violence under any circumstances whatsoever, and it ever insists upon truth."

on Women

"To call women the weaker sex is a libel; it is man's injustice to women."

on War

"Wherever there are wars, wherever you are confronted with an opponent, conquer him with love."

on Enemies

"I recognize no one on the face of the earth as my enemy."

on Equality

"I have never in my life regarded anyone as my servant, but as a brother or a sister."

on Humility

"It has always been a mystery to me how men can feel themselves honored by the humiliation of their fellow beings."

on Swaraj (self rule)

"The Swaraj of our dreams recognizes no race or religious distinctions. Nor is it to be the monopoly of the lettered persons or yet of moneyed men. Swaraj is to be for all, including the former, but emphatically including the maimed, the blind, the starving, toiling millions."

on Travelling Third Class

When asked by a reporter why he always insisted on travelling third class on the railways... "I travel third class because there is no fourth class."

on Prayer

"Prayer is not asking. It is a longing of the soul. It is a daily admission of one's weakness. It is better in prayer to have a heart without words, than words without a heart."

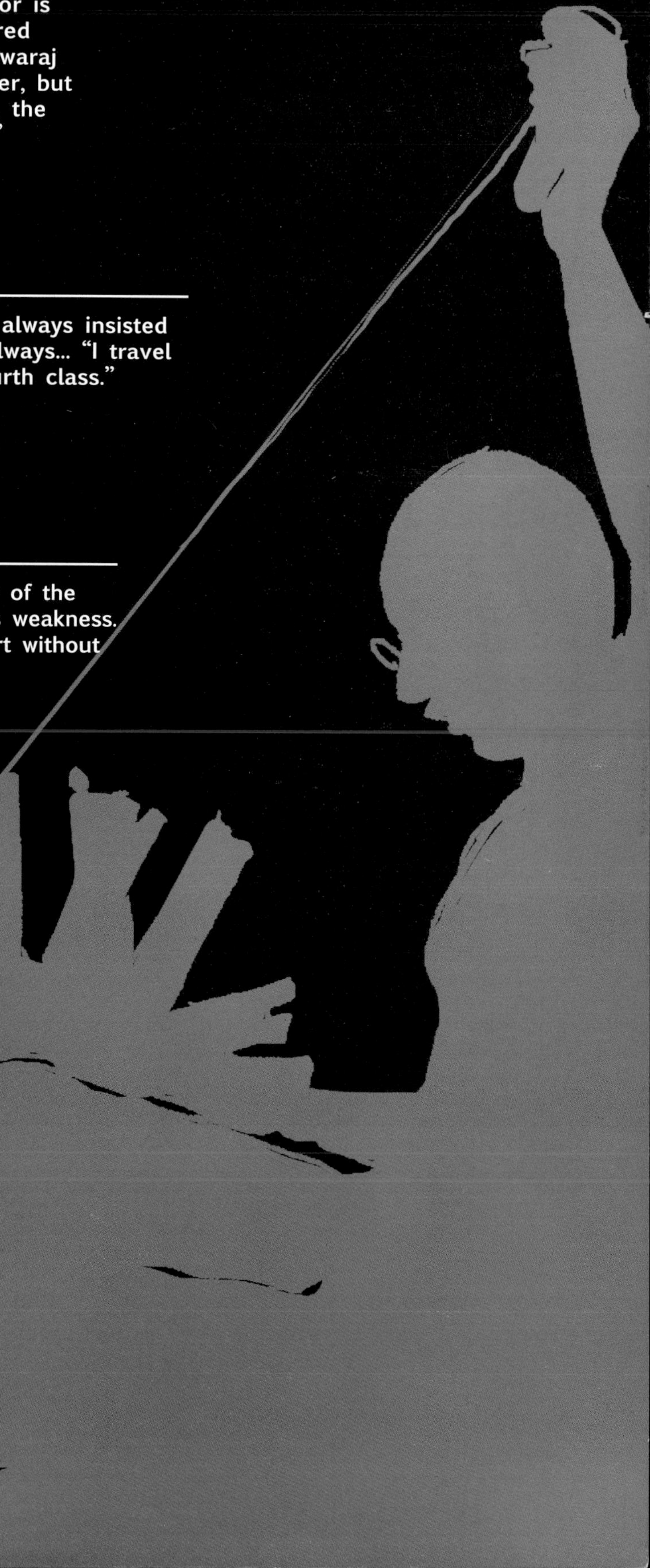

Gandhi

Follow the footsteps
of a great soul.

OCT, 1869

October 2
born in Porbandar.

MAY, 1883

Marries Kasturba
Makhanji.

SEP, 1888

Goes to England to
study law.

JUN, 1891

Returns to India
to practice law.

APR, 1893

Goes to Natal,
South Africa.

MAY, 1894

Founds the Natal
Indian Congress.

SEP, 1906

Protests against
the Transvaal
Government's
Black Act.

JAN, 1915

Returns to India.

APR, 1917

Takes part in the
Champaran agitations.

MAR, 1919

Promotes civil
disobedience
against Rowlatt Act.

FEB, 1922

Non-cooperation
movement ends
following Chauri
Chaura clashes.

MAR, 1930

Launches *Satyagraha*
against salt tax.

SEP, 1931

Takes part in Round
Table Conference in
London.

SEP, 1932

Campaigns on behalf
of the untouchable
community.

AUG, 1934

Resigns from the
Congress Party.

AUG, 1942

Demands that the
British Quit India.

AUG, 1947

August 15
India becomes
independent.

JAN, 1948

January 30
Martyrdom at Birla
House, New Delhi.

More About the Mahatma

There is a wealth of material about Mohandas Karamchand Gandhi available for those readers who would like to know more about his life and works. The following books, movies, documentaries and websites were invaluable to the writer when researching for this book.

BIBLIOGRAPHY

Ravindra Varma: *Gandhi in Anecdotes.* Navajivan Publishing House, 2001.

MK Gandhi and Louis Fischer: *The Essential Gandhi: An Anthology of his Writings on his Life, Work and Ideas.* Vintage, 2002.

Louis Fischer: *The Life of Mahatma Gandhi.* Harper Collins, 2004.

Dr. Ramesh Bhardwaj: *Historic Speeches of Mahatma Gandhi.* Gandhi Hindustani Sahitya Sabha, 2006.

Rajmohan Gandhi: *Mohandas: A True Story of a Man, His People and an Empire.* Penguin Books India, 2007.

Kathryn Tidrick: *Gandhi: A Political and Spiritual Life.* IB Tauris, 2006.

Larry Collins and Dominique Lapierre: *Freedom at Midnight.* Vikas Publishing House, 2011.

MK Gandhi: *An Autobiography: The Story of my Experiments with Truth.* Rupa Publication, 2011.

IN FILM

Mahatma: Life of Gandhi, 1869 – 1948, directed by Vithalbai Jhaveri. The Gandhi National Memorial Fund, 1968.

Gandhi, directed by Richard Attenborough, 1982.

Gandhi: The Early Years, Gandhi: The Rise to Fame and *Gandhi: The Road to Freedom,* BBC Documentary Series, 2009.

ONLINE

http://www.gandhiheritageportal.org
http://www.gandhiserve.org
http://www.gandhimedia.org
http://www.gandhismriti.gov.in

"*The truth of a few will count. The untruth of millions will vanish even like chaff before a whiff of wind.*"

Mohandas Karamchand Gandhi